RELIGION AND ITS RELEVANCE IN POST-MODERNISM

Jack C. Verheyden

RELIGION AND ITS RELEVANCE IN POST-MODERNISM

Essays in Honor of Jack C. Verheyden

Edited by

John S. Park

and

Gayle D. Beebe

The Edwin Mellen Press
Lewiston•Queenston•Lampeter

Library of Congress Cataloging-in-Publication Data

Religion and its relevance in post-modernism : essays in honor of Jack C. Verheyden /
edited by John S. Park and Gayle D. Beebe.
    p.   cm.
    Includes bibliographical references.
    ISBN 0-7734-7284-3
    1. Theology--History--19th century. I. Verheyden, Jack C. (Jack Clyde) II. Park, John
S. III. Beebe, Gayle D.

BT28 .R44 2001
230--dc21

                          2001044060

A CIP catalog record for this book is available from the British Library.

The Edwin Mellen Press   The Edwin Mellen Press
Box 450   Box 67
Lewiston, New York   Queenston, Ontario
USA 14092-0450   CANADA L0S 1L0

The Edwin Mellen Press, Ltd.
Lampeter, Ceredigion, Wales
UNITED KINGDOM SA48 8LT

Printed in the United States of America

Table of Contents

Tribute to Jack Verheyden

Having a good teacher is like having a good compass, role model, and father. As a compass they direct us where we can go to achieve our life goals. In 1990, when I met Dr. Jane Douglas at Princeton while I was doing master's study in theology, I was looking for a doctoral program for nineteenth century theology. Without hesitation, Dr. Douglas said, "Jack Verheyden! Go to Claremont!" After I sent my application, I had a chance to have an interview with him. In my first encounter with him, he carefully questioned my interest and study proposal in theology. He showed his generous concern about my yet un-nurtured proposal. (Normally, when we propose anything, we do not yet know the result of the proposal. But he listened to me with much care and concern.) The first class that I took with him was "Religious Experiences in the Nineteenth Century." Through this class, especially from the section on Schleiermacher, I knew that I would study Schleiermacher for my dissertation. In the second semester of my first year, when I had a chance to ask him about my dissertation topic on Schleiermacher, Dr. Verheyden gave me 1000 pages of *"Christliche Sitte,"* a companion to *"Glaubenslehre"*, by Schleiermacher to read. He assured me, saying, "John, in this book you can swim yourself for the rest of your scholarly life." It was old nineteenth century German writing, which I had never read. In one sentence alone, there may be up to ten relative pronouns. And as some of you may know, some of the pages can hold only three or four sentences. I said "No!" in the beginning, believing that it was an impossible task. After one month of struggling and indecision, however, I decided to take on this impossible challenge. I began to read one page a day everyday. Over the last nine years I have translated over 750 pages. Portions of them are in printing stages for publication now. How much I appreciate the wise guidance and direction that Dr. Verheyden has shared with me from

i

his wealth of knowledge! His compass of wisdom and guidance has been true in its direction and guide of my scholarly life.

Having a good teacher is also like having a good role model in our life. A good role model teaches us what our goals are. I once asked Dr. Verheyden about my intent to publish this magnificent work in Christian theology, *Christliche Sitte*, written by the father of modern Christian ethics. At that time he advised me that, even though publication is important, continuous reading of the German text every single day is more important. "Be habitual in German!" He taught me that being a scholar is to be habitual in the things to which I commit.

He also taught me how to read. My wife and I saw him one day in Claremont Village. Reading a book of Kant held in his left hand, and holding his little dog on the leash in his right hand, we sure hoped that he knew where was going! Reading is his habit, and he reads a great deal. We scholars all know that we should be careful when we talk to him about any book in his areas of scholarship. He knows exactly what is on page 123, the left-hand side of the book, two-thirds of the way down. To every question I had, his single most important question to me was, "Where did you find it and what do you mean by that?" His commitment to scholarship has set a good role model for me.

Having a good teacher is also like having a good father. He teaches us how we can get to our life goals. When I was young, my tradition taught us that the king, our teachers, and our parents have equal authority over us. We were not allowed to call the king, our teachers, or our parents by their first names. Dr. Verheyden has earned my respect and honor not only because of his extraordinary scholarship but also because of his tender fatherly care and concern about my personal life and well-being. He has taught me not merely by asking me to elevate myself up to his level of scholarship, but by standing behind me and next to me. Knowing where I am coming from and what I want to achieve, he has

ii

walked with me every step of the way towards my academic achievements and personal pursuit. He never grew tired of attempting to understand what I was trying to explain. He was never impatient or reluctant, but showing his caring heart he always said, "Say that again!" To me, a teacher is someone who shares his or her life with their students and helps them to grow. Without ceasing, Dr. Verheyden helped me and was also available whenever I needed him. He carefully read my dissertation, perhaps sacrificing sleep to help me finish it on time. With deep gratitude, Dr. Carol Spanier once told me, "Jack read my dissertation in a couple of days in his overwhelmed schedule. This careful thinker and reader, to let me finish my program, devoted himself to me. I was only a student." His paternal care has led me to become who I am today.

Along with his colleagues, friends, and students, I am very delighted that I could start a Festschrift project for him. All of the contributors for this project share their warm appreciation for Dr. Verheyden for all of the things that he has done for each of them.

Dr. Verheyden is a true special blessing of God to all of us. We do thank you, Dr. Verheyden! May God bless you more abundantly in this meaningful new season in your life!

John S. Park, Ph. D.
Assistant Professor in Theology and Ethics
Executive Director of the Los Angeles Regional Center
Azusa Pacific University
Azusa, California

Second Tribute to Jack Verheyden

In the fall of 1990, I came under the spell of Dr. Jack Verheyden for the first time. The occasion was my first Ph. D. seminar as I began my program in modern and post-modern theology. The seminar was Dr. Verheyden's signature course: "The Interpretation of Religious Experience in the 19th Century." I am not exaggerating when I say the course changed the destiny of my program and my life.

Here was a man whose towering intellect and deferential style ranged across the landscape of philosophy and theology drawing together the most amazing syntheses from a pool of discordant ideas and facts. It was a spirited class, simultaneously teeming with brilliant lectures, new discoveries, and fresh insights. I would go on to have three subsequent seminars with Dr. Verheyden as well as enjoying his guidance as chair of my dissertation committee, but it was this first initial encounter that drew me to the magic that is the man.

The collection of essays that follow represent just a small part of Dr. Verheyden's legacy. Each of us has our own stories of particular insights gained, or perspective-changing conversations held, or just plain help received in negotiating the shoals of life's passages. None of these recollections adequately capture the way in which Dr. Verheyden has worked so effectively to bring out the best in each of us. It is never possible to thank a man of this stature adequately, but it is hoped that this volume of essays and the ideas presented here will linger as an enduring testimony to the impact of Jack Verheyden on our life and on our scholarship.

Gayle D. Beebe, Ph. D.
President, Spring Arbor College
Spring Arbor, Michigan

Preface

The multifarious nature of the collection of writings in this volume testifies to the variety of my own indebtedness to those who have influenced me over the past thirty-six years. The many different directions and types of relationships that have helped to shape my own orientation and experience are represented here in principle.

Six of these essays are from colleagues at the School of Theology at Claremont with whom I have most closely worked, John Cobb, Joe Hough, Dan Rhoades, David Griffin, Mary Elizabeth Moore, and Marjorie Suchocki. The latter three I had also taught long ago, and they are joined by nine other former students from the Claremont Graduate School, Avery Fouts, Brad Starr, Gayle Beebe, Helene Russell, Sam Powell, John S. Park, Thandeka, Walt Gulick, and Youngbok Kim. The themes they pursue certainly are ones in which I share an interest and often have participated with them in their explorations. Two scholars from outside Claremont, David Klemm and Hermann Peiter, with exceptional generosity have also contributed with essays dealing with the thought of Friedrich Schleiermacher and Reformation doctrine. Schleiermacher is a figure on whom I have worked for forty years, while as a long time instructor in Christian doctrine to ministerial students I have dealt with a number of issues pertaining to justification ever and again.

I am very appreciative of the time and effort that all of these colleagues of various kinds have given to the production of the essays that comprise this book. Certainly, I never envisioned that my career as a professor would receive an honor such as their work here provides. I would like to engage their essays individually, but space precludes that. I will have to confine my words to them as a group.

My gratitude to you all is deep, indeed!

Jack Verheyden

EXPERIENCE, THOUGHT, AND LANGUAGE
John B. Cobb, Jr.

I

Two centuries ago Christian thought in the West had lost it's grounding. The simple appeal to Biblical authority no longer worked. The equally simple appeal to the evidence for a Creator from the order of nature had also collapsed. Three remarkable German thinkers responded to this situation in quite different ways. Theology, as we now know it in academia, was largely a creation of these thinkers. I refer to the famed trio -- Kant, Hegel, and Schleiermacher.

Kant proposed that thinking about God be grounded in morality rather than in revelation or nature. Although few today follow Kant closely, Ritschlian neo-Kantianism continued the basic project and influenced the social gospel. Today many speak of God only in connection with issues of justice and liberation. Many more share Kant's critique of natural theology and metaphysics as contexts for doing theological work.

Hegel developed a quite new kind of speculative philosophy. His speculation was about thought itself and about human history. In this speculation religion played a large role and Christianity was viewed quite positively. To understand Christianity in its overall role in human history in the past and present has provided a way of doing theology in which it has proved possible to continue to speak of God.

Schleiermacher pointed to religious experience as the basis for understanding Christian faith. He articulated both a doctrine of religious experience in general and an account of the distinctive form it took in Christianity. He depicted this Christian form as the highest and best. Since then, the interest in religious experience has been widespread, and it has provided the basis for understanding Christianity in much of liberal theology.

Subsequently there have been just two developments of comparable importance for theology. Kierkegaard showed the limits of reason as a guide to life in such a way as to justify a decision for Christian faith. This implied that rather than justifying faith in terms of norms of supposedly neutral norms developed external to it, one could take one's stand within the faith and articulate it in its own convincing power.

Finally, in the twentieth century there occurred the linguistic turn. No one thinker stands out as clearly with regard to this turn as in the nineteenth century developments, but Wittgenstein gave it one of its most influential forms. Much theology now takes place on the view that one cannot go behind language to experience or thought. Rather than being an expression of pre-linguistic experience or of thought about an objectively existing world, languages are the comprehensive context of life. Christian language is one such context.

Process theology has some affinities with all of these types, but it does not fit well with any one. It shares with Kantians the sense of the importance of practical reason. Beliefs that do not matter in life and society do not matter. And *how* they matter is of supreme importance. But process theology rejects the view that the concern for practice renders beliefs about the natural world irrelevant. It denies that ethical concerns are independent of speculative thought. And most importantly, it affirms that experience gives us access to a world that exists in and of itself apart from our experience of it.

Process theology appreciates the boldness and breadth of Hegel's speculation. It has much to learn from his type of reflection. However, it misses in Hegel's speculation sufficient attention to the world of nature and is troubled that most Hegelians do not keep closely in touch with scientific developments. It misses adequate empirical testing of the brilliant hypotheses the speculation generates. It is disturbed by the Euro-centrism of Hegel's own thinking and worries that his followers are insufficiently open to the correction and change that should be generated by recognition of the hypothetical character of speculative theories and of the socio-historical location in which one thinks.

Process theology has special affinities with Schleiermacher. For both all reflection, at least with respect to religious matters, should involve close attention to immediate experience. They agree that feeling is the base of this experience. That God is felt and that the feeling of God is of utmost importance to theology is also a point of agreement.

Just because of these marked similarities, it is important to identify differences here in some detail. For process theology, we cannot go far with experience apart from theories about it. These theories can be suggested by examination of human experience, but they can also be suggested by physiological psychology, quantum theory, philosophical epistemology, linguistics, the history of religion, and innumerable other sources. These theories must be tested against immediate experience, but they must also be tested against many other data.

Consider the theory that every occasion of human experience feels God. For Whitehead that theory does not arise directly from the examination of human experience. There are many people who detect nothing in their experience that would initially support this theory. One cannot, therefore, ground belief in God in a previously uninterpreted experience. Indeed, one cannot simply ground it at all. But Whitehead's cosmology called for a source of novel order and ordered novelty operative in all actual entities. In more complex organisms this functions persuasively. The theory illuminates some of the data from the history of religions. If we then attend to personal experience, we can discern the operation of a distinction between what is and what might be and a call to the realization of new possibilities. None of this *proves* the truth of the theory, but it confirms its value as a hypothesis and justifies its provisional acceptance.

That Schleiermacher's own analysis of feeling was informed by theory seems apparent. He described the feeling of God as the feeling of absolute dependence. He then went on to explain absolute dependence as a one-way relationship. We are wholly dependent on God. God is in no way affected by us. Whether people in general can discern in their experience a feeling of total dependence is questionable. That they can discern a feeling that the object of their dependence is in no way dependent on them is exceedingly improbable. Schleiermacher's formulation follows from a long history of Christian theology, from Spinoza's philosophy, and from his own previous speculations. It is not read off of universal human religious experience.

Process theology agrees with Kierkegaard that the position we adopt in life is not justified by any neutral, objective evidence or reason. In each moment we are constituted by a past that is particular to that moment. There is no place to stand outside the flow of events. We are conditioned in many ways by our location in the cosmic and historical process. All our thinking is perspectival. At the same time, we are not the mere products of our situation. Just how we constitute ourselves within the given context is our decision.

With respect to Christian faith we *must* decide. If we grow up in a Christian context we may absorb Christian ideas and values, but this does not constitute us as real believers. Authentic faith requires a decision for faith. There are good reasons to decide to be a Christian, but those who make this decision need to understand that it is just that – a decision. Since the positions adopted by others are also decisions, or the results of failures to make decisions, being a Christian is not less rational than other positions, but it is not a product of reason.

Although process theologians believe that in these affirmations we are close to Kierkegaard, we find much in his thought and influence on subsequent theologians with which we are uncomfortable. We fear the overemphasis on decision when it belittles reason. We want to show the reasonableness of Christian faith rather than depict it as an absurdity. We object also to any depiction of the influence of the past upon us as primarily negative, for example, as bondage. We believe that our inheritance from the past is enriching and empowering as well as limiting and distorting.

Also, with Kierkegaard it seems that to choose to be a Christian is to adopt a set of traditional beliefs many of which are dubious cognitively and ambiguous in their moral consequences. Some of his theological followers have appealed to him to justify holding quite unreasonable, and sometimes harmful, beliefs. Process theology, in contrast, sees an enormous role for critical reflection on the part of Christians with respect to how to change and develop the Christian heritage. Indeed, it sees faithfulness itself as calling for continuous reformulation of the faith and for repentance for much that has been done in its name.

Closely related to this tendency to support traditional beliefs regardless of the plausibility and moral value, is a tendency of Kierkegaard and some of his major followers to treat Christianity as a self-sufficient and clearly-bounded phenomenon. To be a Christian is then seen as excluding the need to learn from other movements. Process theology, in contrast, recognizes that much of the awareness of the need for change in Christian thinking and practice comes from external critics and independent traditions. There is an either/or with respect to whether we will identify ourselves as Christians. But there are thousands of other decisions with respect to understanding what that identification means. Openness to wisdom wherever it can be found and critical rational reflection can and should contribute to those decisions, although they do not determine them.

Process theology agrees with the linguistic turn with respect to the importance of language. The language into which we are socialized as children informs the way we think and feel. It makes us part of a community. We participate in that community largely through speech. What is not named in the language we learn largely eludes us. The meaning of one term is explicable chiefly in relation to other parts of the linguistic system. Apart from a particular language we cannot examine our own experience. Religious experience differs according to the language with which we communicate.

Important as language is, however, process theologians reject the idea that it comprehends the whole of the world in which we live. Infants feel pain and desire before they have language to express these feelings. The argument that, until these are named they do not exist is simply dogmatic, and the dogma in question has seriously negative consequences. It can lead, and has led, to justifying unlimited cruelty to human infants as well as to other animals.

Although most thinking occurs in established language, people do struggle for a word to express an idea or feeling. Sometimes they come across a word that they recognize at once as expressing that idea or feeling. Occasionally, they invent one. The great thinkers usually introduce new language to express ideas that have not previously been thought. Some of this new language becomes widely accepted and enables other people to think these new thoughts.

If language were as ultimate as some representatives of the linguistic turn imply, interreligious dialogue could not occur. It is certainly true that one cannot find equivalent terms in different religious languages. It is true that the explanation of a term used in one religious community is chiefly by relating it to other parts of the linguistic system. It is true that this makes mutual understanding difficult. It is not true that it is impossible. In fact, when representatives of different religious communities listen to one another over a period of time, a great deal of mutual understanding occurs. In successful interfaith dialog participants become aware of features of experience that they had not previously noticed and are grateful to have new names to use for them.

Thoroughgoing advocates of the linguistic turn argue that language has no referential character at all. The arguments for this view take two forms. One form is the philosophical denial that human experience gives us access to a world beyond ourselves. This harks back to Hume and Kant and certain developments from their thought. The other form points out in detail the failure of the claims that words correspond quite simply to things. The meanings of words cannot be isolated from their place in the whole linguistic system. Further, we cannot indicate the thing to which we suppose the word refers apart from other words.

Process theology rejects this denial of a referential element in language. It affirms that there is a real world independent of human knowledge. One of the many functions of language is to highlight features of that real world that the community has found important. It evokes selective attention to these features. Language often requires adjustment as more is learned about that world.

Indeed, for process theology, chronologically and ontologically experience is primary, for primitive forms of experience existed for billions of years before anything we could call thought or language came into being. If human beings destroy themselves and those other animals with complex central nervous systems, thought and language may disappear from the Earth, but there will still be some primitive forms of experience.

Nevertheless, once thought and language are present they affect one another and both interact with experience. In short, for process theology, experience, thought, and language are dialectically related. One cannot appeal to "pure experience" for an argument or a system of belief.

The most significant challenge to this last statement is from Buddhism. Buddhists know that normal experience is deeply affected by concepts. They see this affect as blocking a deeper and truer understanding of reality. They have developed meditational disciplines designed to free the mind of all concepts and to attain to pure experience. There is no doubt about their success in moving in this direction and about the positive value of the results attained. Freed from conceptuality and the illusions it engenders, especially about the self, the meditator is able to let reality be just what it is apart from its meaning to the self.

Some Hindu practices lead to a quite different kind of pure experience. Whereas Buddhist pure experience is total openness to what is given by the world, this Hindu pure experience is totally free of influence from the world. It is a consciousness without data or content.

From the point of view of process theology, one should be very hesitant to deny the reality of extremely unusual forms of experience. It is much easier to understand approximation of these quite different goals than their total attainment; so until the evidence is overwhelming, process theologians are likely to settle for that. The total exclusion from an experience of thought, of language, or of the causal efficacy of the past is hard, indeed, to comprehend.

In any case, normal experience, the only experience most of us ever have, is a product of complex influences of many sorts. Process theologians believe that one of those influences is divine. We also believe that this fact is very important and that much is gained by identifying and cultivating the role of the divine in human life. In this respect we stand in the tradition of Schleiermacher.

II

Section I located process theology in the context of major trends in nineteenth and twentieth century theology. Since the position it adopts can make sense only if much of the most influential philosophy of these centuries is in error, Section II will present a more detailed analysis of experience, thought, and language as understood by process theologians. We are indebted for our understanding of these matters primarily to Alfred North Whitehead.

Whitehead's understanding of philosophy is at the opposite pole from the ordinary language analysis school. That school understands the existing language as adequate and comprehensive, and it undertakes to clarify meaning within its terms. Whitehead regarded this as "the fallacy of the perfect dictionary." He believed that the task of philosophers, like poets, is to discern what has not been noticed and to bring it to light. This requires either that old words be given new meanings or that new words be proposed.

The limitation of existing languages does not imply that they have nothing to contribute. On the contrary, they are depositories of the cumulative wisdom of the race. Much truth is to be learned by studying them.

Nevertheless, Whitehead did not believe that one should derive one's metaphysics from one's language. Most languages express views of the world, derived from sight and touch, that represent the world as composed of substances with attributes. English is one of these languages. Hence, if we derive our philosophical thinking from ordinary English, it will continue this pattern. Since there are now good reasons for believing that events and their relations are more fundamental than substances and attributes, it is important to think *against* language when metaphysical questions are at stake..

In no way does Whitehead thereby discount the importance of language. It is precisely his recognition of its importance that leads him to reflect both on its positive contributions to philosophy and on the way it misleads. As Buddhists have long known, thinking against one's language is a difficult task indeed!

If events are primary, then experiences as such, recognized as events, can constitute the locus of our examination. This replaces the primacy of the examination of the objects of vision and touch that have played so large a role in Western philosophy. Our experience, unlike tables and rocks, presents itself to us as in constant flux. Following William James, however, Whitehead proposed that we speculate that one's experience is not a continuous flow but, instead, that it is composed of momentary occasions rapidly succeeding one another.

Following on this theory, each momentary experience can be seen as largely constituted by the presence within it of past events. The content of an experience seems to be informed by bodily events and through these by external events as well. The view that what takes place in the body, and especially in the brain, informs the moment of human experience seems highly plausible in light of all that we know about physiological psychology and even common sense.

Whitehead calls the way in which one occasion of experience incorporates or internalizes other events within itself "prehension." This idea is central to his whole account of the world, and to understand it takes us a long way into the apprehension of Whitehead's vision as a whole. Unfortunately, we cannot claim to experience this influence of the world in our momentary occasions with much clarity. It seems to remain an idea without experiential grounding. The most immediate prehensions are, presumably, of events in the brain, and of these we are not conscious at all. The way these events affect conscious experience can be considered only in terms of scientific knowledge.

This lack of experiential grounding is qualified by the vague sense of embodiment that takes on vividness and specificity in relation to some parts of the body. Although we do not consciously experience the events in our brain, we are aware of events in other parts of the body and of the way they affect our immediate experience. I feel a pain in my leg and the pleasurable sensations in my palate as I eat. I feel these as located in particular parts of the body but yet as part of my own immediate experience. Reflecting on these helps us understand the prehensive relationship.

Still, the cells in the leg and in the palate are felt only indirectly. Their feelings are transmitted to personal experience through many intermediaries. My suffering or enjoyment with them is not due to a direct prehension.

For this reason we need to turn to the one prehensive relation to which it is possible to attend consciously – the relation of one moment of experience to its immediate predecessor. It is this prehension that gives one the strong sense of identity through time that characterizes most people most of the time. In becoming more consciously aware of this relationship, one has an immediate experiential understanding of what prehensions are and how they function. What is required is close phenomenological attention or guided meditation.

Consider the moment in which you hear the last chord in a musical phrase. That it has the character of completing a phrase implies that as you hear it you are also aware of the earlier chords. In one sense, in this moment you are only hearing the sounds that have just been brought to you by sound waves striking the eardrums and being mediated through nerves to the auditory center in the brain. But in another sense you are still hearing the sounds received in the preceding moments. Your experience in the preceding moments of hearing these earlier sounds is still resonating in the present moment. The preceding occasions of experience are included in the present one. This is what it means to say that the present occasion of experience prehends the preceding one.

Although the present includes the past it never does so exhaustively. The occasion that prehends the antecedent occasions in which the earlier chords were heard does not reproduce every feature of those earlier occasions. Many other features of the past are prehended in the new occasion and selectively synthesized in it. Much is lost in this process.

Nevertheless, the past, especially the immediate personal past, is alive in the present. The present is largely formed by that past. It is what it is because that past was what it was. There is thus enormous continuity in the world in general and in personal experience in particular. What is called "prehension" when viewed from the perspective of the new occasion is called "causal efficacy" when viewed from the perspective of the past. Occasions of experience share in constituting later occasion and thus serve as causes. Hume and Kant could not discover causality in the world because they looked for it in the sphere of what is seen and touched, the realm of objects. Causality can be found experientially only in subjective experience. We experience our own past experience as well as our bodies as causally efficacious in forming our experiences.

A prehension is an internal relation. When internal relations are understood in this way, it is clear that they are asymmetrical. The past is internal to the present. The present is external to the past. The earlier chords are still present as the concluding chord is heard. The concluding chord may be anticipated if the music is familiar, but it is not actually heard until the end.

That the future is not in the present opens the way to considering freedom. The present will participate in shaping the future, and for this reason much about the future can be predicted on the basis of what is known about the past and present. But does that imply that the exact form of the future is already determined by the present situation? Whitehead believed that the evidence of experience is that it is not. An act of experience not only prehends the past; it also decides just how to do so. This is presupposed in the sense of choice and responsibility that play so large a role in human experience but are so often explained away by philosophers. The fact that an occasion prehends its past and is thus causally affected by that past does not preclude its making it own imprint upon the world. It need not simply transmit the past into the future.

We have noted that most of the prehensions that constitute an occasion of human experience are far below the level of consciousness. Conscious experience is but the tip of the iceberg even in wide-awake human experience. We may suppose that many animals have experiences quite similar to ours, in which conscious awareness of aspects of the environment plays an important role. But if we are to take prehension as the clue to causal relations in general, then we must focus on those prehensions that are entirely unconscious. We may then suppose that such prehensive relations exist among the cellular events in our bodies, the molecular events that make up much of the physical and the subatomic events that underlie everything. The hypothesis is that events at all these levels are largely constituted by the inclusion of antecedent events and by some synthesis of them. That means that all these events are to be understood in analogy to human experience rather than in analogy to the way objects appear to us in vision and touch. To incorporate the world is an act, and acts belong to subjects rather than to objects as objective.

In this vision of reality, sense experience is dethroned as the major access to an external world. The philosophical consequences are enormous. Most Western philosophy has assumed that what is given in sense experience, and especially vision, provides the most primitive element in experience of the world. Philosophical reflection pointed out that sensa can give us nothing but phenomena the reality of which is dependent on human experience. Sensa by themselves can tell us nothing about a world outside our experience. In short, they provide no escape from solipsism. A great deal of the philosophy of the nineteenth and twentieth century has been in response to this logic.

For Whitehead sense experience is a complex phenomenon grounded chiefly in the prehensions considered above. These prehensions are, in Whitehead's terms, physical. The events in the external world, say a rug, deflect the sequence of events that we call light to my eyes with a certain pattern of frequencies. The events in my eyes are in turn modified by the light and bring about events in my brain. This is the chain of causal efficacy. The event that is my personal experience at that moment projects onto a contemporary region of space a pattern of colors correlated with the frequencies of the received impulses. These projected qualities are the sensa regarded as primitive in so much philosophy. Whitehead agrees that in themselves these sensa cannot inform us of the independent reality of the world.

On the other hand, Whitehead affirms the common sense view that sense experience does inform us about an independent world. Ordinary sense experience is not simply of the sensa. He calls this aspect "experience in the mode of presentational immediacy." Ordinary sense experience integrates presentational immediacy and causal efficacy. It is an experience of the world there as having the characteristics projected on it. As such, it is both extremely valuable for practical purposes and misleading for philosophical ones.

Normally, when all goes well, there is very little difference between the spatio-temporal region thus colored for me and the locus of events that deflected the light rays toward my eyes. However, they are never exactly identical, and when we are dealing with the heavenly bodies, the difference can be enormous. In all circumstances, there is a considerable difference between the visual sensa projected and the subjective actuality of the entities that compose what is seen.

Our normal experience is of an external actuality characterized in a certain way. Modern philosophy sought to understand the external actuality through the projected colors and found that it could not. Its solution was to deny the actuality or, at least, any human access to such an actuality. The resulting refusal to talk affirmatively about the reality of an external world leads to results that are profoundly at odds with common sense and with what we all in fact believe. For Whitehead, there is an external world that is causally efficacious for our projection of sensa. It is composed of vast congeries of events organized in complex patterns many of which have what Whitehead called social order. The "societies" of events that are actually there are drastically different from the "substances" that philosophers were once accustomed to posit and also from the sensa projected in their regions. Nevertheless, between the sensa and the events there are very important connections and correlations. From sense experience we learn much of utmost importance about our physical environment.

The sensa are examples of what Whitehead calls "eternal objects." In and of themselves they are "eternal" in the sense of having no temporal locus and "objects" in the sense of being totally devoid of subjectivity. They have no existence in themselves, attaining it only as they are objects for some prehending subject. The prehensions of these objects Whitehead termed "mental." Every occasion of experience synthesizes some mental prehensions with the physical ones we have discussed above. Sense experience is a synthesis possible only in complex organisms with central nervous systems and specialized sense organs.

With this sketch of some relevant features of Whitehead's thought, we turn to the nature of language, the major form of communication among human beings. A major function of language is to call the attention of another to some "proposition." For Whitehead a proposition is not a linguistic entity. It is the way some element in reality may, or may not, be. The logical subject of the proposition is some event or society of events. An election or a chair will serve as example. But when we have thought of the society in this way we have already introduced a pattern of eternal objects into the logical subject. In other words we have already identified a proposition. That is that to which we refer, the particular society of occasions abstracted from all its characteristics, may be an election or a chair. In this more exact formulation, "election" and "chair," stripped of their connection to any particular entity, are complex eternal objects. Experiencing these societies of events as possibly having these forms is a propositional feeling.

We are surrounded by innumerable entities that may or may not have innumerable characteristics. Hence we live in a world of propositions. In Whitehead's view, consciousness presupposes the feeling of propositions, that is. feelings of entities in the environment as having, and not having, particular characteristics. We would not be conscious of the grass as green if we did not implicitly contrast green with other colors. To be conscious of green is to be conscious of not-brown, not-yellow, not-red.

Only a tiny number of the propositions that we entertain come to expression in language. Nevertheless, they are basic to language. It is impossible to call the attention of others to more than a very few; so language is used to highlight features of the world that seem important to the speaker and are, in the speaker's judgment, of potential interest to the hearer. If the speaker says something of the health of a friend, the hearer is encouraged to think of that friend and entertain the idea that the friend is well or ill. If the speaker wants to gain the support of the hearer for painting a wall, the hearer is encouraged to think of the wall as having a different color from its present one. If the speaker wants the hearer to share alarm over pollution, the speaker will describe the probable consequences of continuing present lines of action. The hearer will be encouraged to imagine a world different from the present one in diverse ways.

The proposition, or cluster of propositions, evoked to the attention of the hearer will rarely be identical with those in the mind of the speaker. But in most cases they will overlap sufficiently that communication will have occurred. There is no guarantee of this; so the art of good communication requires constant study.

Whereas it is fashionable today to reject the correspondence theory of truth, Whitehead allows it a place. Sentences do not have a one to one correspondence with propositions, so that the truth or falsity of sentences could only be decided by a rather artificial determination of exactly what propositions they are intended or evoked. It is propositions are either true or false. If we require exactness for truth, the vast majority are false, but their error is usually unimportant for the purposes at hand.

In any case, the truth or falsity of propositions does not point to their major function. They are, in Whitehead's language, "lures for feeling." If a sentence uttered by one person leads to another's attention to a particular lure, it has been successful. In the examples above about painting a wall, the proposition about a different color is false. But if it persuades the other to support the re-painting, the speaker's purpose is accomplished.

The clearest examples of true propositions are those dealing with the feeling states of subjects. One may judge by a woman's appearance and actions that she is depressed. One may state this to a third person, evoking a proposition about her state of mind. This proposition may or may not correspond to the actual state of mind of the woman. In short, it may be true or false.

A different question is how its truth or falsity can be determined. The answer here is that absolute certainty is unattainable. One may come close if the proposition is about one's own state of mind, but even here confusion and self-deception are possible. With respect to another person the determination is far more difficult. Nevertheless, the difficulty of determining whether a proposition corresponds with reality does not imply that the question of correspondence is unimportant. In this case, the woman's friends will relate to her according to their judgment of its truth or falsity. This behavior on their part may be of great importance for her future. In the real world we must act on such judgments of correspondence despite their uncertainty.

It may be important to emphasize that the correspondence is not between an element of language and an element of independent reality. The difference between language and actual things is too great for that. The correspondence is between the propositions expressed or evoked by language and the real condition of the entities that constitute the logical subjects of these propositions. Here there must be either correspondence or lack of it.

I have emphasized that the presence or absence of correspondence may not be of major importance in the use of language. Pointing out an additional feature of prehensions can highlight this point. Every physical prehension can be analyzed into its objective datum and its subjective form. It prehends something in the past, but it always does so with some feeling tone. Usually, this largely repeats the feeling tone of the past event. If I am angry in one moment, the prehension of that moment in the next one will be likely to have anger as its feeling tone or subjective form.

For Whitehead, subjective form, primarily in the form of emotion, is the basic actuality of the world. We may think of the objective reality of most of the world in terms of pulsations of unconscious emotion. From the outside we may describe this as the transmission of energy.

Given this ontological primacy of emotion, it is understandable that the subjective form of propositional feelings plays a large role in communication.

One rarely seeks simply to evoke a proposition into the hearer's attention. One wants the hearer to feel that proposition in a particular way. If one describes the kind of world that will result from continued polluting activities, one probably wants the hearer to feel horror at the prospect. If one assures someone that a mutual friend is recovering well from a critical operation, one wants the friend to share one's relief and joy. In addition, there is a good deal of talk in which the propositions involved are less important that the mood of conviviality established.

I am trying to make two main points about language. On the one hand, it has many functions, and evoking propositions that correspond to reality is by no means the most important. Those who have followed the linguistic turn have said much that is correct and illuminating. Their statements evoke interesting propositions that correspond with reality. On the other hand, their denial that language has any connection with an objective reality distorts the discussion. Transmitting information about the world plays a large role in communication.

For Whitehead, then, language is far from being the encompassing world for human beings. Propositions come close to occupying that role, but language can highlight only a few. That means that experience is far more inclusive than language. It also means that thought can outrun language. We entertain many propositions that we do not verbalize.

There is no reason to suppose that all of these propositions can be verbalized in any given language or in all the given languages together. If one attends to features of reality to which others have not yet attended, there is no reason to assume that existing language will be adequate. For example, if in the past people, including philosophers, have not attended to how one moment of human experience is informed by its predecessor, there is no reason to assume that either ordinary language or philosophical language will include words adequate to describe this relationship. If philosophers entertain propositions that others have not entertained, they will need to develop a new language to express them and to evoke them in others.

This is by no means to deny the close connection between thought and language. If one does not find or create language for one's new thought, it is very unlikely that one can do much with it. It will remain a propositional feeling in the penumbra of consciousness with little fruit elsewhere. The insistence that thinking is a linguistic activity is very close to being exhaustively true. Yet the element of error is also important. The growth of language and consciousness depends on thought pressing beyond existing language.

This may be more obvious in scientific language. The breakdown of classical physics with the rise of relativity and quantum theory required the development of language. In my judgment the advance of physics itself has been impeded by too much dependence on existing language. For example, the subatomic world is still described in terms of particles and waves, terms developed in the context of a worldview that does not fit the evidence. The resulting paradoxes might be solved if the evidence were allowed to dictate new thought and a language that would express it better. David Bohm is noteworthy for making this effort.

III

What about God? When sense experience is taken as the primary way in which people relate to what is not themselves, God-talk fares badly! God cannot be experienced through the senses. Hence, those who take sense experience as primal must deny that God can be experienced. If there is to be belief in God at all, it must be based on inference. Arguments for the existence of God, accordingly, have played a major role in Christian history. They continue to have their importance. But standing on their own, apart from supportive experience, they have become unconvincing to most thinkers. The five styles of theology discussed above have arisen in this context.

This statement is least applicable to Schleiermacher. Indeed, in the account above he was presented as affirming a feeling of God. In fact, this is less clear than it seems at first in reading him. Schleiermacher seems to have felt pressure from his intellectual environment to avoid explicitly claiming that the feeling of absolute dependence is a feeling of that on which one is absolutely dependent. Although this interpretation seems to be implied in much that he wrote, there are places where it seems that he wants to avoid the philosophical problems implicit in such claims. The feeling can then be understood in purely subjective terms. Whatever may be the case with Schleiermacher, much discussion of religious experience today, even of theistic religious experience, abstracts from the question of whether anything is objectively experienced.

The situation is very different when physical prehensions as understood by Whitehead are recognized as primary. Theologically there is no reason to deny that there are physical prehensions of God. Philosophically the question is simply one of fact. If God is an actual entity, then God is physically felt in some way in all occasions of experience. The questions are: (1) is there an actual entity that is appropriately named "God;" and (2) if so, what role does the prehension of God play in actual occasions?

Whitehead's positive answer to the first of these questions depends on his analysis of a role for which something that can be called God is needed. He concluded that apart from God pure potentials, eternal objects, can play no role in forming actuality. There is no explanation of how ordered novelty and novel order are introduced into the world. God is both the principle of limitation for the world and the organ of novelty.

This can be understood better on a more personal basis. Apart from God an individual occasion of human experience could be nothing more than the determined outcome of past forces. Its ability to make a decision about how to constitute itself depends on its prehension of possibilities that do not simply derive from the past. God is the reason that it is self-constituting and morally responsible. God is the reason that there is a tension between what is and what ought to be and that there is a lure toward realizing what ought to be.

Normally, the prehension of God is not conscious. Since it is present all the time, it does not call attention to itself. Nevertheless, it is not difficult to bring to awareness some aspects of what has been attributed to God in the preceding paragraph. We can be aware of feeling drawn to be more than we have been or of falling short of being what we might have become. If we imagine what it would be like to be wholly determined by the past, we know that that is not the way we actually experience ourselves. These are pervasive characteristics of experience that are hard to attribute to our prehension of past occasions.

Are there, in addition, conscious experiences of God in which the datum is clearly felt as datum? There are enough reported instances of this sort that those who are open to this line of inquiry are reasonably supported in a positive conclusion. Process theology is not dependent on the reality of such experiences, but it is entirely open to them.

How does language play into these questions? Very importantly. The language with which one is surrounded plays an almost determinative role with respect to those features of one's experience to which one attends. If it leads one to focus on sense data, belittling all else, one is likely to do so. Consciousness of what God does in one's life is, then, extremely unlikely to develop.

If one lives in a context in which God's role in the world is spoken of only in terms of natural and moral laws and reward and punishment, even if the inwardness of the human subject as a possible locus of sinful thought is considered important, one is very unlikely to thematize the role process theologians, following Whitehead, believe that God plays. One may focus on guilt and seek God in connection with that. That will not lead to the experience of God as understood by process theology.

If one lives in a deeply religious context that is not theistic, again, the God of process theology is not likely to be consciously experienced. Buddhists call attention to many of the same features of experience as do process philosophers, but they do not thematize human freedom and moral responsibility or transcendence of the past. In a Buddhist culture these features of our experience are unlikely to be attended to. What Buddhists understand by "God" they reject, as do process theologians. Conscious experience of God as affirmed by process theology is highly improbable in that linguistic world.

God is part of all experience including those whose language obscures God's presence. Those who believe in this God can discern God's presence everywhere. Some who do not recognize God may embody God's activity within them better than most of those who do. Consciousness of God, highly dependent on a suitable language, is not the primary issue. Nevertheless, it has its importance, and for that reason, developing the right theological language to encourage such consciousness also has its importance.

In this whole process, thought is closely bound to language and yet outruns it. Without outrunning it, thought could not reform language in such a way as to encourage attention to the working of God within us. But as it outruns language, it must modify it so as to make use of it. Without a corrected language that is still closely connected with familiar language it cannot evoke in others attention to the working of God within them.

DIVINE ACTIVITY AND SCIENTIFIC NATURALISM
David Ray Griffin

For the past century and a half, the dominant view has been that there is a conflict between science and religion. At the very heart of this perceived conflict is the issue of divine activity in the world. *On the one hand*, the notion that there is a Divine Power that exerts causal influence in the world is presupposed by most if not all religions. This presupposition is clearly central to the biblically based religions: The Hebrew Bible speaks of God as creating the world in a succession of acts, intervening in the histories of the Hebrews and the surrounding nations, and calling the prophets, with one of the prophets having God say, "Behold, I do a new thing." Christianity regards the decisive new thing done by God to be the act of becoming incarnate in Jesus of Nazareth. The idea that God continues to act in the world even after this decisive event is expressed by the Christian doctrine of the Holy Spirit. Islam, while accepting these events of Hebrew and Christian history as authentic acts of God, affirms another decisive act in the calling of Mohammed to be God's prophet. It is not only the biblically based religions, furthermore, that presuppose the notion of divine influence. This notion is presupposed by most primal religions, such as those of Native Americans and Africans. It is presupposed by theistic Hinduism, which is the type of Hinduism accepted by most Hindus. And if the notion of divine action is understood not in an overly anthropomorphic way but simply to mean *some* kind of divine influence in the world, it is even presupposed by many forms of Buddhism.[1] Besides presupposing divine influence in the world, furthermore, most religious thought assumes that reference to this influence plays an essential role in our explanation

---

[1] I have provided support for this assertion in Chapter 7 of my *Reenchantment Without Supernaturalism: A Process Philosophy of Religion* (Ithaca: Cornell University Press, 2000).

of certain aspects of our world. *On the other hand*, the modern scientific worldview, as now usually understood, allows for no divine activity, as least not if such activity is taken to provide an explanation of anything in particular. The notion of "God" or "divine influence" is almost universally said not be an acceptable explanation for any feature of the world. The worldviews of the scientific and the religious communities, accordingly, seem to be in irreconcilable conflict.[2]

The other term in the title of my essay is "scientific naturalism," which I use to refer to the worldview now dominant in the scientific community. Although the term "naturalism" is used in a wide variety of ways, its most basic connotation is simply *the rejection of supernaturalism*. The fundamental meaning of naturalism, more precisely, is the doctrine that there are no supernatural interventions in the world, with a "supernatural intervention" understood to be a *divinely caused interruption of the world's normal causal processes*. Naturalism in this sense can be equated with philosophical *uniformitarianism*, which is the assumption that all events are connected to antecedent and subsequent events by universal, uniform causal principles. This uniformitarian naturalism, which came to be adopted by the scientific community in the nineteenth century, is now this community's most widely presupposed philosophical conviction. It is appropriate, therefore, to use "scientific naturalism" to point to the worldview of the contemporary scientific community. The question of this essay is whether this scientific naturalism is compatible with the kind of divine activity in the world presupposed by most religious belief. My answer is Yes.

---

[2]To put the issue in terms of the theme of the present anthology: *Religious thought*, insofar as it is true to the *experiences* on which most of the religions have been based, presupposes the reality of divine activity in the world. The dominant reading of distinctively *scientific experience* in the past two centuries, by contrast, has led most *scientific thought* to deny the existence of any supernatural interruptions of the world's normal causal processes. The question, to which I will give a negative answer, is whether there is any necessary conflict between these two traditions of experience and thought.

It is now widely assumed, however, that the answer to this question is No. In some circles, this answer is based on the equation of scientific naturalism not merely with the rejection of supernaturalism, as defined above, but also with an atheistic worldview. Although a thorough argument for the compatibility of scientific naturalism with belief in divine activity would need to challenge this equation, arguing to the contrary that the kind of naturalism that is properly presupposed by science need not involve atheism,[3] that argument lies beyond the limits of the present essay, which simply asks whether religious belief in divine activity is compatible with naturalism in the more limited sense of the rejection of supernaturalism.

Even with the question thus phrased, many thinkers would still answer No. By ruling out supernatural interruptions of the world's normal causal processes, these thinkers believe, scientific naturalism is necessarily in conflict with a religious worldview, insofar as religious belief affirms or at least presupposes the notion of divine activity in the world. If this were indeed the case, the conflict between science and religion would be permanent. One would need to choose between them. If one accepts the scientific worldview, with its naturalistic presupposition, one would have to accept the conclusion that religion is incurably false or at least mythological. This is, of course, a conclusion that many students feel forced to accept after a year or two at a college or university. Not all students, of course, are led to this conclusion. Some retain, or even develop, a religious worldview that presupposes divine interruptions of the web of natural causes. Although these students may accept many of the teachings and technological benefits of science, their religious beliefs put them in opposition to the most

---

[3] I have made this argument in *Religion and Scientific Naturalism: Overcoming the Conflicts* (Albany: State University of New York Press, 2000) as well as in *Reenchantment Without Supernaturalism*. In those discussions, I distinguish between a minimal naturalism, which can be called naturalism$_{ns}$ (for "nonsupernaturalistic"), and a maximal naturalism, which can be called naturalism$_{sam}$ (for "sensationistic-atheistic-materialistic"), and then argue that science does not need, and in fact could be more adequate without, the maximal version. In the present essay, only the theism-atheism dimension of this contrast is discussed.

fundamental assumption of the worldview of the scientific community. This is one of the central tragedies of contemporary higher education, that it seems to force reflective students to choose between being religious and being scientific. And this tragedy, of course, simply reflects the wider fact that late modern culture seems to force all reflective people, including college, university, and even seminary professors, to make this choice.

I first review the standard attempts to overcome this problem, all of which, I suggest, are failures. I then point out how these failures are rooted in a traditional assumption about the relation between divine and worldly causation. Finally, I suggest another solution, which rejects that traditional assumption.

The Standard Solutions

Philosophers and theologians have been suggesting solutions to the apparent conflict between scientific naturalism and divine causation for several centuries. Five of these solutions can be considered standard, in that they are well enough known to be widely discussed.

Pantheistic Identity of Divine and Natural Causation

One of these solutions is based on a pantheistic worldview, according to which the terms "God" and "Nature" are simply two different words for the same thing, the universe as a whole. In the seventeenth century, Spinoza affirmed this view with his famous phrase "God or Nature." Given this standpoint, anything can be looked at from two perspectives. On the one hand, everything that happens is produced by natural causes. There are no miracles, in the sense of interruptions of the chain of cause-effect relations. On the other hand, everything that happens can be considered an act of God. By thus affirming a pantheistic identity of natural and divine causation, Spinoza meant to reconcile scientific naturalism with divine activity.

The religious communities, however, have generally considered this pantheistic solution to be unacceptable. The religious sensitivity is based on the conviction that not all events are equally acts of God. For example, Spinoza was Jewish, but most present-day Jews would reject the idea that the activities of Hitler were as fully caused by God as the activities of Moses, Amos, and Jeremiah. Religious believers, in other words, assume not only that God acts in the world, but that this divine activity is *variable*, rather than being the same at all times and places. This notion, that God acts differently in different events, was expressed in the previously quoted prophetic utterance, "Behold, I do a new thing" (Isaiah 43:19).

Paradoxical Identity of Divine and Natural Causation

A second solution has been suggested by some existentialist theologians in the middle of the twentieth century, most notably New Testament theologian Rudolf Bultmann. He agreed with Spinoza that we should not think of acts of God as violations of the natural web of cause-effect relations. Bultmann's famous call to "demythologize" the message of the New Testament was based on his conviction that this idea of divine action is mythological. And he agreed with Spinoza that a nonmythological interpretation requires that we regard divine causation as somehow identical with natural causation. He did not, however, agree with Spinoza's view that we can simply declare in advance that all events are acts of God. Rather, it is only in an existential moment of faith that one can speak of some particular event as an act of God. For example, if my sick child is healed, I may come to see the healing as an act of God, even though I know that the healing was produced by the medicine provided by the doctor. It is not that I think of it as *partly* caused by the medicine and *partly* by God. Rather, as a modern person, I accept the view that every event, even events of extraordinary healing, are *wholly* produced by purely natural causes. Nevertheless, I may also regard it as wholly produced by God. Bultmann realized that this view is paradoxical. Indeed, he used the phrase "paradoxical identity" to describe the relation between divine and natural causation.[4]

This phrase points to the main problem with this solution, which is that we cannot understand what it *means* to say that, although all events are wholly caused by natural causes, some events can be said to be special acts of God. In philosophical language, an event cannot have more than one sufficient cause because a sufficient cause, by definition, is a cause sufficient to bring about an effect.[5] If natural causes are sufficient to bring about a particular effect, there is no room for a supernatural cause.

Language about Divine Causation as Nonreferential

Our first two attempts to reconcile belief in divine causation with scientific naturalism have both involved the notion of two perspectives: From one perspective, an event is purely natural, from another perspective it is an act of God. A third attempt speaks less of two perspective than of two types of language: referential and nonreferential. According to this view, much of our ordinary language is referential. That is, it is intended to refer to objects beyond ourselves, as when we speak of rocks, trees, and planets. By contrast, religious language, especially language about God, is said to be nonreferential. For example, when we confess in reciting a creed that God created the world, the intention is not to refer to a supreme being who brought this world into existence. Rather, it is to express one's attitudes, such as one's awe at the magnificence at the world. To say that God inspired the prophets is to say, perhaps, that one intends to live a life of justice.

---

[4] I have discussed Bultmann's view in a chapter entitled "Paradoxical Identity of Divine and Worldly Action" in *A Process Christology* (Philadelphia: Westminster Press, 1973).

[5] I have discussed this point in relation to bodily and "mental" action in *Unsnarling the World-Knot: Consciousness, Freedom, and the Mind-Body Problem* (Berkeley: University of California Press, 1998), 29-30, 213, 222-23, 232.

One problem with this view is that it simply does not correspond with what most religious people really mean when they speak of divine activity, such as divine creation and inspiration. Another problem is that no religious community based on this understanding of religious language could be self-sustaining. Religious language does, to be sure, have nonreferential functions, such as expressing attitudes and intentions. But those attitudes and intentions are taken to be *appropriate* because of beliefs, expressed in referential language, about the way the world really is. If language about God is said not be refer to anything, then we have no way to say that particular attitudes, such as love and a concern for justice, are appropriate. This third solution, therefore, does not reconcile religious language about divine causation with scientific naturalism.[6]

Scientific Naturalism as Purely Methodological

The first three solutions assume the truth of scientific naturalism as it is usually understood, then seek to reconcile this scientific doctrine with religion by reconceiving the belief in divine causation. A fourth standard solution takes a different approach, saying that it is the notion of scientific naturalism that needs to be reconceived. According to this solution, scientific naturalism should be understood not as an ontological or metaphysical doctrine, according to which supernatural causation never occurs. Rather, scientific naturalism is to be understood as a purely methodological doctrine, which deals with the nature of science, not the nature of the universe. That is, to say that science is naturalistic is merely to say that science by definition, or at least by irreversible convention, restricts itself to tracing natural causes. Science as such, according to this view, neither affirms nor denies the reality of divine causation. It simply does not raise this question, because the restriction to natural causes is inherent in the scientific method.

---

[6]I have argued against the adequacy of nonrealist interpretations of religious language in *Reenchantment Without Supernaturalism*, especially the Introduction and Chapters 7 and 9.

40

In the thought of most of the contemporary advocates of this position, this methodological naturalism is combined with the acceptance of supernatural causation. That is, these advocates believe that reference to divine causation is needed to explain various things, such as the existence and order of our universe, the rise of life, and various biblical miracles. A scientist *qua* scientist cannot refer to divine causation to explain these events, which means that science cannot provide an adequate explanation for them. But this point simply illustrates the fact that science is an inherently limited enterprise. To have an adequate worldview, say these thinkers, we must place science, with its naturalism, within a supernaturalistic framework.[7]

The main problem with this solution is that it fails to reconcile the worldview of the religious community with the worldview of the scientific community. The ideological leaders of the scientific community emphatically do not accept the view that their naturalism is purely methodological. They do not accept the contention that it is fine to affirm supernatural incursions into the world as long as one makes clear that such affirmations are not intended to be scientific statements. Rather, in affirming naturalism, the leading spokespersons of the scientific community affirm the ontological or metaphysical doctrine that no supernatural interruptions of the web of natural causation ever occur, so that all events are, at least in principle, explainable in terms of this web of natural causes.[8] A second problem is that, by returning to the idea of a God who can interrupt the world's causal processes at will, we bring back the traditional

---

[7]I discuss this view, as articulated by various contemporary representatives, in Chapter 3 of my *Religion and Scientific Naturalism*.

[8]This problem is avoided by the consistently deistic version of this position, which says that, whereas God *could* interrupt the world's normal causal processes, God never in fact does so. Although this position--which has been articulated by Rudolf Otto in *Naturalism and Religion* (New York: G. P. Putnam's, 1907) and, less wholeheartedly, by Peter Forrest in *God Without the Supernatural: A Defense of Scientific Theism* (Ithaca: Cornell University Press, 1996)--does avoid the most obvious conflict with scientific naturalism, it is still in conflict with scientific naturalism, insofar as the latter affirms not only that supernatural interruptions never occur but also that such interruptions are not even conceivable.

problem of evil, which asks why this all-powerful God, who could interrupt natural and human causality, allows so much unspeakable evil.

The Rejection of Scientific Naturalism in Favor of Theistic Science

A fifth standard solution casts an even more critical eye on the notion of scientific naturalism. Whereas the fourth solution accepted it as a methodological doctrine while rejecting it as a metaphysical doctrine, this fifth solution rejects it altogether. That is, it says that science, which simply means knowledge, should describe things as they really are. Therefore, if the world and many events within it came about through divine causation, then science, to "tell it like it is," must refer to divine causation. The best science, in other words, would be a *theistic* science. The most well-known version of this view is the fundamentalist position usually called "creation science" or "scientific creationism," which takes the first book of the Bible, understood literally, to be essentially accurate, so that the Earth is only a few thousand years old. A less extreme version of theistic science is represented most vigorously today by attorney Phillip Johnson, whose book *Darwin on Trial* has attracted much attention, and well-known philosopher Alvin Plantinga.[9] In the Plantinga-Johnson version of theistic science, the scientific community's consensus that our world has come about over many billions of years is accepted, but a supernatural act of God is said to be the explanation for the origin of the universe, the rise of life, and the rise of every species of life thereafter. Arguing that this view provides the best explanation of these events, Plantinga and Johnson would overcome the conflict between scientific naturalism

---

[9]Phillip E. Johnson, *Darwin on Trial,* 2nd edition (Downers Grove, Ill.: InterVarsity Press, 1993). See also Johnson's *Reason in the Balance: The Case Against Naturalism in Science, Law, and Education* (Downers Grove, Ill.: InterVarsity Press, 1993). I have discussed these two books in "Christian Faith and Scientific Naturalism: An Appreciative Critique of Phillip Johnson's Proposal," *Christian Scholar's Review* 28/2 (Winter 1998): 308-28. For Plantinga's position, see "When Faith and Reason Clash: Evolution and the Bible," *Christian Scholar's Review* 21/1 (1991): 8-32, and "Evolution, Neutrality, and Antecedent Probability: A Reply to McMullin and Van Till," *Christian Scholar's Review* 21/1 (1991): 80-109. I have discussed the Plantinga-Johnson position in Chapter 3 of *Religion and Scientific Naturalism.*

42

and divine causation by convincing the scientific community to reject naturalism in favor of supernaturalism.[10]

The main problem with this solution, ignoring here the question of its truth, is that there is virtually no chance that the scientific community will accept it, because the rejection of supernaturalism has become the most fundamental metaphysical conviction of the scientific community over the past 200 years. Also, this fifth solution, like the fourth, brings back the traditional problem of evil, which is, in fact, one of the reasons why this position has no appeal to the ideological leaders of the scientific community.

As this brief review of the standard positions suggests, they all fail to reconcile the worldview of the scientific community, with its naturalism, and the worldview of the religious communities, with its notion of divine activity in the world. But why should this be the case? Why should it be impossible to have a notion of divine activity that would be religiously adequate without contradicting the scientific community's assumption that there are no interruptions of the world's normal causal processes? Why, in other words, can there not be a naturalistic notion of divine activity in the world, according to which divine influence is a normal part of the world's causal processes, not an interruption of those processes? There *can*, I suggest, be such a notion. But this alternative notion is not well known due to the continuing impact, reflected in all the standard positions, of the way of understanding the relation between divine and natural causation that was dominant in the Middle Ages. I refer to the scheme of primary and secondary causation. I will next briefly review this scheme in order to show how the conflict between divine activity and scientific naturalism arose.

---

[10]This way of understanding the challenge would probably be accepted, however, only by the Johnson, because Plantinga articulates his position as a defensive strategy, aimed at justifying the right of conservative Christians to hold their beliefs without being able to show that they are more plausible than opposing beliefs.

The Scheme of Primary and Secondary Causation

According to the scheme of primary and secondary causation, God is the *primary* cause of all events. Being omnipotent, God's activity as primary cause of all events makes God the *sufficient* cause of those events; no supplementation by other causes is needed. However, God usually does not bring events about unilaterally, but through *secondary* causes, now more commonly called *natural* causes. These secondary or natural causes are *also* sufficient cause--as long as attention is focused on the *nature* of the events that are brought about, on their *whatness*. If, by contrast, the question of the *thatness* of the events is raised-- namely, why a world, with its chains of causal events, exists at all--one must then refer to God, as the creator and sustainer of the whole universe. But if one ignores this more radical question--of why there is anything rather than nothing--one need not refer to God to give a complete account of most events. Divine causation, accordingly, is usually restricted to the invariable activity of sustaining the universe. It is usually not variable causation that is constitutive of the nature or whatness of worldly things and events. For the normal course of events, accordingly, a science limited to secondary or natural causes can in principle be complete.

This scheme has been very appealing to both scientists and theologians. On the one hand, it has allowed scientists to ignore theological ideas in developing their detailed accounts of how the world works. On the other hand, it has allowed theologians to defend the uniqueness of divine causation. Arguing that divine and natural causation occur on "different levels," theologians could say that "God is not one cause among others"--that divine causation is not to be treated as simply one more type of finite causation. This scheme, accordingly, allowed theologians and scientists to operate autonomously, with each protected from possible conflict with, and thereby interference from, the other.

There was, however, one snag. The doctrine, as I said, was that God *usually* brings about effects through secondary or natural causes. In a *few* cases, God was said to bring about the effects directly, without using secondary causes as instruments. The most obvious of such cases were the miracles in the Bible and the lives of the saints. Indeed, a miracle was *defined* as an event brought about directly by God as primary cause, without the employment of secondary causes. But the list of events produced directly by God's primary causation also included events not usually classified as miracles, such as the creation of the world, the creation of life, the creation of the various species of plants and animals, the creation of the human soul, the inspiration of the prophets and the biblical writers, and the incarnation in Jesus. Given all these events that were not explainable in terms of natural causes, there could not really be a fully naturalistic science of either nature or history.

This was so because of the most fateful implication of the primary-secondary scheme for thinking about the relation between divine and worldly causation. According to this scheme, to speak of any divine influence that is constitutive of the nature of events in the world was *ipso facto* to speak of a supernatural interruption of the chains of natural causes and effects. Because most events were said to be fully explicable, at least in principle, without reference to any variable divine influence, the affirmation that some such influence played a constitutive role in particular events implied that this divine influence interrupted the causal principles involved in most events. For example, to say that the prophet Jeremiah's experience of God's call was constitutive of his experience was to say that God's causal influence on Jeremiah in those moments was different in kind from God's causal influence in most human experience. Likewise, if we say that the creation of life involved divine activity beyond the undifferentiated divine influence that sustains all beings in existence, we have to say that the creation of life involved an interruption of the causal principles involved in most events. This position, which is embodied in the fourth and fifth of the standard solutions reviewed earlier, was widely accepted by scientists, philosophers, and theologians in the eighteenth and nineteenth centuries.

Those who were imbued with the spirit of the scientific enterprise, however, became increasingly reluctant to accept the idea that there were gaps in the chain of natural causes that needed to be filled by supernatural causation. These thinkers came, in other words, to reject the "God of the gaps." Given the primary-secondary scheme for thinking of the relation between divine and worldly causation, this denial of supernatural interruptions implied pantheism, or atheism, or at least the deistic idea that, after creating the universe, God did *all* things through secondary or natural causes, never acting to fill a gap in the nexus of natural causes. This deistic solution was central to the uniformitarianism famously championed by Charles Lyell, according to which our explanations of past events should assume no causal factors not operative today.

Lyell, however, illustrated the difficulty that thinkers had in fully leaving supernaturalism behind, given a worldview in which any affirmation of variable divine influence in the world entailed a supernatural intervention. Lyell believed that fresh divine influence was necessary to explain the origin of the human mind. Divine intervention, he said, added "the moral and intellectual faculties of the human race, to a system of nature which had gone on for millions of years without the intervention of any analogous cause." This meant that we must "assume a primeval creative power which does not act with uniformity."[11] Lyell, in other words, thought that there was still one gap to be filled.

It was on this point that Charles Darwin broke with his older friend. In a letter to Lyell, Darwin rejected the idea of divine additions to explain the distinctive capacities of the human mind, saying: "I would give nothing for the theory of natural selection, if it requires miraculous additions at any one stage of descent."[12] Darwin still believed in a creator God, thinking evolution intelligible only on the assumption that God, in creating the universe, had built in laws of

---

[11]Lyell's statements are quoted in R. Hooykaas, *Natural Law and Divine Miracle: A Historical-Critical Study of the Principle of Uniformity in Geology, Biology, and Theology* (Leiden: E. J. Brill, 1959), 114.

[12]Francis Darwin, ed., *The Life and Letters of Charles Darwin*, 2 vols. (New York: D. Appleton, 1896), 2: 6-7.

evolutionary development. But Darwin insisted on a consistently deistic view, with not a single supernatural interruption of these laws.[13]

This rejection of supernatural causation, furthermore, was soon applied to the origin of the universe itself, so that Darwin's followers rejected his deism in favor of complete atheism. It is this late modern worldview, with its atheism, that is generally equated with scientific naturalism today. The denial of supernatural gap-filling is taken to mean the denial of *any* divine influence in the world. It is this assumption that led thinkers holding the first three solutions to redefine the notion of divine causation so radically that it is no longer recognizable by religious believers. And it is this same assumption that has led advocates of the fourth and fifth solutions to hold that, to do justice to religious belief, they must reject not only the atheism of the late modern worldview but also its naturalism, thereby reaffirming the medieval and early modern idea of supernatural interruptions of the world's normal causal processes. It was in these ways that the scheme of primary and secondary causation led to the present impasse, in which it seems impossible to do justice both to the scientific community's naturalism and the religious community's belief in variable divine influence in the world.

---

[13]Because this essay is for a volume in honor of Jack Verheyden, I cannot resist pointing out that Darwin's rejection of Lyell's exception had been anticipated by David Friedrich Strauss's rejection of an exception in Friedrich Schleiermacher's position. In one passage, Schleiermacher had said: "It can never be necessary in the interest of religion so to interpret a fact that its dependence on God absolutely excludes its being conditioned by the system of Nature" (*The Christian Faith*, ed. H. R. Mackintosh and J. S. Stewart [New York: Harper, 1963], 178). However, in a discussion of the origin of the life of Jesus (398-415), Schleiermacher maintained that Jesus's perfect God-consciousness is understandable only on the assumption that divine causation protected him from the kinds of sinful influences to which the rest of us are subject. Strauss, who from his Hegelian position regarded any such exceptions to be impossible, criticized Schleiermacher for affirming one. While acknowledging that Schleiermacher "limits the miraculous to the first introduction of Christ into the series of existences, and allows the whole of his further development to have been subject to all the conditions of finite existence," Strauss argued that "this concession cannot repair the breach, which the supposition only of one miracle makes in the scientific theory of the world" (*The Life of Jesus Critically Examined*, translated by George Eliot, edited by Peter C. Hodgson [Fortress Press, 1972], 771).

Naturalistic Theism

I turn now to a new way of understanding divine causation that has been developed in the twentieth century, a way that overcomes the impasse that resulted from the scheme of primary and secondary causation. This new way was suggested by William James, at the end of *The Varieties of Religious Experience,*[14] but it was first fully worked out by Alfred North Whitehead, whose philosophy became the basis for the movement known as "process theology."

This Whiteheadian way of thinking of divine influence can be called "naturalistic theism," because divine causation never interrupts the world's normal pattern of cause-and-effect relations. There is, nevertheless, variable

---

[14]I refer to the position that James called "piecemeal supernaturalism" (*The Varieties of Religious Experience* [New York: Longmans, Green, and Co., 1902], 520), according to which we experience "ideal impulses" originating from an "unseen region" (516). In calling it *piecemeal* supernaturalism, James was contrasting his position with what he called the "universalistic supernaturalism," by which he meant transcendental idealists and others who "obey the Kantian direction enough to bar out ideal entities from interfering causally in the course of phenomenal events" (520). Whereas James himself "finds no intellectual difficulty in mixing the ideal and the real worlds together by interpolating influences from the ideal region among the forces that causally determine the real world's details," for the universalists "the world of the ideal has no efficient causality, and never bursts into the world of phenomena at particular points" (521). Explaining his reason for considering this universalistic supernaturalism religiously inadequate, James said: "Our difficulties and our ideals are all piecemeal affairs, but the Absolute can do no piecework for us" (522n). James's own position, by contrast, is that the ideal world *can*, by means of the "ideal impulses" mentioned above, "get down upon the flat level of experience and interpolate itself piecemeal between distinct portions of nature," thereby entering into "transactions of detail" (521, 522). Given my way of distinguishing between naturalism and supernaturalism, James's position is a form of (theistic) naturalism, not supernaturalism, because, thanks to James's panpsychism (499), he could affirm that the "ideal impulses" received by human beings are high-level forms of a kind of divine influence pervading "the whole universe" (517). He characterized his position as a form of supernaturalism, however, because he defined "naturalism" as the view that there is nothing beyond the world known through sensory perception. Given that definition, his belief in an "unseen region" meant that his position had to be called a version of supernaturalism. As James himself put it: "If one should make a division of all thinkers into naturalists and supernaturalists, I should undoubtedly have to go . . . into the supernaturalist branch" (520). This choice of terms was unfortunate, however, because most readers will almost inevitably interpret it to entail supernatural interruptions of the world's basic causal processes, as does John Mackie in *The Miracle of Theism: Arguments for and against the Existence of God* (Oxford: Clarendon, 1982). Having defined miracles as "divine interventions which have disrupted the natural course of events" (13), Mackie explicates James's piecemeal supernaturalism to mean that "the supernatural must enter into 'transactions of detail' with the natural--in other words, the sorts of interventions that we have defined miracles to be" (182). The correct characterization of James, I am arguing, is as a naturalistic theist who, by virtue of his acceptance of divine "piecework," affirmed variable divine influence in the world.

48

divine influence in the world, because variable divine influence is part of the normal pattern of causal relations. In the early modern view, the universe was thought of as a more or less fully self-sufficient machine, with God sustaining it from outside and perhaps intervening occasionally. In Whiteheadian process theology, by contrast, God is the "soul of the universe,"[15] constantly interacting with all of its parts, somewhat as our minds or souls interact with our bodies. To develop the analogy: In our bodies, each of the units is constantly receiving information from other parts: Cells, for example, receive information from molecules, from organelles, and from other cells. But they also receive information from our minds or souls. Likewise, our souls are constantly receiving information from our various bodily members and from other souls. If there is a mind or soul of the universe, then it would be natural to assume that we are also constantly receiving influences from this source.

In terms of this framework, we can do justice both to scientific naturalism and to the religious belief in variable divine causation. Scientific naturalism is affirmed, because uniformitarianism is endorsed: No event is to be explained in terms of a type of divine causation that does not occur in all other events. Rather, divine influence is *formally* the same in all events. Whitehead expresses this point in his technical language by saying that God provides an "initial aim" for each event. Receiving a divinely-rooted aim toward an ideal possibility, in other words, is part of the normal pattern of causal relations.[16] In this sense, divine action is uniform.

---

[15]Charles Hartshorne, in developing and modifying Whitehead's idea of God, has used the term "panentheism," which affirms that the world exists in God (*Man's Vision of God and the Logic of Theism* [Hamden, Conn.: Archon Books, 1964], 348), and has referred to God as the World Soul (*Omnipotence and Other Theological Mistakes* [Albany: State University of New York Press, 1984], 59). Although neither of these terms was used by Whitehead himself, they can both, I have argued in Chapter 4 of my *Reenchantment Without Supernaturalism*, appropriately be used for characterizing his conception of God as well.

[16]Whitehead's doctrine that every actuality receives a divinely provided initial aim--which he originally called an "ideal consequent"--(*Religion in the Making* [New York: Macmillan, 1926], 156-58)--seems to be his development of James's suggestion, discussed in note 14, that God influences the world in terms of "ideal impulses." That Whitehead was, like James, affirming variable divine causation is shown by his statement that God provides "particular ideals relevant to

This view, nevertheless, can also do justice to the religious belief in divine causation. In the first place, process theology says that divine causation is a factor in every event in the universe--never a fully-determining factor, to be sure, but a real causal factor.[17] In the second place, although this divine causation is *formally* the same in all events, it is variable *substantively,* that is, *in content.* By analogy, your mind's influence on your body is formally always the same, as your mind provides instructive information to various parts of the body by means of influencing the brain. But this influence is variable in content, as your mind provides one instruction for your left hand, another instruction for your right hand, another for your vocal cords, and still other instructions for your heart, lungs, and stomach. In a similar way, the ideals or initial aims provided by God for different parts of the world would differ in content. Whitehead expressed this notion by saying that the divine aim is always towards the best possibility for that particular situation.[18] This idea provides a basis for expressing the biblical notion that God does new things from time to time.

Process theology's naturalistic theism does rule out a few ideas that some religious people have believed. For example, it rules out the idea that God has acted in one religious tradition in a qualitatively different way than God has acted in other religions. But why, sinful arrogance aside, should anyone today want to maintain that idea, which has been the source of so much tragedy? It also rules out the idea that God can completely determine any particular event in the world. But that is the idea that has created an insoluble problem of evil, thereby being

---

the actual state of the world" (159) and his later affirmation of "particular providence for particular occasions" (*Process and Reality,* corrected edition, edited by David Ray Griffin and Donald W. Sherburne [New York: Free Press, 1978], 351). Hartshorne, in fact, explicitly makes the connection in relation to this latter affirmation, saying that Whitehead thereby exemplified James's piecemeal supernaturalism ("Whitehead's Idea of God," in Paul Arthur Schilpp, ed., *The Philosophy of Alfred North Whitehead,* 2nd edition [New York: Tudor, 1951], 513-59, at 530).

[17] James had already emphasized this point, not only saying that "the unseen region is not merely ideal, for it produces effects in this world" (*The Varieties of Religious Experience,* 516), but then adding: "'God' is a causal agent as well as a medium of communion, and that is the aspect which I wish to emphasize" (517n).

[18] *Process and Reality,* 84, 244.

responsible for much of the agnosticism and atheism in the world. This naturalistic theism also rules out the idea of miracles, *if* miracles are defined as supernatural interruptions of the world's normal causal processes. It does not, however, rule out the kinds of events that have usually been thought of as miracles, such as extraordinary healings,[19] and it does not rule out the notion that divine influence plays a role in such events. It merely holds that the divine influence in such events is not formally different from that in all other events. Although such events are extraordinary, therefore, they are not supernatural-- which is the interpretation usually presupposed by those involved in psychosomatic and parapsychological research.

In concluding this essay, I will point out how this idea of naturalistic theism can be helpful to the scientific community. Thus far, I have been pointing out its benefits to the religious communities, suggesting that it, besides reconciling the religious belief in variable divine activity with scientific naturalism, can also avoid the problem of evil and overcome the primary basis for religious arrogance. But this idea of theistic naturalism can be equally helpful to the scientific community. The reason this help is needed is that the scientific community, by virtue of having thus far equated scientific naturalism with atheism, has been unable to explain a wide range of phenomena. For example, this atheistic form of scientific naturalism cannot explain the extraordinary order of

---

[19]It might be thought that my contention in note 14--that James's position is not, according to my definition of supernaturalism, a species of it--is contradicted by his statement that his piecemeal supernaturalism "admits miracles" (*Varieties of Religious Experience*, 520). In affirming miracles, however, James did not mean violations of the normal causal principles of the universe. Rather, having spent a significant portion of his life engaged with the phenomena of psychical research, he argued that we need a scientific worldview that would allow these phenomena to be regarded as fully natural, albeit exceptional, occurrences. He said, for example: "Science, so far as science denies such exceptional occurrences, lies prostrate in the dust for me; and the most urgent intellectual need which I feel at present is that science be built up again in a form in which such things may have a positive place" (*William James on Psychical Research*, edited by Gardner Murphy and Robert O. Ballou [New York: Viking Press, 1960], 42). I have argued elsewhere, in a journal that James helped found, that Whitehead's philosophy can provide the basis for a position that would fill this need ("Parapsychology and Philosophy: A Whiteheadian Postmodern Perspective," *Journal of the American Society for Psychical Research* 87/3 [July 1993], 217-88).

the universe, especially the apparent "fine-tuning" that made it possible for our universe to bring forth life. It cannot explain the directionality of the evolutionary process, in particular the direction toward richer modes of experience. It cannot explain the novelty that has kept appearing in physical, biological, and cultural evolution. It cannot explain the significant jumps that have, according to the fossil record, occurred throughout the evolutionary process. It cannot account for the excessive beauty that has occurred throughout the process, meaning beauty that cannot be explained in purely Darwinian, functionalist terms. With regard to human experience in particular, this atheistic version of naturalism cannot explain the objectivity of logic and mathematics, an issue that has been at the center of the philosophy of logic and mathematics in our century. It cannot explain the objectivity of moral experience. And it, by virtue of denying the possibility of genuine religious experience, cannot explain the universality and persistence of religion.

Although I cannot discuss any of these controversial claims in this essay, I do address them at some length in *Religion and Scientific Naturalism* and *Reenchantment Without Supernaturalism*.[20] In those works, I express my agreement with Plantinga and Johnson that science could be improved by becoming theistic. My proposal differs from theirs, however, in rejecting a return to supernaturalism. What we need, I suggest, is a theistic science based on a *naturalistic* theism. If such a development were to occur while at the same time the theistic religious communities came to eschew supernaturalism in favor of a naturalistic form of theism, the apparent conflict between scientific naturalism and the religious belief in divine activity would be seen to be just that--merely apparent. Religious experience and thought on this issue would, in other words, no longer be regarded as in conflict with scientific experience and thought.

---

[20]The various problems related to evolution are treated most fully in *Religion and Scientific Naturalism*, while the remaining issues are treated most fully in the other book.

BEYOND THE REACH OF LANGUAGE: ASSESSING RELIGIOUS EXPERIENCE AS A GUIE TO LIVING WELL
Walter B. Gulick

During the past two centuries, one's own experience has often been suggested as the necessary foundation upon which a good life, an authentic existence, may be built. This emphasis on personal experience is to be expected during an era in which individualism has become the standard form in the Western world of defining the self and engaging the world. The principle of the primacy of personal experience has roots in Greek, Renaissance and Reformation thought, but it was firmly fixed as a general cultural principle first during the age of Enlightenment in terms of autonomy and then in the Romantic era in terms of personal feeling and expression. While few today would deny that the evidence of personal experience is vital to autonomous, authentic living, that strong consensus dissipates when the personal experience is reported to be religious in character. The issue to be explored in this article is the extent to which religious experience may legitimately be relied upon as a guide to meaningful existence.

I

Within Christianity, Protestant thinkers have been more insistent than Catholic theologians on the significance of religious experience as a basis for authentic faith and practice. At the beginning of the 19th century, Friedrich Schleiermacher was especially influential in the way he appealed to experiences of absolute dependence as the irreducible reference point for personal piety and theological construction. Later, Rudolf Otto understood numinous experiences to provide the basic data which religious thought and practice developed and articulated. William James collected examples of ways ordinary people claimed to have had their lives change because of such religious experiences as a conversion, a dramatic encounter with something uncanny, a mystical experience, prayer answered, or a paranormal experience.

For theologians, the appeal to religious experience has had a protective as well as a constructive function. It has been used to counter the criticisms of a Feuerbach, Freud or Durkheim, each of whom in some way emphasized the noncognitive, projective quality of religious thought and stressed the emotional satisfactions rendered thereby. If one personally encounters God, proponents of religious experience retort, one has first hand acquaintance with a religious reality that no amount of second hand criticism, whether philosophical, psychological or sociological in nature, can render suspect. Yet in recent years, much has been written which casts doubt on the capacity of religious experience, however characterized, to serve legitimately as a grounding for the way one lives. Chief among the criticisms of religious experiences has been the claim that they are irremediably subjective – subject to arbitrary interpretation and shaped by the narrow, haphazard context of a single life.

The claim that religious experience is unavoidably subjective has been typically developed in two ways, one personal and one social in nature. Each critique may be put in the form of questions.

(1) When one experiences the divine, has one truly encountered a reality beyond one's own psychic makeup? Or are Feuerbach and Freud essentially correct in asserting that religious encounters arise from deepseated emotional needs and make use of the mind's imaginative or projective qualities?

(2) Is there any evidence to think that there is something more to spiritual experience than the imaginative vision provided by the language and practices of a religious tradition and its supportive culture? Or is one's experience necessarily limited to and perhaps even evoked by the concepts and beliefs to which one has been exposed, so that one's religious experience necessarily is an individualized mirroring of one's culture?

It is not necessary to view the personal and social critiques as disjunctive alternatives, for each may contain elements of the truth. However, it is the social critique, emphasizing the constitutive and functional roles of language, which, primarily through the influence of the later thought of Wittgenstein, has had the greatest influence in the past several decades. Three of its leading proponents are anthropologist Clifford Geertz, theologian George Lindbeck, and philosopher of religion Wayne Proudfoot.

In this article, I will take issue with some aspects of the view of language held by the social critics. I have dealt elsewhere with the strengths and weaknesses of Geertz's views[21] and will not repeat that analysis. Rather I will focus especially on the thought of Lindbeck and Proudfoot. It is my overriding aim to rescue the notion of religious experience as a reasonable ground of authentic decision making, although I save the notion only at the expense of some cautions and qualifications. Based on a review of background considerations affecting religious experience and its analysis, I'll offer some criteria to take account of when evaluating the meaning of the religious experience.

II

George Lindbeck argues that the concepts, doctrines, and canonical texts which jointly embody a religious tradition also articulate the meaningful worldview within which the religious adherent dwells. I fully concur. However, his emphasis on fidelity to a text-based worldview means that in practice he is suspicious of those (the "liberals") who regard experience as a primary authority. "Liberals start with experience, with an account of the present, and then adjust their vision of the kingdom of God accordingly, while postliberals [Lindbeck counts himself as one] are in principle committed to doing the reverse."[22] The Lindbeckian postliberal is first of all faithful to the language-constituted religious

---

[21] See Walter B. Gulick, "Reconnecting Geertz's Middle World," *Soundings* LXXI (Spring, 1988), 113-153.

[22] George A Lindbeck, *The Nature of Doctrine: Religion and Theology in a Postliberal Age* (Philadelphia: The Westminster Press, 1984), pp. 125-126.

tradition and then speaks prophetically to the world from that tradition. That is, the postliberal does not wish to begin from a position already compromised by the contemporary world.

Postliberal ideas as advocated by such persons as Hauerwas, Willimon and Placher as well as Lindbeck have had a decided impact on Christian education. Postliberal thinkers would like to substitute the stories of the Bible for the sorts of stories pervading our culture through the influence of the media. In advocating a return to a catechismal approach to religious education, postliberalism ironically appears similar to the preliberalism of another lover of language, Horace Bushnell. In Bushnell's nineteenth century version of a cultural-linguistic view, children were to be taught the language of faith from an early age so that they would never know they were anything but Christians. Lindbeck would differ by educating children to perceive their difference as Christians from the prevailing culture. Yet neither Bushnell nor Lindbeck provides a place for the passion that makes religious identity a matter of real concern to the individual. Why should children adhere to a postliberal Christian identity when the exciting stuff for most youngsters occurs in the culture at large? Is a moralized version of David and Goliath or Daniel and the lion's den really superior to a moralized story about Pokemon? And do we really want to return our children to a worldview where evil spirits are exorcized, loaves are magically multiplied, and the faithful yearn to touch a garment to be healed? Might not conformity to this religious worldview be purchased at the too costly price of (1) establishing a gulf between the person's everyday Biblical worldview and competing worldviews, especially the scientific/technological worldview, and (2) engendering feelings of guilt if other perspectives are explored? To be sure, traditions respecting diversity, appreciation for nature, and the like, can be found within the richness of Biblical traditions, but highlighting these traditions would suggest one's reading of the Bible is already "contaminated" by current cultural concerns.

Lindbeck's antagonism toward religious experience finds expression through his categorization of theories of religion and doctrine into three types:

propositional, experiential-expressive, and cultural-linguistic. He dismisses a propositional view quite quickly but spends a good bit of space refuting the experiential-expressive view, which he sees as dominant in our time. He traces this view back to Schleiermacher as its founder.

> Thinkers of this tradition all locate ultimately significant contact with whatever is finally important to religion in the prereflective experiential depths of the self and regard the public or outer features of religion as expressive and evocative objectifications (i.e., nondiscursive symbols) of internal evidence.[23]

He believes experimental-expressivism inadequate to deal with the relation between religion and experience because it mistakenly postulates a realm of experience beyond the reach of language. How could there possibly be significant prereflective experience, he asks, when significance itself is a product of reflection and the use of language? The cultural-linguistic view remains as the satisfactory alternative.

Wayne Proudfoot develops Lindbeck's embryonic critique much more fully with respect to religious experience. He shows that Schleiermacher's religious ultimate, the feeling of absolute dependence, makes sense only as a particular outworking of the Judeo-Christian notions of creation and providence. The divine "whence," to which Schleiermacher's feeling of absolute dependence is referred as source, is an intentional object which may or may not exist but which cannot even be conceived as a possibility without fairly sophisticated belief. Proudfoot concludes that Schleiermacher "is correct to view primary religious language as the expression of a deeply entrenched moment of consciousness but incorrect to portray that moment as independent of thought and belief."[24] With this conclusion I can only agree.

Unfortunately, however, Lindbeck and Proudfoot go so far in combating experiential-expressivism that they tend to undercut the essential role of feeling

---

[23] Ibid., p. 21.

[24] Wayne Proudfoot, *Religious Experience* (Berkeley: University of California Press, 1985), p. 36.

and emotion in vital religious belief and practice. In so emphasizing the inescapable communicative role of language they dance on the edges of Hegelian pan-rationalism. Proudfoot reveals the shortcomings of his own views when he speaks of "the impossibility of transcending language in order to discover some aspect of experience which is innocent of conceptual assumptions or grammatical practices."[25] While it is true that no cognitive articulation of experience to oneself or others is possible apart from language, it is false that we have no experiential ways of transcending language. For language is rooted in and dependent upon the felt (the schematized) dimension of consciousness. When we fumble to find the right words to express a schematized notion, we experience how the felt dimension of experience serves as a standard for and guides the articulate dimension. Yes, cognitive significance is a product of reflection and the use of language, but also crucial for determining how best to live are issues of emotional significance originating in somatic regions beyond the reach of language.

III

In order to explore more concretely the worth of religious experiences, let us examine one such experience. Because we are exploring whether religious experience is a reliable ground for authentic living, it would be helpful to select an experience which did in fact significantly influence a person's way of life. It might also be advantageous to choose an experience outside familiar Christian circles to ensure the experience has a freshness to it and is not subjected to premature theological evaluation. Lame Deer's account of his first vision quest meets these criteria. As one following the traditions of the Sioux, Lame Deer entered into this vision quest seeking an answer to a pressing question: Would he be granted the power to be the medicine man he longed to be? The visions he received confirmed his vocational aspirations during this rite of initiation, as he makes clear in his own words.

---

[25] Ibid., p. 229.

Sounds came to me through the darkness: the cries of the wind, the whisper of the trees, the voices of nature, animal sounds, the hooting of an owl. Suddenly I felt an overwhelming presence. Down there with me in my cramped hole was a big bird. The pit was only as wide as myself, and I was a skinny boy, but that huge bird was flying around me as if he had the whole sky to himself. I could hear his cries, sometimes near and sometimes far, far away. I felt feathers or a wing touching my back and head. This feeling was so overwhelming that it was just too much for me. I trembled and my bones turned to ice. I grasped the rattle with the forty pieces of my grandmother's flesh. . . . I shook the rattle and it made a soothing sound, like rain falling on rock. It was talking to me, but it did not calm my fears. I took the sacred pipe in my other hand and began to sing and pray: "Tunkashila, grandfather spirit, help me." But this did not help. I don't know what got into me, but I was no longer myself. I started to cry. Crying, even my voice was different. . . . Slowly I perceived that a voice was trying to tell me something. It was a bird cry, but I tell you, I began to understand some of it. . . . I heard a human voice too, strange and high-pitched, a voice which could not come from an ordinary, living being. All at once I was way up there with the birds. . . . A voice said, "You are sacrificing yourself here to be a medicine man. In time you will be one. You will teach other medicine men. We are the fowl people, the winged ones, the eagles and the owls. We are a nation and you shall be out brother. You will never kill or harm any one of us."[26]

Through this experience, Lame Deer's hopes were answered. He received the power to be a medicine man and encountered the guardian spirits, the birds, to rely upon when he was in need. He gained thereby a meaningful religious identity even though the course of his life reveals that he never achieved a stable occupational identity. He made it clear that this religious experience was indispensable for establishing the terms of meaning in his adult life.

Certainly as Lame Deer experienced his vision quest, there was no willful element of subjectivity in it. Phenomenologically, he experienced things beyond the ken of his conscious imagination. The voices came to him; he did not simply imagine them. Yet many are the sorts of interpretations which, in some way or other, deny that the manner in which he experienced his visions can adequately explain them. I'll briefly outline three such explanatory approaches.

---

[26] John Fire/Lame Deer and Richard Erdoes, *Lame Deer, Seeker of Visions* (New York: Simon and Schuster, 1972), pp. 15-16.

First, there is what might be termed the psychological/physiological sort of explanation. It would term his visions hallucinations. According to this explanation, Lame Deer's hallucinations were encouraged by the nature of the discipline required in a vision quest: four day and nights without food or water. Not only were the visions evoked by physiological processes well known to be associated with fasting, they were hastened by the sensory deprivation Lame Deer experienced while wrapped in his star blanket in the vision pit. The specific hallucinatory content would appear to be a form of wish fulfillment. Lame Deer was confirmed in his wish to be a medicine man.

Does such an explanation increase our understanding of Lame Deer's experience, or does it merely explain it away? I think it does a little of each. The psychological/physiological explanation enlightens us about some processes which quite plausibly underlay and supported Lame Deer's experiences. The explanation is helpful so long as it is not thought that such an explanation is sufficient to account for all levels of the experience, including Lame Deer's explanation. To suggest that delusions decisively influenced the course of a thoughtful, sane person's life is to fail the test of complete explanation. If it is concluded that the experience was only an hallucination and could therefore be ignored, then truly the experience was more explained away than explained.

While psychological/physiological explanations seek to uncover causal mechanisms in behavior, notice the peculiar nature of causality involved in these explanations. They work only retrospectively: a person x experiences event y, and causal mechanism z explains why. But causal mechanism z (for instance, sensory deprivation) cannot be successfully used to predict what the subject will experience during the occasion or in the future. Thus it lacks the predictive quality that is characteristic of causality as understood in the natural sciences. In this regard, a psychological/physiological explanation is not really different in kind that the "spiritual" explanation Lame Deer used to account for his experience. It too has causal elements ("the winged ones communicated with me") and is retrospective (the account emerged out of subsequent interpretation by the sponsoring medicine man, Chest, and a lifetime of reflection by Lame Deer), and it too lacks the ability to predict specific future experiences. But Lame Deer's account is able to render meaningful the particular details of what he experienced in a way that simply labeling the experience an hallucination cannot.

The cultural details involved in Lame Deer's first vision quest are ignored in a psychological/physiological account. Perhaps an anthropological account would better illuminate why Lame Deer experienced what he did. Insights from anthropology will be plumbed to provide our second type of explanation.

Lame Deer, it would be suggested by the anthropologist Victor Turner, was passing through the liminal stage of an initiation ritual in that part of his account we just examined. Rituals structure processes of change and render them less threatening to transitory person and society alike. Initiation rituals provide personal instruction about adult customs and responsibilities. Their symbolism is such that the individual experiences death as a boy and rebirth as a man. Thus Lame Deer began his vision quest by shedding his boyish clothes and entering his first sweat bath. Here he was purified of his old ways and his mind was emptied for new insights. On the vision pit hill he remained naked in the womb-like pit awaiting his birth as a man. He was separated from his extended family for the first time. During the liminal period in the vision pit he relied upon symbols of the support of his family: the star blanket his grandmother made for him, the peace pipe used by generations of vision questers, the gourd rattle containing the pieces of his grandmother's flesh sacrificed so his quest might be successful. Yet in a totally strange environment he had to face powerful visions himself. Emotions overwhelmed him in this transitional stage. Crying, even his voice was different. Yet he finally received the tokens of a new adult identity. The birds were to be his totemic protectors. A vision of his great-grandfather, Lame Deer, appeared before him, and this revered ancestor urged him to replace his boyish name with his own powerful adult name. With these visionary gifts, Lame Deer's independence, his new adult identity, was sealed.

Such an anthropological account of Lame Deer's religious experience is quite illuminating. We understand far more about the details of the vision quest through such an explanation than we do through the psychological/physiological explanation. But do we receive any insights concerning the questions which propel our inquiry in this essay? Was Lame Deer's experience actually a species of subjective projection even though it seemed otherwise to him? Was it a responsible act on his part to allow his life's course to be so greatly influenced by what he experienced? The anthropologist does not have much to say about these questions.

We have already previewed the third explanatory approach that I'll delineate, the sort of explanations offered by George Lindbeck and Wayne Proudfoot. Lindbeck, we saw, believes religions are usefully understood as analogous to languages and their correlative forms of life. Like languages, religions function "as idioms for the construction of reality and the living of life." Their doctrines are used as "communally authoritative rules of discourse, attitude. and action."[27] Lindbeck also affirms that experiences can affect religious doctrine and practice; religion and experience are dialectically related, although he stresses that cultural factors are more significant than inner experiences in shaping life.[28]

But what of Lame Deer's experiences? He was not, per Proudfoot, simply applying religious conceptuality to a neutral state of arousal, was he? Potent visions seized him and *caused* a violent emotional response that was life shaping. Lindbeck, however, would point out the role of Lame Deer's vision quest sponsor, the medicine man Chest. Even before the sweat bath, Chest helped prepare Lame Deer for what might transpire. Thus the vocabulary with which Lame Deer was equipped to interpret his experience was traditional and culture-bound. Right before his vision of the birds, he heard the hooting of an owl. Because birds were recognized by the Sioux as common agents of the divine, especially among medicine men, might not Lame Deer's conceptual framework

---

[27] Lindbeck, op. cit., p. 18.
[28] Ibid., pp. 33-34.

have been almost pre-programmed to convert bird activity into religious experience? Lindbeck could also point out the authority Chest was given to interpret Lame Deer's experience when Chest came to retrieve him after four days and nights. "He would give me something to eat and water to drink and then I was to tell him everything that had happened to me during my *hanblechia*. He would interpret my visions for me."[29]

As we saw, Proudfoot applies Lindbeck's cultural-linguistic approach to religious experiences. He concludes that the "distinguishing mark of a religious experience is not the subject matter but the kind of explanation the subject believes is appropriate."[30] Of great import in interpreting experience as religious experience is the attribution of the cause of the experience. "Beliefs about the causes of one's experience are themselves constitutive of the experience."[31] Lame Deer, thinking in Sioux categories, assumed that Wakan Tanka, the Great Spirit, was the ultimate cause of his visions, although the specific spirits of things in the vicinity of the vision pit were believed to be the immediate causes. His experience was constituted as a religious experience in that he never even considered questioning that his visions were of divine origin; his interest was in finding out what their spiritual message was for him. Lindbeck and Proudfoot, however, are no more able to offer normative spiritual guidance to Lame Deer as to how to respond to his experience than were the anthropologists. Indeed, their approach to explanation is far closer to an anthropological than a theological approach. Proudfoot's urging of a naturalistic explanation of religious experience, grounded in his hermeneutics of suspicion, would seem irrelevant to Lame Deer as he pondered his future.[32]

---

[29] *Lame Deer*, p. 16.

[30] Proudfoot, op. cit., p. 231.

[31] Ibid., p. 114.

[32] To be sure, Proudfoot understands that at one level of analysis an experience must be described in the conceptuality by which the subject identifies it. "To describe the experience of a mystic only by reference to alpha waves, altered heart rate, and changes in bodily temperature is to misdescribe it." (p. 196) Proudfoot thus wants to avoid what he calls descriptive reduction even as he embraces the notion of explanatory reduction (p. 197). Yet both types of reduction are oriented

64

Now a delineation of the subjective nature of Lame Deer's religious experience can be offered. The most fully subjective features of the experience are the emotional responses Lame Deer made to the various features of his vision quest. But it should be noted that the features of the vision quest are designed to evoke individualized emotional responses. As is well known, personal transformation (as from a boy to a man) is most likely to occur in times of emotional crisis. Being completely alone for the first time would surely elicit fear. Sensory and nutritional deprivation would evoke visions which would in turn elicit awe. So the emotions experienced would be unmistakably subjective, but their evocation would be a cultural achievement designed to ensure that the lesson learned would be firmly imprinted on the initiate's memory.

The religious categories available to Lame Deer would, as Lindbeck and Proudfoot claim, help constitute the experience for him, especially as reinforced by Chest's interpretation. So Lame Deer's experience would be subjective in the sense that it would surely be dramatically different than that which an atheist, an evangelical Christian, or a Zen monk would experience if each had replaced Lame Deer in the same vision pit and undergone the same sequence of external events.

Both the personal and social critiques of religious experience have been shown to have merit. Insofar as religious experiences are suffused with emotion, they are personally subjective; insofar as they are dependent on cultural concepts for being understood and acknowledged as significant, they are socially subjective. Because the experiences are shaped by subjective factors, it would seem as if they are incapable of being *known* as objective, as real. Does it not follow that religious experiences are unreliable and inadequate sources upon which to build a life? Was not Lame Deer mistaken or deluded to view his first vision quest as providing experientially verified grounds for knowing he should become a medicine man?

---

toward providing an explanation of the event, which is not what Lame Deer would be interested in. He would be concerned with meaning, not explanation.

IV

All right, Lindbeck and Proudfoot have demonstrated that religious experiences necessarily are conceived through cultural concepts that render them socially subjective – so what? This means they have demonstrated that religious experiences do not give one direct, immediate access to the real, so that Schleiermacher's hope that experience might play a foundational and persuasive role for any unbiased person cannot be sustained. But the validity of feelings of absolute dependence or other types of religious experience is not thereby eliminated. For in addition to the three levels of interpretation just presented, there are other perspectives which might self consistently be adopted. I will briefly mention a fourth perspective, a theological interpretation, and then in the balance of the essay set forth a fifth level of analysis, an existential perspective attuned to issues of meaning.

From a theological perspective, the first three levels might all be affirmed but subsumed to a yet more primordial perspective, the activity of God. It might be claimed that God acts through psychological and cultural means to carry out God's will. Alvin Plantinga's view is consistent with this point; he claims that religious experiences may be affirmed as properly basic, to be taken as they are experienced, seen as contributing through the work of the Holy Spirit to a Christian's understanding of the way God is involved in the world.[33]

How confusing the assessment of religious experience must be to one who has been significantly exposed to religious concepts but who is unclear about what to believe. Can religious experience assist such a person? At this point a brief excursus is called for. The basic point of the excursus is this: any assessment of experience must involve subjective elements. The fact that religious experiences are shot through with personal and social varieties of subjectivism is therefore no reason not to take these experiences seriously.

---

[33] Many works of Plantinga could be cited in support of this claim; his most recent book is *Warranted Christian Belief* (New York: Oxford University Press, 2000); see pp. 175 ff.

66

The first part of the excursus is practical and commonsensical. It asks what sorts of experiences would be most reliable for determining how one best should live. Should one read a sampling of books about great figures of the past and rationally decide which qualities one would like to adopt? But we know that humans are not rational beings along the lines of this caricature of decision making. One's decisions about who one is and how one should behave arise in a variety of ways in which rationality is often subservient: through trial and error, stubborn self assertion, admiration of someone's qualities, reaction against a rival, calculation of what is to one's advantage, and so on. Often behavior is adjusted because of experiences of failure or pain. Surely most of the occasions during which a person decides what she stands for and how she should live involve emotionally significant crises or challenging experiences. And surely the arsenal of cultural concepts a person has acquired will help that person articulate the options available and underwrite any decisions made. Religious experiences, we have seen, are emotionally robust and shot through with cultural categories. So why should lessons drawn from such experiences be denigrated as subjective any more than lessons drawn from other sorts of emotional encounters? Would not religious concepts, refined through centuries of reflection, tend to be less subjective than the popular cultural terms of the day, whether provided by soap operas, self help books, or back fence gossip?

The second part of the excursus is theoretical. From the perspective of the analytic tradition, John Searle has written helpfully of the Network of cultural and personal information each person has interiorized and the Background of abilities, involved in thinking.[34] Mark Johnson has further developed the notion of the Background to emphasize its embodied character and the susceptibility of thought to be shaped by metaphors, many of the most important of which have to do with

---

[34] See *Intentionality: An Essay in the Philosophy of Mind* (Cambridge: Cambridge University Press, 1983), Chapter 5.

bodily orientation (up-down, foreground-background, in-out, etc.).[35] These metaphorical thoughts contribute to the Background and shape our sense of ethical propriety and religious reality.[36]

The thought of Michael Polanyi is an especially rich resource for those seeking to understand how Background considerations influence human meaning making. Although Polanyi does not use the language of Background in his wide ranging reflections on how meaning is engendered and experienced, his explications of tacit knowing, the fiduciary dynamics of communal decision making, the embodied from-to structure of consciousness, and the emergent nature of knowledge as seen in evolutionary perspective all enrich one's understanding of the factors involved in producing and assessing knowledge and belief claims.[37] His analyses indicate that there are many factors other than culturally mediated ones involved in shaping experience.

In a series of articles, I have elaborated on Polanyi's ideas and argued that human cultural meaning emerges out of a *from-via-to* framework of human consciousness.[38] The *from* indicates our felt pre-articulate access to sensations, skills, motivations, drives, and the schematized results of previous learning. Out of this Background symbols are evoked by our most insistent feelings; symbols (above all, words) are the translucent *via* component of human consciousness, organized by grammatical rules to bring mute feeling into articulate expression.

---

[35] See *The Body in the Mind: The Bodily Basis of Meaning, Imagination, and Reason* (Chicago: University of Chicago Press, 1987), p. 190, for instance.

[36] On morality, see Mark Johnson, *Moral Imagination: Implications of Cognitive Science for Ethics* (Chicago: University of Chicago Press, 1993), passim, and for a summary of the implications of an embodied mind for ethics and religion, see George Lakoff and Mark Johnson, *Philosophy in the Flesh: The Embodied Mind and Its Challenge to Western Thought* (New York: Basic Books, 1999), pp. 556-568.

[37] Polanyi's magnum opus is *Personal Knowledge: Towards a Post-Critical Philosophy* (New York: Harper Torchbooks, 1964). Another of his works particularly important for the theme of this essay is Michael Polanyi and Harry Prosch, *Meaning* (Chicago: University of Chicago Press, 1975).

[38] See especially Walter B. Gulick, "Polanyi's Theory of Meaning: Exposition, Elaboration, and Reconstruction," *Polanyiana* II:4-III:1 (1992-1993), 7-42, but also "The Meaningful *and* the Real in Polanyian Perspective," *Polanyiana* VIII:1-2 (1999), 13 and "Beyond Epistemology to Realms of Meaning," *Tradition and Discovery* XXVI:3 (2000), 27, 34.

Through such integration we experience focal meanings, the *to* dimension of consciousness. Such meanings satisfy to a greater or lesser degree our felt need for expression and communication, and they provide a means whereby a person can mobilize energies in the pursuit of goals. Those most deeply satisfying meanings will likely evoke an emotional response, and their lessons will be internalized, thereby becoming resources for future meaning construction.

Experiences of what I term *existential meaning* arise out of occurrences most heavily marked by the satisfaction or frustration of personal interests, goals and values. There are two primary components of positive experiences of existential meaning that need to be highlighted: the involvement of one's values, goals, or interests – what matters to one – and their satisfaction or enhancement in the event, a satisfaction experienced with emotional intensity. Life itself is felt to be meaningful when it is suffused with experiences of existential meaning.[39] Positive experiences of existential meaning are what impart zest, direction, and pleasure to existence. Religious experiences are often highly flavored with existential meaning because such experiences deal with issues about which humans care a great deal: life and death, the best way to live, guilt and forgiveness, salvation.

It should be evident that there is far more in the Background and the production of meaning than Lindbeck or especially Proudfoot acknowledge. Proudfoot claims that emotions are a neutral form of physiological arousal which are identified as a specific emotion through a culturally influenced attribution of causality in relation to a culturally interpreted context. G. William Barnard effectively criticizes the psychological theory from which Proudfoot derived his understanding of attribution.[40] The from-via-to structure of consciousness within which meaning is constructed highlights the role language plays in the

---

[39] See Walter B. Gulick, "The Thousand and First Face," in Daniel C. Noel, *Paths to the Power of Myth: Joseph and the Study of Religion* (New York: Crossroad, 1990), 29-44, for a more detailed discussion of existential meaning.

[40] See Barnard's "Explaining the Unexplainable: Wayne Proudfoot's *Religious Experience*," JAAR LX:2 (Summer, 1992), 232-238.

construction of meaning (in the *via* dimension and also as schematized in the *from* dimension) but also takes account of the following factors which exist wholly or partially outside the play of language: the on-going projects, material objects, practices, and events which shape the context within which the experience occurs; the felt quality of the experience itself (feelings are not simply neutral, but highly differentiated); the salient skills and stock of schemata which an individual can draw upon to shape and interpret experience; the individual's emotional world orientation (including needs, vulnerabilities, and drives); and the already constituted patterns of relationships to others which influence expectations and avoidances.

The excursus is complete. I conclude that what is needed for assessing the legitimacy of religious experiences are criteria rich enough to encompass their many dimensions of subjectivity. Strictly speaking, what is needed is advice about what factors should be consulted and evaluated in the drawing of a *lesson* from religious experience, for over the long term it is the meaning of the experience, its lesson, rather than the details of the experience, which is dwelt in and influences future decision making. I offer four significant subregions of experience to attend to when assessing the lesson's meaning, subregions mentioned in the excursus as contributing to the construction of meaningful experience. Different criteria of assessment are embedded in each subregion.

V

First, and of greatest immediate import, the lesson must seek to grasp and, insofar as is possible, articulate the felt experience of *existential meaning* produced by the experience. What sorts of feelings, connections to basic interests, does the experience body forth? Are they affirmative? Life enhancing? If so, this represents an initial reason for embracing the experience and digging for its lesson(s). But experiences of negative existential meaning can also carry important messages that need to be heard. If the experience produces weak feelings of existential meaning, it is probably not worth spending much time pondering its import.

We have seen that experiences of existential meaning are thoroughly subjective in both the personal and social senses already adumbrated. They elicit strong emotions and bear on important personal values. But they are not felt simply as restricted to some monad of inner awareness. Emotions are visceral. As embodied, they energize one and connect one with different aspects of the world. They are impregnated with cognitive structure.[41] Moreover, the emotions one experiences in existential meaning are calming and engaging as well as passionate or violent. One may experience existential meaning of a religious type while viewing the baptism of a child as well as when setting out on a crusade – in peaceful meditation in a garden as well as in the heat of a conversion experience. The lessons one draws from each experience will likely connect us beyond ourselves in time as well as space. In bringing to the fore one's values and goals, they connect us to the abstract residue of earlier lessons.

Second, the lesson one draws from an experience of existential meaning ought to be open to the qualities of reality and otherness in the experience and seek to capture what is new to one. This criterion honors what is real or artfully crafted over what is hyper-real or arbitrarily imaginary. It celebrates the bracing quality of encounters which teach one about structures and processes of the real. The more complex the things one engages (to a point), the more fully one's capacities are challenged, and the more exhilarating is one's experience. Albert Borgmann speaks of focal things as those complex entities which have the greatest power to draw one out of oneself and to open up practices that sustain the experiences of existential meaning initiated by one's first encounters with the

---

[41] Two recent works strike me as particularly insightful in the way they set forth the reciprocal relation of emotion and cognition: Antonio R. Damasio, *Descartes' Error: Emotion, Reason, and the Human Brain* (New York: Putnam's Sons, 1994), especially Chapters 7-8, and Catherine Z. Elgin, *Considered Judgment* (Princeton: Princeton University Press, 1996), especially Chapter 5.

focal things.[42] For instance, wilderness is a focal thing with the power to challenge one and reorient one's thought. In contrast, engagements with commodities and technological devices tend to be thin and oriented toward immediate gratification rather than sustained engagement. Mutatis mutandis, similar comments pertain to one's interactions with other people. Generally speaking, encounters which engage the otherness of the other are more profound than conventional meetings or casual relationships. In sum, lessons are instructive and invigorating to the extent that they search out and incorporate new insights from what is other and real.

Third, the lesson drawn generally needs to comport well with previous lessons learned and with the authorities which have proven worthy of honor in one's life. This criterion has both personal and social dimensions and is perhaps most fully consistent with Lindbeck's point of view. Lessons that threaten personal integrity would bear careful scrutiny, and lessons that set one in conflict with the traditions and communities one honors are especially suspect. This criterion has to do both with plausibility and consistency. It is important not to draw the boundaries of what is plausible, what is real, too narrowly, however. In addition to the empirical realities of the physical world, lessons must acknowledge the cultural realities of custom, preferences, and taboos. But it must also be recognized that on rare occasions one will undergo overpowering experiences that overturn previous allegiances, that transform one's basic paradigms. Such archetypal experiences require massive amounts of reflection and reorganization of thought. Through such efforts that new personal coherence of thought and action may emerge. It is also the case that some experiences may remain enigmatic; life is not always experienced as a unified whole.

Fourth, the lessons we draw need to take into account perspectives other than our own in general and the lessons resident in the great moral traditions in particular. Harmonious lesson drawing must be more than an individual exercise;

---

[42] Albert Borgmann, *Technology and the Character of Contemporary Life: A Philosophical Inquiry* (Chicago: University of Chicago Press, 1984), pp. 196ff.

it should seek out ideal relationships with other persons and the environment and thereby ensure that one's experience of existential meaning is not aberrant or community destroying. What best ensures that all interests and perspectives are taken into account is that one adopt something like the moral point of view advocated several decades ago by Kurt Baier or the veil of ignorance of John Rawls. The moral point of view is basically ecological in nature: all components in a system and envisaged consequences are to be considered when discerning what conclusions should be drawn from an experience. In seeking to carry out the universality and reciprocity entailed in the moral point of view, persons should employ empathetic understanding of the positions of the persons affected by the ethical decision making and be ready to discuss differences according to the principles outlined in Habermas' notion of communicative competence.

To sum up, an experience is trustworthy as a guide if it offers lessons which are emotionally satisfying and fulfill important personal values; are open to and learn from what is different in the experience, what savors of the real; are coherent with what one knows of the world, what is plausible; and can be affirmed when the moral point of view is applied to the lessons. These are pragmatic considerations which can be used to assess all experiences; issues of truth and ontology are largely beside the point vis-a-vis matters of meaning. Religious experiences tend to stretch the boundaries of personal satisfaction, reality and coherence. Some religious experiences may not fit comfortably with previous experiences, or may challenge one's sense of reality. For instance, the experience may be emotionally satisfying but culturally unacceptable, or be consistent with one's values but lead to conflict with other people. There is a tragic dimension to life. There is also an ambiguity to life such that we must often choose between alternative interpretations without adequate insight as to the [43]implications and consequences of acting upon each lesson.

How would Lame Deer's experience measure up when assessed in terms of these Background and contextual contributors to meaning? Clearly the vision quest was laden with existential meaning for Lame Deer. He encountered life changing aspects of otherness in the experience; assessments of reality may be bracketed when the meaning of an experience is at stake. Certainly the lessons he derived from the experience are consistent with the authorities he honored. By consulting Chest and other Sioux elders he ensured that his experience was moral – indeed, praiseworthy – in the eyes of those in his community. Thus the lessons Lame Deer derived from his religious experience are defensible.

I conclude with three cautions. First, my argument has provided no grounds for making inferences about the structure of reality from the nature of one's religious experience. The reification of a spiritual experience is a venture in faith, not a logical inference. Second, even if a religious experience overwhelms us with awesome force, that fact provides no warrant for transforming what is absolute for an individual into what is absolute for all. And third, while this essay has attempted to justify taking religious experiences seriously, it has not argued that interpretation of the meaning of the experience is all that is of interest. Many types of interpretation are useful. Indeed, the examination of Lame Deer's vision quest illustrates the following claim, paradoxical to a traditional rationalist: a religious experience may simultaneously be language dependent, hallucinatory, culturally real, and personally meaningful.

THEOLOGICAL THINKING, THE AMERICAN EXPERIENCE, AND THE IDEA OF THE UNIVERISTY
Joseph C. Hough, Jr.

From medieval times to the present, the history of theology and the history of the university have been closely intertwined. In the case of the medieval univerities, it was clear that their founders saw them as instruments in God's ordering of society alongside the state and the church. The university was to act in such a way as to balance the pretensions of the church, on the one hand, and the state on the other. Actually university faculties played a mediating role in some of the major disputes within the church, and even disputes between the church and the state, throughout medieval times. The Reformation did not change this understanding of the university in any significant way. Calvin, who thought about social institutions in his notion of a "Chrisitian society" in terms of the offices of Christ, cast the university in the role of the prophetic office of Christ, while the state served the kingly office and the church the priestly office.

In America, however, theological thinking about the university took its own peculiar turn. From the establishment of Harvard straight through to the founding of the University of Chicago, the university has been understood in the context of a mission to construct a Christian social order.

1. Education for a Learned Ministry.

"The Calvinist and Puritan churches of eighteenth-century America," writes Douglas Sloan, "were rooted in a tradition that had long placed a high value on learning and education. From the time of the Reformation the Protestant notions of the authority of scripture and the priesthood of all believers had greatly encouraged the idea, strongly held in early New England, that every man should be able to read and write."[44] Moreover, they came to the New World with a vision for a new society, a Holy Commonwealth of persons, whose piety would be manifest in the orthodoxy of their religious beliefs and practices, but whose piety would also lead them to develop the kind of competence for leadership that would ensure the prosperity and advancement of the new commonwealth. The decision to establish Harvard college, then, was a response to their divinely appointed vocation. The founders of Harvard were graduates of Cambridge, a center of Puritan influence during the seventeenth century. Not surprisingly, they brought their idea for a college with them from England. Steeped in the tradition of Cambridge and the theology of Calvin, they tried to re-create in the new Cambridge what they knew on the banks of the Cam. They brought with them the love for classical learning which shaped the curriculum at Cambridge. But they also carried the deep suspicion of orthodox theology which their Puritan forbearers in Cambridge had developed in relation to the reigning theological paradigms of the official English church. Moreover, like their Calvinist forbearers in Geneva, they believed that the whole of society should be founded upon and ordered by biblical teaching.

The initial purpose of the founders was to build a college which would provide a learned ministry for the churches, but in light of their perception of the vocation of the community, they understood the ministry in much broader terms than the clergy. If the mission of the people was to establish a New Jerusalem, the entire holy and royal priesthood of this people of God should be thoughtful, learned and pious. Public service by all sorts of dedicated leaders in a Holy Commonwealth was ministry, and the early devotion to education reflected this theological understanding. The course of studies was the same for all. For the most part, it reflected the classical studies of Cambridge, except that theology was not to be taught in the university. It was assumed that the creation of an ethos of

---

[44] Douglas Sloan, *The Great Awakening and American Education*, New York: Columbia University, 1973, 11.

piety would sustain orthodoxy, so the study of scripture and regular prayer and worship were to be practiced by all outside the classroom. Thus, while it is clear that they understood that learning was to be in the service of piety, it was not to be a piety developed by the teaching of any official theology. It was, rather, to be a piety cultivated and sustained by individual and corporate religious practices. The rules of the college were quite specific. The student was to "consider the main end of his life and studies to know God and Jesus Christ which is eternal life."[45]

What was required for a learned ministry and orthodox laymen alike was the study of the ancient trivium and quadrivium, together with the languages required for the reading of classical texts and scripture. Thus, while the ethos of the college was geared to promote true piety, the course of study was designed to discipline the mind so that the graduate could put learning to the service of Christian commonwealth. Most professors were ministers who were seen to be the prophets laboring in the tradition of those who struggled to transfer the learning of the ages bequeathed to Abraham, to Greece, Paris, and Cambridge.[46] The Puritans had, at least to some degree, maintained the legacy of the medieval tradition.[47] This was hardly surprising, since Paris, after all, was the mother of Cambridge.

The aim of the founders of William and Mary was, like that of Harvard's founders, to educate a learned clergy and a core of cultured and pious leaders for the new society who would dedicate themselves to public service. In this case, the inspiration was drawn from Oxford instead of Cambridge, and the call for a university educated leadership was not cast in terms of ministers for a New Jerusalem. The founders of William and Mary were interested in a permanent

---

45   Charles F. Thwing, *A History of Higher Education in America*, New York, D. Appleton, 1906, 34.

46   *Ibid.*, 1-49; See also Robert Handy, *A Christian America*, New York, Columbia University, 1984 edition, 6, 11; Williams, *op. cit.*, 143-157; and John Brubacher and Willis Rudy, *Higher Education in Transition*, New York, 1977 edition, Chapter 1.

47   Brubacher and Rudy, *op. cit.*, 7.

supply of educated Anglican priests and leaders for public institutions who were both pious and cultured, much more in the mode of England than the grand vision of Geneva.[48] In both cases, however, the colleges were seen to be instruments in the service of established piety. In this sense, William and Mary, like Harvard, owed much to the medieval idea of the university.

This medieval pattern was not long to survive in America. Yale and Princeton added a new dimension to the rationale for the new American college: "the pursuit of denominational survival in an environment of religious diversity."[49] The rapid increase in the religious diversity of America undermined the possibility of any unified Christian conception of society under an established church. More and more rival groups established competing colleges, and confessionalism had its day. But the dearth of resources and students, together with developing religious pluralism, required a search for some sort of religious detente. Thus, by the middle of the eighteenth century, religious tests for admission to colleges were non-existent and toleration was extended even to diverse religious practices on many college campuses.[50]

The developing tolerance did not extend to curriculum patterns. The other eastern colleges taught much the same subjects as were taught at Harvard, at least until about 1765. After that, however, a series of modifications were introduced which broadened the curriculum offerings significantly. Still the classical pattern together with an emphasis on mental discipline persevered, and the residential college system inherited from Cambridge and Oxford was duplicated everywhere. Religion dominated student life, and Christian orthodoxy was the norm. College education was liberal education for leaders in a Christianized society, even though

---

[48] Rudolph, op. cit., 7.

[49] Ibid., 8.

[50] Brubacher and Rudy, op. cit., 8-9.

not all of the Christians meant the same thing when they imagined what it was for a society to be Christian.[51]

2. Education in the Service of God and Country

Though this pattern of education remained dominant in the colleges throughout the colonial period, there was, at no time, general agreement that it was the best kind of education for the new world. It was elitist, and that did not go down well among the democratically-minded colonials. It was classical, and that did not suit the practical bent of many of the new Americans. Critics began to agitate for change. As early as 1749, for example, Benjamin Franklin argued for the founding of a college in Pennsylvania clearly secular and directed toward the practical needs of a growing population in the new world. In the constitutional statement of the new college there was no mention of religion, the church, or the ministry.[52] Soon after the founding of the College of Pennsylvania, Thomas Jefferson, most likely influenced by the Philadelphia model, proposed for William and Mary a similar model. Both Jefferson and Franklin believed that education for Americans should focus on "useful knowledge." In Jefferson's case, it was the needs of the present time in the history of a newly-forming nation which should be the primary focus of college and university education. To design a university curriculum which would meet his standard of utility, Jefferson argued, it would be necessary to eliminate much of what had been taught in European universities and American colleges and to substitute new subjects, because the current needs of Americans were not related to the old curriculum. Such subjects as Greek and Latin, moral philosophy, and divinity would be eliminated from the course of studies, and in their place would be added such subjects as law, anatomy, natural philosophy, police work, medicine, and modern languages. Interestingly enough, Jefferson also thought

---

[51] *Ibid.,* 14, 22, 23 and 42ff.

[52] Thwing, *op. cit.,* 112ff.

that history was a useful subject because of the practical lessons it could teach Americans about being good judges of the present and future actions of public leaders. This, in turn, would make them better citizens in the new democracy.

In contrast to the founders of William and Mary and Harvard, Jefferson was adamant that there be no domination of the university by any religious groups, nor would he allow any religious groups to veto choices of faculty. Though early in his educational career he had become disaffected from traditional religious beliefs, it is not likely that he allowed his private beliefs to determine this particular policy recommendation for the university. He steadfastly claimed that he did not allow his personal views to intrude on his policy considerations.[53] Jefferson, himself a religious man, had no objection to the establishment of centers of worship near the campus, but he wanted no sectarian intrusions into the organization and internal ethos of the university itself.[54] He was fearful of the contentiousness which he had witnessed in the denominational struggles to impose orthodoxy in Virginia, and he was determined that this divisive spirit would not destroy either the freedom or the quality of the new university. This same opposition to sectarian control probably led him to exclude the faculty of divinity from his plan for the university because of his fear that a divinity school would be especially a matter of contention between the warring religious groups. This non-sectarian pattern ran counter to that of earlier state universities where denominational groups had succeeded in applying religious tests for the faculty and where it was common for students to be required to attend daily prayers and occasional Bible study. It is not at all surprising that this aspect of Jefferson's proposal generated heated opposition from religious leaders interested in

---

[53] Dumas Malone, *Jefferson, the Virginian* (Vol 1 of *Jefferson and His Time*) Boston, Little Brown and Co., 1948,275.

[54] On Jefferson's religious beliefs see Robert M. Healey, *Jefferson on Religion in Public Education*, New Haven, Yale University Press, 1962, 17-39.

protecting the minds of the students from the onslaught of unorthodox and godless teachers.[55]

Shortly after Jefferson became governor in 1749, his proposals for William and Mary were introduced.[56] The reforms were not well received, so it was not until the founding of the University of Virginia in 1818 that Jefferson's dream of a new university for a new nation was at least partially realized. Combining a dedication to the Enlightenment canons of scientific excellence with a devotion to the cause of education for the good of the new republic, he founded the first state university clearly under public control and fully secular in its curriculum.

Jefferson was not alone in his challenge to the reigning model of the colonial college. George Tichnor and Philip Lindsley, both enamored of the new German university pattern, tried to effect reforms respectively at Harvard and at the ill-fated University of Nashville. Both of these men were in close contact with Jefferson's experiment at the University of Virginia. In New York, another group of reformers opted for a new parallel course of study inspired by the launching of the University of London in 1828. Theirs was a proposal for a professional approach to scientific studies, one which would meet the practical needs of an expanding economy in the new nation at a level of sophistication which might enable America to achieve a leadership position in applied technology.[57]

It should also be noted also that in 1757 the federal government had already made its first "land grant" to the Ohio Company for the endowment of a university in the Ohio territory. The management of the endowment was assumed by the state of Ohio in 1804, setting a precedent for almost all of the western

---

[55] See Daniel J. Boorstin, *The Lost World of Thomas Jefferson,* Chicago, 1981 edition, 213f. See also Brubacher and Rudy, *op. cit.*, pp. 147ff.

[56] Thwing, *op. cit.,* 112-116, 192, 202.

[57] Rudolph, *op. cit.,* 116-130.

states.[58] These newly emerging state universities were strongly influenced by Jeffersonian ideas. The needs of the surrounding communities figured prominently in their curricula, and they were governed by public policies and, for the most part, financed with public funds. Because they were supported by public funds, there were immense pressures on them to meet an ever expanding number of educational and practical needs for more of the population. If Jefferson challenged the prevailing and uniform pattern of classical studies with his new university at Virginia, the new state universities were very early forced to abandon his focus on an educated elite and to respond to the rising demand for the democratization of education throughout the nation.

In all of this ferment, there emerged a strong critical challenge to the old classical pattern of education characteristic of the early colonial college. Sensitivity to this challenge led to the publication of the famous Yale Report of 1828, authored by President Jeremiah Day and Professor James L. Kingsley. Though they admitted that the classical college curriculum was imperfect and called for "gradual" change, they affirmed the essential features of the traditional college curriculum. "The two great points to be gained in intellectual culture," the authors contended, "are the discipline and furniture of the mind; expanding its powers, and storing it with knowledge." The sort of study that should be characteristic of the college would focus all of the mental faculties on the subject matter of instruction, namely, science, literature and the ancient languages. The aim of this mental discipline was to form in the student a "balance of character" and the capacity to communicate ideas. The college in this way would best serve society not by teaching the specifics of professional practice, but by laying the foundation for all of the professions represented in the college by separate schools

---

[58] Brubacher and Rudy, *op. cit.,* 153-154.

of law, medicine and theology.[59] The authors also concluded that the range of professional instruction appropriate for the university was very narrow. Training for agriculturalists, engineers and business men was not properly the concern of the college or university. These matters, they argued, could best be learned on the farm, in the business or in the factory.[60] With that conclusion the pressures for democratization of university education were rejected and the traditional aristocratic pattern was re-affirmed.

Yale was extremely influential, and the report was supported by Princeton. Together these two institutions were able to shape decisively the course of study in most American colleges other than the state universities. They thus were able to stem the tide of reform until well after the Civil War.[61] Nevertheless, the harbingers of change had already inspired their prophetic followers, and the days of the old college pattern were numbered. Foreshadowed in these early developments was the complete revolution in university education that occurred at the end of the nineteenth century, a development to which we shall return later.[62]

3. Education, the Kingdom of God and Christian Civilization

It was not only the conception of education that was changing in America. Early in the colonial period, it had become evident that the regionally established churches could not survive the growing protests and strength of dissident religious groups. Baptists effectively challenged the pressure for uniformity in Massachusetts and Virginia, and Presbyterians struggled with the Anglicans for control in Virginia. The Quakers came to America as anti-establishmentarians. Their belief in the universal availability of the "inner light" to all humanity led

---

[59] The Yale Report is reprinted in Richard Hofstadter and Wilson Smith, editors, *American Higher Education: A Documentary History,* Chicago: University of Chicago Press, 1961, Volume I, 275f.

[60] *Ibid.,* 282.

[61] Rudolph, *op. cit.,* 131f.

[62] Laurence Veysey, *The Emergence of the American University,* Chicago, Chicago University Press, 1965, Chapter I.

them to be strong advocates of freedom for all sorts of nonconforming religious belief. The Unitarians also challenged the Puritan and Congregational hegemony in Massachusetts and other parts of New England. This early movement toward religious diversity was given greater impetus by the first Great Awakening, a religious revival that added large numbers of converts to religious groups such as the Baptists and Methodists, both of which were anti-establishmentarian by conviction.

The new sectarians found support from colonial leaders like Jefferson and Franklin, both of whom were deeply influenced by the Enlightenment assault on all sorts of religious orthodoxy and religious authority. It was Jefferson's Virginia Bill for Establishing Religious Freedom (a work which he valued second only to the Declaration of Independence)[63], which signaled the end of established churches in America and spurred the movement toward legal protection for the free exercise of religious practice, a movement that led to the First Amendment provisions in the new American Constitution. By the time that these provisions became the law of the land, religious pluralism was a reality everywhere.[64]

In all of this diversity, however, the various fledgling denominations had one thing in common. They believed in education. As Douglas Sloan has pointed out, "when Jonathan Edwards expressed his conviction that an advancement in learning had preceded and gone hand in hand with the recovery of 'true religion' in the Reformation, he was simply repeating an attitude already commonplace among Protestants."[65] To be sure, the confidence in education did not always extend to that provided at Yale and Harvard, but even the "new side Presbyterians" who found Yale and Harvard too liberal moved quickly to establish the College of New Jersey. Their faith in education as an important means of achieving their Christian social ideals had not diminished even though their suspicion of Yale and Harvard had been aroused by rumors of liberalism.

---

[63] Malone, *Jefferson, the Virginian, op. cit.,* 279-280.

[64] Handy, *op. cit.,* 13ff.

[65] Douglas Sloan, *The Great Awakening, op,cit.,* 12.

By the end of the eighteenth century, the College of New Jersey had a president who thought that education was more important than conversion in shaping human character and the social order.[66]   At the beginning of the nineteenth century, then, there had developed in America a wide Protestant consensus on the importance of education. As Robert Handy has written, "A literate populace was understood to be essential so that all could read the scriptures and be informed about the advances of civilization."[67]

This developing Protestant theory of education was very vague. It had to be, given the deep tensions which existed between the various Protestant denominations. However, vagueness has never been an obstacle to Protestant moral fervor, so it was with considerable confidence that Protestants marched alongside each other during the early nineteenth century, enthusiastically supporting education and simultaneously pursuing their own particular visions of a Christian civilization.[68] This enthusiasm for education inspired the Protestant denominations to build colleges, and build them they did! Under the impact of a second religious awakening and the rise of the home missionary movement, they indulged in an orgy of college building which enticed even the most anti-intellectual sects and denominations.[69]   Altogether, more than 180 successful attempts were made to found colleges during the period from 1820 to the end of the Civil War. Many more attempts failed. Even if one takes account of colleges founded by non-religious groups, the denominational enthusiasm for college building was quite astonishing.[70]

At the same time, the enthusiastic support for education was emerging from other quarters as well. I have already indicated that Jefferson was one of the

---

[66] Douglas Sloan, *The Scottish Enlightenment and the American College Ideal*, New York, Columbia University, Teachers College Press, 1971, 157.

[67] Handy, *op. cit.*, 34, see also 27ff.

[68] Handy, *op. cit.*, 37.

[69] Rudolph, *op. cit.*, 52-58.

[70] Donald G. Tewksbury, *The Founding of American Colleges and Universities Before the Civil War*, New York, Columbia University, Teachers College Press, 1932, 16.

early leaders. Deeply influenced by Newton, Locke and Bacon, he was, like Benjamin Franklin, the embodiment of the spirit of forward-looking Enlightenment thinkers in America who were opposed to arbitrary authority and who believed that human beings were capable not only of progress but perfectibility as well. His was not a shallow optimism. He was too steeped in the classics to fall prey to that fallacy, but he did believe that with education individual persons could experience remarkable development and improvement of their capacities, and he advocated providing every possible educational opportunity to those capable and willing to study. His 1779 "Bill for the More General Diffusion of Knowledge" called for a system of education which would include at least three years of free education for every child in Virginia. This, Jefferson thought, would help to insure wise and honest government and prevent tyranny.[71] In other words, Jefferson, along with other supporters of democracy, advocated the broadening of educational opportunity as a way of creating a body of citizens who could make intelligent political choices and maintain democratic political institutions in perpetuity.

Jefferson's early effort failed, but he persisted even after his return to Virginia from the presidency. In 1817, he drafted a revision of his earlier proposal for a comprehensive primary educational system for Virginia. That effort failed too, though advocates of education in the legislature were able to salvage the proposal for the University of Virginia.[72]

The Jeffersonian spirit was becoming pervasive in America during the early years of the nineteenth century. As in Europe, there was a growing hope for human progress.[73] Profoundly impressed by the discoveries of the natural

---

[71] Malone, *Jefferson, the Virginian, op. cit.,* 282f.

[72] Dumas Malone, *The Sage of Monticello*, (Volume 6 in *Jefferson and His Time*) Boston, Little Brown and Co., 1981, 233f.

[73] Material in the following paragraphs is taken from my essay entitled, "The Loss of Optimism as a Problem for Liberal Christian Faith," in Robert S. Michaelsen and Wade Clark Roof, eds., *Liberal Protestantism*, New York, Pilgrim Press, 1986, 147-152.

sciences and their potential to open the secrets of nature, the leading thinkers of the time quickly became determined to apply the powers of the human mind to the persisting problems of human health and industrial development. They soon expanded their horizons to human behavior and the problems of social organization as well. The world, natural and social, was seen to be malleable. Everything in the world was open to human investigation, and the exploration of the nineteenth-century philosophers unveiled to them a panorama of immense possibilities. Things could be better, and they were. Of that, few of the participants in the enthusiasm of the Enlightenment had any doubt. Human ingenuity could intervene to change history and nature. No longer were human beings simply responders to the mysterious forces and spirits of the universe. They were now the lords of nature and the subjects of history. As their reason was liberated from the fetters of superstition and fear, they could lead human beings toward a future of progress for their good and the good of future generations.

In America, this confidence about the future emerging from the Enlightenment was supported by an optimism rooted in the life experience of white persons who came to the New World. This was true in America in a way that it never was in Europe. Here the future was opened not just by the preaching of visions inspired by scientific discovery, but also by the telling of hundreds of life stories about the opportunities for beginning a new life that had been actualized among simple folk who had seized on the vast resources that were available in the new world and relentlessly pursued the freedom of the open frontier. By the end of the nineteenth century the stories of their lives had been shared many times over. Nearly every white person had heard or told a success story about new beginnings and had shared dreams about new possibilities out there on the frontier. "Nothing in all history has ever succeeded like America, and every American knew it. Nowhere else on the globe had nature been at once so rich and so generous, and her riches were available to all who had the enterprise to take them and the good fortune to be white."[74] To the average white American, "progress was not...a philosophical idea but a commonplace of experience."[75]

Material progress was not the only common characteristic of American experience. The Americans had struggled to inaugurate a widely participatory society in which each white American could experience a growing sense of participation in the decisions about rules and laws governing his social life. From the congregations of the religious and the hundreds of other voluntary associations to the rules prescribing the processes of Government decision-making, the white male Americans were subjects of their lives and history in a manner heretofore unknown.

Thus was born secular "democratic faith," an informal shared belief system which Crane Briton has identified as the only form of this-worldly utopian thinking in Western history to gain widespread acceptance of the many.

Central to this democratic faith is the view that a suitable physical and social environment can be devised and put into practice so that what in the West has been considered evil can be vastly diminished, perhaps eliminated... Furthermore, the necessary changes in the bad environment, though they must be planned and preached by an enlightened minority, will--must in a democracy--be ratified by the majority of the people and even will, after the necessary universal education, be initiated by the people.[76]

From another perspective too, America's faith was different from that of Europe. The Enlightenment of Europe had been for the most part, anti-church. In America, from the beginning, it was not universally so. Even in Europe the symphony of optimism generated by the Enlightenment was not altogether strange music to Christians, particularly those of the Calvinist side of the Reformation. They had a strong belief in the God of Israel, who had promised a messianic age

---

[74] Henry Steele Commager, *The American Mind*, New Haven, Yale Univerity Press, 1950, 5.

[75] *Ibid.*

[76] Crane Brinton, "Utopia and Democracy," *Daedalus*, Spring, 1965, 348-366.

of unparalled peace and prosperity. This is not to suggest any easy compatibility between traditional Protestant beliefs and the Enlightenment. The relationship was always uneasy and much of the time it was downright hostile. Yet the Reformers knew that authentic biblical faith had always been filled with hope. That hope, grounded in the conviction that God was sovereign over all the cosmos; belief in God's creative action to bring forth the world; and the proclamation of God's active intervention in human history in the incarnation of Christ, had always engendered images and visions of a redeemed future for nature and history. Thus, although the Protestant Reformers were profoundly pessimistic about human nature and, therefore, about the immediate future possibilities for nature and history, they never lost sight of God's promise for a new age, a new future and a new kingdom.

For the most part, that new kingdom was not of this world. It would take shape in another world beyond this one or at the end of it. Yet, as Ernst Troeltsch observed in his study of the social teachings of the churches, the gospel idea itself contained within it assumptions about persons and God that would cause it to venture often " on the most searching interference with the social order."[77]

Furthermore, at Geneva, a theocratic experiment was attempted, and the Marian exiles from Britain, who resided there for a time, were stamped by that experience. As a result, there developed among the English Puritan Reformation groups what A. S. P. Woodhouse has called "the method of analogy," by which faithful Puritans extrapolated political judgments from theological visions about the order of life in the Christian community.[78]

Those intrepid Puritans, who left England to come to America in the New World came, then, not only for religious freedom. They came anticipating a new political experiment, one that would be a light to the nations and one based on

---

[77] Ernst Troeltsch, *The Social Teachings of the Christian Churches*, vol. 1, trans. Olive Wyon, New York, Harper Torchbook, 1960, 86.

[78] A. S. P. Woodhouse, ed., *Puritanism and Liberty*, London: J. M. Dent and Sons, 1938, 60f. See also Michael Walzer, *The Revolution of the Saints*, New York, Atheneum, 1968.

their own perceptions of the proper rules of God for human communities, both in church and in society. They came hopeful that in this new world something genuinely new could occur. Their vision was, as it were, of the coming Kingdom of God in America.

At some point during the nineteenth century in America these religiously-based hopes for a new future and a new world merged with the new images of the future of humanity emanating from the projects of the new sciences; the vision of boundless natural material prosperity promised by the resource-rich American continent; and fascination with the experiment with egalitarian democratic political institutions. Thus, even as American democratic faith emerged as a secular phenomenon it was never anti-religious. Most Americans, religious or not, affirmed the importance of religion for the new social order. Even Jefferson, the persistent opponent of orthodox religion and theology, believed that the teachings of Jesus were the most inspired of all ethical teachings.[79] In fact, most Americans thought that the general acceptance of Christianity was one of the major reasons for their success. They were special objects of divine favor.[80]

To be sure, the evangelicals who were dominant in American life did not become too sanguine about the depravity of human beings. The sinner stood in need of conversion. But the converted sinner who saw the light easily became a recruit for the building of the Kingdom. The most serious sort of judgment about human sins, therefore, was no barrier to the coming of the Kingdom. Having been properly confronted by sin and having been shaken firmly over the fiery pit, the converted sinner understood that the practice of piety required involvement in the kind of social reform that would bring in the Kingdom.[81] But equally important,

---

[79] Malone, *Jefferson, the Virginian, op. cit.,* 109.

[80] Commanger, *op. cit.,* 163-164.

[81] See Timothy Smith, *Revivalism and Social Reform,* Nashville, Abingdon Press, 1957; See also the introduction in Willian G. McLoughlin, ed., *The American Evangelicals 1800-1900,* New York, Harper and Row, 1968.

God was raising up persons who had "Christian instincts," even if they did not participate in organized religion.[82]

Thus Walter Rauschenbusch would write:

All history becomes the unfolding of the purpose of the immanent God who is working in the race toward a commonwealth of spiritual liberty and righteousness. History is the sacred workshop of God. There is a pre-sentiment abroad in modern thought that humanity is on the verge of profound change, and that feeling heralds the fact. We feel that all this wonderful liberation of redemptive energy is working out a true and divine order in which our race will rise to a new level of existence.[83]

Rauschenbusch was not unaware of the ambiguity of history, but that ambiguity for him was a temporary phenomenon.

It is unjust to Christianity to call our civilization Christian, it is unjust to our civilization to call it un-Christian. It is semi-Christian. Its regeneration is in process, but it has run in streaks and strata, with baffling inconsistencies and hypocrisies...but insofar as the process has gone, it will warrant us in taking the completion of the job in hand with serene confidence... The largest and hardest part of the work of Christianizing the social order has been done.[84]

Although Rauschenbusch himself never quite said that the Kingdom would come on earth completely, the possibilities were certainly promising. Some of his followers were not even that careful about their claims. In fact, for a time, to be a Christian in America was to believe in America as God's historical experiment in human redemption.[85]

The theological perspective of Rauschenbusch was based on three central convictions. First, the God of biblical faith was the God who acted in history, in and out of the church, and the action of God in history was for the sake of human good. Second, God was absolutely sovereign over history, and that was the basis for hope about human progress in history. Third, Christian piety was not only a

---

[82] Walter Rauschenbusch, *Christianizing the Social Order*, New York, MacMillan, 1916, 122.

[83] *Ibid.,* 121.

[84] *Ibid.,* 123-124.

[85] H. Richard Niebuhr, *The Kingdom of God in America*, New York, Harper and Brothers, 1937, 192f.

matter of personal, moral, and religious behavior; it was also identified with participation in and support of progressive movements in history, particularly those movements that had the force of democratizing the major institutions of society. God was acting in history, in American history particularly, progressively to bring in the Kingdom of God on earth, and that work was already becoming manifest in educational institutions.

An American consensus in support of education was evident. Both religious Protestants and non-religious children of the Enlightenment shared the conviction that education was extremely important for civilization. The civilization whose cause they championed was one in which dedication to democracy and dedication to "Christian" morals went hand in hand. For the progressive theologians of the time, the emergence of a truly democratic civilization in America was thought to be evidence that God was working to bring about the Kingdom promised in the Bible. As Rauschenbusch said, history is the "sacred workshop of God." In this way, Protestant enthusiasm for education was impelled not only by the desire to have a literate faithful flock who could read the scriptures. Since education was so important to the development of a democratic society, it was also a necessary component for the coming of the Kingdom of God. Alexander Campbell, a leader of the Disciples of Christ spoke for most Protestants when he argued that Protestantism, universal education and free republican institutions were much the same thing.[86]

Unfortunately this shared consensus in support of education never included agreement on the role of religion in the universities. The disagreement first surfaced when Jefferson's efforts to establish the University of Virginia met with the opposition of certain Protestant leaders on the grounds that there was no place in that university for the teaching of religion or even the cultivation of piety. In the West it was primarily the partisans of the private denominational colleges who stubbornly resisted the founding of public institutions of higher education,

---

[86] See David Harrel, Jr., *The Quest for a Christian America: The Disciples of Christ and American Society to 1866,* cited in Handy, *op. cit.,* 37.

primarily because they did not want the competition with their own colleges. But they also had the same apprehensions as their colleagues in Virginia. They were successful in preventing the state of Illinois from establishing a university for a number of years. In states where their opposition was overcome, they struggled always to secure control over the state institutions, a tactic used successfully in relation to the earlier state universities such as North Carolina and Georgia.[87]

The consequences of religious groups' opposition to the establishment of state universities were far-reaching. It reinforced in all of the new state universities the Jeffersonian aversion to any control of the universities by religious groups. Moreover in the long run, as we shall see later, it helped to create tensions which, for a time, made the teaching of theology and religion in those universities problematic.

In most cases, however, the denominational opposition to the state universities did not diminish the conviction of most nineteenth century university leaders that Christianity was important for the life of the American universities. After all, it was for the service of the nation that the state universities were created, and it never occurred to many university leaders that service to America was anything but service to a civilization that was Christian at its core.

An interesting case in point was Henry Tappan, president of the University of Michigan from 1852 until 1863. He was an ordained clergyman and a strong advocate of the necessity for nurturing Christian faith and for supporting belief in the divine inspiration of the Bible in the university. He even went so far as to prescribe daily prayers and courses of lectures on Christian morals in the university itself. While Tappan was a steadfast opponent of ecclesiastical control of the university, he believed that all human organizations should benefit from "the presence of benign and charitable religion" and that university professors should be "men of piety." That could happen without the presence of formal theological study. The pursuit of theological questions would be informal and, in

---

[87] Brubacher and Rudy, *op. cit.,* 154-57.

time, participation in religious practices was to become totally voluntary. But both religious conviction and religious practice in the university remained important, because it was true religion that was the foundation for the kind of basic humanity that should be one of the outcomes of a university or college education.[88] It was in this same spirit that James Angell, a successor to Tappan at Michigan, could argue that the "Christian spirit, which pervades the laws, the customs, and the life of the State, shall shape and color the life of the University, that a lofty, earnest, but catholic and unsectarian Christian tone shall characterize the culture which is here imparted." What he envisioned was a university whose faculty would be composed of "secure, gifted, earnest, reverent men, whose mental and moral qualities will fit them to prepare their pupils for manly and womanly work in promoting Christian civilization."[89] Daniel Coit Gilman had named the university, the agent of knowledge, as one of the five great agencies promoting Christian civilization. The universities, he said, were "truly religious." The influence of university study was "favorable to the growth of spiritual life, to the development of uprightness, unselfishness and faith."[90] As with Angell, the faith promoted by the university was non-sectarian and vague, having to do not with the "ebb and flow" of dogmatic beliefs but with the "deep mysteries" underlying all knowledge and faith.[91]

The convictions of Tappan, Angell, and Gilman about the importance of religion for the life of all human organizations, particularly the university, was fairly typical of American academic leaders of the early nineteenth century. After all, as late as 1865, approximately ninety per cent of all university presidents were

---

[88] Henry Tappan, "The University: Its Constitution and Its Relations, Political and Religious," and *University Education*, excerpts of which are reprinted in Hofstdter and Smith, vol 2, *op. cit.*, 507,539.

[89] James B. Angell, *Selected Addresses*, New York, Longman's Green, and Co., 1912, 29-31.

[90] Daniel Coit Gilman, *The Benefits Which Society Derives from Universities*, Baltimore, Johns Hopkins Uinversity Press, 1885, 5, 17.

[91] *Ibid.*, 18.

recruited from the ranks of the Protestant clergy.[92] They shared not only the conviction of their fellow Protestants about the importance of education for religion and for the progress of the nation. They also shared in the broad assumption that hope for a vital American civilization lay in the promotion of the Christian religion. In other words, their vision for the future of America was a vision of a Christian America. It is, therefore, not at all surprising that university presidents often spoke of their institutions as centers for the promotion of Christian civilization.

Of all the nineteenth century university leaders of the universities, none was more clear about the relationship between America, democracy and true Christianity than William Rainey Harper.[93] Harper, who became the founding president of the University of Chicago in 1892, was formed in the crucible of American evangelicalism, critical Bible study, and the passion for reform that was in the air at the time of the rise of the Progressive Movement in America. It was, however, the Bible which most clearly shaped Harper's vision of the university.

Harper's conception of the purpose and function of the university contained all of the themes characteristic of the developing consensus on democracy, Christianity and America. In his study of history, he found important evidence of human progress. That progress had been an upward movement toward higher and higher human possibilities, leading to the emergence of democracy. Harper prophesied that as a culmination of this movement there would follow twenty centuries of the "time of America," in which mankind would test the spirit of democracy and its institutions.

In this time the university was to play a major role. Seizing upon ideas he had learned from John Heyl Vincent, a leader of the Chautauqua movement in New York, Harper developed a vision of the university which would involve not only collegiate and advanced instruction, but extension work, the upgrading of

---

[92] Veysey, *op. cit.*, 7.

[93] In the following section on William Rainey Harper, I have relied almost exclusively on the excellent book by James P. Wind, *The Bible and the University*, Atlanta, Scholars Press, 1987.

pre-collegiate education, and a series of university sponsored publications which, though based on the most scientific scholarship, would be written in such a style and manner that they could become available to interested non-specialists. Harper, like Jefferson before him, believed that the American people must be educated if they were to succeed in the great democratic experiment. In fact, Harper argued, the first and foremost policy of democracy was to be education. The relationship was reciprocal. The university was to be the agency for the deliverance of the people from the shackles of the past to the new future age.

This symbiotic relationship between the university and democracy, was, Harper argued, thoroughly grounded in history. He believed that the university and democracy had developed side by side from the time of the medieval universities. They were, after all, the places where people of all nations could come together to study those things that really mattered. These early universities were associations of free men, who sought knowledge for the sake of addressing the great questions before human civilization.

Turning to his biblical vision, he likened the university to the prophets of Israel. Like the prophet Elijah, who read the signs of history for the word of God to the people, the university, too, would point to those signs of history which revealed that democracy was indeed the fulfillment of the "laws of life." Like Isaiah, the university was to be the bringer of hope to the masses of persons in the cities and great industrial centers, thus "soothing the spirit" of the people who were anxious and deprived. In fact, the whole nation would become a great "temple of democracy," and the university would exercise the priestly functions of preserving the traditions and interpreting the mysteries of the temple. It would do so by maintaining an unswerving devotion to the truth and by constantly pressing beyond the discordant notes of conflict in the society toward a harmonious new pluralism. The university, true to its nature as an association of free persons devoted to addressing the great problems of civilization, would press ever toward an expanded vision of the "brotherhood of man." Thus, while the primary vocation of the university was the education of leadership for every field of activity, its larger vocation was nothing less than the messianic vocation of bringing the salvation of democracy to a wider and wider circle of humankind. [94]

Some of Harper's contemporaries, like John Dewey, had made the same connection between democracy, a common faith and the university, but none of them had grounded this connection in a theological vision. Harper, like Rauschenbusch, believed that God was working in history. There was no doubt that the work of God was manifest in the coming of democracy. Moreover, in Harper's view, God had created the university, even as she had created in Israel a chosen people. Neither was an end in itself. Both of them had a divinely appointed mission and a promise. The mission was deliverance, and the promise was that all nations would be blessed by the faithful performance of that mission. The mission would not be accomplished with ease. It was, in fact, a torturous task to lead humanity forward. For this reason, the university, like the anticipated messiah of Israel, should be the institution that "suffers" for the sake of the world.

This vision was not based on any naive understanding of the Bible. Harper represented the best of biblical scholarship in the nineteenth century. He was a superb teacher and a very competent student of all the semitic languages as well as Greek. Harper's theological understanding of the university, then, was based on scientific study of the scripture employing the most sophisticated research methods available.

Harper was convinced that his study of the Bible had provided him with insight into the meaning of history and the pattern of life which constituted the highest hope for humanity. If the study of the Bible had led him to his own vision, it seemed reasonable to him that the same sort of scientific and sophisticated study of the Bible as history and literature should be at the heart of the modern university if it was to fulfill its divinely determined vocation. Therefore, Harper's Chicago opened with a divinity school and a graduate school, and the study of the Bible was central in both institutions. It was provided for in

---

[94] *Ibid.*, 128.

the normal course of ministerial studies in the divinity school, and in the graduate school, the more sophisticated study of the Bible was lodged in Semitic Studies. This move by Harper was to prove very important for the future of religious studies in the university. He, as much as anyone, secured a firm footing for the "scientific" study of religion in curricula of both private and state institutions of higher education.

Harper's theological vision was manifest not only in his sweeping theological conception of the university, in the university's related basic institutional structure and its initial curricular emphases, it was also manifest in Harper's insistence that the manner in which the vocation of the university was to be pursued was by providing for its students the kind of freedom to learn that would enable them to pursue their own vision of a higher life. They were also to be inculcated with the sense of vocation which was to characterize the university itself. They, who were so privileged to study in the temple, would themselves "suffer" for the people. If democracy was God's gift of hope to the world and America was the place where that gift would be tested and perfected, then those who were to be leaders were to be servants. They were to go forth from the university as missionaries in the service of God and society. The ideal of service to God had always been present in some form or another in American thinking about higher education, but as we shall see later, it was soon to take a secular form. Increasingly the legitimation of the university was not to be cast in terms of its service to God but to society.

Even though much of what he did was anticipated by other university leaders, the comprehensiveness of the Harper experiment and its subsequent impact upon college, seminary and university life has led many commentators to accord to him a unique place in the history of higher education in America. What has been almost completely unnoticed, says James Wind, was "the missionary character" of all of Harper's work. "Whether attempting to reform the Chicago public high school system, raiding the faculty of a sister institution, or handling another bequest for a building, Harper was striving for nothing less than the redemption of America."[95] His was the last great theological vision of the university in America, and it was the only uniquely American one. For Harper, the university was the servant of American democratic civilization, and his deepest conviction was that this very civilization was at least the harbinger of the Kingdom promised to Israel and to Christians as the heirs of biblical faith. Promoting the study of the Bible and promoting American democracy, then, were integrally related. Both were in the service of God's work for the world.

Harper's theological vision never captured the imagination of university leaders in general. By the end of the nineteenth century, few of the key leaders in the emerging American universities thought very much about the direct connection between the promotion of the Christian religion as such and the promotion of Christian civilization. To be sure, most of the reformers were religious men, but they were not theologians. Religion for them had become more rational and ethical. As John Bascom put it, "Religion is not so much the foundation of morals, as morals the foundation of religion."[96] In a sense, nineteenth century Americans began to make a religion out of ethics. Their universities were at the pinnacle of an educational system promoting a civilized society. For them civilization incorporated certain Christian values and ideals, but their notion of a Christian society was characterized by decent morals, democratic values and stability. When they championed the Christian religion, it was more likely because they thought that religion helped to promote these general social goods.

Their thinking probably reflected a subtle shift in the use of the term Christian civilization, one which took place, according to Robert Handy, just after 1860. In the earlier version of Christian civilization, it was Christianity which was the hope of civilization. It was the "best part of civilization," the redemptive element in history. Before the end of the century the emphasis had

---

[95] *Ibid.*, 124.

[96] Quoted in Veysey, *op. cit.,* 202, 203.

shifted to American democracy itself--partly at least because it was understood to have absorbed the spirit of Christianity. Thus the churches now began to be assessed in relation to their contributions to the religion of democracy.[97] In fact, most of the university reformers of the late nineteenth century were dubious about the contributions of organized religion to the future of genuine Christian civilization. Even Harper shared this pessimistic assessment of the churches, pointing out that they were often hostile to the "superior ideas" of Christianity, namely, democracy.[98]

During the latter half of the nineteenth century, war, reconstruction, massive immigration, urbanization and industrialization had combined to change the face of America. In the process, it rendered the old concept of a Christian civilization obsolete. That conception grew out of the consensus on values that emerged in white Anglo-Saxon Protestant rural and small town America. Like the Puritan society that preceded it, it gave way to a new kind of social and religious pluralism.

As these changes took place, the discussion of the purpose of the university also took a decidedly different turn. The old American college idea came under increasingly vigorous attack from the reformers of several stripes. The pursuit of these reforms generated the most creative debate over the theory of the university in American history. In all of this, there were continuing vague references to the service of Christian civilization in presidential speeches from time to time. But most of the discussion went on without any reference to religion or theology at all.

---

[97] Handy, *op. cit.*, 95-96.
[98] Wind, *op. cit.*, 127.

KNOWING GOD AND LIVING FULLY
Mary Elizabeth Mullino Moore

As I packed books to move from my theological home in Claremont, Jack Verheyden waxed eloquent on our similar theological moorings, a surprising topic given the very different emphases of our work. He ruminated on his coming retirement, noting that the two of us had brought a unique emphasis on religious experience in theology. An odd comment, I thought, but I was destined to ruminate on his words for many months to come. The occasion of Professor Verheyden's retirement opens an opportunity to reflect on a set of questions that have been important to him for at least 40 years, and on an array of responses that he has shared with many generations of students. How do we know God? What do we know? And how does that knowing interplay with the deepest experiences of our lives?

At the heart of this essay is the yearning to explore the interdependent relationship between knowing God and living fully. Epistemological questions about knowing God cannot be separated from questions of human religious experience, nor can religious experience be considered independently from knowledge of God. As a feminist woman deeply committed to the flourishing of God's creation, I would further argue that all human experience, not just experience labeled as "religious," contributes to knowing God, and whatever we know of God shapes our experience. On the surface, this seems like an obvious claim, but followed to its limits, it suggests that we cannot individualize or compartmentalize knowledge of God, nor can we assume that human life is a separate field from theology. We cannot bracket life from religion as some advocates for secularity would claim, nor can we bracket theology from biblical, historical, or social scientific studies, as some advocates for the study of religion would argue. Whatever form of secularity or religious study that we attempt will be laced with theological assumptions (or more broadly religious assumptions about the world and spiritual realities), whether we open those assumptions for reflection or not. Are we not better scholars if we are honest in examining the theological passions that underlay our living and scholarship?

Certain features mark the trajectory of Jack Verheyden's work on these questions. While this article is not a review of his work, it is focused on many features of knowing God that have captured Professor Verheyden's attention, with particular reference to three of his theological mentors—John Calvin, Friedrich Schleiermacher, and John Wesley. No attempt is made to repeat Verheyden's emphases in a literal way, but rather to acknowledge his interest in inquiries about God and the similarity between his emphases and the ones named here.

Five features of knowing God are identified in this chapter: multifarious, engraved, sensate, personal, and convictional. Paired with each feature of knowing God is a corollary feature of living fully. Recognizing these correlations and their mutual influence is the central concern of this chapter. To pair features of knowing God and living fully is to critique much contemporary theological work, which focuses on theological constructs without self-consciousness about the experiential forces that influence and underscore a given concern. Even many contextual theologians, as they reflect on the influence of a particular socio-historical context, fail to acknowledge the interactive influence between a people's religious experience and their theological assertions.

MULTIFARIOUS KNOWING: OPENING TO CREATION, REDEMPTION AND TRANSFORMATION

To speak of knowing God as multifarious is to quote Jack Verheyden, who argues that John Calvin is "right in contending that the knowing of God is multifarious."[99] He appeals particularly to Calvin's delineation of different ways of knowing God, which are distinctive emphases representing "different aspects

---

[99] Jack Verheyden, "The Knowledge of the Existence of God in Protestant Theology," *Dialogue and Alliance*, vol. 1, no. 1 (Spring 1987), 39.

of the one God." More specifically, in this essay, Verheyden appeals to the distinction Calvin makes between knowledge of God as Creator and knowledge of God as Redeemer. He notes further that Calvin delineates three ways by which people come to a conviction of God as Creator: an internal sense of divinity (immediate apprehension of that which is "inscribed" or "engraved" on the human mind); an external attending to the likeness of God in the magnificence and order of the world; and alertness to the human conscience and its inherent knowledge (however corrupted) of right and wrong.[100] Marked as these pathways are by sin, they are true ways of knowing God. Another pathway is important, however, because of the power of sin, and this is the knowledge of God as Redeemer, made known through Jesus Christ and the Holy Spirit, and testified to in the Old and New Testaments. These multiple ways of knowing God represent "a variety of lamps which light one's way to God."[101]

Verheyden contrasts the more limited, albeit insightful and ingenious, approaches to the knowledge of God in Samuel Clarke, Immanuel Kant, Friedrich Schleiermacher, and Karl Barth. All of these figures, in their own distinctive ways limit the pathways to one, focusing on only one lamp.[102] For Clarke, the lamp is "the structure and order of the world as rationally inferred."[103] For Kant, it is a conviction born of the human sense of moral duty.[104] For Schleiermacher, it is the internal sense of divinity, or religious consciousness.[105] And for Barth, it is the acknowledgment of God as revealed in Jesus Christ, contrasting such knowledge of God as Redeemer with what Calvin called knowledge of God as Creator, and recognizing only the former as true.[106] In short, the two basic pathways of knowing God, as delineated and elaborated by Calvin, are focal

---

[100] Ibid., 27-28; cf: John Calvin, *Institutes of the Christian Religion*, trans. Ford Lewis Battles, ed. John T. McNeill (Philadelphia: Westminster, 1960), 35-47, esp. 43-44.

[101] Verheyden, 28.

[102] Ibid., 29-39.

[103] Ibid., 31.

[104] Ibid., 34.

[105] Ibid., 36.

[106] Ibid., 38.

points for later philosophers and theologians as well, but the successors are often more limited in their understandings. The genius of Calvin's work is to point to the multifarious ways of knowing God.

This discussion begs the question of how the multifarious knowledge of God is related to living fully. Certainly, the most obvious implication is that people will come to know God as they open to God's movements in creation, redemption, and transformation. God is revealed in the wonders of the universe— the stars and sea, the pebbles and mountains, the plants and animals of every kind, and the people of every size and shape. God is also revealed in the redemptive work of Jesus Christ. And God is revealed in the human conscience. Calvin attends less explicitly to the possibility of knowing God in movements of transformation—liberation, deliverance, reconciliation—but these are likewise essential to knowing God multifariously.

Just as opening to God enhances the possibility of living fully, practices of living fully lead people into deeper and broader experiences of God. As people explore a mountain trail or watch a sunset, study the biblical witness to Jesus Christ, listen to and follow their conscience, participate in acts of transformation, they are opening to God. These encounters with God will also open them to deeper engagement with life and more vital encounters with the world. This does not mean that people will have altogether pleasurable experiences of God and the world, but surely people will experience intensity, vitality and hope in the multifarious search for God and the opening of self and community to full living.

ENGRAVED KNOWING: ATTUNING TO THE INTERNAL INFINITE

We have already noted that Calvin refers to knowing God through directly apprehending what God has engraved on the human mind. While Friedrich Schleiermacher uses a different language, he paints a similar picture, suggesting that religious feeling emerges from the impress of the infinite; the feeling of absolute dependence is itself a consciousness of God.[107] This suggests that the infinite is present in the finite, and a finite being can even sense that presence and be guided by it. This suggests further that, in every human encounter with God's creation, the imprint of God's infinitude is present; therefore, to know God is to experience the fullness of life. The converse might also be argued: to experience life fully is to know God. The point here is that, when one assumes that God's infinite presence is somehow engraved on human life and on the rest of creation, then, by extension, one suggests that knowing God and living fully are deeply intertwined.

In yet another language, we turn to John Wesley's emphasis on prevenient, or preventing, grace. For Wesley, this is fundamental to understanding how God is active in the world, moving in persons long before they are aware of it. Prevenient grace is that which awakens the conscience and opens the way for God's justifying and sanctifying grace. In a real sense, one can say that prevenient grace is engraved on human hearts; it is the first way that a human being comes to know God. People are able to apprehend God because of this presence that stirs inside. As in Schleiermacher, Wesley makes no dichotomous distinction between God and the world. Certainly the two are not the same, but both affirm that God is engraved on the world and people are able to discern God—with immediacy and surety—as a result.

This discussion of engraved knowing suggests that God is internal to human lives and to all of God's creation. If people are to be open to such knowing, they need to be attuned to their inner being and respectfully alert to the inner being of others. Such attunement is not to be equated with humanistic psychology, but it does bear resemblance to transpersonal psychology and even more to mystical and monastic religious traditions. To acknowledge engraved knowing is to be aware of the mysterious infinite that dwells within each being,

---

[107] Friedrich Schleiermacher, *On Religion: Speeches to its Cultured Despisers*, trans. John Oman (New York: Harper and Brothers, 1958), 88-90; *The Christian Faith*, vol. 1, trans. H. R. Mackintosh and J. S. Stewart (New York: Harper and Row, 1963), 12-18, esp. 16-18.

106

known in part ("in a mirror dimly," I Corinthians 13:12, NRSV) but always tugging to be known more fully.

Living fully is, thus, a response to the inner tug of the infinite engraved on our being. It is a feature of knowing marked by immediacy. Schleiermacher recognized the immediacy of religious feeling, which Verheyden summarizes as "more immediate than either thinking or acting."[108] John Wesley increasingly shifted his own understanding of faith, describing it in terms of direct spiritual experience; he never repudiated his earlier emphases on faith as reason and faith as trust, but the emphasis changed decidedly.[109] The liberation theologian Gustavo Gutierrez bears a similar sensitivity; he argues that contemplation and practice precede reason and speech in the work of theology.[110] For such widely divergent theologians to agree on the importance of primal spiritual experience is striking, compelling human attention to the internal infinite. At the same time, all of these theologians focus largely on spiritual depths within human beings, being less attentive to the internal infinite within the rest of creation. The perspective offered here broadens the idea of engraved knowing to include that which is engraved in the whole universe, within which God dwells and through which God can be known.

Drawing from an emphasis on engraved knowing, the desire to live fully begins to shape life practices. Living fully is enhanced by prayer and meditation, as by careful listening to the intuitive nudges within our souls and the intuitive nudges of others. It is further enhanced by being present to the nonhuman natural world. Attunement is an art to be cultivated—a way of being in the world that

[108] Verheyden, 35; cf. Schleiermacher, *The Christian Faith*, 6-7.

[109] Rex D. Matthews, "'With the Eyes of Faith': Spiritual Experience and the Knowledge of God in the Theology of John Wesley," in Theodore Runyon, ed., *Wesleyan Theology Today: A Bicentennial Theological Consultation* (Nashville: Abingdon, 1985), 406-415.

[110] Gustavo Gutierrez, *On Job: God-Talk and the Suffering of the Innocent*, trans. Matthew J. O'Connell (Maryknoll, N.Y.: Orbis, 1993), xiii-xiv. Gutierrez elaborates this point: "God is first contemplated when we do God's will and allow God to reign; only after that do we think about God. To use familiar categories: contemplation and practice together make up a *first act*; theologizing is a *second act*. We must establish ourselves on the terrain of spirituality and practice; only subsequently is it possible to formulate discourse on God in an authentic and respectful way" (emphasis his, xiii).

opens people to what God has engraved. These engravings bear grace, and they have potential for transforming our lives from the inside out.

Attending to engraved knowing, especially when focused on that which God engraves within each person, has its limitations. This accent can lead people to focus on transformation that is rooted and lodged first in the internal, individual, intimate community, and human depths; only then does transformation move toward external, communal, global, and ecological realities. The power of such knowing is that it can be truly transformative; the danger, when separated from other features of knowing God, is that it can be distorted into self-justification, self-preoccupation and anthropocentrism. In short, engraved knowing and multifarious knowing are powerful complements of one another.

SENSATE KNOWING: FEELING THE WORLD

This leads naturally, but not inevitably, to another feature of knowing God—sensate knowing. This is not a separate kind of knowing, but a significant quality of all knowing, a characteristic that can be nurtured and honed. This quality is more fully developed by poets and people of color and women than by Calvin, Schleiermacher, and Wesley. These three thinkers, however, have not neglected sensate knowing; at times, they sharpen their readers' senses through their effusive writing. For example, in Schleiermacher's early romantic period, he awakened the senses of his readers to the immediate environments of human experience.[111] In his more explicitly theological writings, however, he wrote more formally and abstractly of creation and God's relationship to it.[112] Further, his emphasis was decidedly human. Immediate self-consciousness and the feeling of absolute dependence were understood as uniquely human experiences. These same experiences were elevated as the source of religious knowing and the clearest pointers to the infinite.

---

[111] Friedrich Schleiermacher, *Christmas Eve: Dialogue on the Incarnation*, trans. Terrence N. Tice (Richmond, Va.: John Knox, 1967). This is a particularly good example of Schleiermacher's environment-rich writing of this period.

[112] Schleiermacher, *The Christian Faith*, 142-156.

No one is more eloquent than John Calvin in painting a picture of God's imprint on creation. Calvin claims that God is self-disclosing "in the whole workmanship of the universe."[113] Thus, people see God whenever they open their eyes. God's essence and divineness escape human perception; however, Calvin adds: "But upon [God's] individual works he has engraved unmistakable marks of his glory, so clear and so prominent that even unlettered and stupid folk cannot plead the excuse of ignorance."[114] Even with this strong emphasis on creation's glory, we find that Calvin does continue the dominant Christian emphasis on making distinctions between humans and beasts. He argues that religious impulses are human, not belonging to the rest of creation, and whereas people can experience awe before God's creation, the fullness of God's grace is conveyed in the free acts of God, radically distinct from, and unbounded by, the creation.

John Wesley, writing later, is bold at points in recognizing God's presence in the world, a presence conveyed through the larger creation.[115] Yet, Wesley is well remembered for his reticence regarding the untrustworthy human body and human senses. We see in Wesley an inability to embrace sensate knowing beyond a general acknowledgment.

For attention to the senses as a way of knowing God, we might turn to recent writings of women instead. Consider Chung Hyun Kyung, for example. Chung describes Asian women's spirituality and theology as embodied, grounded in the life of people, especially poor people, and attentive to the embodied nature of biblical stories (as of Jesus and Mary). She explains that theological method

---

[113] John Calvin, *Institutes*, 52; cf. 51-68.

[114] Ibid. Calvin believes that this knowledge of God is awesome but not sufficient; therefore, he proceeds immediately to a discussion of the necessary guidance of Scripture.

[115] John Wesley, Sermon 77, "Spiritual Worship," *The Works of John Wesley* (Nashville: Abingdon, 1984 ff), 3:95; Wesley, Sermon 23, "Upon the Lord's Sermon on the Mount, III," *Works*, 1:513-514, 516-517; Theodore Runyon, *The New Creation: John Wesley's Theology Today* (Nashville: Abingdon, 1998), 200-207. Runyon describes this accent in Wesley, recognizing that ecological consciousness was quite different in Wesley's world than in the present one. Nevertheless, Runyon summarizes Wesley's understanding with these words: "This vision of God is a vision of all creation *in* God, and God *in* all of creation" (emphasis his, 206).

begins with women's storytelling, which she describes as "embodied truth."[116] Women talk about their concrete experiences and broken bodies.

One can find strong embodiment in the Psalms as well, sometimes in a lament or protest and sometimes in joyful thanksgiving. The psalmists speak from a culture far closer to the earth and sacred place than our present world, especially more so than the modernist Western world. Consider a psalmist's prayer for help: "Hear my prayer, O Lord; let my cry come to you . . . For my days pass away like smoke, and my bones burn like a furnace. My heart is stricken and withered like grass; I am too wasted to eat my bread" (Psalm 102:1, 3-4, NRSV). This psalm of lament is matched with psalms of celebration, such as Psalm 19: "The heavens are telling the glory of God; and the firmament proclaims [God's] handiwork" (19:1, NRSV). In both Chung and the psalmists, we see sensory pictures of tragic devastation and salvific beauty. God is present with those who suffer, and God's creation reveals and incarnates the Creator. This is far from pantheism, but it does reveal the strong strand of panentheism within Jewish and Christian traditions.

If sensate knowing is a feature of knowing God, then living fully has much to do with awaking the senses and trusting them to reveal God. These senses include the most obvious ones, seeing and hearing, but also the less obvious sense of smell and the more neglected or maligned touch and taste. For the Christian community, full living would mean full use of the senses. This includes the more conventional spiritual practices, such as enjoying the visual beauty of God's creation and the harmonies of music; it also includes the smells of incense and spices. But sensate knowing cannot stop with these more common practices.

Consider the practices that are absent from Christian sensory reflection and practice. Despite the sacramental quality of eating in biblical tradition, almost no theological attention has been given to taste, whether the sour vinegar Jesus tasted on the cross or the sweet wine and bread shared at Jesus' table.

---

[116] Chung Hyun Kyung, *Struggle to Be the Sun Again: Introducing Asian Women's Theology* (Maryknoll, N.Y.: Orbis, 1990), 104, cf: 85-114.

Likewise, the church has a long history of devaluing sexuality and attributing it with value only as it serves another purpose, first in procreation and later (with less emphasis) in companionship. It is no wonder that touch has rarely been named and, even more rarely understood, as a way of knowing God. If we take sensate knowing seriously, we will foster full living by way of the senses: movement and touch; eating and taste; exploring the earth through smell; listening to sounds of the universe (both natural and human-made); and seeing the most tender and tiny, and most bold and grand, sights in God's creation.

PERSONAL KNOWING: RESPONDING TO GOD'S CLAIM ON ONE'S LIFE

Another feature of knowing God is personal knowing, grounded in persons' encounter with wonder, whether internal or external, biblical or natural, delight-filled or terrifying. Here we meet a dominant focus of Western theological thinking, particularly in the European and European-American trajectories of theology. Knowing God is understood as the work or blessing of one person at a time, with communal and ecological realities being understood as helpful or hurtful to that personal experience, but not primary forms of religious experience.

The focus here will not be on a full critique of personal knowing, which has been elaborated with vigor in recent years. The focus instead will be on the value of personal knowing, with reflections and corrections on some of the limitations. Consider the emphases of Calvin, Wesley, and Schleiermacher—all European men but from different times and places (16th century France and Switzerland, 18th century England, and 18th-19th century Germany respectively). Each of these men discusses the power of personal knowing—knowing that overwhelms, transforms and empowers men and women. This personal knowing, in fact, confronts individuals with God's claim on their lives and calls them into fuller living and giving of themselves in the world.

At the same time, this is a limited perspective. Such thinking dominates thinking in the United States context still, where "personal" is most often equated with "individual." Even well-intentioned people, for example, cannot grasp the Native American's sense of self, grounded in a people or tribe or clan. Even when outsiders make sincere effort to understand, they judge indigenous persons by their individual qualities and ignore their communal relationships; with such an approach, outsiders can never understand Native people, for whom community is the primary reality. One sees similar misunderstandings in the political arena. When white men in the United States use such terms as "reverse discrimination" or "glass ceilings" for men, they betray their individualistic assumptions. They seem to be saying that people are not embedded in cultures and that all people begin with the same opportunities and individual freedom to become whatever they wish. Similar assumptions also appear in religious arenas. Further, the music, art and religious practices of diverse cultures are often understood as the background from which individual spirituality grows, with little or no recognition of the communal passions, attachments and commitments that grow from these communal practices.

Reflection on personal knowing needs to encompass both individual and communal aspects of the personal, namely, those revelations and passions that emerge as persons experience the fullness of their lives in moments of separate silence (which is never truly separate) and moments of communal gathering (which is never without individuation). If we can but recognize the uniqueness of each individual within the person's unique communities and cultures, we can encourage a more full-bodied personal knowing. Personal knowing is always both individual and communal, but if we impose worldviews that focus on only one or the other, we will skew personal knowing into something less than it is.

If we value personal knowing in all of its fullness, we will discover that living fully has to do with responding to God's claim on one's life. This claim comes to us in our individuality and connectedness; thus, the practices that nourish and hone personal knowing and full living are those that draw strength and wisdom from our aloneness and from the many communities and cultures to which we belong. This is not to say that all aloneness, communities and cultures are good. It is only to say that they are part of our unique personhood—sources of our lives to be appreciated, critiqued, and transformed.

CONVICTIONAL KNOWING: LIVING WITH COURAGE AND RISK

We turn now to one last feature of knowing God—convictional knowing. Naming this feature is filled with hidden humor, especially in a festschrift essay for Jack Verheyden, whose life is marked with convictions spoken with clarity and power. If people know only one thing about Professor Verheyden, they probably know of his convictions, held firmly and persistently. What may be less obvious is the intimate connection that these convictions have with his assumptions about religious experience and theology. With this personal observation in the background, we turn now to examine convictional knowing.

Convictional knowing is experience of God that overcomes, persuades, proves, and awakens. Relating with God can take many convictional forms: People experience being convicted; they are also guided to live by their convictions; finally, their convictions influence their further experiences of God. The Latin root of the word "convict" is "convincere," meaning to overcome or conquer. The trajectory of meaning still carries the warring tone of this root, but it also includes meanings less oriented to an antagonist who seeks victory over others. The trajectory of meaning includes elements of persuading, proving, and awakening.

Convictional knowing of God includes all of these. To know God is to be overcome (overawed) by God and God's creation; it is to overcome dominant or conventional ways of explaining, experiencing, and acting in the world. To know God is to be persuaded and to persuade others of new dimensions of life. To know God is to prove a way of believing, acting, and being in the world; it is also to be proven in one's experience as a self-conscious self and a child of God. To know God is to be awakened to mysterious dimensions of life and to awaken new commitments for living. In short, convictional knowing has to do with religious experience that affects people (actively influences them) and is effected by them (actively proclaimed by their words and deeds). Convictional knowing overcomes, persuades, proves, and awakens.

This introduction clearly does not say that convictions are rigid and unchanging, nor that convictional knowing is warlike and conquering. Simply stated, it says that knowing God shapes a way of understanding and living in the world, and the way we understand and live in the world shapes our experience of God. This double-natured reality is best communicated by a living example. When John Wesley faced a crisis of faith during and after his Georgia sojourn, he sought the counsel of Peter Bohler. According to Wesley's journal dated 5 March 1738, Bohler advised him with these words: "'Preach faith *till* you have it, and then, *because* you have it, you *will* preach faith'" (emphasis in the original).[117] We see here a mutual influence expressed between the act of asserting faith and receiving it. This is not a simple matter of works' producing faith; in fact, this journal entry appears in the midst of Wesley's reflections on, and yearning for, faith as an experience of assurance that comes only from God. The words of Bohler, which Wesley took to heart and which eventuated in inspired congregations and his own "heart-warming experience," is simply that faith and works are more intimately connected than the Protestant faith vs. works rhetoric would suggest.

One can trace the trajectory of the Wesleyan movement and see the continuing complexity of convictional knowing. Wesleyan people have often held together convictions that are typically torn apart in Protestant theological discourse. For example, John Wesley, with his brother Charles and other colleagues, was convinced that people could grow in holiness and that the quality of their lives could be improved. This represents a deep knowing, which eventuated in his doctrinal and ethical convictions—belief in the possibility of

---

[117] John Wesley, *Works*, 18:228.

perfection in human life and commitment to working actively to improve the quality of life for all persons. His active work was focused in many directions: protesting slave trade, preaching to miners and other poor and oppressed people, writing to politicians on behalf of the elderly, supporting a network of classes and bands to support spiritual renewal, founding educational institutions, and so forth. One can see that Wesley's belief in God's care for every soul, and his trust in God's ability to do miracles in human lives, were not abstractions. These beliefs grew from convictional knowing, and they helped shape his doctrinal formulations and active involvement with many aspects of individual and social life in his time and place.[118]

One sees similar patterns of convictional knowing in John Calvin, who proclaimed his convictions, reshaped the life of Geneva Protestants around these convictions, and framed one of the most comprehensive and lucid doctrinal statements ever written within the Christian tradition (*Institutes of the Christian Religion*). One sees the patterns, also, in Friedrich Schleiermacher, who was a scholar-pastor, committed in his ministry of preaching, lecturing and teaching, as in his efforts to reshape and set new directions for theological education. In all three of these men, one can identify many ways in which their experience of God and the world shaped their doctrinal and ethical convictions, sending them forth with vigor (even enthusiasm) to communicate those convictions in word and deed.

What is thus far implicit in this discussion is that religious and moral sensibilities, doctrinal formulations and ethical principles rise from God and

---

[118] The connections between Wesley's experience of God, theological commitments, and ways of living are evident in his writings and in the historical documentation of his ministry. One of the more direct and lucid comments on these connections has been made recently by Kenneth L. Carder. He says, "Wesley was obsessed with knowing God, living the reign of God, and proclaiming and teaching the truth of God made known in Jesus Christ and through the Holy Spirit." [Carder, "What Difference Does Knowing Wesley Make?" in Randy L. Maddox, ed., *Rethinking Wesley's Theology for Contemporary Methodism* (Nashville: Kingswood Books, Abingdon, 1998), 23.] Carder continues this emphasis by focusing on the heart of Wesley's work, noting that "what matters is not intellectual *thought about God* but the *shaping of life by the reality and presence of God*" (emphasis his, 24). See also: Randy L. Maddox, "Reclaiming an Inheritance: Wesley as Theologian in the History of Methodist Theology," ibid, 215-217, 220-226; and Theodore H. Runyon, "The Importance of Experience for Faith," in Randy L. Maddox, ed., *Aldersgate Reconsidered* (Nashville: Kingswood Books, Abingdon, 1990), 93-107.

experiences of God. Once formed, these then influence further experiences of God and further examination and reformulation of theology and ethics. Curiously, this suggests the inverse of Immanuel Kant's assumption that the inherent moral sense of human beings points to God.[119]

What is less obvious on the surface of this discussion, but implied in the complex nature of convictional knowing, is that people experience God differently in different cultures. If we take this seriously, we will not be surprised that diverse convictions emerge as diverse human communities experience God. People experience themselves as being convicted (in the language discussed above) within their distinctive cultural contexts. Within those same contexts, but with new perspectives born of religious experience, they are inspired to live by their convictions. Finally, their convictions influence their further experiences of God. The convictions that arise from diverse cultural contexts may, in turn, reshape those contexts, especially as the convictions are formed, challenged and reformed by the religious experience of a people. Just as faith and works cannot be dichotomized, neither can cultural experience and the experience of God.

Taking seriously the interplay of being convicted, living by convictions, and being transformed by convictions, one concludes that living fully is nourished by convictional knowing and vice versa. On the surface, this seems like a happy affirmation, but convictional knowing sometimes requires more of people than they are willing to give. The rewards of convictional knowing and living by convictions are more often the rewards of integrity than those of success, fame and comfort. Convictional knowing often leads to the sacrifice of personal wishes and the loss of comfortable worldviews, theological convictions, and moral standards. In short, it leads to transformation that can be experienced as a

---

[119] Verheyden, 31-34; cf: Immanuel Kant, *Religion within the Limits of Reason Alone*, trans. Theodore M. Greene and Hoyt H. Hudson (New York: Harper & Bros., 1960), 142; cf: 142-151. Kant's corpus is more complex than indicated here, but his central idea is strongly relevant to this discussion, namely, that human consciousness of moral obligation points people to divinity, the source of moral duty. For Calvin, Wesley and Schleiermacher, the experience of God (or God-consciousness in Schleiermacher) precedes this sense of moral duty. In all of these men, however, the interconnection is upheld and emphasized.

quaking of the earth. Likewise, full living in the world might challenge the experiences of God that have become familiar and easy. We, therefore, conclude this section with the obvious: In light of convictional knowing, full living is living with courage and risk.

CONCLUSION

The intimate relation between knowing God and living fully suggests a dynamic interplay among religious experience, theological formulations and ethical living. The most obvious challenge in this essay is to recognize the complexity of knowing God and living fully. It is also the challenge of understanding interactive relationships, moving beyond simple cause-and-effect thinking (e.g., theology produces ethics or culture determines theology) or dichotomous formulations in theology, such as faith and works or theology and culture.

Implicit in this discussion is the importance of wrestling and struggle. Easy separation of theology from ethics, or Godly matters from worldly matters, or God-knowledge from world-knowledge can be actively destructive to knowing God and living fully. As much as a community may be tempted to focus on only one aspect of these tangled realities, the task of wrestling with complexity is incumbent on human beings. The demands of poverty and hurt in the world evoke from sincere seekers a more challenging experience of God. Similarly, the human encounter with God's fullness evokes a more challenging awareness of the world and a more demanding ethical response. Acknowledging these relationships turns us to the values of much feminist discourse. Oddly enough, this discourse can build fruitfully (albeit suspiciously and critically) upon the work of the very people who have been the focus of this essay (three white men embedded in cultures of white male dominance).

Many have already begun this work, but much more will be needed in the future. One particularly helpful example is Rebecca Chopp. Acknowledging her debt to the Wesleyan tradition, Chopp recognizes how that tradition of systematic theology "focuses on grace-filled Christian living."[120] In so doing, she addresses the complex relationships discussed in this essay. From this recognition, she proposes a shift in defining theology "from mastering a closed system of doctrine to constructing open spaces for living"; this leads Chopp, then, to propose a Wesleyan feminist emphasis on "the expression of grace in the moments of empowerment, critique, and transformation in prophetic Christian movements."[121] This is but one example, but a powerful one. Epistemology moves back and forth in the lively interchange between past and present, knowing God and living in the world.

The real challenge of this essay is to move beyond simplistic theological and ethical discourse, and to call forth full-bodied religious experience in relation to full-bodied living. The fact that this is difficult is obvious, visible in the ease with which theologians and religious scholars ignore connections and make efforts, often quite sophisticated, to bifurcate. Even more important, the idea that knowing God and living fully are deeply connected is actually dangerous, demanding of us more courage than we may think possible. The promise is that the very challenge is met with the magnificent promise of living more fully with God and the world.

---

[120] Rebecca S. Chopp, "Anointed to Preach: Speaking of Sin in the Midst of Grace," in M. Douglas Meeks, ed., *The Portion of the Poor: Good News to the Poor in the Wesleyan Tradition* (Nashville: Kingswood Books, Abingdon, 1995), 101.

[121] Ibid., 101-102.

DOCTRINE IN CHRISTIAN LIFE[122]
Marjorie Hewitt Suchocki

The importance of doctrine in the life of the church is both individual and corporate, for doctrine is our way of expressing intellectually and gratefully the identity which is given to us by the grace of God in Christ Jesus. Doctrine is both the collective wisdom of our intellectual responsiveness to the grace of God, and the individual's creative appropriation of that wisdom. Out of this interplay, doctrine continues to be newly expressed, thus continuously creating the Christian tradition.

Doctrine differs from revelation. Revelation is the manifestation of God in time, given to us primally in Jesus Christ. Doctrine is the human endeavor to interpret what this means in our lives of faith and faithfulness. Revelation is a manifestation; doctrine is an interpretation. Revelation is a person; doctrine is a paragraph. Writing those paragraphs, thinking those paragraphs, and transforming those paragraphs is essential to the living nature of the tradition. This task of critically appropriating the tradition through the continuous work of expressing the doctrines of the church belongs to the church as a whole, and to the individual members of that church. It is a task belonging deeply within the heart of what it is to be a Christian.

For Christian faith involves the whole of who we are--our emotions, our bodies, our minds. John Wesley has a wonderful little passage to this effect in *A Plain Account of Christian Perfection*: "Persons should use, to the glory of God, all the powers with which they were created. Now, they were created free from

---

[122] An earlier version of this essay was delivered as a lecture to ministers at Candler School of Theology. I have chosen to rewrite the address as an essay in honor of Jack C. Verheyden because the essay reflects several things that have pervaded Verheyden's own life and thought: his Wesleyan heritage, his conviction that the worship of God is central to all Christian life, and the importance of theology in the life of laity as well as clergy.

any defect, either in understanding or affections."[123] Wesley's immediate reference in this passage is to Adam, but the implication for all of us remains the same, despite the fact that we can make no claim of being "free from any defect either in understanding or affections." On this point, Wesley continues the passage by outlining the difficulties of reason in our present as opposed to created condition, so that "..it is as natural for us to mistake as to breathe, and we can no more live without the one than without the other."[124] Despite these defects, however, we are still called to use our minds as well as our emotions to the glory of God.

In this essay I build on Wesley's statement by suggesting four distinctive themes for the place of doctrine in Christian life. 1) The development of Christian doctrine is a dynamic activity that belongs to every age, every Christian. 2) Since we must confess defects in our understanding, the development of Christian doctrine is a fallible enterprise. 3) All expressions of doctrine are framed within the context of grateful praise to God. 4) The adequacy of our intellectual responsiveness to God's grace through our doctrines is to be measured by the extent to which our expressions of doctrine both parallel and increase our ability to love God and neighbor.

Doctrine as Dynamic

The role of doctrine in the life of the church is no abstract intellectual exercise--it is our development of the life of faith with our minds as well as our hearts. It is part of the fullness of our salvation in this world's history, and it is an expression of who we are in Christ with pragmatic effects in the quality and course of our lives. It bespeaks and empowers our identity in Christ.

Thus the development of doctrine is our interpretive responsiveness to the grace of God revealed to us in and through Jesus Christ. As such, doctrine is a dynamic activity that is not the province of one generation alone. To the contrary,

---

[123] John Wesley, *A Plain Account of Christian Perfection* (London: Epworth Press), p. 69. I have taken the liberty of putting Wesley's words into gender inclusive language.
[124] Ibid., page 70.

it is part of the identity of the church, and thus it is a task given to every generation.

If individuals are to develop all the powers with which they are created to the glory of God, it is also the case that the church as a whole must likewise do so. But to be alive is to continue to think, to explore, to ponder. This means that while part of our exploration is to probe the thinking of the generations who have preceded us, we dare not relegate the thinking of the church to a mere repetition of the past, as if the call to interpret God's revelation were time dated. And in fact the very witness of our tradition is that each generation absorbs the expressions of the past, but transforms them in ever rich expressions of each generation's own peculiar perspective. When I teach theology to my seminarians, I do not teach them Ignatius of Antioch and close the books. To the contrary! While teaching the history of the theology of prayer we begin with second century theologians Tertullian, Cyprian, and Origen, then move to the desert fathers, to Augustine, to Irish monks, to Anselm, to Francis, to Hildegard, to the Beguines, to Thomas Aquinas, to Calvin, to Jeremy Taylor, and finally end with Wesley--not because there is no one further to study, but because we come to the end of the semester. Is each thinker a mere repetition of the previous ones? Of course not! Otherwise we would not have bothered to read them. Each represents a variation on the understanding of the theology of prayer, sometimes in direct contradiction to one or more of the previous theologies, and other times in complementarity. Is the issue, then, which theologian was correct? How impoverished our study would be if that were our criterion for studying this rich history! Rather, we learn what a rich and varied history we have with regard to the church's understanding of prayer. And the very richness of diversity in our tradition places upon us the demand that we, like our forebears, enter into what is now our task of giving intellectual expression to our life in Christ.

While I have used the illustration of the theological interpretation of prayer, I could easily use any doctrine of the church--trinity, incarnation, the transcendence and immanence of God, the nature of grace, the work of salvation, the nature of revelation. Whenever I teach a seminar on a particular doctrine I always assign students the task of looking into our history and discovering in what ways, and how, and why our forebears in the faith have expressed this doctrine. And invariably what my students find is not invariability, but variability. There is no one way to express any doctrine, which means that we are called in our own time, in faithfulness to our past, to think deeply into our tradition in transformative ways.

Doing theology belongs to every generation. And if theology devolves into no more than rote repetition of one of the ways our forebears thought, then we have turned theology into shibboleths, and reneged on our call to develop our intellectual life to the fullest of the powers with which God created us. For our Christian identity is no finished thing, no once-upon-a-time reality. It is a dynamic, living, zestful process of ever interacting with the gracious God who does not leave any generation bereft of the call and the empowerment to think into its faith. To be sure, thinking sometimes differs radically from the thinking of the past. But is this not one of the reasons for the various forms and denominations of Christianity? Many a theologian so differed from the past that a new way of being the church came into being. The point is not conformity with grace received by others in the past, but faithfulness to God's call in every generation to express anew our interpretive responsiveness to God's gracious salvation given to us through Jesus Christ. And this salvation, like the manna of old, is to be gathered and expressed daily in living continuity and transformation of our rich and varied past.

The Fallibility of Doctrine.

Since the development of doctrine is a human activity in response to God's graciousness, it is an activity that reflects our finite condition: our enculturation in a particular time and place, and the finite nature of our intellects. Far from being a weakness of doctrine, this is its livingness and its strength. Too often we have had a misplaced affection for timelessness, as if God had somehow fallen into error in creating us as such thoroughly temporal creatures. We have bemused ourselves with the so-called comfort of thinking that our minds could transcend our temporality--that thought tainted by time is impure and unworthy of theology. Or, because theology speaks of our perceptions of God, and we perceive that God is eternal and unchanging, that our thoughts of God, to be quite right, must also be eternal and unchanging. Such attitudes implicitly accuse God of a certain messiness by plunging our intellects into time, a messiness that we ourselves can "correct" by claiming that our human thoughts can attain to timeless truth. The idolatry that clings to such an approach to doctrine tempts us into worshiping our thoughts about God rather than God's own self, who--as Scripture is wont to tell us--is more than our thoughts can think.

But consider the import of God's incarnation in Christ for our doing of theology, our development of doctrine. We learn, to our wonder, that the infinite can become manifest in the finite, that the glory of God can embrace time. Indeed, we are so accustomed to portraying Jesus as a humble Galilean clothed in homespun cloth that we forget the wonder of it. God can speak to us in and through the stuff of culture. But the God who does this in first century Palestine is a God capable of speaking to us through any and every culture. We are given timely truths, not timeless truths. The incarnation bespeaks a God who can be immanent in all times and places, even our own. Therefore we should not despise the way one's culture enters into the way one speaks theologically. To the contrary, culture belongs to our humanness, and through it a God who is no stranger to incarnation can speak to us. We are called, I suspect, to rejoice that God is expressible through the stuff of our own time.

To make this more concrete, let me speak to my own mode of developing doctrine, which is through the categories of process thought. Unlike earlier ages, we now live in a time when the interdependence of all things and the relativity of time are commonplaces of how we interpret our world. Just as Augustine used the philosophies of his day to express Christian faith, even so we, in faithfulness are called to use the understandings of our own age in service to Christian faith. From the perspective of being immersed in Christian scriptures and tradition, and from the livingness of my faith, I use process thought to develop doctrine. But I would laugh to think there is any ultimacy to process categories! They are useful to me and others, as Plotinus and Plato were to Augustine, and Aristotle to Aquinas, and nominalism to the Reformers, and Enlightenment sensitivities to Wesley. But process is no more ultimate than Plotinus or Plato or Aristotle or nominalism or Enlightenment or any other structure of human thought. It does not necessarily have universal appeal, and in its own time it, like its predecessors, will be superseded as a useful vehicle for expressing our human responsiveness to God's grace. By using process thought I do not worship a "process" God--I worship the living God whom I know through Jesus Christ, expressed faithfully in my own time through categories appropriate to my own time. To use process thought is to interact transformatively with the tradition--but this is so with whatever structure of human reason is used.

But this leads to another aspect of what it is to bespeak God's grace through the means given to our intellectual capacities. John Wesley said that under the conditions of finitude, no person "can at all times apprehend clearly, or judge truly."[125] It is pride to think that human formulations are infallible, and such a perception has led to some of the most egregious sins of the Christian church. In the name of infallible doctrine we have persecuted, tortured, and murdered those who had the audacity not to agree fully with our own mode of expressing Christian faith. To make our own thinking synonymous with God's thinking is to put ourselves in the place of God, and to bow down and worship the sorriness of our own little minds rather than the greatness of the God with whom we have to do. In our own day we no longer torture and murder bodies--but I fear we easily fall into the same tactics with regard to the spirit. Whenever we find ourselves filled with hatred toward those whose theological expressions differ from our own, we must beware the sin of idolatry.

---

[125] Ibid.

If in fact we are fallible; if in fact it is not possible to live without making mistakes, then we are called to humility in all of our doctrinal development. Consider the paradox: If one accepts the fact that our minds are fallible, and that it is not possible for any human being to be infallible, then one must recognize that one is wrong about something. The question is, which something? In the nature of the case, we cannot know it, for if we knew it, we would cease thinking that way. By definition, then, to be a fallible creature doing theology and developing doctrine is to be subject to error in one's doctrine.

There is no loophole by saying this is exactly how Wesley, or Calvin, or Luther, or Aquinas, or whoever developed doctrine, and therefore one is without error in such and such a point. The old saw that God has no grandchildren (which some of us realize could be a great impoverishment, even of Deity) comes into play with the dictum that every generation is responsible for thinking anew about what it means to receive the grace of God in Jesus Christ. Thus we cannot escape error by flying to the past, for our forebears were also fallible. Doctrine is a human intellectural responsiveness to the grace of God, and partakes of our fallible human situation. Therefore, it behooves us to be humble about our theologies, open about our doctrines. Oddly enough, to recognize this is to be freed from the impossible and intimidating task of developing an infallible theology. It is to be released into the joyous task of playing with our intellects, like some game of holy tag: "is it like this, God? What if I say it this way? That way? Ah, God, can I plumb the depths of grace one more time to say the unsayable, and worship you with the saying?"

If Wesley was right, God calls us to develop our intellectual powers to their fullest, to the glory of God. But the fullest of our intellectual powers is yet finite, bound by perspective, time, place, prejudice, habit, custom, culture. To develop doctrine knowing these conditions is to enter the joy of thinking the unthinkable--it is holy play. To be sure, the very finitude of our ways of expressing doctrine calls upon us to study the ways of the past and the resources of the present. It is not an "anything goes" task, but a transformative task marked by a particular tradition, even as our thinking faithfully moves that tradition to a new place. To think transformatively is the stuff of Christian faithfulness.

The Grateful Praise of God.

The above leads, of course, to my third point. While doctrine is the intellectual aspect of our responsiveness to God, it cannot be separated from the fullness of gratitude that pervades our whole being. Thus all expressions of doctrine are framed within the context of grateful praise to God. For only consider: Doctrine is our intellectual responsiveness to God's grace. It is our way of interpreting that grace in our own experience, our own time. As such, doctrines always point beyond ourselves and our own fallibility to the God to whom we so fumblingly respond. Is it the doctrine of the trinity we wish to explore and to express anew within the context of our time and place? Fundamentally, the trinity says that within the depths of the divine nature God is already communal, everlastingly so, and that we experience the communality of God in three "moments" of grace: our createdness, our redemption, and our sanctification. The how of our expressing this is infinitely variable. Several years ago Joseph Bracken and I edited a book of essays in which nine theologians each used the relational structure of process thought to express the relational nature of God as trinity.[126] Of course there were overlaps in the essays, but the surprise in editing that book was the radical diversity even among persons using the same basic structure of thought within a common Christian traditional trajectory. The point is not the diversity of ways that obtain to express how it is that we express God within the Christian tradition in a trinitarian way, but that this God we express is for us in Christ Jesus. God is for us! Is that not amazing; is that not an absolute wonder? Today, in this world of relativity physics, in this world set within a galaxy within a universe of unimaginable dimensions, the God of this universe is *for* us. To even attempt to express how this God is trinitarian is to be overcome with gratitude not only that we, in all our finitude, can find ways to talk

---

[126] Joseph Bracken and Marjorie Hewitt Suchocki, eds. *Trinity in Process* (Continuum, 1995).

about God, but that the God of which we speak is one whom we existentially know.

I suggest that one of the functions of doctrine is to increase our wonder at the grace and glory of God. We are so habit prone; we are so capable of rendering things familiar, even the things of faith, and in many respects this is well and good. To be pulled into the task of developing our intellectual lives of faith challenges us and shocks us ever anew into the absolute wonder of God.

Is it the doctrine of incarnation we wish to express? Again, in this universe so vast in space, the God we worship not only pervades it through omnipresence, but also "erupts" within it in a singular manifestation of divine love. That God--that God!--should share our condition for the sake of our salvation is the action of God to which our doctrines of the incarnation point. How we express incarnation is variable--in what sense is God revealed in Jesus Christ? There has been such a variability of answers to that not-so-simple question! But *that* God is so revealed fills us with wonder and gratitude, even as we struggle to express anew the experienced reality.

What does the cross mean? There has been no single doctrine affirmed concerning this question within the history of the church. We are challenged to answer the question not by rote, but by thinking deeply into our living experience of God's salvation in the context of our texts, tradition, and contemporary world. Can we think into this without being overcome with wonder and gratitude that the question is even given? What we try to express with our halting words is the wonder of the universe: that God, *God*, is for us, and that we have discovered/encountered this through the witness to Jesus Christ and of Jesus Christ.

To do theology, to be engaged in the development of doctrine which belongs to every age, is to be plunged anew into the wonder of God for us. This intellectual activity, then, expresses the development of our intellectual powers in living responsiveness to God's grace. As such, it is a vehicle for profound gratitude and joy. Doctrine is not a labor of rote recitation of dead truths of the past; nor is it a simple recovery of what past generations said. It is the living responsiveness with our intellects to the God of past, future, and present; it is an activity that evokes and expresses intense joy and intense gratitude.

The Criterion of Love.

If theology is variable; if it is a fallible and finite activity involving our intellectual responsiveness to the grace of God, what sorts of criteria do we use in developing theology? Is it an every-person-for-him-or-herself sort of exercise? Is it an "anything goes" activity? And if it is done in every age, in transformative continuity with the past, what provides the continuity? What is to prevent us from dropping whole doctrines that no longer speak to us? What criterion do we use?

I speak within the Wesleyan tradition. This tradition has graced us with the famous quadrilateral--theology is done within the resources of scripture, tradition, reason, and experience, which then offer guidance for the contemporary formulations of theology. But this does not exactly answer the question. The doctrine of the trinity, for example, is not in scripture; it emerges in the tradition. It is consistent with some aspects of scripture and inconsistent with others; it is a case of a doctrine entering the tradition transformatively, going beyond the given resources of its past. And some doctrines within the tradition are dropped from some of the branches of the tradition: The ubiquity of Christ was once such a critical doctrine that it spawned wars, but today it hardly raises an eyebrow. Supralapsarianism instigated profound and profoundly heated debates--but I suspect not even the most hide-bound traditionalist would worry to find someone for or against it. Predestination is an example of a doctrine deeply influential in those following the Calvinist traditions, but not so for those of Wesleyan persuasion. Clearly we can each have favorite doctrines from either scripture or tradition that we are quite convinced must always be given faithful expression, but in the nature of the case a bit of arbitrariness can be detected. If theology is the human intellectual responsiveness to the grace of God experienced in Jesus Christ, and if variability and fallibility attend our human intellectual ways, then what we find through the guidelines of scripture, tradition, reason, and experience are precisely that--guidelines, not iron-clad criteria.

But I suggest that there is indeed a criteria attendant upon all our doctrinal developments. Perhaps the criteria is uniquely applicable to one who is as deeply influenced by Wesley's *A Plain Account of Christian Perfection* as I am, but nonetheless I offer it--and it is the criterion of love. Wesley teaches us that God creates and redeems us for the sake of the love that is available in Christ, and that love of God and neighbor is the ultimate fulfillment of salvation. Love is no sentimentalism in Wesley--love is an active caring for the well-being of others, it is the wellspring of our emotional, intellectual, and physical responsiveness to God. Love is rejoicing service; it is an intent toward inclusive well-being. Love is the content of salvation: It is evoked within our human selves in grateful response to the boundless love of God, manifest for us in time past, present, and future.

Craig Dykstra, in an address published by the Association of Theological Schools, borrows a phrase from Martha Nussbaum to discuss theology and theological education, and the phrase is "love's knowledge."[127] By it he indicates that the intellectual life of the Christian is not about abstractions; it is not about absolute intellectual certainty; it is not about cold analytical reasoning. Christian knowledge is that which is known and grasped in love.

I think he is profoundly right, and that just as our development of doctrine should naturally evoke in us a profound gratitude and praise of God, it is also the case that our development of doctrine should bear the fruit of furthering our growth in love. If so, then the criteria by which we can test our doctrines is not the criteria of an inaccessible infallibility, but the accessibility of love. Do our ways of expressing what God has done for us in Christ Jesus lead to a deeper caring for all God's creatures? Does it lead us to richer forms of human

---

[127] Craig Dykstra, "Love's Knowledge: Theological Education in the future of the Church and Culture." An Occasional Paper published by The Association of Theological Schools in The United States and Canada. Pittsburgh: 1996.

community? Does it contribute to reflecting God's own image of love more faithfully both individually and communally?

An alternative way of expressing the criterion would be this: Does our way of expressing what God has done for us in Christ lead to ill-being for any aspect of earth or its creatures? To the extent that it does, we need to revisit our doctrines to ask at what point and why ill-being is implied. The issue is subtle, and I can illustrate it with the worst possible illustration since it is the most volatile and controversial illustration in contemporary church life. Do our doctrines lead to persecution of persons whose sexuality is oriented toward their own gender rather than toward the opposite gender?

There are several doctrines involved in such an issue, perhaps the most central is the doctrine of sin--our expression of that from which God has redeemed us in Christ. Is homosexuality a sin? Some argue vociferously "yes!" and others argue vociferously "no!" The pros and cons have been gloriously argued, and amply show that more than intellectuality is involved in one's theological opinions and doctrines. Both sides claim scriptural authority for their answer, which shows that scripture alone is seldom the final arbiter or criterion of theology. And of course both sides of the controversy would claim that theirs is the one meeting the ultimate criterion of love: Those arguing for the sin of homosexuality strongly feel that the well-being of the homosexual involves renouncing their sin, and therefore denouncing homosexuality is the most loving response; those arguing that homosexuality is part of the God-given diversity of creation strongly feel that social persecution of homosexuality is against their well-being, and that the criterion of love is best met by accepting the homosexual as a brother or sister in Christ. Those who argue that homosexuality is a sin that requires rejection of homosexuals from God's ordained service on the basis of their being sinners must answer the peculiar question of why this sin is somehow more sinful than the other sins that afflict us, which do not prevent ordination; those who argue that homosexuality is not a sin must answer to those passages in our texts which identify homosexual acts as sinful. In other words, the criterion of love alone, while lovely in the abstract, is a little more thorny when applied to contemporary issues in theology around which there is great diversity of opinion. Love is no easy criterion.

Yet for all this I still maintain that it is a criterion that binds us, even in our diversity. We are called to apply the criterion in multiple modes. First, does our expression of doctrine increase our wonder and gratitude and praise and love of God? In what ways? Second, does our expression of doctrine increase our appreciation of one another in the community called church? Can we love those who disagree with us--not abstractly, but concretely, such that we can speak together caringly even in our disagreements? Can the effect of our thinking deeply into faith, even in the most controversial of issues, be such that our care for one another is increased? And I submit that true care for the other is not the demand that they become a relative clone of oneself, but that their own subjectivity and integrity and difference from oneself shall be a matter of affirmation rather than condemnation. Do our doctrines lead us to more deeply caring communities, such that "they shall know we are Christians by our love"? And thirdly, do our expressions of doctrine lead to greater care for God's own earth and all its creatures? Do our doctrines lead us into an echo of Wesley's "One of the principal rules of religion is, to lose no occasion of serving god. And since [God] is invisible to our eyes, we are to serve [God] in our neighbour: which [God] receives as if done to Godself in person, standing visibly before us"?[128]

Are our doctrines not only ways of expressing our interpretation of what God has done for us in Christ Jesus, but are they ways of deepening our appreciation and care for those beyond our familiar circles of caring? I don't mean by the criterion of love that we never get testy with one another. But deeper than the testiness is a respect, regard, and affirmation for each other that flows from our shared identity in Christ. And ultimately, of course, our disagreements

---

[128] Wesley, *Op. Cit.*, p. 103

perform an essential service: They keep us aware of human fallibility, and therefore of our own fallibility, and protect us from worshiping our doctrines instead of worshiping the God before whom all our doctrines will one day fall away in the infinite joy of wisdom born of fully redeeming love.

In the fallibility of our living, the answers to our questions concerning doctrine will always be more or less, but despite the difficulties, I suggest that love should be the guiding criterion of all our theological thinking. Doing theology, and developing doctrine, is not the same as doing philosophy. It is not thinking for the sake of thinking. It is a living expression of a living faith; it is a faithful response to God by loving God with our minds as well as our hearts; it is part and parcel of the stuff of our Christian identity. And since our Christian identity is for the sake of increasing the love of God and God's creatures within ourselves and our communities, then those things that make for that identity are rightly brought under the criterion of love.

So let me conclude by expanding upon my initial statement. The importance of doctrine in the life of the church is both individual and corporate, for doctrine is our way of expressing intellectually and gratefully the identity which is given to us by the grace of God in Christ Jesus. Doctrine is the collective wisdom of our intellectual responsiveness to the grace of God; it is the human endeavor to interpret what this means in our lives of faith and faithfulness. It is a task belonging to the church as a whole, and to the individual members of that church. It is a task belonging deeply within the heart of what it is to be a Christian. And it is a task that in its very doing will deepen our faith, increase our love, and join our voices to that cosmic choir of all creation singing everlastingly the praise of God.

JACK C. VERHEYDEN: GLIMPSES OF A UNIVERSE
Thandeka

Jack C. Verheyden is the Great Disrupter of my life. A man with scant patience for the smoothly developmental outlines of academic advance, Jack interrupted my doctoral student outlook like a large rabbit with a pocket watch in hand as he rushes off to tea. His appearance in my life gave me a glimpse of a universe where sharp breaks and revolutionary reversals are given the time of day.

I met this disrupter of conventional consciousness seventeen years ago when I took his course on Schleiermacher and Kierkegaard to prepare for my qualifying exams in theology. This class, so I thought, was *pro forma*. All theology students had to take a qualifying exam on nineteenth-century theology. His course fit the bill. So my cohorts and I signed up for it in order to prepare for "the exam."

The disruptions began on day one. At the end of the first class session, one of my classmates, who was expected to lead the class discussion on Schleiermacher's *Speeches on Religion* the following week, approached Jack after class and asked what his focus should be. He was a cautious student and didn't want to make analytical errors. Jack, noting that he had thought about the *Speeches* for decades, wanted to know what the student might see on his own. Perhaps he would discover something Jack had not considered. Jack, in a word, said "no." The student would have to make his own discoveries.

I was shocked. Never had I come across such a direct affirmation of the integrity of a student's intelligence *before* it had been shaped by the professor's own style and thoughts. My classmate looked as surprised as I felt, and he quickly left the room. We had received a message from the man I now began to think of as a disrupter of conventional discourse. I had learned the first lesson of protocol for this class: dare to think.

Lesson two came several weeks later when my turn came for a class report. I presented a synopsis of Kierkegaard's analysis on the nature and meaning of anxiety. Using my professional background as a broadcast journalist and dramatist, I commenced with an account of a supposed conversation between Schleiermacher and Kierkegaard (a mini-drama) on their own personal experiences of anxiety and then turned to a careful textual analysis of Kierkegaard's *Concept of Anxiety*. Jack later complimented me on the thoroughness and rigor of my analysis and he took delight in the play.

One of the doctoral candidates in the class, however, was perturbed that a mere doctoral student who was also female and African American could undertake such a difficult project with such panache and skill. His attack against me started, but was immediately blocked.

"Let Sue, I mean, Miss Booker complete her thought," Jack said interrupting the student.[129] Jack's comment was astonishing because he always referred to his students by their last names attached to a formal title. And we always referred to him as *Professor* Verheyden. (I did not begin to call him Jack until after I had graduated and continued to work with him as I prepared my dissertation on Schleiermacher's *Dialektik* for publication.).

Our professor, as all of us knew, did not make such "slips." Both the student and I immediately interpreted the slip for what it was: an act of protection. Jack had notified all of us that I had his support. In short, I was off limits as a class target of derision. Thus I learned that for Jack Verheyden, difference was a good thing. I could dare to know.

My ideas could be challenged but I would not be attacked. Like Alice, whose day had been disrupted by the sudden appearance of a rabbit with a pocket watch, I followed Jack to his office for student office hours.

---

[129] Desmond Tutu, formerly the Archbishop of Cape Town, South Africa, had not yet given me the name "Thandeka."

As I entered his office, the usual markers of reality fell away. There was not one flat surface in his office—except for the floor—that was not covered with books and papers. Bookcases were stuffed to overflowing with books and manuscripts. Essays, articles, papers, and journals abounded. Chairs were used as file cabinets. It seemed as if everything with print on it had been read and then set aside to mark by location its encounter with Jack's mind. Stories about Jack's mind were legion among his students. My favorite was that he had memorized the entire Encyclopedia Britannica by the time he was five. (He has a photographic memory.)

Clearing a place for myself on one of the chairs, I told him that I wanted to know more about the structure of Schleiermacher's thought. The people in Schleiermacher's world were never alone, I said. Each person was always linked to another. To know oneself meant to also look "objectively for an Other." Self-consciousness was not a strictly private affair. Particularity occurred in community. Each of us co-existed with an Other. What did this mean? Are we so constructed that we are never fully alone? Where "in" me did I meet this Other? Where could I find Schleiermacher's phenomenology of self-consciousness?

Jack smiled. "Schleiermacher's *Dialektik,*" he finally said.

I had never heard of this text. "It's in German," Jack said.

And so my work with Jack as my dissertation adviser began. Jack, I quickly discovered, believed that Schleiermacher's outlook was "much too smoothly developmental." As summarized in his introductory essay to Schleiermacher's *The Life of Jesus*, Jack believed that Schleiermacher's outlook did not allow for "sharp breaks, revolutionary reversals, and crises waged in fear and trembling."[130] I sought those disruptions in Schleiermacher's work and found them at the under-theorized core of his philosophic work. I argued first in my

---

[130] Jack C. Verheyden, "Introduction," Friedrich Schleiermacher's *The Life of Jesus* (Philadelphia: Fortress Press, 1975), lv.

dissertation and then in my book on Schleiermacher,[131] that these disruptions are the mystical dimension of his work. They are the eruptions in human consciousness that indicate the presence of an Other.

I consider my ongoing attention to this disruptive fact of consciousness Jack C. Verheyden's major legacy to me. Presently, I have begun work on a systematic theology of human consciousness to give a full account of this fact as the basis for a doctrine of human nature. Doctrines of the church, sin and salvation, God, evil, and the Eschaton will be developed from this first doctrine. Not surprisingly, my work begins with an analysis of human consciousness by Wilhelm Dilthey, the master phenomenologist of human consciousness who was not only Schleiermacher's biographer, but also applied Schleiermacher's insights to the social sciences. I offer the following reflections on Dilthey's analysis of consciousness in honor of my Great Disrupter of conventional thought.

*   *   *

Wilhelm Dilthey studied disruptive thought in order to understand the interdependence of identity and difference. His analysis of human consciousness was the focal point of the project. This is not surprising because human consciousness, according to Dilthey in his *Introduction to the Human Sciences*,[132] is our primordial condition of knowing. It is the *sine qua non* of human awareness. If consciousness is absent, nothing can be known. Every object, every feeling is a fact of consciousness (248). But every object is also more than this. It is distinct from human consciousness, and as such, is objectively real. Dilthey thus invites us to investigate the real from the standpoint of human consciousness.

Two premises govern Dilthey's initial investigation. First, everything human beings know about reality is a fact of human consciousness. This does not

---

[131] Thandeka, *The Embodied Self: Friedrich Schleiermacher's Solution to Kant's Problem of the Empirical Self* (Albany: The State University of New York Press, 1995).

[132] William Dilthey, *Introduction to the Human Sciences. Wilhelm Dilthey: Selected Works (Volume 1)*, ed. Rudolf A. Makkreel and Frithjof Rodi (Princeton: Princeton University Press, 1989). Further references to this work will be made parenthetically with page numbers in the text of this essay.

mean that reality is *only* a fact of consciousness. Rather, this claim means that the only way *human beings* know external reality is *as* a fact of consciousness.

Second, everything exhibited as consciousness—perceptions, memories, objects, representations of objects, concepts—is psychological (263-4). The independence of external reality is not the issue here. The task is to understand *inter*dependence, how external reality is known *as* but cannot simply be reduced *to* a fact of human consciousness.

To understand this congruence between conscious fact and discreet object, Dilthey asks us to pay attention to what happens when we touch a part of our own bodies:

> When our hand grasps a part of our body in which a feeling is
> located, or a muscular tension is felt, or when our eye follows a
> movement, then inner states and representations of sense fuse into
> a stable framework of contiguous intuitions which belong at one
> and the same time to our self and to our body (346).

When, for example, my hand touches my body, I feel (= self) and am felt (= body). The coincidence of these two events of feeling and being felt is the human experience of congruence, which Dilthey defines as the *I* (345-6). The term *I*, according to Dilthey, refers to the human experience of the unity of these two disparate feeling states. We can think of this experience as our psychic-somatic congruence.[133] The *I* that thinks about feelings (percepts) is the same I that feels the object of its thoughts (affects).

Dilthey uses a second example to identify the difference between affect and percept as distinct but united facts of consciousness. He begins this analysis with a discussion of his experience of listening to a Beethoven symphony:

---

[133] My use of the term "psychic-somatic congruence" is based on a vivid, post-Freudian theory about psychic-somatic congruence that is remarkably consonant with Dilthey's basic perspective, by D. W. Winnicott, "Mind and its Relation to the Psyche-Soma," published in *Through Paediatrics to Psycho-Analysis: Collected Papers, D. W. Winnicott* (New York: Brunner/Mazel, 1992), 243-254.

138

The play of moods with which I accompany the Eroica Symphony is distinct from the succession of tones itself. The kind of consciousness involved in these moods is wholly different from that involved in following the tones. Both the tone and my delight in it are facts of consciousness, but the ways in which they exist in consciousness are different Hearing and taking delight in the tone are both experienced reflexively as states of the subject who becomes aware of them. But the tone emerges in consciousness as a fact distinct from and independent of the self. It stands over against the self as its object. In the nexus of psychic life, hearing and taking delight in the tone thus becomes constituents of the self that perceives and experiences, while the tone becomes a constituent part of the external world which confronts the listening subject as something distinct (254-5).

Dilthey reminds us in this example that human consciousness begins as a self-enclosed event. He claims that his mood of delight while listening to the symphony does not have an external referent. His mood is simply a state of himself, an affect. Affect, according to Dilthey, is the simplest form of human consciousness. Affect is the feeling-of-oneself, the sensing-of-self, or the finding-oneself-being-affected (257). Affect is "self-feeling" (350), Dilthey's first referent for the term *self*. According to Dilthey, reflexive awareness, as an affective experience, is the original form of consciousness (255). It is "being-for oneself, life" (339). The content of Dilthey's awareness is his own feelings.[134]

---

[134] Psychoanalytic theorist W. R. Bion makes a strikingly similar point when discussing Freud's definition of consciousness as "a sense organ for the perception of psychic qualities." Elaborating upon this definition, Bion notes that by restricting the term "consciousness" to the meaning conferred on it by Freud's definition, "it is possible to suppose that this consciousness produces 'sense-data' of the self... [In this limited consciousness as so defined, all] impressions of the self are of equal value; all are conscious." These impressions or first "thoughts" of the self then require an apparatus to deal with them. Thinking, Bion thus argues, is "called into existence to cope with thoughts." See Bion's essay, "A Theory of Thinking," in *Melanie Klein Today: Developments in Theory and Practice, Volume 1: Mainly Theory*, ed. Elizabeth Bott Spillius (New York: Routledge, 1988), 178-186.

Dilthey now argues that his mood of delight differs only in intensity as he listens to the tones. "It is as if the content were being illuminated and highlighted" (254). The luminescent quality of his inner life is his definition of a human mood.

The next stage of Dilthey's analysis breaks out of this enclosed circle of self-feeling by focusing on the tones of the music rather than the moods of the listener. *Hearing* the tones, Dilthey argues, is given to consciousness in a different manner than that of being the mood. We follow the sound, but we are the mood. The directive or "vector" quality of following the tones is felt as a kind of "pressure on feeling and of resistance to the will which reveals an activity outside me" (342). In other words, there is a nudge to (re)direct attention, an interruption of a mood that seems involuntary and thus abrupt. We can think of the will as this abrupt shift of focused attention. It is a disruption of the self-enclosed consciousness by the impress of something exterior to it that opens up human awareness to the surrounding world.

This pressure on and resistance to the will breaks moods, throttles affect, reverses expectations, and alters directions. As a disruptive pressure and resistance, it marks the presence of an object, an other, something felt. The perceptual content (the tone) is thereby posited in consciousness as objective, as something distinct from and independent of the self. It is heard—felt—as that which has impinged upon feeling and shifted its directional vector. This disruption is the difference within consciousness that stands over against the self as the object of its attention (255). However, the act of hearing the tone belongs, like the mood of delight, only to the self (343). The tone itself, on the other hand, is a constituent part of the external world (255). Thus a reflexive awareness (the hearing-self) accompanies and is part of the reflection (the tone as the object the self hears).

What has Dilthey accomplished by means of this example and analysis? It is easy to state what he has not accomplished. He has not proved conclusively that the tone he hears entails an external reality distinct from his self. He has, however, indicated the way in which the possibility of such a claim can be established purely by means of a phenomenological analysis of consciousness. The ground for this possibility pertains purely to a fact of consciousness.

This is Dilthey's major achievement. By means of a purely internal analysis of human consciousness, Dilthey establishes a leeway that lets him affirm human experience as an interactive process with objects distinct from the self. He can conclude that the first reference for the self as an affect-laden feeling-of-oneself does not constitute complete self-consciousness (350). A further condition must arise for the completion of this experience of self-awareness (350).

Dilthey calls this additional necessary condition a Thou—something that is outside the self. The first form of this Thou is an object (350). This object appears in consciousness as a percept. In the above example, the percept is the tone the self hears.

Dilthey's analysis of the structure of hearing the tone thus leads him to conclude that hearing contains within it a mediated knowing: "The passive [something heard] contains within itself the existence of the active [something impressing itself upon me]" (342). He also notes, however, that both the mediated and unmediated awareness are experienced together, simultaneously, as part of the same fact of consciousness. Following the logic of his own analysis, Dilthey is confronted with a new question: How are these two distinct modes of consciousness within the same fact of consciousness reconciled and experienced simultaneously as the same event? Dilthey solves this riddle through an analysis of the experiential content of the word "I."

When the child first says "I," Dilthey contends, this expression does not identify a singular, isolated self, but a self already in relationship to a "Thou." The term "I" is simply a linguistic expression for the twofold structure of the fact of consciousness which preceded it. "I" and "Thou" mean someone speaking and someone being spoken to—Thou refers to the absent one spoken about (351). The ego as a "representation of the I exists only relative to the representation of a Thou. One posits oneself only by positing a world, and the most important event for the development of the self, which is introduced here as something new, lives in the representation of another self" (347).

Every encounter with something or someone exterior to the self, Dilthey argues, is an encounter with a Thou—an "other" distinct from the self. Such encounters constitute the basic condition of self-consciousness[135]: the experience of the other as an inextricable aspect of the experience of the self.[136] Difference (the *Thou*) is embedded in the very center of self-consciousness.[137]

Difference, in Dilthey's scheme of things, is thus the great disrupter of consciousness. It is the appearance of another, a Thou. As a disrupter of insulated feelings and seamless expectations, conventional strategies are dashed. When the disruption is great, we are reminded that sharp breaks and revolutionary reversals in human consciousness must be given the time of day. When such disruptions expand our self-definition without reducing the other to the terms of our own identity, we know that we have met a teacher.

---

[135] Developmental psychologist Daniel Stern refers to this central fact of human engagement and relationship as *interaffectivity*. It is an awareness of the core sense of self as already engaged with the core sense of another. This awareness begins as a body-based awareness of another through the resonance of feeling states, developed expectations, and experienced differences. See Stern's *The Interpersonal World of the Infant* (New York: Basic Books, 1985).

[136] This descriptive language of Dilthey has been adopted by contemporary intersubjective psychoanalytic theory. Intersubjective theorists Robert D. Stolorow and George E. Atwood, for example, suggest that "The analyst is aware of the nature of interpretation as 'the discovery of the I in the Thou' (Dilthey)..." Dilthey is referenced here because these theorists trace their own psychoanalytic theories back to him. They have thus replaced classical Freud drive theory with a theory of the organization of the child's experience as a property of the child-caregiver system of mutual regulation. The recurring patterns within this developmental system of mutual, intersubjective transaction result in the establishment of invariant principles that organize the child's subsequent experiences. See Stolorow and Atwood's essay, "Toward a Science of Human Experience," in *The Intersubjective Perspective*, ed. Stolorow, Atwood and B. Brandchaft (Northvale, NJ: Jason Aronson Inc., 1994).

[137] Dilthey's references to I and Thou are reminiscent of Martin Buber's book *I and Thou*. Dilthey was Buber's teacher.

On Nineteenth Century Theology

A PHENOMENOLOGY OF RELIGIOUSNESS A[138]
Avery Fouts

In the fall of 1989, I had the privilege of taking Jack Verheyden's seminar on Kierkegaard. By the end of the course, I had yet to come to terms with Religiousness A and its point of distinction from the ethical sphere of existence. In this essay, I discuss these issues as I presently understand them. Dr. Verheyden's approach often includes asking a few probing questions and then leaving the student to grapple with the respective text(s), an approach particularly appropriate when dealing with Kierkegaard. So if the content of this discussion does not honor Dr. Verheyden's career in some way, my hope is that my grappling with the writings of Kierkegaard, a thinker in whom I am confident we both feel a kindred spirit, will do so.

Whatever the relationship between Soren Kierkegaard and Johannes Climacus, one thing is for certain: the account of Religiousness A presented in the *Concluding Unscientific Postscript* is no mere thought experiment; every page drips with existence. It is the story of an individual at the crossroads between time and eternity who, in an infinite effort to escape despair, attempts to fulfill absolutely the ancient maxim found at Delphi: Know thyself. In the course of things, it is learned that the absolute fulfillment of this maxim (and simultaneously the absolute liberation from despair) is an ontological impossibility. But with the integrity of the self as an existential premise, it is discovered that the *truth* of an eternal happiness must yet be accepted, for "life becomes confused and comfortless, unless the expectation of an eternal happiness

---

[138]My thanks to David Isaacs for reading a draft of this paper.

regulates and calms it."[139] Even though such an individual is more than aware that an eternal happiness is an objective uncertainty, and even more aware of this than those who can demonstrate it on the blackboard, in silent reply the appeal is made to existential necessity. Such an individual understands all too well the parson who prepares his sermons while walking on the Jutland heath that "only the truth which edifies is truth for you."[140] Of course, there is also Religiousness B to consider, but "Religiousness A must first be present in the individual before there can be any consideration of becoming aware of the dialectical B."[141]

In the *Philosophical Fragments*, an exclusive disjunction is presented contrasting two ways of learning of things eternal.[142] As particularly revealed in the *Postscript*, scenario A represents pagan philosophical thought and scenario B represents Christianity. In scenario A, all pagan philosophical thought is broadly subsumed under the Socratic doctrine of recollection in which a finite individual naturally possesses knowledge of things eternal and learning of them is a matter of recollection. This scenario is inclusive of post-Kantian Idealism, for those in this tradition also assume they have natural access to things eternal through speculative philosophy. In scenario B, the individual does not possess knowledge of things eternal, having no natural resources for doing so; and once having had access to things eternal through faith but having lost it through sin, the person now totally depends upon revelation from the god who has entered time.

Although scenario B is intended to be Christianity, nowhere are they equated. For instance, while scenario B is an imaginative construction, "whether what was imaginatively constructed was therefore Christianity is another

---

[139]Soren Kierkegaard, "The Expectation of an Eternal Happiness," in *Edifying Discourses: A Selection*, ed. with introduction by Paul Holmer and trans. David F. and Lillian Marvin Swenson (New York: Harper Torchbooks, 1958), 124.

[140]Soren Kierkegaard, *Either/Or*, trans. Walter Lowrie (Garden City, New York: Anchor Books, 1959), Vol. II, 356.

[141]Soren Kierkegaard, *Concluding Unscientific Postscript to Philosophical Fragments*, ed. and trans. Howard V. Hong and Edna H. Hong (Princeton: Princeton University Press, 1992), vol. I, 556.

[142]Soren Kierkegaard, *Philosophical Fragments/Johannes Climacus*, ed. and trans. Howard V. Hong and Edna H. Hong (Princeton: Princeton University Press, 1985), 9-36.

question, but this much was gained by it, however, that if modern Christian speculative thought has categories essentially in common with paganism, then modern speculative thought cannot be Christianity."[143]

This contrast between pagan philosophical thought and Christianity in scenarios A and B prevents a simple transition to Religiousness A and Religiousness B, respectively. While Religiousness B represents Christianity, Religiousness A does not without qualification represent pagan philosophical thought. Kierkegaard confesses that in subsuming all the latter under the Socratic doctrine of recollection, he has turned Socrates "into a speculative philosopher instead of what he was, an existing thinker who understood existing as the essential."[144] And while a speculative philosopher (*per se*) ignores existence, the individual of Religiousness A, like Socrates, accentuates existence.[145] As a matter of fact, since Socrates is "in the truth in the highest sense within paganism," he presumably stands at the end of Religiousness A without ever having had to embark explicitly upon it due to his extraordinary inwardness.[146] Nonetheless, a speculative philosopher and the individual of Religiousness A do have something in common; both parties seek things eternal only within the parameters of natural knowledge, both operating only in the sphere of reflection. Therefore, Religiousness A is "not speculation but nevertheless is speculative."[147] While a speculative philosopher mistakenly, and in self-forgetfulness, thinks a vantage point *sub specie aeterni* has already been attained, the individual involved in Religiousness A, in intense self-awareness, *actually* seeks to climb out of time into eternity in search of such a perspective.

An understanding of Religiousness A presupposes some understanding of Kierkegaard's anthropology. Several times in the *Postscript*, it is remarked that a

---

[143]CUP, 368.
[144]Ibid., 206.
[145]Ibid., 570-71.
[146]Ibid., 204.
[147]Ibid., 570.

human being is a synthesis of the infinite and the finite.[148]   But the place where this is best expressed is in the opening paragraphs of *The Sickness Unto Death*:

A human being is spirit. But what is spirit? Spirit is the self. But what is the self? The self is a relation that relates itself to itself or is the relation's relating itself to itself in the relation; the self is not the relation but is the relation's relating itself to itself. A human being is a synthesis of the infinite and the finite, of the temporal and the eternal, of freedom and necessity, in short, a synthesis. A synthesis is a relation between two. Considered in this way, a human being is still not a self.[149]

Here the three pairs of contrasting terms, "of the infinite and the finite, of the temporal and the eternal, of freedom and necessity," describe the two components of the self, each with three dimensions. One component is infinite, eternal, and free; the other is finite, temporal, and necessary. These two components are basically the transcendental ego and the object, respectively, the latter including one's own body. Loosely considered, empirical reality is conditioned by space and time, and is necessary in the sense that objects therein are constrained by the law of universal causality mandating that every event be determined by a preceding cause. From this point of view, the object is finite, temporal, and necessary. The transcendental ego transcends empirical reality and in this sense transcends the finite, the temporal, and the law of universal causality. From this point of view, the ego is infinite, eternal, and free.

Considered as a mere *intentional* "synthesis of the infinite and the finite," the human being is a mere "relation" between these two components. So construed, the human being is not yet a "self," properly speaking. Rather, the potential "self" must maintain equilibrium between the two components in order for the "self" to come into existence as "spirit." This task is likened to driving a

---

[148]See, for example, ibid., 302.

[149]Soren Kierkegaard, *The Sickness Unto Death: A Christian Psychological Exposition for Upbuilding and Awakening*, ed. and trans. Howard V Hong and Edna H. Hong (Princeton: Princeton University Press, 1980), 13.

team of two horses, one Pegasus, the other an old nag--the infinite and the finite, respectively.[150] Of course, a team of two horses needs a driver, and the infinite side of the synthesis is the driver. The infinite possesses partial self-transcendence by way of reflection and thereby is able to realize that it is constituted by the respective synthesis and requires equilibrium in order to escape despair as spirit. This partial self-transcendence enables the infinite to "relate itself to itself." So the "self" is "not a relation," but is "a relation that relates itself to itself or is the relation's relating itself to itself in the relation."

The "relating itself to itself" can be construed as the infinite's relating itself to the finite, but, more properly, this should be construed as the infinite's own relating itself to itself. In other words, the infinite *qua* infinite must relate itself to itself in order then to relate itself appropriately to the finite. Having been established by God, however, the whole relation is a "derived, established relation."[151] Therefore, the infinite cannot absolutely relate itself to itself, requiring absolute self-transcendence. As a result, it resides in anxiety because it can never lay hold of itself nor do away with itself: "How does spirit relate itself to itself and to its conditionality? It relates itself as anxiety. Do away with itself, the spirit cannot; lay hold of itself, it cannot, as long as it has itself outside of itself."[152] When the self yearns to do away with itself, we have the sickness unto death; when the self yearns to lay hold of itself, we have the "ethical and ethical-religious." Let us begin with a brief word concerning the ethical.

The Ethical Sphere of Existence

Religiousness A is characterized as ethical-religious, for phenomenologically it is identical with the absolute ethical choice prescribed in *Either/Or*, albeit differing in interpretation. According to the *Postscript*,

---

[150]CUP, 311-12.

[151]SUD, 13.

[152]Soren Kierkegaard, *The Concept of Anxiety: A Simple Psychologically Orienting Deliberation on the Dogmatic Issue of Hereditary Sin*, ed. and trans. Reidar Thomte in collaboration with Albert B. Anderson (Princeton, Princeton University Press, 1980), 44.

> the ethicist in *Either/Or* had saved himself by despairing, had terminated hiddenness in disclosure, but in my opinion there was a discrepancy here. In order to define himself in the inwardness of truth . . . he nevertheless made it appear that by despairing, in the despair itself, he *uno tenore* [without interruption], as it were, found himself. If it were to be pointed out clearly in *Either/Or* where the discrepancy lies, the book would have needed to have a religious instead of an ethical orientation and would already have said all at once what in my opinion should be said only successively. . . . The discrepancy is that the ethical self is supposed to be found immanently in despair, that by enduring the despair the individual would win himself.[153]

The fact is that the ethical self *cannot* be found immanently in despair. Finding oneself by absolutely despairing is indeed interrupted—the infinite discovers that it cannot absolutely lay hold of itself in order to despair of itself absolutely thereby gaining itself. Put another way, the absolute "Either/Or designates the choice by which one chooses good and evil or rules them out," that is, the choice to be either an ethical or an esthetic individual, respectively.[154] At the point of this choice, despair has intensified to "a doubt of the personality," marked by the esthete's desire to choose a different personality absolutely.[155] Establishing oneself *absolutely* as an ethical personality, however, is not a mere choice to be ethical in the present moment in some particular situation; rather, establishing oneself *absolutely* as an ethical personality is a choice entailing no lapses into the esthetic way of life at *any future moment* from the point of choice. One only becomes reflectively aware of living an esthetic life *after* one has been living it; therefore, one must prevent this sort of ignorance of oneself in the future. Such a choice mandates that the self get behind itself, as it were, in order to monitor all its future activity--in effect uniting reflection and willing. The self must choose itself absolutely.

> But what is it, then, that I choose--is it this or that? No, for I choose absolutely, and I choose absolutely precisely by having chosen not to choose this or that. I choose the absolute, and what is the absolute? It is I

---

[153]CUP, 257-58.

[154]Soren Kierkegaard, *Either/Or*, ed. and trans. Howard V. Hong and Edna H. Hong (Princeton: Princeton University Press, 1987), Part II, 169.

[155]E/O, trans. Lowrie, 215; see also E/O, trans. Hong, 211.

myself in my eternal validity. Something other than myself I can never choose as the absolute, for if I choose something else, I choose it as something finite and consequently do not choose absolutely. Even the Jew who chose God did not choose absolutely, for he did indeed choose the absolute, but he did not choose it absolutely, and thereby it ceased to be the absolute and became something finite.[156]

This passage will become clearer as we go; suffice it here to say that choosing oneself absolutely requires the infinite to relate itself to itself absolutely, an ontological impossibility, and is tantamount to self-creation. The absolute ethical choice is therefore incapable of fulfillment; "the ethical is then present at every moment with its infinite requirement but the individual is not capable of fulfilling it."[157]

The decisive expression for this same impossibility within Religiousness A is the consciousness of total guilt. But Judge William, having testified that he has despaired, implies that he is already aware of total guilt; he comments that ". . . only when I choose myself as guilty do I absolutely choose myself, if I am at all to choose myself absolutely in such a way that it is not identical with creating myself."[158] It therefore is no accident that the last essay in *Either/Or*, introduced by Judge William, is a sermon from the aforementioned parson in Jutland who realizes that there is "edification implied in the thought that as against God we are always in the wrong," that is, always guilty.[159]

Presupposing the language of guilt, one absolutely chooses oneself only through repentance; repentance "is the only condition he wants, for only in this way can he choose himself absolutely."[160] In the attempt to fulfill the absolute ethical choice, the infinite side of the self is turned toward itself; with repentance, there is a return to the finite, but not to the esthetic sphere of existence—at least

---

[156]E/O, trans. Hong, 214.
[157]CUP, 266.
[158]E/O, trans. Hong, 216-17.
[159]E/O, trans. Lowrie, 343.
[160]E/O, trans. Hong, 216; see also 248.

as life used to be lived. The ethical task is marked by self-assertion, and even though absolute freedom is not possessed, freedom nonetheless is revealed by total guilt.[161] So, with a newly found sense of freedom, the person who chooses himself ethically chooses himself concretely as this specific individual, and he achieves this concretion because this choice is identical with the repentance, which ratifies the choice. The individual, then, becomes conscious as this specific individual with these capacities, these inclinations, these drives, these passions, influenced by this specific social milieu, as this specific product of a specific environment. But as he becomes aware of all of this, he takes upon himself responsibility for it all. . . . And this choice is freedom's choice in such a way that in choosing himself as product he can just as well be said to produce himself.[162]

Repenting and choosing oneself as product entails freely accepting one's past; in this way whatever has befallen one is transformed from necessity to freedom.[163] This is why "the person who lives ethically has a memory of his life," while "the person who lives esthetically does not have it at all."[164] All in all, the individual who repents has discovered that beginning "in the beginning" on either the side of the infinite or on the side of the finite is impossible.[165] The individual through repentance has "come to himself, since he does not assume that the world begins with him or that he creates himself."[166]

The Task of Religiousness A

Religiousness A, or the ethical-religious, originates from the esthetic sphere of existence. The various esthetic stages are summed up in this way: "All the stages have this in common, that the reason for living is that whereby one immediately is what one is, because reflection never reaches so high that it

---

[161]CUP, 534.
[162]E/O, trans. Hong, 250-51.
[163]Ibid., 250.
[164]Ibid., 230.
[165]Compare SUD, 68.
[166]E/O, trans. Hong, 258.

reaches beyond this."[167] The esthetic self is bereft of a consciousness of the eternal dimension of itself, the infinite not yet disassociated from the finite. The absence of this consciousness for a potential spirit alters consciousness, producing an unhealthy, despairing immediacy in which the finite defines life; the finite is that whereby one immediately is what one is and is thereby the reason for living. Existential weight resides in the finite; purported happiness and peace of mind depend on what transpires therein.

The finite *per se* is not the difficulty, but rather *how* one is related to the finite constitutes the problem. As a result, and most likely by way of a misfortune, the esthete who possesses the existential wherewithal discovers through self-reflection that the finite is being absolutized. The esthete is "absolutely within relative ends," treating things finite as things eternal.[168] Things finite are not things eternal, however, and therefore "it is a contradiction absolutely to will something finite, since the finite must indeed come to an end, and consequently there must come a time when it can no longer be willed."[169] With this realization, there is a natural attempt to gain equilibrium within the self. In so doing, it is further realized that, in order to temper an unhealthy immediacy, existential security must be anchored in something that transcends the finite, in something eternal, which can be willed *all the time* and for its own sake--an absolute *telos*.[170] The individual chooses this path, for in order to escape despair, by existential necessity, at this point there is no other path to take.

The required anchor is the individual's *own* eternal happiness, the individual's *own* immortality. If this life is not all there is, then things finite can be treated as they should be—as finite. An eternal happiness is the individual's *own* highest good, the individual's *own* absolute *telos*. Moreover, anchoring oneself in an eternal happiness is not to think about it, but rather to *will* it,

---

[167]Ibid., 191.
[168]CUP, 461.
[169]Ibid., 394.
[170]Ibid.

154

"transforming one's own existence into a testimony to it."[171]   And since life is lived in the temporal *all the time*, so to speak, in order *always* to enjoy a healthy immediacy, an eternal happiness must be willed *every moment*, that is, willed absolutely. The task of Religiousness A then is set as follows:

> The task is to practice the absolute relation to the absolute *telos* in such a way that the individual strives to reach this maximum: to relate himself simultaneously to his absolute *telos* and to the relative—not by mediating them but by relating himself absolutely to his absolute *telos* and relatively to the relative. The latter relation belongs to the world, the former to the individual himself, and it is difficult simultaneously to relate oneself absolutely to the absolute *telos* and then at the same moment to participate like other human beings in one thing and another.[172]

While an absolute *telos* can be so willed, for it is not an element among things temporal, the question will become whether an individual who is constituted by the temporal can so will the absolute *telos*.

Religiousness A takes place wholly within the confines of consciousness, for "true inwardness does not demand any sign at all in externals."[173]   This venture of true inwardness is described in terms of three expressions: the initial, the essential, and the decisive. We will examine each in turn.

The Initial Expression

The "initial expression" of Religiousness A is renunciation of the finite.[174] This activity is also expressed in terms of resignation: "In immediacy, the individual is firmly rooted in the finite; when resignation is convinced that the individual has the absolute orientation toward the absolute *telos*, everything is changed, the roots are cut. He lives in the finite, but he does not have his life in it." As a result, whether the world offers everything or takes everything away, the

---

[171]Ibid.
[172]Ibid., 407.
[173]Ibid., 414.
[174]Ibid., 404.

individual accepts it with an "Oh, well" and "this 'Oh, well' signifies the absolute respect for the absolute *telos*."[175]

Since the task of Religiousness A mandates that the individual live in the finite, albeit properly related to it, resignation is not renunciation of the finite *per se*. Rather, resignation is the renunciation of the unhealthy immediacy infecting consciousness. The individual who makes such a choice, while never ceasing earnest interaction with the finite, engages in a certain state of detachment from it, signified by the "Oh, well."[176] And to the degree that one has renounced the finite, to that same degree one possesses absolute respect for, and absolute orientation toward, the absolute *telos*: "resignation has made the individual face or has seen to it that he faced toward an eternal happiness as the absolute *telos*."[177]

Religiousness A "demands a transparency of consciousness that is acquired only very slowly."[178] The account of Religiousness A offered in the *Postscript* traces this increase in self-knowledge as the individual goes deeper into consciousness. As we will see, the individual in Religiousness B goes forward into time, but even within the parameters of Religiousness A, the individual goes forward into time to a certain extent. Even for Religiousness A, and speaking of the absolute distinction between the absolute *telos* and the finite, "the word is continually 'forward,' and as long as it is 'forward' the point is to practice the absolute distinction, the point is to have gained a proficiency in doing it more and more readily and a good self-awareness."[179] The individual at the point of gaining proficiency in making this absolute distinction surely *already* possesses the respective self-knowledge. One wonders then if this self-knowledge is originally gained in the "great moment of resignation."

Just as in the great moment of resignation one does not mediate but chooses, now the task is to gain proficiency in repeating the impassioned

---

175Ibid., 410-11.
176See ibid., 471-72.
177Ibid., 400.
178Ibid., 427.
179Ibid., 411.

choice and, existing, to express it in existence. So the individual is certainly in the finite (and the difficulty is indeed to preserve the absolute choice in the finite), but just as he took away the vital power of the finite in the moment of resignation, so the task is to repeat this.[180]

Using this same expression, a parable is told of a king who still wears his crown regally in his third decade of rule, but out of respect for the absolute *telos*, the crown "dwindles into insignificance as it did that time in the great moment of resignation."[181]

We take it then that the account of Religiousness A offered in the *Postscript* is a phenomenology of the "great moment of resignation" in which one attempts to fulfill absolutely the task of Religiousness A, thereby learning the parameters within which one can engage in self-transformation within immanence; one can then gain proficiency in repeating the impassioned choice— although, at best, all that can be done here is a "feigning" of self-transformation.[182]

The Essential Expression

One who embarks upon Religiousness A ideally seeks equilibrium within the self, between "existing finitely" and "existing infinitely."[183] Existing finitely defines the esthetic sphere, and while attempting to move out of this stage of existence by fulfilling the task of Religiousness A, the self unbeknownst to itself now turns toward existing infinitely. Religiousness A is a "daring venture" by which one "becomes infinitized."[184] In this infinitized state, one runs into concrete difficulties that constitute religious suffering, the "essential expression" of Religiousness A. There is a suffering that comes with renunciation of the

---

[180]Ibid., 410-11.

[181]Ibid., 410.

[182]Ibid., 433.

[183]Ibid., 420.

[184]Ibid., 423. Compare Judge William's claim that absolutely choosing oneself infinitizes; but again it is *only* in repentance that one can infinitely choose oneself: see E/O, trans. Hong, 223-24.

finite, and a suffering that comes with absolutely relating oneself to the absolute *telos*. Following the *Postscript*, we shall examine the latter first.

For a self composed of the infinite and the finite, willing the absolute *telos* means that the will must orient itself toward the infinite since this is the direction of that which transcends things finite.

Existence is composed of the infinite and the finite; the existing person is infinite and finite. Now, if to him an eternal happiness is his highest good, this means that in his acting the finite elements are once and for all reduced to what must be surrendered in relation to the eternal happiness.[185]

Moreover, "the absolutely differentiating one relates himself to his absolute *telos*, but *eo ipso* also to God."[186] While the absolute *telos* does not fall within the finite, neither does God. So when existentially appropriating the conception of God, transforming existence into a testimony to God, consciousness takes on the same phenomenological constitution as one absolutely related to the absolute *telos*.[187]

Specifically stated, in order to gain the needed existential security by relating oneself to something that transcends the finite, that absolute *telos* must exist. For a self composed of the infinite and the finite, there is only one thing other than God that transcends the finite, the infinite. The absolute *telos* is the infinite itself: "to will absolutely is to will the infinite, and to will an eternal happiness is to will absolutely, because it must be capable of being willed at every moment."[188] In the words of Judge William, the absolute *telos* is "I myself in my eternal validity." In order then for a self to will the absolute *telos* absolutely, the infinite must relate itself to itself absolutely, attaining objective certainty of an

---

[185]CUP, 391.

[186]Ibid., 413.

[187]This is why it often seems that 'eternal happiness' and 'God' are used interchangeably in the treatment of Religiousness A

[188]Ibid., 394.

eternal happiness through a direct apprehension of its own immortality. Since this is impossible, the religious suffering under discussion comes from being "hindered from absolutely expressing the absolute relation to the absolute *telos*."[189] Here the "individual has discovered the boundary," and the spiritual trial of suffering "expresses the response of the boundary against the finite individual."[190]

If such were possible, according to the principles of classical theism, there would be a coincidence of consciousness and existence for such a spirit, and the maxim to know thyself would be absolutely fulfilled. According to these classical principles, however, there is only one entity for whom this pertains—God. Likewise, it is a constant theme in the *Postscript* that the identity of thought and being is the principle of speculative philosophy. And although not many theological details are given to us, it is urged that this principle holds true only for God, not for existing individuals; for instance, "the agreement between thinking and being, . . . is indeed actually that way for God, but it is not that way for any existing spirit, because this spirit, itself existing, is in the process of becoming."[191] Therefore, the individual striving to relate absolutely to an eternal happiness is attempting to be God, or *at least like God*. In the discussion of suffering, the possibility is considered of a god who falls in love with a mortal woman. Assuming that love can only take place between equals, it is postulated that the woman "would make one desperate attempt after the other to elevate herself" to the god; she would attempt to make herself an equal to the divine.[192] Analogously, "if, through his knowing that this suffering indicates the relation, an existing person were able to lift himself above the suffering, he would then also be able to transform himself from an existing into an eternal person, but that he

---

189Ibid., 432.
190Ibid., 459.
191Ibid., 190.
192Ibid., 490.

will no doubt leave alone."[193] As a matter of fact, this is Kierkegaard's ultimate point: if a temporal individual cannot somehow self-elevate to the level of eternity, then eternity must lower itself into time.

The same hindrance equally applies in the case of God. According to the *Fragments*, the understanding cannot even think the absolutely different; it cannot absolutely negate itself but uses itself for that purpose and consequently thinks the difference in itself, which it thinks by itself. It cannot absolutely transcend itself and therefore thinks as above itself only the sublimity that it thinks by itself.[194]

Consonant with St. Thomas, in order to think the essence of God, one would have to be God.[195] The understanding cannot apprehend God directly, rendering God finite, so God can only be thought of in terms of "the sublimity that it thinks by itself" (namely, *via negationis* or *via eminentiae*[196]). Therefore, when the conception of God is existentially appropriated, the will must turn toward the infinite, and in order for the will to relate itself absolutely to God, the understanding must "absolutely transcend itself" in the process.

Now let us turn to the suffering that comes with renunciation of the finite. The basis of this suffering is that in his immediacy the individual actually is absolutely within relative ends; its meaning is the turning around of the relation, dying to immediacy or existentially expressing that the individual is capable of doing nothing himself but is nothing before God, ... In immediacy, the wish is to be capable of everything, and immediacy's faith, ideally, is in being capable of everything; . . . .[197]

Before renunciation of the finite, one of the manifestations of an unhealthy immediacy, at least for individuals such as Napoleon, is faith in being capable of doing everything.[198] Since the infinite has not yet been disassociated from the

---

[193]Ibid., 452.
[194]PF, 45.
[195]St. Thomas Aquinas, *Summa Theologica*, Pt. 1, Q. 2, art. 1.
[196]PF, 44; see also SUD, 122.
[197]CUP, 460-61.
[198]Ibid., 462.

finite, the finite has not yet been disassociated from the infinite; therefore, particularly for outwardly-directed, ambitious individuals, things finite become 'limbs of the soul.'[199] The religious individual here, however, has already realized the futility of such a faith and is renouncing it. In the midst of dying to this immediacy, the individual suffers by coming to express existentially the religious truism that (without God) "a human being is capable of nothing at all."[200]

At first glance, it seems odd that in renouncing an unhealthy immediacy, one would end up in a worse state, contracting a "sickness" in which one is capable of nothing at all. But Kierkegaard says that the ethical helps an individual out but only by first making things worse, "helps him out of the frying pan into the fire."[201] Put another way, from the perspective of Religiousness B, as we will see, Religiousness A is despair; therefore, the self by increasingly trying to save itself actually increases its despair.

In one of his edifying discourses, "Man's Need of God Constitutes His Highest Perfection," Kierkegaard deals with this same theme. He proposes that "the highest of human tasks is for a man to allow himself to be completely persuaded that he can of himself do nothing, absolutely nothing," both outwardly and inwardly.[202] Outwardly, due to the contingencies intrinsic to the finite, "the world about us is unstable, every moment admitting of a change to its very opposite."[203] As a result, there is no guarantee that any act can be brought to fruition, even a worthy one. So given that an individual has no absolute control over the finite, in this sense, one can do nothing regarding external events. With this realization, an individual has difficulty making a beginning, getting caught in the paralyzing contradiction of wanting to do something yet realizing that it may

---

[199]See St. Augustine, *On Free Choice of the Will*, trans. Thomas Williams (Indianapolis: Hackett, 1993), 26.
[200]CUP, 473.
[201]Ibid., 429.
[202]Soren Kierkegaard, "Man's Need of God Constitutes His Highest Perfection," in *Discourses*, 151.
[203]Ibid., 160.

never come to pass. But this experience provides spiritual medicine, for when the individual does act in the light of the respective realization, the "burning desire" for things outward is eliminated.[204]

Inwardly, the issue is not an inordinate concern with external things but with self-generated difficulties. An individual "creates in his mind the temptations of glory and fear and despondency, and those of pride and pleasure and defiance, greater than the temptations that meet him outwardly."[205] To rid oneself of such dangers, however, one must go to battle with oneself, overcoming oneself by oneself. But, seemingly speaking of the infinite requirement of the ethical, Kierkegaard observes that while "withstanding oneself" is possible, an absolute overcoming of oneself by oneself is impossible.[206] Since an individual then can do nothing either outwardly or inwardly, a human being is capable of nothing at all.

The content of this particular discourse may very well be what Kierkegaard is trying to tell us in the *Postscript* about the suffering integral to dying to immediacy. But it is not clear to me that it is. Indeed, the individual described in the *Postscript* likewise has difficulty making a beginning, but the language and existential gravity suggest that Kierkegaard is speaking of a version of an infinitized will. According to *The Sickness Unto Death*,

> every human existence that presumably has become or simply wants to be infinite, in fact, every moment in which a human existence has become or simply wants to be infinite, is despair. For the self is the synthesis of which the finite is the limiting and the infinite the extending constituent. Infinitude's despair, therefore, is the fantastic, the unlimited, for the self is healthy and free from despair only when, precisely by having despaired, it rests transparently in God.[207]

In this context, infinitized feeling, infinitized knowing, and infinitized willing are each characterized as having "become fantastic." A will that has

---

[204]Ibid., 164.
[205]Ibid., 168.
[206]Ibid.
[207]SUD, 30.

become fantastic has lost contact with the limiting factor of finitude and has therefore become "volatilized," and in so doing "does not continually become proportionately as concrete as it is abstract," with the result that one cannot carry out "the infinitely small part of the work that can be accomplished this very day, this very hour, this very moment."[208] The religious sphere of existence is discussed in this context.

The God-relationship infinitizes; but this may so carry a man away that it becomes an inebriation, it may seem to a man as though it were unendurable to exist before God—for the reason that a man cannot return to himself, cannot become himself. Such a fantastic religious individual would say (to characterize him by putting into his mouth these lines), "That a sparrow can live is comprehensible; it does not know anything about existing before God. But to know that one exists before God—and then not to go crazy or be brought to naught!"[209]

Consistent with this characterization of an infinitized personality before God, the suffering individual described in the *Postscript* is "absolutely captive in the absolute conception of God" (or eternal happiness), for appropriating this conception "is not to have the absolute conception en *passant* but is to have the absolute conception at every moment." The absolute conception of God consumes the individual like the fire of the summer sun, and this is not a matter for "laughter and joking." Given such a state, Kierkegaard avows that it is no wonder that for the pagans "the God-relationship was the harbinger of madness." As a result, the individual has engaged in the "cessation of immediacy" and is more "captive" than "the bird in the cage, the fish on the beach, the invalid on his sickbed, and the prisoner in the narrowest prison cell" for "absoluteness is not directly the element of a finite existence." Moreover, the religious person lies in the finite as a helpless infant; he wants to hold on to the conception absolutely,

---

[208]Ibid., 32.

[209]Soren Kierkegaard, *Fear and Trembling and The Sickness Unto Death*, trans. Walter Lowrie (Princeton: Princeton University Press, 1941; reprint, 1974), 165; see also SUD, trans. Hong, 32.

and this is what annihilates him; he wills to do everything, and while he is willing it, the powerlessness begins, because for a finite being there is indeed a meanwhile. He wills to do everything; he wants to express this relation absolutely, but he cannot make the finite commensurate with it.

This "religious person has lost the relativity of immediacy, its diversion, its whiling away of time—precisely its whiling away of time."[210]

The key to understanding this suffering is the powerlessness felt in making a beginning and the relationship of this state to time. Kierkegaard says that the individual who undergoes this suffering will "slowly, but then finally" become captive in the absolute conception of God. Then, in a note, he tells us that the expression "slowly, but then finally" is an "imaginative form in connection with the vanishing of time."[211] This is to say, he paradoxically uses temporal terms to express the vanishing of time. Analogous to the absolute ethical choice, the suffering individual is attempting to relate absolutely to the absolute *telos* so that in *every future moment* from the point of choice, there will be no lapses into the esthetic way of life. To such an individual, "the least loss is an absolute loss," and "the slightest regression is perdition."[212] But this infinitizes the self; the self pulls away from the temporal in the direction of the infinite. The constraints of the finite are then lost, the relativity of immediacy and its whiling away of time. The individual then wills in accordance with this infinitized state; while strenuously willing to do everything in order to express "the absoluteness of the religious,"[213] the will cannot become concrete, cannot *take the time*, to do anything. Simply put, the individual is trying to jump over time, as it were, and will as God wills who does not have to worry about the constraints of the temporal. This explains the paradoxical juxtaposition of strenuous willing and powerlessness; willing against the constraints of time results in incapacitation in

---

[210]For the whole of the respective characterization in this paragraph, see CUP, 483-85.
[211]Ibid., 483.
[212]Ibid., 416-17.
[213]Ibid., 483.

which one "once again stands at the beginning," prompting the individual to "come to himself, understand himself."[214]

Evidence of this interpretation is the illustration of the person who goes to bed "weeping not because he could not sleep but because he dared not stay awake any longer."[215] Such a person, while working on a project of some sort, impatiently desires to stay awake to work on it. But being temporal, sleep is needed, so the person goes to bed, albeit weeping because willing absolutely against the constraints of time is hopeless. It is quickly pointed out, however, that this example is only something relative "in comparison with the religious person's absolute relation to the absolute" and therefore is not the suffering of dying to immediacy but is nonetheless "something of this sort."[216]

The suffering of dying to immediacy is discussed in the context of taking an outing to the Deer Park. If one is incapable of something as trivial as this, it is easy to see that one is capable of nothing at all. But the experienced powerlessness does not pertain solely to the diversion of the Deer Park. Rather, complete powerlessness is first experienced; and then one should "now try to add going out to the amusement park."[217] Moreover, it sometimes sounds as if Kierkegaard is merely agreeing with those in the monastic movement. Even though he praises those in the monastic movement for attempting to relate themselves absolutely to God, he criticizes them for trying to do so in an outward way, ceasing finite activities such as taking outings to the Deer Park and devoting themselves to other finite activities such as prayer. It is Kierkegaard's mind that sacrificing participation like other human beings in one thing and another is an enthusiastic attempt "to be like God."[218] Yet he agrees that relating oneself absolutely to the absolute *telos* cannot be joined together with taking an outing to the Deer Park, and this is why he sometimes sounds as if he is merely agreeing

---

[214]Ibid., 485.
[215]Ibid., 485.
[216]Ibid., 486.
[217]Ibid., 484.
[218]Ibid., 492.

with the monks who have *no time* for outings. But Kierkegaard goes further in realizing that relating oneself absolutely to the absolute *telos* necessitates having *no time* for any finite activity whatsoever. An inward orientation, designed to allow participation like other human beings in one thing and another, equally results in an enthusiastic attempt to be like God.

Even though the conception of God has led to this "crisis of sickness," this same conception can strengthen the individual—only God can exist infinitely.[219] Learning this lesson includes at least five elements. First, absolutely relating oneself to the absolute *telos* is an ontological impossibility; nonetheless, immortality must yet be *assumed* in order to maintain integrity with the finite. The individual has discovered in time that "he must presuppose himself to be eternal."[220] Second, since the identity of thought and being does not hold for a finite entity, the relation to an eternal happiness is defined by suffering "just as the certitude of faith that relates itself to an eternal happiness is defined by uncertainty."[221] Concerning the latter, the highest reward in temporality is "the *expectancy* of an eternal happiness."[222] Third, in what amounts to the same thing phenomenologically, absolute self-transformation is also an ontological impossibility. Since an absolute relation to the absolute *telos* cannot be established, a human being "in temporality cannot endure to lead uninterruptedly the life of eternity."[223] Therefore, an unhealthy immediacy cannot be absolutely alleviated—or, at least a healthy immediacy cannot be guaranteed in *every future moment*. One faces the day-to-day struggle of dying to immediacy which "is so prolonged and regression to it so frequent that an individual very rarely succeeds in making his way through it or in having overcome it for a long time."[224] In the face of this struggle, resignation must be continually repeated with an orientation

---

[219]Ibid., 488.
[220]Ibid., 573.
[221]Ibid., 455.
[222]Ibid., 402.
[223]Ibid., 491.
[224]Ibid., 460.

toward the absolute *telos*. Fourth, and on a more positive note, since the individual has passed through the state of being capable of nothing at all, a deeper understanding that "outward activity" cannot be directly brought about by the will is possessed. This helps take away power from an unhealthy immediacy, aiding the elimination of all existential income from the finite.[225] Fifth, although the maximum equilibrium within the self (Religiousness B) has not been attained, there is now more than there was. Suffering reveals that existing infinitely has been attempted and is not a viable option for an existing individual; but it is only through making such an attempt that one can come to reside between existing finitely and existing infinitely, acquiring a certain equilibrium where the ethical "must intervene regulatively and take command."[226] Thereby, rather than willing infinitely, the individual learns to make a decision and begin a task in time, becoming "concrete in what has been experienced."[227] And, paralleling Judge William, "through the decision in existence, an existing person, more specifically defined, has become what he is."[228] Or, as stated elsewhere, the self has infinitely come back to itself; in order to become concrete, there must be "an infinite moving away from itself in the infinitizing of the self, and an infinite coming back to itself in the finitizing process."[229] Overall, the individual has learned humility before God.[230]

The Decisive Expression

The decisive expression of Religiousness A is the consciousness of guilt,[231] the initial awareness of which is described in this oft-quoted passage.

---

[225]Ibid., 506.
[226]Ibid, 488.
[227]Ibid., 489.
[228]Ibid.
[229]SUD, trans. Hong, 30
[230]CUP, 493.
[231]Ibid., 533.

In existence, the individual is a concretion, time is concrete, and even while the individual deliberates he is ethically responsible for the use of time. . . . Even at the moment the task is assigned, something is already wasted, because there is an "in the meantime" and the beginning is not promptly made. This is how it goes backward: the task is given to the individual in existence, and just as he wants to plunge in straightway . . . , and wants to begin, another beginning is discovered to be necessary, the beginning of the enormous detour that is dying to immediacy. And just as the beginning is about to be made here, it is discovered that, since meanwhile time has been passing, a bad beginning has been made and that the beginning must be made by becoming guilty, and from that moment the total guilt, which is decisive, practices usury with new guilt. The task looked so grand, and one thought "like for like"; as the task is, so must the person be who is supposed to carry it out. . . . [N]ow the existing person is really in agony—that is, now he is in the existence-medium.[232]

The first thing to notice in this passage is that since the ideal of the identity of thought and being does not hold for an existing individual, there is a temporal interval for a finite entity between accepting a task in thought and the actual bringing it to pass through the will.[233] If this ideal were an operative principle for an existing individual, thinking and willing would coincide.

If what is thought were actuality, then what is thought out as perfectly as possible, when I as yet have not acted, would be the action. In this way there would be no action whatever, but the intellectual swallows the ethical.[234]

So after accepting in thought that the absolute ethical-religious choice needs to be made, which entails accepting the ethical-religious as the standard for life, the individual has to begin as guilty, for in the respective interval, such a life

---

[232]Ibid., 526-27.
[233]See ibid., 488.
[234]Ibid., 338.

168

is not lived. This is "why in pure ideality the transition from thinking to being is so easy, for there everything is at once."[235]

An individual could admit this but hope to live an ethical-religious life *every future moment* from the point of choice. But the same disjunction between thought and being creates problems here as well, and this brings us to the remainder of the above passage, which basically recapitulates the course of Religiousness A. Just when the individual wants to begin, it is discovered that a temporal person cannot *simultaneously* fulfill the two prongs of the task: one must *first* die to immediacy and *then* absolutely relate oneself to the absolute *telos*.[236] But just as the beginning is about to be made here, it is discovered that a bad beginning has occurred, revealed by the passing of time. In *initially* renouncing the finite, the individual attempts to exist infinitely, incurring an infinitized will; the passing of time reveals that the will has gone abstract and made a bad beginning. It is realized that the task initially set forth *has not* been fulfilled. When the individual, however, joins the conception of God together with the conception of this guilt, "the category of guilt changes to a category of quality."[237] It is realized that the task initially set forth *cannot* be fulfilled. The task and the individual are incommensurate, not "like for like." This is the consciousness of total guilt, and this is why the individual is in agony; there is no "beginning all over again" so that in *every future moment* from the point of choice, an ethical-religious life will be lived.[238] As a matter of fact, it is here that the religious life properly begins, for "the totality of guilt-consciousness in the single individual before God in relation to an eternal happiness is the religious."[239]

---

[235]SUD, trans. Hong, 94. Kierkegaard here is specifically speaking about the relationship between thinking and willing.

[236]CUP, 431-32; see also 526.

[237]Ibid., 530.

[238]Ibid., 533.

[239]Ibid., 554. For reasons of space, one of the issues omitted here is how the individual in Religiousness A acquires the conception of God. We can say, however, that although Religiousness A can take place within Christendom (ibid., 557), it is probably best to construe the God of Religiousness A as a pantheistic Deity. The doctrine of creation plays an important role in the

The individual yet wants to exist infinitely, because not to do so is tantamount to a concession to insecurity and guilt. The consciousness and pang of total guilt, however, come not so much from the thought of future lapses into the esthetic realm, but rather from the fact that it is inherently impossible for the self to live up to the task of Religiousness A that guarantees no such lapses. This is why to begin in time is an admission of guilt and appears as retrogression: "compared with the totality of the task, to carry out a little of it is a retrogression, and yet it is an advance when compared with the whole task and carrying out none of it at all."[240]

It is difficult to escape the notion that finitude prevents the task of Religiousness A from being fulfilled. If so, it seems the individual "must be able to shove the guilt onto the one who placed him in existence or onto existence itself."[241] The question is anticipated with the response that "it can never occur to someone who is essentially guiltless to shove guilt away from himself, because the guiltless person has nothing at all to do with the category of guilt."[242] Even so, the real issue is why the individual should be considered guilty in the first place. The reason is that even though finitude prevents fulfillment, the consciousness and pang of total guilt come from the self's inability to live up to its *own* ideal.

The continuation of the consciousness of total guilt, or the "eternal recollecting of guilt," could lead "to insanity or to death," but the individual "will seek to find the minimum of forgetfulness needed for enduring."[243] The individual does not need to forget absolutely, for "the totality of guilt-consciousness is the most up building element in Religiousness A."[244] The fact that the absolute *telos* cannot be grasped is a "repelling relation" and total guilt

transition from Religiousness A to Religiousness B, and Kierkegaard points out that the only consistent position outside of Christianity is pantheism (ibid., 226).
[240]Ibid., 527.
[241]Ibid., 528.
[242]Ibid.
[243]Ibid., 536-37.
[244]Ibid., 560.

consciousness is a "repelling reaction of a repelling relation." Yet total guilt consciousness presupposes a relation of immanence between the self and the absolute *telos*, "but has it only in an annulled possibility, not as one annuls the concrete in order to find the abstract but as one annuls the abstract by being in the concrete."[245] In other words, through the eternal recollection of guilt, the possibility of attempting to become infinite is annulled.

There still needs to be a full break with immanence, and this for two reasons, one ontological and one practical. Ontologically speaking, there is still "a possibility of an escape, of a shifting away, of a withdrawal into the eternal behind . . . as if everything were not actually at stake."[246] In the final analysis, "let the world's six thousand years of history be true or let it not be true—in the matter of his happiness it makes no difference one way or the other to the existing person, because he rests ultimately in the consciousness of eternity."[247] As we will see in a moment, this is the *untruth* of Religiousness A. Practically speaking, the self is burdened with an inordinate self-consciousness; the self cannot quite forget itself, since it is only through "one's own powers," through renunciation of the finite, through suffering, and through the eternal recollection of guilt, that one maintains the equilibrium here available.[248]

The Break with Immanence

The break with immanence comes with Religiousness B. The latter has a "retroactive effect" on Religiousness A, revealing that the most significant truth of Religiousness A is actually untruth. One cannot enter Religiousness B from the standpoint of Religiousness A, because "if there is any remnant of immanence, any eternal qualification remaining in the existing person, then it

---

[245]Ibid., 533.
[246]Ibid., 572.
[247]Ibid., 578.
[248]Ibid., 429.

cannot be done."[249]   Through revelation, however, the self discovers that it has been created and therefore naturally possesses no eternal determinant; it is naturally impossible to climb from time into eternity, even at the point of death. This truth was not available in Religiousness A. Not only was absolute self-transparency not possessed, but also an individual's having no eternal determinant would have never entered the mind of one operating solely in the sphere of reflection, for this "cannot be thought."[250]

With the aforementioned annulled possibility having become an impossibility, the individual still requires an anchor in an eternal happiness. Now, however, the individual "must go forward; to go backward is impossible."[251]   If blessed with the condition of faith, the person can move "forward in order to become eternal in time through the relation to the god in time."[252]   In so doing, one becomes a "new creature," something which begins with the "miracle of creation" and "happens to someone who is created."[253]

---

[249]Ibid., 576.

[250]Ibid., 574.

[251]Ibid., 208-09

[252]Ibid., 583-84.

[253]Ibid., 576. In one place, Kierkegaard says that the doctrine of hereditary sin does not depend on revelation (see SUD, trans. Hong, 156). In the *Postscript*, however, hereditary sin seems to be the fact that one has been created (CUP, 208). This latter view squares with *The Concept of Anxiety*, for even though therein hereditary sin is closely associated with anxiety, there would be no anxiety if the self were not a "derived, established relation."

SHELLING AND TILLICH ON GOD'S RELATION
TO THE WORLD
Sam Powell

Introduction

Tillich often acknowledged his debt to F.W.J. Schelling; the influence of the latter on Tillich is evident in many ways. Unfortunately, familiarity with Schelling's thought has never been extensive in the English-speaking world. In part this is a function of the unfinished nature of his work. Having produced no definitive statement of his system, he was eclipsed by G.W.F. Hegel and others. In part, it results from the fact that Schelling's thought never affected a mass audience as did Hegel's through its influence on Marxism. However, without an acquaintance with Schelling's thought and its influence on Tillich, Tillich's doctrine of God and of God's relation to the world cannot be rightly understood. In particular, the existential dimension of his theology will be interpreted humanistically, as though Tillich were primarily a theologian of human culture or religiosity. His doctrine of God will be largely ignored. Only when Tillich is seen in relation to Schelling will interpreters be likely to regard him as a *theologian*.

The purpose of this essay is to contribute to our understanding of Tillich's theology by demonstrating his indebtedness to Schelling, particularly with regard to the doctrine of God. I will first point out their similarities, then their differences. Finally, I will argue for the superiority, in certain respects, of Schelling's doctrine of God to Tillich's.

Before launching into the exposition, it may be helpful to indicate briefly why Tillich's and Schelling's doctrines of God are worthy of consideration. They deserve attention because theological discussion today is again focusing on matters to which they can contribute, notably God's relation to the world. The closing decades of this century have witnessed a burgeoning interest in theories of divine action, in the relation of science to religion, and in the prospects for a theology of nature. Each of these issues presupposes an understanding of God's relation to the world. This is a subject to which Schelling, Tillich and the entire idealist tradition in which they stood devoted considerable attention. Too often in today's discussion about science and theology naive assumptions prevail, assumptions whose limitations have already been exposed by Tillich and others. This is not to claim that the idealist conception of God and of God's relation to the world is above reproach. This essay will exhibit some ways in which Tillich himself was highly critical of his idealist heritage. Nonetheless, this tradition possesses resources that can be profitably used today. At the very least, the questions that this tradition found pressing are still relevant today: What does it mean to declare that the existence of the universe is contingent? What does it mean to speak about God's freedom? Is there teleological development within the universe? Can Christian eschatology make any sense at all in today's scientific understanding of the universe?

Points of Agreement Between Schelling and Tillich

There are at least three important points of agreement between Schelling and Tillich. First, both God and world are constituted by a set of opposed principles and by the relations among them. Tillich referred to these principles as the ontological elements; Schelling called them potencies. Second, these qualities are found in God in perfect harmony and God's life is constituted by the harmonious dynamics of these qualities. God is living because God's nature combines the identity and difference of the qualities in an eternal harmony. Third, the world differs from God in that it is characterized by a disharmonious tension between the qualities. As a result, it is marked by brokenness. The world participates in God's being because it is constituted by the same qualities that constitute the divine life, but it does so in a distorted and fragmentary way.

The first point of similarity between Schelling and Tillich is that both God and world are constituted by a set of opposed principles and their relations. This introduces Schelling's doctrine of potencies. There are, he asserted, three powers within God's nature. One is the power of love. Schelling denoted this power with the symbol "A."[254] However, love, because it "does not seek what is its own," cannot exist alone. It requires a ground, something to support it. Hence there is a another power, the power of selfhood and subsistent being, symbolized by "B." With these two powers, "the being which is love may subsist as independent and be for itself."[255] However, although love requires the principle of selfhood, these two powers are opposed to one another. The power of love is "the outflowing, outspreading, self-giving essence" of God; the other power is the "eternal power of selfhood, of return unto self, of being-in-self."[256] By the power of love the divine nature is eccentric and outgoing; by the power of selfhood God's nature is centered and self-grounding. Despite this opposition, God's nature is not simply the eternal antithesis of these powers; it is also their eternal unity. "It is indeed *one and the same* [divine nature] which is the affirmation and the negation, the outspreading and the restraining."[257] We must, therefore, speak of a third power in God, the unity of the first two.[258] This unity is the first two powers in their identity and their difference. It is their unity, but a unity that does not annul their distinctive properties. As a result, God's nature is complex:

God's nature is twofold: first, negating power (B), which forces back the affirming essence (A), secretes it inwardly as passive; second, expansive,

---

[254] Schelling also called this potency A², to signify that this is God's nature raised to a higher power. For the same reason, he calls the third potency A³.

[255] F.W.J. Schelling, *The Ages of the World*, trans. Frederick deWolfe Bolman, Jr. (New York: Columbia University Press, 1942), 96-97.

[256] *Ages*, 97.

[257] *Ages*, 98-99.

[258] Schelling went to great lengths to ensure that we do not understand this unity to be a dialectical one. In other words, the powers are original principles; none is derived from any other. *Ages*, 97-98.

self-communicating essence [A], which on the contrary suppresses in itself the negating power [B] and does not let it come to outward effect.[259]

Here is Tillich's comment on Schelling's view: Schelling construed two or three principles in the ground of the divine, the unconscious or dark principle, the principle of will which is able to contradict itself [corresponding to B], on the one hand, and the principle of logos, or the principle of light, on the other hand [corresponding to A].[260]

These same principles are present in Tillich's theology. Schelling's first potency (B), the power of selfhood, becomes in Tillich's system the abyss in God, the principle of depth and power. This is the basis of God's being God. It is the ground and power of being of all that is.[261] For both Tillich and Schelling this first power gives God substantial reality; it is that by which God eternally conquers non-being.[262] The second potency (A) becomes in Tillich's thought the principle of meaning, designated by the term *logos*. It is the principle of structure, definition, creativity, and revelation.[263] Schelling's third potency, the unity of the first two, appears in Tillich's theology as Spirit, which is the actualization and unity of the principles of power and meaning.[264] These principles of being recur, according to Tillich, in life. Life includes three elements: self-identity, self-

---

[259] *Ages*, 101.

[260] Paul Tillich, *Perspectives on 19th and 20th Century Protestant Theology*, ed. Carl E. Braaten (New York: Harper & Row, 1967), 149.

[261] Paul Tillich, *Systematic Theology*, 1:250-251.

[262] It may be helpful for the reader to note that Tillich's comments on non-being and negation within God are somewhat confusing. He described the element of depth in God (which corresponds with Schelling's first potency [B] as being the power of resisting non-being (1:250) and expressly linked this power with the "self" pole within God, including self-transcendent vitality (dynamics) (1:249). Yet he also identified the principle of form as that by which being has the power of resisting non-being (1:199). Further, in his comments on Schelling he identified Schelling's first potency with the principle of dynamics and as the aspect of non-being and negation within the divine life (1:189 and 1:246). So, the first principle (dynamics) is both the principle of non-being and also of the overcoming of non-being. This is confusing. So is his identifying first dynamics then form as the principle by which non-being is overcome.

[263] *Systematic Theology*, 1:251.

[264] *Systematic Theology*, 1:249-251.

alteration and return to one's self.[265] Here again we can see Schelling's three potencies. Self-identity corresponds to the power of selfhood [B]. Self-alteration corresponds to the outgoing power of love [A²]. Return to self corresponds to the unity of the first two potencies [A³]. This is why, according to Tillich, God may be called the living God. "He is the eternal process in which separation is posited and is overcome by reunion."[266]

Like God, the world is, for Schelling and Tillich, also structured according to these powers of being. For Schelling, both the physical universe and human history are governed by the relations of the potencies and by the sequence of their actualization outside of God's nature.[267] For Tillich, "God is the ground of the structure of being."[268] All the polarities of being and the elements and functions of life that we find in the finite world are found primordially in God. In fact, it is best to say that God *is* this structure of being. For both Tillich and Schelling, the finite realm is grounded in God in the sense that there is a common ontological structure that both share. Or, more accurately, God is the ontological structure of powers in which the world participates.

The second point of similarity between Tillich and Schelling is that, in God, the powers are found in a perfect and eternal harmony. For Schelling, the potencies, each being the antithesis of the others, cannot co-exist without some mediation. In themselves, each strives to be and to assert itself and to negate the others. Without some resolution of the tension inherent in their conflicting striving, the divine nature would be wild and chaotic, without order. The resolution, which is an eternal one, takes the form of the establishing of a

---

[265] *Systematic Theology*, 3:30-32. It should be noted that Tillich's exposition of self-transcendence does not make effective use of self-identity, self-alteration, and return to self.
[266] *Systematic Theology*, 1:242.
[267] *Ages*, 199.
[268] *Systematic Theology*, 1:238.

hierarchy of the potencies.[269] In this hierarchy, the first power (B) assumes the lowest position, the second power (A^2) takes the middle position and the third power (A^3), the unity of the first two, takes the highest. This order of the powers is important because when, in the act of creation, the powers are set outside of God's nature, their hierarchical ordering determines the chronological course of development in the physical universe and in human history. In God's nature, however, there is an eternal hierarchy of powers that establishes a dynamically stable divine nature. Schelling did admit the bare possibility that the hierarchy could dissolve, with the potencies resolving back into a state of disharmonious contradiction. In fact, however, this is merely an abstract possibility for God. Such a condition has reality only as a something that God has eternally posited as past.[270] Of course, this past is not a temporal moment in the past, for God transcends the passage of time. Instead, this past is conceived as a possible state that God eternally overcomes through an act of will.[271] Consequently, this possible state of disharmony is not unimportant for Schelling. It is a reality for God, one that is eternally overcome. By an eternal act God resolves to maintain the dynamic stability of the divine nature.

Although Tillich concurred with Schelling on the main point, he did not go as far as Schelling on subsidiary matters. The main point is that the powers that constitute the divine life exist in God in eternal perfect harmony:

> The polar character of the ontological elements is rooted in the divine life, but the divine life is not subject to this polarity. Within the divine life, every ontological element includes its polar element completely, without tension and without the threat of dissolution.[272]

But Tillich did not affirm some of Schelling's other theses. He betrayed no inclination to represent the polar elements within God in a hierarchical way.

---

[269] *Ages*, 128-130. Schelling's account is complicated by his opinion that this hierarchy is created by a sense of longing among the powers, a longing occasioned by the presence of something in God even higher than God's nature. This higher element is God's freedom.

[270] *Ages*, 142.

[271] *Ages*, 153-155.

[272] *Systematic Theology*, 1:243.

Whereas for Schelling the harmonious co-existence of the potencies depends on their being ordered in a hierarchy, for Tillich the co-existence of the polar elements "without the threat of dissolution" in the divine life is apparently without condition. He thus lacked Schelling's conviction that the eternal harmony of the powers in a hierarchy is, as it were, a contingent fact. Tillich did indeed allow for talk about God's eternal conquering of the negative within the divine being,[273] but the non-being in question relates to the element of dynamics--one of the polar elements--within God.[274] The relation, within God, of being to non-being is the relation of the "world" pole of the ontological structure to the "self" pole, of meaning to power.[275] While this relation is highly significant in Tillich's theology, it is quite different from Schelling's thesis. Schelling's claim is that God's eternal act of overcoming is a matter of harmonizing the potencies by establishing them in a hierarchy. For Tillich, God's eternal act of overcoming consists in conquering the power of non-being, which is linked with the "self" pole of the ontological elements. As we will see later in this paper, this difference from Schelling has a large effect on Tillich's theology. It means that God's freedom is treated in very different ways by Tillich and Schelling.

The third point of agreement between Schelling and Tillich is that, in distinction from God, the world exhibits the ontological structure of the powers in a disharmonious form. According to Schelling, the creation of the world occurs when God, by a free although timeless decision, externalizes the potencies that

---

[273] *Systematic Theology*, 3:404.

[274] Recall that Tillich understood the first potency in Schelling's philosophy to represent the dynamic element that is also a "negative element in the ground of being which is overcome as negative in the process of being-itself" (1:246). Tillich also expressly linked non-being and finitude to the "self" side of the ontological structure: "Selfhood, individuality, dynamics, and freedom all include manifoldness, definiteness, differentiation, and limitation. To be something is not to be something else" (1:190).

[275] See *Systematic Theology*, 1:189 and 1:246, where Tillich interpreted Schelling's doctrine of the potencies in terms of the negative element within God. But Tillich never mentioned Schelling's concept of God's past, that disharmonious state of the powers that God eternally posits as past and overcome.

180

constitute the divine nature and allows them to collapse out of their state of hierarchical harmony. In this collapsed state, they revert to their natural state of opposition to one another. They cannot co-exist in this state, for each contradicts the others as it strives to assert itself. Since they cannot co-exist, their respective strivings produce a history, first in the physical universe, then in human history, in which the potencies sequentially assert themselves and gain dominance.[276] This sequence of the potencies' self-expression in nature and history mirrors their hierarchical ordering in God's nature: first the dark power of self-hood (B), then the lucent power of love (A^2), finally the third, unifying power (A^3).[277] The result is that the course of cosmic history mirrors the nature of God, except that whereas the potencies exist in God in an eternal harmonious hierarchy, they exist in the world initially in a state of contradiction and sequential development. And yet, the eternal hierarchy functions as a *telos* for natural and human history, for the goal of this history is the establishing of a hierarchy of the potencies in the finite universe as it subsists eternally in the divine nature. The evolutionary development of organic being, culminating in the appearance of humanity, and the subsequent history of humanity are marked by the gradual triumph of the second power (love) over the first power (selfhood). At the end of history, when the second power has completely subordinated the first to itself, the third power (the perfect unity of the first two) will become actualized in the world.[278] In this way, the powers will relate themselves to each other in the finite as they do eternally in the divine nature.

Tillich likewise held that the world reflects the powers of God's being but without the harmony that exists in God. Like God, the finite world includes an element of nonbeing. But whereas for God nonbeing is included only as something that is eternally overcome, in the world nonbeing constitutes a threat to

---

[276] *Ages*, 191.
[277] *Ages*, 197.
[278] This is the subject of Schelling's lectures on mythology and revelation.

being.[279] In the finite world being is limited by and opposed to nonbeing.[280] Likewise, life, under the conditions of finitude, is ambiguous: The unity of life "is threatened by existential estrangement, which drives life in one or the other direction. . . . Self-integration is countered by disintegration, self-creation is countered by destruction, self-transcendence is countered by profanization."[281] Tillich and Schelling are agreed, then, that the structures that are found in God without disruptive tension are found in the world in a tensed, separated way. However, as noted previously, Tillich did not see the harmony of the powers in God as a function of their hierarchical ordering. As a result Tillich had no interest in interpreting the course of cosmic and human history as a development of the dynamics inherent in the powers.

Tillich's Differences From Schelling

One important difference between Tillich and Schelling concerns their views of eschatology. Briefly put, Tillich did not share Schelling's eschatology as expounded in the latter's *Philosophy of Revelation.*

As noted above, Schelling understood the act of creation to consist in God's decision to externalize the potencies. By this I mean that the hierarchy of the potencies is allowed to dissolve and they are allowed to relapse back into a state of contradiction. Of course, this could not happen in God's eternal nature; instead it occurs outside of God. The potencies are given an existence independent of God's nature and apart from the harmony that subsists in God. In this way, a finite world comes about. In this relapse into contradiction, the potencies lose their harmonious co-existence based on their placement in a hierarchy. But a problem arises, for each power strives to be. Since they

---

[279] *Systematic Theology*, 1:246-247.
[280] *Systematic Theology*, 1:189.
[281] *Systematic Theology*, 3:32.

contradict one another, this striving is equivalent to the attempt by each to subdue the others. Each wishes to be without restriction by the others. This tensed situation is impossible. But without the establishing of a hierarchy, the only way in which the contradictory powers can exist at all is for their manifestation to occur sequentially. One power will be followed chronologically by another, each in turn becoming dominant. But what is the sequence? It follows the hierarchical order of the powers in God. The eternal hierarchy orders the appearance of the powers in time. The first power (selfhood) asserts itself into being, followed by the second power seeking to gain dominance over the first. This process transpires first in the inorganic world. In the early history of the universe there is just inert matter, which represents the unchallenged dominance of the power of selfhood and the virtual exclusion of the eccentric power of love (A^2). Gradually, however, the second power (A^2) begins to overcome the first (B). The process of this overcoming is manifest in the rise of living forms. Its initial culmination occurs when human spirit first arises out of matter. In the emergence of spirit from matter, the outgoing power of love has gained a preliminary victory over the inward power of selfhood.

However, with the appearance of humanity, the process begins to repeat itself. At first selfhood dominates as humanity gives in to the power of selfhood, a fact pictured in the Biblical story of the fall into sin. Only gradually in the course of human history does the power of love gain ascendancy. Another provisional victory of the second power over the first occurs in the person of Jesus Christ, in whom the power of selfhood is voluntarily subordinated to love. This conscious abnegation of selfhood is, Schelling believed, the meaning of the Christian doctrine of the condescension and humiliating death of the Son. Jesus Christ therefore is the second power in its full historical development. But even this victory of the second power in Jesus Christ is still preliminary, for it must be actualized in all humanity. Eventually, this actualization will occur. When it does, the third power will have arrived at its full historical development. This will be the age of the Spirit, when the powers will again be established in a hierarchy, for the first will have been overcome (although not destroyed) by the second, allowing the third to come into historical being as the perfect identity and difference of the first two. At that eschatological moment, the harmony of the potencies in the world will mirror the eternal hierarchy of the potencies in God.

We can see that Schelling's philosophy includes a vigorous eschatology. The sequence of the powers in their temporal development determines first the history of nature and then the history of humanity. This development is teleological. It aims at bringing the finite world to a state in which it mirrors God's own nature. This development is also Trinitarian. The Son and Holy Spirit, as persons, have a temporal becoming. Although grounded in the eternal nature of God, their existence as persons happens as a result of the dynamics of the powers. The Son's personhood comes about when in Jesus Christ the second power finally overcomes the first in the realm of human history. The Spirit's personhood awaits the eschatological moment when this triumph of the first power over the second is universal.

When we turn to Tillich's understanding of eschatology, we find a quite different view. For one thing, Tillich's idealism is of the chastised sort. He was hesitant to make sweeping claims, in the manner of Hegel and Schelling, about world history and its alleged progress.

> The nature of trends . . . should prevent any attempt to establish historical laws. Such laws do not exist, because every moment in history is new in relation to all preceding moments. . . . The existence of chances, balancing the determining power of trends, is the decisive argument against all forms of historical determinism--naturalistic, dialectical, or predestinarian.[282]

This quotation states clearly enough Tillich's sentiments. History has trends but not laws. The experience of novelty and chance militates against the idea of laws.

---

[282] *Systematic Theology*, 3:327. See also 3:328: "Because it is the character of historical causality to be creative and to use chances, it cannot be said that a universal structure of historical movement exists."

184

But even if there are no laws of history, can there still be a teleological development of history? This is the crucial issue for Tillich's relation to Schelling. Schelling's philosophy does not make use of the concept of law. It is guided by the dynamics of the potencies, but there is nothing deterministic about this process. However, Schelling's system is unashamedly teleological. The cosmos is moving toward the day when the historical conflict of the potencies will be overcome. Specific moments in world history (e.g., the appearance of humanity and the existence of Jesus Christ) are interpreted as anticipations of the eventual victory of the second power over the first. However, for Tillich it seems that history is not in any sense teleological. He stated that "there is no progress where individual freedom is decisive." For this reason, while there may be progress in the cultural side of human life, there can be none in the moral-religious side.[283] Even in the cultural sphere there can be no progress "beyond the classical expressions of man's encounter with reality."[284] This is true all the more with respect to the revelatory experience. It "is always what it is, and . . . in this respect there is no more or less, no progress or obsolescence or regression," although there can be progress in the "degrees of clarity and power with which the manifestation of the Spiritual is received."[285] It is evident, then, that history is not progressive for Tillich as it is for Schelling. Furthermore, Tillich eschewed any sort of historical eschatology in which there would be a final culmination and consummation of history. History does have a *telos*, but it is eternity and Tillich expressly denied that this eternity is a future state. "It is always present."[286] For Tillich each moment stands as close to and also as far from the fulfillment of history as does any other. Just as Creation and Fall are not spatio-temporal events, so "there will be no utopia in the future."[287]

---

[283] *Systematic Theology*, 3:333.
[284] *Systematic Theology*, 3:334.
[285] *Systematic Theology*, 3:337.
[286] *Systematic Theology*, 3:400.
[287] *Systematic Theology*, 2:44.

As a measure of Tillich's difference from Schelling in particular and from idealism in general, we may consider his critique of Hegel. Tillich faulted Hegel's essentialist thinking for asserting that "non-being has been conquered in the totality of the [Hegelian] system [and that] history has come to an end."[288] For Tillich, eschatology is never fully realized. "Being is [always] finite, existence is [always] self-contradictory, and life [always] is ambiguous."[289] Although revelation can bring a degree of healing and harmony to the disruption between essential being and existence, the ambiguity of life remains.

As a further indication of Tillich's uneasiness with Schelling, we may note that he declined to embrace Schelling's notion of a historical becoming of the Trinitarian persons. Schelling's understanding of the Trinity depends on his belief that the potencies in history undergo a process of development. While Tillich, like Schelling, allowed that the finite world participates in the divine powers, he emphatically did not think of these powers, in their manifestation in the finite world, as developing or as having any *telos*. Instead, in Tillich's system they have a somewhat static character. He allowed that the powers have a certain order in God (since God as Spirit is the unity of the elements of abyss and *logos* and thus presupposes them) but as noted previously he did not relate this ordering to any teleological development in natural or human history. This strategy effectively distinguishes Tillich from Schelling, for whom the Son and Holy Spirit are the complete actualizations of the potencies in history.

Accordingly, Tillich also did not employ Schelling's conception of God's actualization in world history. For Schelling, the decision by God to create a world by externalizing the potencies and allowing them to relapse back into a state of contradiction means that something happens to God. God enters the sphere of actual being. Of course, Schelling also held that God did not need to

---

[288] *Systematic Theology,* 2:24.
[289] *Systematic Theology,* 1:81.

create the world. The actualization of which he speaks is not a remedy of some deficiency in God. On the contrary, he insisted that God's being is full and complete in itself. He affirmed the possibility that God could have remained eternally in the fullness of the divine nature and freedom. As a result, the creation of the world was ascribed by him to an act of God's freedom. Nonetheless, once God freely decided to create the world, God does not remain unaffected by that decision, for the potencies that constitute the world are God's own potencies. Consequently, the history of nature and of humanity is the history of God's actualization, as the powers strive toward their eventual, teleological ordering in a hierarchy that mirrors God's eternal nature. Tillich, on the contrary, did not represent God as becoming actual through any process in the finite world. Although God is living and is "the eternal process in which separation is posited and is overcome by reunion,"[290] this process does not transpire teleologically in the finite world. Tillich did not describe God as, in the act of creation, passing over into the world and as depending (in any sense of the word) on the world. We must judge, then, that Tillich's theology, in comparison to Schelling's, is far less teleologically oriented and that his view of God is less historically oriented.

There is another important respect in which Tillich differs from Schelling. That is their respective views of God's freedom. Schelling was insistent on the distinction between God's nature and God's freedom. It forms the cornerstone of his positive philosophy, which he extolled as vigorously as he denigrated a merely negative philosophy of necessity. "Freedom and necessity are in God. . . . [Yet] the two are not the same. What a being is by nature and what it is by freedom are two quite different things."[291] God's freedom performs two functions in Schelling's system. First, it is responsible for the orderly hierarchy of the powers

---

[290] *Systematic Theology*, 3:242. Tillich did state of the "eternal identity of God with himself . . . [that it] does not contradict his going out from himself into the negativities of existence and the ambiguities of life" (3:405). This does suggest an idealist conception of God entering into the finite world and becoming in its processes. However, Tillich had already consciously declared his interest in balancing this dynamic view of God with the medieval emphasis on the element of form in God (1:247-248). Hence the near total reluctance to ascribe any sort of becoming to God.
[291] *Ages*, 95-96.

in God's eternal nature;[292] second, it is the ground of the creation of the world.[293] I wish to focus on this second function, for it will throw into clear relief Schelling's differences from Tillich. God's essence (God's necessary nature, consisting in the potencies, plus God's freedom) might have remained in itself, unrevealed. Schelling believed that this essence of God can be described philosophically; such a description forms the content of the negative philosophy, which is the knowledge that we can have about God by the exercise of human reason. However, God can also create and thus be revealed. This revelation introduces the possibility of the positive philosophy--the knowledge of God that is inaccessible to pure reason.

> If life progresses from here on [i.e., beyond the necessity associated with God's essence], this progress is only by virtue of a free divine resolution. The godhead can persist peacefully in that equilibrium between attraction [B] and repulsion [A²]. Nothing compels it to annul that equilibrium, or to come forth from itself in the one way or in the other. Consequently, if the godhead took the part of being [i.e., by creating a world and coming to be through that world]. . . then the resolution for that could come only from the highest freedom.[294]

The creation of a world, then, as noted previously, results from God's freedom. Of course, this divine freedom is not to be thought of as just like human freedom. Yet it does bear a resemblance to human power of choice:

> A being is free in that it does not have to reveal itself. To reveal one's self is to act, just as all acting is a self-revelation. The free, however, must be free [either] to halt at mere ability, or to pass over into act.[295]

The point is that God is bound by no necessity to create the world. There is no deficiency in God's essence that requires the creation of a world. The act of creation by which God is revealed is an utterly free one. Of course, the actual

---

[292] *Ages*, 127-128.
[293] *Ages*, 96.
[294] *Ages*, 189.
[295] *Ages*, 194.

188

content of this revelation is not arbitrary. It depends on God's nature, for as noted previously the revelatory course of natural and human history follows the sequence of the powers.[296] However, it is free, at least in the sense that it is not necessary. As a result, the existence of the finite world is radically contingent. It has no ground of existence in itself and its grounding in God's nature depends on an act of God's freedom.

The matter is far different for Tillich. For Tillich, freedom is one of the ontological elements of being, grounded in the fundamental structure of self and world. As has already been noted, Tillich held that in God the polarities of this structure are without tension. God's freedom is perfectly balanced by destiny:

> The divine life is creative, actualizing itself in inexhaustible abundance. . ..
> Therefore it is meaningless to ask whether creation is a necessary or a
> contingent act of God. Nothing is necessary for God in the sense that he is
> dependent on a necessity above him. . . . Nor is [the activity of] creation
> contingent. It does not 'happen' to God, for it is identical with his life.
> Creation is not only God's freedom but also his destiny.[297]

There is every reason to think that Schelling would agree with Tillich's view of creation as he described it here. For Schelling creation is neither necessary for God nor something that has happened accidentally to God. However, whereas for Tillich freedom is one of the polarities, balanced by destiny, for Schelling freedom is not part of God's nature at all. It is instead contrasted with God's nature and with the potencies in which it consists. God's freedom stands above God's nature as a sort of "supergodhead."[298] Whereas Tillich regarded freedom as part of God's nature (the polarities of being), Schelling distinguished God's freedom from God's nature (the potencies). Tillich accepted Schelling's general portrait of God's nature as the harmonious relation of opposed powers. However, he identified freedom with the "self" pole of the ontological elements,[299] thereby associating God's freedom with the first potency (B) of Schelling's philosophy.

[296] *Ages*, 200.
[297] *Systematic Theology*, 1:252.
[298] *Ages*, 123.
[299] *Systematic Theology*, 1:164.

For Schelling, however, God's freedom is something over and above not only the first potency but all the potencies. Ironically, although Tillich credited Schelling with overcoming Hegel's essentialism[300] and with developing a positive philosophy, he himself diminished the importance of the chief anchor of the positive philosophy, the freedom of God. He did so by making freedom relative to destiny, whereas Schelling sought to make God's freedom absolute.

Tillich did occasionally approach Schelling's view that there is in God something beyond the ontological elements. For example:

> As the actualization of the other two principles [power and meaning], the Spirit is the third principle. Both power and meaning are contained in it and united in it. The third principle is in a way the whole (God *is* Spirit), and in a way it is a special principle (God *has* the Spirit as he has the *logos*).[301]

We can see here a distinction between 1) Spirit as a third ontological element alongside the first two and 2) Spirit as the totality of the ontological elements. But this is essentially the same as Schelling's view that the third potency (A^3) is on the one hand one of the potencies and on the other the perfect unity of the first two. Even though Tillich thought of the Spirit as in some sense distinct from the ontological elements, he did not identify freedom as the essential feature of Spirit. God's freedom never transcends God's nature but is instead always in harmony with and relative to God's destiny. As a result, God is far less spontaneous than in Schelling's system. Further, in Tillich's view the world loses the radical contingency that Schelling ascribed to it, because its existence does not seem to depend on an act of God's freedom.

---

[300] *Systematic Theology*, 2:24.
[301] *Systematic Theology*, 1:252.

Conclusion

Tillich's doctrine of God is highly influenced by Schelling's philosophy; however, it differs in two very important respects, eschatology and freedom. It is my opinion that it suffers because of his neglect of certain aspects of Schelling's thought that he was aware of but chose to ignore. In the remainder of this essay I would like to suggest why in these respects Schelling's view is to be preferred to Tillich's.

With regards to eschatology, I have noted that Tillich had a severely chastened eschatology, one in which there is no teleological movement of history. Eternity is always equally present to each moment of history. For Schelling, on the contrary, the doctrine of the powers explains the course of development in nature and in history. The initial dominance of the first power (B) over the second (A^2) accounts for the chronological priority of nature to humanity. The eventual triumph of the second power over the first yields, among other things, a Christology with a substantial content. Of course, it is possible to be too sanguine about the course of history. Tillich's restrained eschatology has much to recommend it. Yet we do not have to embrace the full measure of Schelling's eschatological triumphalism to acknowledge that his view of the potencies and their role in history makes better sense of Christology than does Tillich's theory of the polarities. In comparison with Schelling's Christology, Tillich's view appears static, idealistic and a-historical. "The Christ" seems to be an ideal type that Jesus fits into rather than a power in history that finally emerges in the person of Jesus Christ. Naturally, I am not endorsing Schelling's philosophy as providing in itself an adequate Christology. However, it does seem that Schelling's philosophy captures better the Christian sense of a struggle in history between opposing powers and the possibility of the triumph of one over the other. Schelling's attempt to interpret the history and characteristics of both nature and history in terms of the dynamics of the potencies is particularly impressive. Although a contemporary theological or philosophical interpretation of the natural world or of history would have to take into account a far more sophisticated level of scientific knowledge than was available to Schelling, his thought contains resources that may be useful for any such interpretation.

I have also noted Schelling's assertion that the world results from a free decision of God. This freedom implies the radical contingency of the world. Although the general course of nature's evolution and of history's development is fully rational according to Schelling, the sheer existence of a finite world is not rational. It is not necessary. The created world might not have been. Tillich, on the contrary, acknowledged freedom and contingency *within* the world but seemed to hesitate on the contingency *of* the world. On the one hand, he wrote of the phenomenon of ontological shock, when we feel the force of the question, Why is there something and not nothing at all.[302] This shock seemingly points to the world's contingency. On the other hand, he did not expressly endorse Schelling's thesis that the world might not have been and that it rests on an act of God's will. To be sure, Tillich rejected Hegel's conception of the world's logical necessity; he discouraged any thought of the world being in any sense a necessary actualization of God. And as already noted, he denied that the act of creation is for God anything necessary or arbitrary. But his comment about the experience of ontological shock is revealing: "Thought must start with being; it cannot go behind it. . . . Thought is based on being, and it cannot leave this basis."[303] This statement tacitly denies what Schelling affirmed, namely that thought should and can go behind being and behind the necessary nature of God, for in addition to God's nature there is God's primordial will. Contrary to Tillich, Schelling suggested that we can ask the question, Why is there something instead of nothing? and receive an answer. Tillich, by confining thought to being, committed himself to the negative philosophy whose limitations Schelling sought to transcend. Schelling's confidence that an answer can be obtained is based on

---

[302] *Systematic Theology*, 1:163.
[303] *Systematic Theology*, 1:163.

his conviction that God's freedom and decision to create must be taken into account. Hence, for Schelling, the question of the world's existence is not merely an index of our existential situation but also points us toward the freedom of God. Which of the two, Tillich and Schelling, should we follow in this matter? Each position has its own cogency. Tillich's purpose in balancing freedom and destiny is clear and reasonable. He wished to move beyond a simplistic dichotomy of contingency and necessity and to argue that this dichotomy is resolved in God's prefect harmony between freedom and destiny. Schelling's motivation is also commendable. In the wake of Hegel he strove emphatically against any rationalistic view of creation that would locate the ground of creation in some sort of necessity or in God's nature. Understandably, he emphasized God's freedom. The question, then, is whether Tillich's or Schelling's conception is to be preferred, given contemporary theological and scientific commitments.

Current scientific cosmology does not settle the matter. One may, within the bounds of scientific theories, maintain the contingency of the universe, especially with cosmologists refusing to speculate on the state of things prior to the Big Bang. At the same time, contemporary cosmology also allows the possibility of multiple universes or of states of reality prior to the Big Bang, ideas that suggest the eternity and perhaps necessity of matter in some form. Contemporary science allows for but does not compel the judgment that the existence of the universe is contingent. Further, Christian doctrine does not fully settle the issue. Although clearly against the notion of any necessity of the world, theologians long ago recognized that the world is not the result of an *arbitrary* act of God's will. Any doctrine of freedom must take this into account as well.

Perhaps a more fruitful way of resolving the issue is to ask whether Tillich has preserved what Schelling regarded as the central insight of the positive philosophy--the transcendence of God's freedom. For Schelling, the freedom of God is something different from God's nature as embodied in the potencies. For Tillich, freedom is one of the polarities and accordingly is balanced by God's destiny. Both Schelling and Tillich grant that there is within God an element of freedom. The question is whether we prefer Schelling's view that this freedom transcends God's nature or Tillich's that freedom is a part of God's nature. Is freedom one of the ontological categories or does it transcend the categories?

In my judgment, Tillich may have failed to appreciate the need to distinguish freedom from nature. Although the distinction can certainly be overdone, it is a necessary distinction if the Christian doctrine of grace is to be preserved. The doctrine of grace declares that our existential standing before God means transcending (although not contradicting) our natural existence. Our life in God is to an extent discontinuous with our everyday life in the world. Further, the Christian tradition has long maintained that entering into this relation with God is an exercise in true freedom in cooperation with grace. As a result, I think that we should side with Schelling and regard freedom as transcending nature and not as a part of nature. This is not to deny that there is a dynamic aspect of nature. On the contrary, nature has its own form of spontaneity. But it is to deny that our true freedom is simply a component of our natural being. Our true freedom transcends the spontaneity of our nature. And what is true of us must be true all the more of God, if indeed human being is grounded in God's being.

The strength of the tradition in which Schelling and Tillich stood is its attempt to make sense of God's relation to the world. It does so by regarding the world as structured by the same principles that constitute God. In this way, it avoids representing God as a being that is external to the world and who relates to the world as an external agent or cause relates to an effect. The way forward in contemporary attempts to discuss divine action and God's relation to the world can be hastened if theologians will attend to thoughts of Schelling, Tillich and others in this tradition. Although their thoughts cannot today be simply adopted without refinement or alteration, their general approach has much to recommend it. It may yet provide the best resources for theology's engagement with the natural sciences.

ETHICS, CREATION AND LIFE
Dan Rhoades

Introduction

Consider this anomaly. Christian theologians accepted the burgeoning humanism of nineteenth century Western culture, but rejected evolution and much new scientific knowledge about humans. Clearly, the doctrines of creation and imago Dei prompted both responses, for they set humans apart from nature, and indicated a status of infinite worth. These theological presuppositions were even the basis for "natural theology", for nature was only understandable and meaningful within these anthropocentric parameters. But the modern sciences steadily eroded these theological doctrines. It is time to reject anthropocentrism, and embrace a naturalistic theology.

This article begins with a critique of the doctrines of creation and the imago Dei, as articulated by Reinhold Niebuhr. He is certainly a famous proponent. It will be argued that these doctrines are dualistic, anthropocentric, and interpret nature with a political model. These doctrines also evoke forms of piety which exacerbate the problems.

The second part of the article will develop some alternative concepts and sensibilities grounded in more naturalistic concepts. Herbert Spencer's philosophy of evolution will provide a nineteenth Century launching pad, followed by a constructive formulation.

I. On Creation

For Niebuhr, the concept of creation is born in human experience, by a "...sense of reverence for a majesty and of dependence upon an ultimate source of

196

being." [304] He interprets Romans 1:19-20 as follows: "The fact that the world is not self-derived and self-explanatory and self-sufficing but points beyond itself, is used as evidence for the doctrine of Creation and to point to the glory of the creator."[305] Naturalism is "…forced to reduce man to the level of nature."[306] But nature must be interpreted in terms of mere chance and caprice, or it must be related to a more ultimate realm of freedom. Thus, the "mythical or supra-rational" concept of creation ex nihilo preserves the transcendence and freedom of God. It also measures man "…in a dimension of depth which is initially suggested by the structure of human consciousness, and by the experience of a reality more ultimate than his own, which impinges on his freedom."[307] Humans are created in the image and likeness of God (imago Dei). They are finite, but their special creation sets them apart from the rest of nature. These few statements should suffice, but it is well to remember that salvation history is also imaged as a new creation. Creation itself will be transformed into the Kingdom of God by the triumphant return of the messiah.

Some Cognitive Difficulties

The doctrine of creation establishes an absolute differentiation between Creator and creation. The result is a dualism between infinite/finite, eternal/temporal, mind/body, and spirit/flesh that extends throughout the cosmos. Rosemary Ruether, among others, has documented the negative consequences of dualism in gender, ethnic, religious, and class relationships.[308] Furthermore, creation is by God's command, an act of absolute power. Nature is so powerless that it could not exist for a moment without God's sustaining power. God's

---

[304] Niebuhr, Reinhold, *The Nature and Destiny of Man,* (Louisville, Ky.: Westminster John Knox Pr., 1996) p. 131.
[305] Loc.cit. *pp. 132-3.*
[306] Ibid.
[307] Ibid.
[308] Ruether, *New Woman, New Earth,* (New York: Seabury Press, 1975)

sovereignty is clear, but it is bought at the expense of any independent natural vitality.

God is also rational Spirit, and guarantor of truth, principles, purposes and values. If meaning, and human freedom, depend on the doctrine of creation, as Niebuhr argues, then the attachment of theologians, and believers alike, would be understandable. Also, God gives humans "dominion" over nature, and the responsibility of stewardship. Nature is understood "from the top down", and humanity is at the center. In his messianic interpretation of the new creation, Jurgen Moltmann discusses the "doctrine of the house". It is difficult to imagine a clearer symbol of anthropocentric parochialism than the final domestication of nature into our home.[309]

Anthropocentrism also tends toward the conquest of nature.[310] That project gained increased intellectual, cultural and technical power in modern times. Faith in human mastery is so great that technology seems to have a life of its own. If religion is to play a constructive role, believers must stop worshipping a god fashioned in their own image.

The doctrine of the sovereignty of God increases the problems exponentially. The irony of a political interpretation of the processes of nature is clear, as are many of its difficulties. When a political metaphor is used to interpret nature, two fundamentally different spheres are confused. Nature is robbed of its vitality and potency, and theology finds itself only a step removed from a mechanical interpretation. Also, the problem of evil is focused on the unfairness of life, and any distinction between misfortune and injustice is made very difficult. The Hebrew and Christian traditions are replete with theological

---

[309] Moltmann. Jurgen, *God in Creation,* (San Francisco: Harper and Row, 1985)
[310] Gustafson, James, *Ethics from a Theocentric Perspective,* (Chicago: University of Chicago Press, 1981-84)

efforts to honor God's goodness in spite of the problem of evil, without much success.[311]

The projection upon nature of a political/moral system based on justice is absurd, no matter how justice is interpreted. Life is not fair, and a moment's reflection tells us that such a "moral" universe would be without grace, and unbearable. Morality itself would be easily confused with prudential self-interest, which is Satan's charge against Job's goodness in the council. (Job 1:9-12) Nor does morality deserve such a lofty throne at the expense of so many other values.

When sovereignty was transposed into an eternal principle, it legitimated temporal rulers through most of Western history. Historically, it has almost been a theological principle that God's rule set limits upon political power. But history tells a different story, at least in the main. In fact, the most powerful religious impact of God's just rule has been the concept of God's all knowing judgment upon individuals, and the religious nurturing of sensibilities of sin, especially for disobedience to authority. Therefore, freedom, liberation, hope, and the political struggle for justice have had to work against the symbolism of a divine kingship.
Some Problematic Sensibilities

It has been said that polytheism constructs a god out of every divine appearance, but monotheism recognizes in all these mysteries the same God experienced in personal confrontation. While Hebrew and Christian communities affirmed monotheism, both claimed to be the elect people of God, and then claimed that their God was the God of creation. Yahweh was the just deliverer of the Israelites from Egypt, and the holy One of Israel, who established a holy people. Later, monotheism and doctrine of election co-existed. The early Christians saw their election in Jesus the Christ, and claimed to be the `new Israel', the holy people of God. In the prologue to the Gospel of John, this same Jesus was proclaimed to be the `Word' who was in the beginning with God. In both cases, the exclusive sensibilities of the elect specified the nature of the

---

[311] See Griffin, David,*God, Power, and Evil,* (Lanham, Md.: University Press of America, 1990)

creator, and assured that the creator was none other than their God. There were exceptions in the prophets and wisdom literature, but the dominant traditions have remained intact for thousands of years. For Christians, matters were made worse by their religious imperialism. It is difficult to imagine a religious sensibility, other than the claim of being God's elect, that could have more potential for evil. Unfortunately, it has a long record of actualization.

But God is also holy. Rudolph Otto, in the Idea of the Holy, says that the holy is the predominant religious feeling and affection in Hebrew and Christian religion. He believes that the religious feeling of holiness is evoked when the numinous is experienced as objectively present. Ironically, he cites Abraham, in Genesis 18:27, as an example of a creature consciousness that is submerged and overwhelmed by its own nothingness before an overpowering God.[312] The citation is odd, since Abraham has just argued with God, and said, "Shall not the judge of all the earth do what is just?" It's also odd because the patriarchs were probably among the early free human leaders.

But who could deny that holiness is a profound, ineffable, religious feeling? Or that it requires an absolute and exclusive devotion which includes submission and obedience to the almighty God? But there is more. Otto argued that the mysterium tremendum was grounded in demonic dread in primitive religions, where it could easily be experienced in all sorts of connections. The awfulness which made the blood run cold and the flesh crawl could spread like a contagion. Of course, Otto interprets the tremor, terror, and holy fear in Biblical religions on a different plane. The fear of the Lord is the beginning of all wisdom, and the wrath and jealousy of God are both described and legitimated in terms of the ineffable and irreducible experience of the holy.

However, the tremendum must also be developed in terms of 'might' and 'absolute overpowering,' which are the basis for the "...feeling of one's own

---

[312] Otto, Rudolph, *The Idea of the Holy*,(New York: Oxford University Press,1970), p.9

submergence, or being but 'dust and ashes' and nothingness." [313]   Humility becomes self-depreciation and powerlessness. Nature is under an absolute royal dominion. God commands, and claims absolute loyalty, self-abnegation, and self-identification with God's rule. The order of creation tends to be static and universal, and morality is reduced to duty and obedience. Once again, the sensibilities evoked by these images reflect a life, history, and cultural imagination that is more a part of the problem than the solution.

Two points may be highlighted. First, God's supernatural being is affirmed on the basis of a religious dread, and awe, in the presence of the numinous. Indeed, Otto argues that the natural man is unable to shudder, or feel horror, in the real sense of the terms.[314] This concept of the holy is also the basis for attributing human feelings, such as wrath and jealousy, to God. Second, holiness, sacrifices, and (ritual) purity go hand in hand. The sacred is marked off from the profane, and the pure assiduously separated from the impure. Even when defilement is defined in spiritual terms, as purity of thoughts, intentions, and what comes out of the mouth, the dualism between natural feelings and religious sensibilities remain.[315] The psyche is split by a perfect spiritual purity with regard to love, sex, and happiness. The split is soon re-enforced by religious ceremony and moral law. A similar split between these religious affections and altered cognitive understandings of nature is inevitable.

The Human Condition: Sin, Guilt, and Original Sin

It is not surprising that an emphasis on God's holiness and majesty would define sin as pride, thinking too highly of one's self, idolatry, and rebellion. Niebuhr's focus was upon the will to power among nations and institutions on the collective level, but the impact of this view on personal existence remains. Niebuhr seems to assume that humans are Promethean sinners. They do not do many things very

---

[313] Loc. cit., pp. 19-20

[314] Loc. cit., p. 15

[315] See Matt. 15: 10

well, but they are great sinners. A naturalist would tend to argue that humans are very mediocre sinners. Humans haven't shown any creativity as sinners. They haven't come up with new sins, but have repeated the same stupid ones (inertia). New technical skills increase the terror and scope, but the inability to tell the difference between an ordinary bomb and a hydrogen bomb is still a matter of inertia.

Niebuhr's theology certainly evokes guilt. But guilt has not been an effective constraint upon sin in the past, and its excessive role has often cast a pall over pious folks. It certainly should not be cultivated as such a primary religious sensibility. Wonder, mystery, beauty, goodness, energy and graciousness also abound. Idolatry in our time may be the restriction of worship to a supernatural God. For we meet God in I-Thou relations between ourselves, others, and our natural world.[316] In days of old, an altar for worship was built wherever God was encountered.

Original sin is certainly bound up with the mysterium tremendum of divine holiness. As a state of existence it cannot be understood in terms of the commission of particular sins. Guilt is generalized, mystified, and intensified in a context of awe and dread. Dietrich Bonhoeffer wrote that existentialists, like Methodists, try to convict us of our sin so that they can bring us to God.[317] They insist that precisely because we think we are healthy, we have the worst form of sickness—unto death. We are even more guilty because we don't feel guilty.

Consider the difference it would make if these matters were viewed from a more naturalistic perspective. If the power and vitality to sustain life were itself perceived as natural, then the interplay, tension, and conflict between finitude and freedom could be embraced. Wholeness and individuality would not be torn

---

[316] Buber, Martin, *I and Thou,* (New York: Scribner, 1958)
[317] Bonhoeffer, Dietrich, *Letters and Papers from Prison,* (New York: Macmillan, 1962) p. 196

asunder by definition, and finding the sacred unknowable precisely in the taken for granted everyday world would be a primary religious exercise/experience.

With such a coming of age, free life would become a form of worship. It would be affirmed as responsive, sensitive, imaginative and accountable. Empowerment, too, would be an act of faith, with an equal respect and hope for all. Such a piety would reject any theology that created a chasm between God, the world, and humanity. It would seek for wholeness, and act for its enhancement in every way it could. But it would reject any claim to wholeness that denied its own particularity.

II. An Alternative: Evolution

One can hardly mention creation without an association with evolution. A sketch of some of Herbert Spencer's nineteenth century ideas may serve as a springboard for discussion. Spencer developed a distinction between an unknowable power, and manifestations of that power that were knowable in their likeness and difference.[318] Humans find it necessary to represent the unknowable in some idea, image, or metaphor. In fact, both religion and science construct trans-empirical generalities that must be perpetually adapted in response to change.[319] Spencer calls for humility before the immensity and greatness of that which we vainly strive to grasp, because of the "...incommensurable difference between the Conditioned and the Unconditioned."[320]

Religion enables humans to cope with the fundamental mysteries of life. Religions are adaptable and relative, but they all contain a deeper truth, and point to the mystery "...that the power that manifests itself in consciousness is but a differently conditioned power which manifests itself beyond consciousness."[321]

---

[318] F. Howard Collins, *An Epitome of the Synthetic Philosophy,* (London: Williams and Norgate, 1889), p.14

[319] Ibid.

[320] Loc. cit., p.14

[321] Spencer, Herbert, *Principles of Sociology, Part IV,* Ecclesiastical Institutions, (London: Williams and Norgate, 1885), p.838

Religious symbols have evolved from homogeneity to heterogeneity, from simple to complex, and from the indefinite to the definite. The result is a proliferation and hierarchy of gods and spirits without qualification. With increasing knowledge, religious mythology goes through a process of dissolution, and there is an increasing adaptation that integrates and concentrates supernatural power-- and eliminates increasing elements of anthropocentric characterization. Naturally, Spencer envisions the continuation of that process, including all those more elevated human capacities that presuppose a series of states of consciousness. All these are"... inconsistent with that omnipresent activity which simultaneously works out an infinity of ends."[322]

Yet Spencer denied that science was dissipating the most profound core of religion, vis., openness and responsiveness to the mystery of existence. Whether one looks to biology, geology, or astrophysics, one finds that whenever science dissolves one mystery, new ones are created. To understand how Science and religion express opposite sides of the same fact--the one its near and visible side, and the other its remote or invisible side--becomes our problem."[323] "But one truth must grow even clearer...Amid the mysteries which become the more mysterious the more they are thought about, there will remain the one absolute certainty, that he is ever in the presence of an Infinite and Eternal Energy, from which all things proceed."[324]

Spencer's views of evolution/dissolution reflect the principles of the indestructibility of matter, the continuity of motion, the persistence of force, and the transformation and equivalence of forces. Given these laws, there is an unceasing redistribution of matter and motion throughout the universe. Evolution consists of a predominant integration of matter, and dissipation of motion. Dissolution involves a predominant absorption of motion, and disintegration of

---

[322] Loc. cit.. p.836

[323] Collins, Loc. cit. p.5

[324] Spencer, Loc. cit., p. 843

matter. When evolution is uncomplicated by other processes, it is simple. When secondary changes go on due to differences in the circumstances of aggregates, evolution is compound. It results in a transformation of the homogeneous to the heterogeneous, and renders its heterogeneity increasingly definite.[325]

The reasons for this unceasing redistribution of matter and motion are the instability of the homogeneous due to exposure to diverse incident forces, which sub-divide with a multiplication of effects. When equilibration has been accomplished in an aggregate, there may be further transition stages toward equilibrium, but rest (inorganic) and death (organic) are the ultimate limit of the changes constituting evolution. Dissolution is the opposite change, which every evolved aggregate undergoes, sooner or later.

> This rhythm of evolution and dissolution, completing itself during short periods in small aggregates, and in the vast aggregates distributed through space completing itself in periods which are immeasurable by human thought, insofar as we can see, universal and eternal..."[326]

Matter, motion, force, and consciousness are all modes of the same inscrutable and eternal power of the universe, from which all things proceed.

This outline of Spencer's thought indicates that evolution opens up an overwhelming vista of multiple, overlapping, interconnections influencing development over time. Humans are offspring of the universe, a manifestation of the inscrutable energy that surrounds them, and flows from within. Body, soul, and mind are all natural. Theology errs when it rends them asunder. Everything that is, or has been, or will be, is also a manifestation of that power, and is so intricately interdependent that it is not possible to treat individuals (particulars) as the simple basic unit.

Metaphors for a Theology of Nature

---

[325] Collins, Loc. cit., Preface by Spencer, pp. viii & ix
[326] Loc. cit., pp. X & XI

This article has focused more on root metaphors than upon metaphysics. It has also attended to the cognitive, affective, and cognitive implications of the metaphors explored. From this perspective, while Spencer's thought is quite dated, his emphasis upon the necessity of symbols, and humility before the mystery of life, is very appealing. All symbols are culturally limited, but those chosen should at least point beyond anthropocentric images, and leave no doubt that the Power/Energy they envision is more inclusive than persuasion.

The metaphors of generation, evolution, dissolution, and re-generation have historically had great religious significance, and they certainly have the advantage of more accurately reflecting human experience of the mystery of life. Whatever else may be said, existence has been generated for all entities by a cosmic process, which has evolved for ages prior to the appearance of humanity, and will continue without humans for ages more. These metaphors offer a natural basis for a vision of universal relatedness, for a common inheritance, and a deep, rich, ecologically conceived environment through time. Evolution also introduces change and process in the most direct fashion. Since the inscrutable energy in the universe is manifested in all these matters, the heartbeat of theological dynamics comes from within the natural. That encourages empirical investigation, an imaginative probing of the mysteries of the universe, and a quest for novel insights that puts humanity in its proper perspective.

Evolution is followed by dissolution. None chose to live, and all will die. From an anthropocentric perspective, death is a great evil, and there is no point in the process that is without possibility for misfortune. Yet dissolution greatly enhances the potential for innovation and change. It is a most significant passage, which clears the way for new generations and novelty, while leaving its inheritance as a bequest from the past. Dissolution enables re-generation, that new beginning which carries the past within itself, while opening to a novel future.

Death is difficult for humans to accept with serenity, as one of those things they cannot change. Death may evoke submission, rebellion, resentment, or technological efforts to overcome the limit. But with serenity comes a different perspective, celebrated by some believers, mystics, and naturalists. Humans are offspring of the universe, just like the trees and the stars. We belong here. But life and death are the heartbeat of the universe. Any static concept of conservation is obsolete. Faith on Earth responds with trust, confidence and hope to the immense, mysterious and rich universe that surrounds and sustains us.[327] Judaism and Christianity have always considered these metaphors with great distrust, though others have found greater religious significance in them than in the creation myths. The greatest barrier to their use in Christian circles is precisely the charge of idolatry. But this religious taboo has had a paralyzing cognitive and affective impact in relation to this world, our bodies, sexuality, and death.

One metaphor in relation to the universe is that all entities are heirs, or joint-heirs, with an inheritance passed on through all generations. For all its limits, the metaphor of kinship points to an interrelation that extends through space and time. While kinship and inheritance language have always been conceived as a profound tie, they have also been perceived as an exclusive bond, often involving enmity. So they are fraught with danger. They have long been used to make exclusive claims, especially in the name of Christ. And they have almost universally been grounded in sexist traditions.

However, our bodies bear witness to another truth, for ontogeny recapitulates phylogeny. Modern science has exposed us to the depth and breadth of our kinship beyond our species. Indeed, our common inheritance extends to the ends of the universe. Kinship still has exclusive connotations, but with increasing knowledge, the truth about its potential for inclusiveness will become more obvious. Kinship must become a religious sensibility if its power for

---

[327] Niebuhr, H.R., *Faith on Earth,*(New Haven and London: Yale University Press, 1989)

bonding is to be realized. Of course, kinship includes all sorts of negative as well as positive relationships. But kinship is a fundamental tie that bonds/binds us, and it is unwise to allow either conservatives or liberals to narrowly define it.

Kinship is one of the few things that transcends death, since life and death create diverse rhythms as the heartbeat of the universe. Everything is what it is as much by the inheritance it leaves behind as by the inheritance it received. Self-identity among humans tends to be sought in the specifics of the inheritance they have received. But life challenges any attempt to cling to one's parochial self as a proper reckoning of one's true integrity. Parochial identities are enlarged and enhanced by an integrity that loses/finds itself in ever more complex networks of relationships. When one thinks of the scope of such a mystery, one is filled with wonder, and a different kind of awe. In a strange new way, it is the discovery of our bodily reality that demands a new spirit and mind among us. Of course, values cannot simply be read off the facts. But radical changes in understanding must influence the formulation of value systems. In a relational view, values always include an objective as well as a subjective pole. The question is whether the relation between them is a "fitting" one.

The Sensibilities of Joint-Heirs
The metaphor of joint-heirs generates a sensibility about life as an inheritance, granted to each generation for safe keeping, enhancement, and endowment for the next generation. Each entity is valued in its own right, as well as for its contribution to the ecosystem. Its kinship, or the fact that it belongs, may be traced through a rich natural ecology. Each particular entity is dealt a different hand, with different social valuations. But each is a player, as well as a card--a participant with its own degree of influence within the whole.

Aldo Leopold was at least partly correct when he argued that a thing is right when it tends to preserve the integrity, stability, and beauty of the biotic community. It is wrong when the opposite is true. [328] It is the inclusive, dynamic, ecosystem that the metaphors of kinship and inheritance call into view in a highly value oriented way. While each entity is valued in itself, Garrett Hardin has argued that unregulated freedom in the commons brings ruin to all. Nor is there a technical solution to this problem. The morality of an act is the function of the state of the system at the time it is performed.[329] Responsibility for the future also requires a moral basis.[330] Perhaps the images of heirs, joint-heirs, and guarantors may provide a partial basis for an ethical conversation dealing with all these concerns.

These metaphors of inheritance must be developed together. All entities are birthed in the image and likeness of the universe. Every endowment and right that accrues to each entity is given in and through its natural conditions and connections. The metaphor of heirs, whose inheritance is jointly held, describes this situation well. It also carries a moral freight. Being joint heirs indicates indebtedness to both past and present entities that have generated and sustained one's existence, and a corresponding gratitude for the gift. Or it may point to an unjust withholding, even with regard to the necessities of life. Being joint heirs entails negative as well as positive evaluation. It also points to a duty as the guarantor of the inheritance for future generations. Finally, it indicates a status that establishes the worth, rights and potential of each entity on universal and inalienable grounds, and not on dualistic, anthropocentric, or supernatural terms.

The majesty and mystery that is encountered in the universe is the One who surrounds and sustains life, movement, and being—is encountered in the midst of life. Nothing is alien to an heir, and nothing can ultimately isolate one. The metaphor of the heirs captures something of the corporate understanding of

---

[328] See Leopold, Aldo, *A Sand County Almanac,* (Schwartz. N.Y.: Oxford University Press, 1949)

[329] Hardin, Garrett. *Exploring New Ethics for Survival,* (New York: Viking Press, 1972)

[330] See Jonas, Hans, *The Imperative of Responsibility,* (Chicago: University of Chicago Press, 1984)

the Jewish Testament, and something of the individuated status of heirs from the Christian Testament. But it does so on a more naturalistic basis.

Yet our discussion of endowment and inheritance must be analyzed in terms of its historical and cultural development, no matter what dimensions are considered. For example, gender difference is a matter of endowment. But cultural systems have interpreted, defined roles, honored, dishonored, and distributed opportunities and rewards in grossly unfair ways. These patterns have been generated and evolved by societies, and can just as clearly be changed and regenerated. The same is true of social systems for the distribution of power, status, wealth and resources.

A more naturalistic perspective opens up all questions about "inheritance" in a decisive way. It does so, first, by underlining the fact that all entities are heirs, and joint-heirs. The constitution of the U.S.A. has spoken for over two centuries about the inalienable rights of human beings as a basis for freedom and justice. It remains to clarify one's rights and duties to the entities and ecosystems that surround and sustain humanity. This requires a focus upon the complex patterns of interdependence across space/time. New sensibilities must enable humans to claim and prize this inheritance for all, to act as guarantors for future generations, and to work for the regeneration of all nature.

While biblical accounts emphasize that God is the only true owner, so that God has a right to do what God wills, believers are accountable because they are not owners (stewards). In a word, ownership means absolute freedom without accountability. Of course, human owners have always assumed divine prerogatives, and capitalism tends to establish the principle. Joint-heirs, contrary to tradition, view ownership as essential to maturity and responsibility. Without a pattern of ownership that protects one's rights with respect to one's body, beliefs, associations, and property, both responsibility and accountability are difficult. However, ownership is always constituted within some more comprehensive framework of justice. Joint-heirs would clearly place their priority on a pattern of justice that has a demonstrated capacity to meet the claims and needs of all, while providing a ground for defining and protecting the rights of each heir. These views are a fundamental requirement of an ecological vision.

"Owning" and prizing our inheritance requires a new awareness of our kinship, and a greater openness to corporate and co-operative responsibility. The pattern of joint heirs is inclusiveness, liberation, justice, participation, solidarity, and regeneration. But this way has a narrow gate, which is the acknowledgement that we have been unjust heirs, who have adapted too easily to American culture. The model for the later is the prodigal son, who was certainly not a prodigal because he ended up with the pigs. He was a prodigal the moment he sold his inheritance for a sum of money, and left all the rest behind. If he had become a millionaire, he would still have been a prodigal, for prodigality wastes all that it has received on self-indulgence. Its pattern is private appropriation, accumulation, greed, hierarchy, oppression, elitism, and waste. Prodigality has taken on corporate and global dimensions, in the form of an untrammeled race to sell our inheritance for a mess of money. It is time to reclaim our inheritance. What must be fostered are images that focus our attention on the claims of all the heirs, and generate a genuine passion for their protection and regeneration.

KIERKEGAARD'S DIALECTICAL DANCE: SPHERES OF ESSENCE
Helene Tallon Russel

INTRODUCTION

No study of the nineteenth century could be truly complete without attention to Kierkegaard's imaginative conceptualization of being. This essay briefly examines Kierkegaard's view of what it means to become oneself. Kierkegaard's spheres of existence contain the key to his view of human existence. His thought is scrupulously existential. Knowing oneself for Kierkegaard does not correspond to knowledge in the traditional sense. For him, truth is existential; it "is subjectivity." Truth is not about knowledge, but about living, choosing, relating, repenting, believing, willing, and loving. How do you know what you know? Kierkegaard answers, By living.

In this article on Kierkegaard, I examine his conceptualization of human existence through his notion of multiple spheres of existence and his understanding of the dialectical factors in the self. First, I will briefly describe these three spheres and their relationships to each other. Then I will critically analyze interpretations of these spheres within current Kierkegaard scholarship, culminating in my own interpretation. I describe Kierkegaard's complex dialectic, starting with his discussion in *Sickness Unto Death (SUD)* of the dialectical form of the interrelationship of the elements of existence, the finite and the infinite, et al. I argue that Kierkegaard's thought is thoroughly dialectical, by which I mean, relational and processive. I apply this dialectical form to the form of the relationship of the spheres to each other. The spheres relate to each other dialectically, both objectively in Kierkegaard's conceptualization of existence, and subjectively in the lived religious sphere. By highlighting the spheres' processive nature and progressive development toward greater inclusiveness, I show that his dialectic is the foundational element in, and the key to unlocking, the mysteries of his notion of the synthesis of human existence and the spheres.[331] The content of the spheres, the nature of the spheres, the very ontological reality of the spheres is **dialectical**. The contribution to Kierkegaard scholarship here is twofold. First, I am interpreting Kierkegaard's conceptualization of human existence as a non-harmonious synthesis of the finite, the infinite, and their relationship to each other. Second, I am applying Kierkegaard's theological anthropology to the relationship of the spheres of existence. In so doing, the relational character and the processive form of his understanding of subjectivity becomes apparent.

"How does one become a Christian?" is the inquiry upon which Kierkegaard's entire authorship hinges. He believes that the Danish practice of assuming that one is a Christian, simply by means of a Danish birth, is the "monstrous illusion we call Christendom." [332] He argues against the assumption of such an easy road to religious salvation. Rather, becoming a Christian is the most difficult of all tasks. Becoming a Christian entails becoming subjective, which is movement in and through all the spheres of human existence toward willing to become oneself. His authorship shows the details, the depths, and the breadths of each sphere from inside out.

OVERVIEW OF THE SPHERES

Kierkegaard expresses his conception of human existence by demonstrating three stages or spheres of existence, which reflect different modes and models of living. The three distinct spheres, or forms of how to live -- how to be related to the facts and processes of one's existence, are the aesthetic, the ethical, and the religious stages. Two of these three spheres also contain two sub-spheres, or poles. The aesthetic sphere consists of the immediate pole and the

---

[331] It is also the key to understanding Kierkegaard's employment of pseudonyms. But this is a different paper.

[332] Kierkegaard, *The Point of View of My Work as an Author* (New York: Harper Torchbook, 1962), p. 6.

reflective pole.[333] Also, the relationship of the two poles in the religious sphere, religiousness A and religiousness B, creates a polarity within the religious sphere. This complex structure and content of each of the three spheres is a primary aspect of the complexity of Kierkegaard's view of human selfhood.

In *Either/Or*, first published in February 1843, Kierkegaard illustrates the first spheres: the aesthetic and the ethical.[334] The aesthetic sphere of existence is characterized by its emphasis on the immediate. Here the focus is on the immediate moment of the closest external object of immediate stimulation, as in gratification, satisfaction, pleasure, and even sorrow. The aesthetic sphere is "immediate" also in that it lacks mediation, or reflection. It does not choose itself or know itself. The one who lives in the aesthetic realm does not reflect upon his/her own life or self. He is unaware of himself, unreflexive, and oblivious to the world around him, including his own external behavior. The self's immediate experience is determinative, there is no self-examination, or self-reflection and thus, no self-knowledge of any true decisions. The only concern is with the immediate experience in the moment. The lack of reflective decisiveness makes the one in this sphere not actually a self, but a chaotic, inconsistent and unpredictable conglomeration of human impulses. There is no genuine selfhood since there is no mediation either by decision, and/or by reflection. As Louis Dupre' says:

> The aesthetic never commits himself, and thus never becomes a self, since the self is essentially a choice, an active relationship to oneself....[335]

In *Either/Or* volume one, Kierkegaard shows the reader the scattered self of the aesthetic sphere, by demonstrating the way a scattered self sees life. He

---

[333] C.f. Mark C. Taylor, *Kierkegaard's Pseudonymous Authorship*, (Princeton, New Jersey: Princeton University Press, 1975). pp.76-77.

[334] The third, the religious, is present, but only implied in the Judge's sermon.

[335] Louis Dupre', *Kierkegaard as Theologian, the Dialectic of Christian Existence*, (New York: Sheed and Ward, 1963), pp.42-43.

illustrates the form of disunification and inconsistency present in the aesthetic realm by including essays on many different topics, with many different tenors. These essays range from "The Immediate Stages of the Erotic or the Musical Erotic" and "The Diary of the Seducer," to "The Rotation Method" and "The First Love." The aesthetic includes not only pleasure, but also pain, as seen in the essay, "The Unhappiest Man." Only the superficial aspects of pleasure and pain are considered personally, and only for the moment. The following example illustrates A's themes of despair and feelings of meaninglessness mixed with humor:

> My view of life is utterly meaningless. I suppose an evil spirit has set a pair of spectacles upon my nose, of which one lens is a tremendously powerful magnifying glass, the other an equally powerful reducing glass. [336]

The aesthetic realm is recognized by its form, not just its content. Its form is like a stream that wanders this way and that, purely reacting to the resistance of the rocks and earth. The analogy is not exact in that the stream may eventually create its own path by carving its way into the earth. This ability is not present for the aesthetic. Instead, one living in the aesthetic sphere is entirely affected by the external stimuli. It simply flows as the wind blows.

The aesthetic sphere has two phases or poles: the immediate pole of the aesthetic sphere and the reflective pole. The first mini-sphere within this first sphere is utter immediacy. It is illustrated by the non-reflective immediate experience of Don Juan, who enjoys the pleasure of any woman who is present. Next is the reflective pole of this sphere, which includes philosophers, who may reflectively think about the realities of other peoples' lives without examining their own lives.

For the development of a self, this sphere must lead to the next one: the ethical, which will be characterized by decision. But it won't be an easy

---

[336] Soren Kierkegaard, *Either/Or*. (Princeton, New Jersey: Princeton University Press, 1944). Vol. I p.19.

transition, as Dupre' tells us that the aesthetic sphere "bears within itself the germ of its own destruction."[337] By this Dupre' means that the quest for absolute pleasure and comfort in the aesthetic sphere cannot lead to any pleasure and comfort in the long run, for despair and meaninglessness surround the one who, by his refusal to choose himself, chooses despair. Dupre' continues, "If the aesthete has followed his attitude to its ultimate consequences, there is nothing left for him to choose other than the despair into which he has brought himself."[338] The only way out of this existential despair is *through* the despair. A decision *for* the despair will inadvertently lead one out of this sphere, and into the next one, the ethical sphere. By choosing oneself one brings "an absolute element into his existence: in his commitment to despair he constitutes a relationship to himself."[339] This decision of the person in aesthetic sphere is like the enzyme necessary for the digestion of the aesthetic pleasures into the ethical nutrients of selfhood. In *Either/Or* B, Judge William bids the aesthetic author to choose despair, for at least he will have acted decisively.

The ethical sphere, in contrast, demonstrates thoughtful reflection, self-awareness, and careful decisions based on universal norms of society. It is about one's relations with others. It is concerned with universal norms of behavior, with questions such as, *what is right to do, for any person in this situation?* An individual determines his/her course of action in this sphere by what is reasonable and what is in accord with the universal norms of appropriate behavior. The universal is the dominant mode here. These decisions are made with commitment and with the assuredness of logical thinking. Here a person's self is "self-made," by her decisions, into a singular, consistent, unified self. Decision is the operative word here, as Judge William demonstrates when he bids his friend in the aesthetic

---

[337] Dupre', p.43.
[338] Dupre', p.43.
[339] Dupre' p.43.

sphere, "Choose thyself,"(a play on Socrates' "know thyself.") The Judge expands his understanding of the significance of choice, the primary characteristic of the ethical sphere, "That which is prominent in my either/or is the ethical. It is therefore not yet a question of the choice of something in particular, it is not a question of the reality of the thing chosen, but of the reality of the act of choice."[340] It is **that** you choose, **that** you participate in the becoming of what you are becoming, that is essential for the ethical.

Note that the primary sources of the ethical sphere, Judge William in *Either/Or* B and *Fear and Trembling*, are relational in context. Kierkegaard explains the ethical in counter-distinction to the aesthetic and the religious spheres.

The third sphere is the religious sphere, primarily concerned with relationality. One's relationships to oneself, to one's decision, to God are the determinative questions. While the ethical sphere emphasizes **that** one decides, the religious sphere emphasizes **how** one **relates**. The religious sphere includes aspects of both of the other spheres, such as the aesthetics' emphasis on the needs of the particular individual and the careful self-reflection of ethical. The religious person does not make decisions based solely on the universal norms of society, or on the logic of reason, nor on the external relations of humans to each other. But decisions are made. These decisions are often made in "fear and trembling," since there is no external norm or systematic rule to tell an individual what is the "right" decision, only the individual's own faith and discernment. The religious sphere is the one most concerned with "the individual," and with the absolute. Kierkegaard is careful not to conflate the universal and the absolute. One's relationship to the universal is external and the same for all, while a person's relationship with the absolute is particular and individual. The experience of subjectivity is the focal point in this sphere. When Kierkegaard says in his *Point of View for My Work as an Author*, that all his works are an expression of his

---

[340] Kierkegaard, *Either/Or*, Vol. II p.149.

religious vocation, he means that he writes all of his works for the purpose of evoking subjectivity within his reader.[341] Subjectivity is a necessary prerequisite for becoming a Christian. He is not primarily concerned with philosophical clarity and the truth of facts as D. Z. Phillips[342] argues; rather, his main concern is to evoke this *subjectivity*. The double movement of objectivity and subjectivity distinguishes the religious sphere, which is the core of Kierkegaard's dialectic. *Fear and Trembling* gives us a paradigmatic example of this movement of faith in the religious sphere. First Abraham, the exemplar of faith, must renounce the finite for the sake of infinite, and then he must return to the finite in love.[343]

Kierkegaard explicitly introduces the religious sphere in *Fear and Trembling,* first published in October 1843, in contrast to the ethical sphere. Later, in *Concluding Unscientific Postscript* (*CUP*), first published in February 1846, religiousness B, is articulated as distinct from religion in general, which is referred to as religiousness A.[344] Also in *CUP*, Climacus suggests intermediate stages between the stages: irony between the aesthetic and ethical, while humor lies between the ethical and the religious spheres. Further, there has recently been talk of three subdivisions of the religious sphere, not just two. Richard Schacht argues for Religiousness A (Socrates), Religiousness B (Christian), and a stage between the two (Abraham).[345] While Merold Westphal also detects a third stage

---

[341] Kierkegaard, *The Point of View*, p. 6.

[342] D.Z. Phillips, "Authorship and Authenticity: Kierkegaard and Wittgenstein," *Midwest Studies in Philosophy*, XVII (1992). (pp.177-193.) p.186.

[343] Kierkegaard, *Fear and Trembling*.

[344] Although it should also be noted that Kierkegaard begins working out the religious B sphere even before *Concluding Unscientific Postscript* in his Edifying Discourses, but he does not distinguish this sphere by name until *Concluding Unscientific Postscript* (Princeton, New Jersey: Princeton University Press, 1974.).

[345] Richard Schacht, *Hegel and After*. Pittsburgh: University of Pittsburgh Press, 1975.

in the religious sphere, he suggests that it lies beyond that of religiousness B.[346]

Interpreting Kierkegaard's Spheres

The most appropriate method of interpreting the relationship and meaning of the spheres of existence is in dispute among Kierkegaard scholars. Mark C. Taylor organizes the Kierkegaardian scholarship on the interpretations of the spheres of existence into four major approaches:

(1) Stages in Kierkegaard's own development;

(2) Stages in the development of world history;

(3) Ideal personalities;

(4) Stages in the development of the individual self; [347]

Taylor goes on to provide a sampling of each of these approaches, indicating that the first method is the most common. Josiah Thompson's book, *The Lonely Labyrinth,*[348] is a fitting example here. In this work, Thompson believes that Kierkegaard's philosophy is a symptom of his sickness. He believes that Kierkegaard writes to become healthy, through trying on these various modes of approaching life, in hopes of finding the one most suitable for him. The second way of interpreting the spheres is generally considered outdated. The third view of the stages is still fairly common. It views the spheres as paradigms for how to live. Kierkegaard's purpose in this view is believed to be simply, to put forth the different options, and ask the reader to choose. However, says Taylor, if this view is taken alone, it "greatly oversimplifies Kierkegaard's insights."[349] This approach neglects the obvious value given to the development toward the religious sphere in Kierkegaard's thought as a whole. It also neglects the relationship of the

---

[346] Merold Westphal, "The Teleological Suspension of Religiousness B." *Foundations of Kierkegaard's Vision of Community*. Eds. George Connell and C. Stephen Evans. Atlantic Highlands, N.J.: Humanities Press, 1991.

[347] Taylor, pp.62-63.

[348] Josiah Thompson, *The Lonely Labyrinth: Kierkegaard's Pseudonymous Works*, (Carbondale, Illinois: Southern Illinois Press, 1967).

[349] Taylor, p. 69.

spheres to each other present within one person. George Connell's interpretation, which we will examine in detail below, exemplifies this approach while also venturing into the next approach.

Finally, the fourth approach Taylor mentions, views the spheres of existence as stages through which one passes along one's maturation toward the highest mode of living: Christianity. This approach is the one with which Taylor personally finds the most cadences. Taylor claims to utilize elements from the third and the fourth group of interpretation in his explication of the complexity of Kierkegaard's view of selfhood and the stages, but he emphasizes the developmental interpretation of the "stages." Taylor uses the words "developmental" and "stages" in his representation of most of the scholarship's approaches to the spheres and consistently through out his book on Kierkegaard's authorship. He argues that the term "stages," which he uses, is the most helpful term since "it gives more emphasis to the developmental character of Kierkegaard's dialectic."[350] Taylor's emphasis of the term stages and their progressive movement through time to the exclusion of the inter-relational characteristic of these realms of existence is due in Taylor's significant use of the concept of time to focus his analysis of the differences and relationship of the stages. He asserts that Kierkegaard's "arrangement of the stages of existence and the primary characteristics of each stage depend on his conception of time. . ." [351]

Taylor argues that the various stages of existence are divergent ways of trying to attain equilibrium between the three pairs of existential elements, temporality and eternality, finitude and infinity, and possibility and necessity. Each attempt that fails to attain this equilibrium ends in despair. The more dis-equilibrium, the greater the despair, the greater the dread, and the greater the sin. These attempts toward equilibrium represent the stages and are organized as a

---

[350] Taylor, p.62, note.
[351] Taylor, p. 267.

developmental process in which the self becomes more individuated.[352] The more individuated a person is, the better self one is. The movement from one stage to the next reflects a qualitative development in one's dexterity with the ambiguities of life and a development of individuation. The final stage, Taylor suggests, is the one with the most balanced relationship between these questions of existence.

While Taylor's analysis of Kierkegaard's understanding of the spheres of existence is thorough and more than adequate in most regards, his approach is lacking in its brief treatment of the dialectical relationship of the existential elements and the stages of subjectivity itself. I agree with Taylor that the dialectics of the existential elements examined in *SUD* provide the key to understanding the stages or spheres of existence. However, the connection between these elements of existence (finitude and infinite, eternal and temporal, and possibility and necessity) and the spheres of existence is more profound than Taylor suggests. His view examines only the external relationships of the elements, and misses the subjective side of the dialectic. He argues that the way a person relates the polarities of the eternal and the temporal determines his or her current sphere or stage of existence. I suggest that the spheres of existence are related to each other in the very same way that the elements of existence are related to each other (and to that relation itself): dialectically. Taylor's interpretation of Kierkegaard's objective in *SUD* to establish a harmonious and actual equilibrium minimizes the significance of the dialectic in Kierkegaard's view of existence. I suggest the inclusion of both the quantitative and the qualitative dialectics. I will develop this suggestion in greater detail below.

Another Kierkegaard scholar, George Connell, interprets Kierkegaard's spheres in terms of unity and oneness. He believes that Kierkegaard's "stages of existence" are expressions of distinct types of selves. In this regard his interpretation fits in Taylor's categorization of Kierkegaard scholarship discussed above. In *To Be One Thing*, he argues that "each of the stages, subdivisions of the

---

[352] Taylor, p. 7.

stages, and intermediate positions in the Kierkegaardian 'phenomenology' may be characterized by its way of accepting or rejecting the imperative of self-unification."[353] Connell believes these stages or selves are distinguished from each other by their relationship to oneness. Furthermore, he argues that Kierkegaard understands human selfhood as that which is made by each individual human's efforts "to be one thing." The goal of human existence then is to be a unity, one thing. To attain this goal, a human must "will one thing." In so doing she makes her will into an essential unity, by conforming it to the will of that which is One, or God. Connell believes, and rightly I think, that Kierkegaard understands the dynamic of will and unity to be as follows: when a person wills an object, her will becomes conformed to the form of this object. Thus, Connell sees that Kierkegaard believes that a person can be a unity at her essence by willing an object that is essentially a unity itself, one thing.

Let's examine the first sphere as an example of how unity is the crux of Connell's interpretation of Kierkegaard's spheres of existence. For Connell, the aesthetic sphere is best understood in terms of how an aesthete responds to this call. Connell sees the aesthete as the type of "self" that is led away from the unity of selfhood by his immediate reaction to whatever is most readily available or captivating at the time. In the aesthetic sphere the person's self is disunified. He is related to the divine imperative to be a unified self in an aesthetic way, as in an immediate, non-reflective, momentary existence. Further, the aesthetic self is not one thing because the object of its will is many different things. (Or one might say it has many different objects of its wills.) Connell considers the existential problem of the aesthete to be that he has a "fundamentally divided personality."[354] Connell highlights the juxtaposition of the aesthetic sphere with what he calls the perfect unity of the religious sphere and argues that it is an

---

[353] George Connell, *To Be One Thing* (Macan GA: Mercer, 1985), p. 37.
[354] Connell, p. 95.

expression of Kierkegaard's own intimate struggle between the temptations of the aesthetic sphere and the religious sphere. He believes that Kierkegaard personally felt the tension between the powerful draw of the aesthetic sphere on the one hand, and the oneness of the unity of self, found in the religious sphere, on the other. These two opposite energies provide the tension that drives this dialectic. The dialectic then, is viewed as a negative necessity.

Connell's view is problematic for several reasons. First, his hermeneutical approach focuses exclusively on the unity of a person's essence or soul. While Kierkegaard is concerned with the "willing one thing" of *Purity of Heart*, he does not argue that the polar elements of existence are brought together in a synthetic unity, nor does he argue that these elements are related to each other by the sheer force of an individual's will. Connell fails to differentiate Kierkegaard's concern in *Sickness Unto Death (SUD)* for "willing to become oneself" from Kierkegaard's concern in *Purity of Heart* for "willing one thing." In Connell's view Kierkegaard argues that the human self must "constitute itself as an essential unity in the face of the disruptive action of the world,"[355] by willing one thing, which is willing the Good. Note the difference between this formula which is from *Purity of Heart*, and the formula from the text on the self, *SUD*, which calls for the self to be "willing to become oneself as transparently grounded on the power that constitutes one before God."[356] Connell has conflated these two formulas. "Willing the good, or one thing" is not the same as "willing to **be**, or to **become**." He has also confused Kierkegaard's understanding of actuality and possibility: he has replaced Kierkegaard's becoming with Connell's being, identifying willing with a static being. This is a misunderstanding not only of Kierkegaard's primary critique of Metaphysics and Danish Lutheran practice, but also of his purpose in *Purity of Heart*.

---

[355] Connell, p. xiv-v.

[356] Kierkegaard, *The Sickness Unto Death*. (Princeton, New Jersey: Princeton University Press, 1970). p.162.

In *Purity of Heart*, Kierkegaard names willing one thing as that which opposes the double-mindedness of sin and that which is the essence of being pure of heart. Connell argues that the opposite of "double-mindedness" is willing to be one thing. This is incorrect. Kierkegaard describes double-mindedness, not as the state of having more than one part within oneself, but as doing the good for the wrong reasons. It is deceiving oneself into believing that one is doing the good for the sake of the good, when actually, one is doing the good out of fear of punishment or for the reward, or to feel good about oneself. Kierkegaard's discussion of barriers to purity of heart is best understood when taken in the context of searching one's soul for the barriers that inhibit us from knowing our selves as individuals before God. He writes it for the expressed purpose of preparing a Christian for the sacrament of confession. The point is not to will one thing; the point is to be pure of heart, which means to know oneself, wholly as an individual before God. Purity of heart is a religious matter, and the "ethics" discussed in the book are ways to help an individual examine and purify his heart, so that he can become conscious of himself before God. Kierkegaard 's primary concern here is not to will to be one thing.

This confused identification leads Connell to miss the processive character in Kierkegaard's view of authentic selfhood. Kierkegaard emphasizes **becoming** oneself, not **being** one thing, or even being oneself. This issue is part of Kierkegaard's argument with Hegel, which focuses on the mode of truth and being. He reads Hegel as building a vast, interconnected and perfect (unchanging) System. Kierkegaard's response is as follows:

> Everything said in Hegel's philosophy about process and becoming is illusory. This is why the System lacks an Ethic, and is the reason why it has no answer for the living when the question of becoming is raised in earnest, in the interest of action. In spite of all that Hegel says about process, he does not understand history form the point of view of becoming.... It is therefore impossible for a Hegelian to understand himself by means of his philosophy, for his philosophy

224

helps him to understand only that which is past and finished. [357]

Kierkegaard believes that human reality can only be comprehended in the middle of existing, not by reflecting about the fixed principles of the past of human culture while sitting still in the proverbial armchair. He argues that human existence looks quite different from the point of view of the existing individual than it does from the objective eyes of reason and philosophy. He believes that human reality is in the mode of "becoming" not in the fixed mode of "being," as he writes of "willing to **become** oneself before God,"[358] and "[A] self, every instant it exists, is in process of becoming."[359]

Kierkegaard thinks that Hegelian metaphysics and the Danish Church share the same misguided assumptions that reality is fixed. He tells a story about the Danish Christians to illustrate this similarity. (Of confusion about the essence of human existence as becoming): The Tame Geese. Kierkegaard says that the unwillingness of the geese to fly when all they do is talk about "the lofty destiny" of flight that the Creator had given the geese is like the hypocrisy of Christendom.[360] They proclaim that humanity is not yet complete as each individual Christian will come to the stature of Christ, but they do not practice this task of becoming a Christian. Instead, Danish Christendom sees that one is automatically a Christian via a Danish birth. This "monstrous illusion" ignores the truth that one becomes a Christian: it is a **task**, and the most difficult task of all. Furthermore, it is the only task worth pursuing in this human existence.

Connell also misunderstands another one of Kierkegaard's primary philosophical and theological points, that truth is subjectivity. He says that Kierkegaard's claim that "Truth is Subjectivity" is an expression of Kierkegaard's

---

[357] Kierkegaard, *CUP*, p.272, note.
[358] Kierkegaard, *SUD*, p. 163.
[359] Kierkegaard, *SUD*, p.163.
[360] Bretall, *Kierkegaard Anthology*, (New York: The Modern Library, 1970). p.433

"conviction that the self must constitute itself as an essential unity."[361] Connell sees this formula as meaning that a person must be one thing in order to be a self. But Kierkegaard's view of the subjectivity of the religious sphere (which is a prerequisite of becoming a Christian) is not a synthetic unity or "one thing." It is not abstract or fixed. It is willing to become who one is, in all the ambiguity of existence. It is relating polar elements in tension to each other. It is acknowledging both one's guilt as a sinner in despair and one's unique worth as one for whom God died. The subjectivity of the religious sphere is not a systematic unity. Religious existence is characterized by multivalency and movement, in which one holds together the contradictions of existence. It is the constant forth and back motion of the dialectic. Connell's approach to the spheres misses these significant aspects of Kierkegaard's theological anthropology.

THE DIALECTICAL RELATING OF THE SPHERES

The approach I offer here brings together several of these approaches with a fundamental difference: The spheres of existence are not only a developmental processes, but rather, the spheres are inter-related dialectically, in the here and now, within the existing individual. My constructive view of Kierkegaard's spheres of existence differs from Taylor's view primarily in my emphasis on the dialectical form of the spheres, in contrast to Taylor's developmental stages. My interpretation also differs significantly from Connell's contention that the goal of Kierkegaard's religious sphere is to be one thing. Contrarily, I argue that the religious sphere is multivalent, dynamic and relational.

First, let's examine Kierkegaard's dialectic. I focus on his discussion in *SUD* on the relationship of the three pairs of existential elements that make up the self. I also touch on his development of the idea of the dialectic in *CUP*. Then I will apply the dialectic to interpreting the spheres of existence.

---

[361] Connell, p. 9.

Kierkegaard's use of the term dialectic is intricate. The term dialectic is a general philosophical term synonymous with dialogue and debate within the norms of logic, as well as being used in particular ways by Socrates and Hegel. Socrates' dialectical method of asking questions was to elicit the recognition by the dialogue partner that he doesn't really know anything. It is a negative task. Plato employs a polar dialectic that is a "two-fold process involving synthesis. . . and division."[362] In this movement of thought, ideas are placed together according to their similarities, while at the same time, divided from each other according to their differences. Hegel's dialectic is more one-sided in that it is always synthesizing. For Hegel, the dialectic is the progressive movement of ideas throughout history toward greater and greater conscious awareness of the great idea of the Spirit. Hegel's dialectic has been described as the march of the thesis which meets its opposite, the antithesis, and the two are unified in the synthesis, which then becomes the next thesis to start the process again. While these thinkers influence Kierkegaard's use of the term dialectic, he also develops the term uniquely in his own thought. Most distinctly, he ascribes dialectical meaning to existence, not exclusively to ideas.

The dialectic in Kierkegaard's authorship is complex, forming both the content of his thought, such as the relationship of the existential elements, and also the form of his polemical method, such as the mode of his pseudonymous authorship. His authors are related to each other by name and by argument. He creates a web of interrelated authors/characters who dialogue among themselves. Further his method is dialectical in that he desires to engage his reader in a conversation.

His existential use of the concept dialectic is expressed most explicitly in both *Sickness Unto Death* and *Concluding Unscientific Postscript*. In *SUD* Kierkegaard asserts that the human self is constituted by three pairs of irreconcilable elements: the finite and the infinite; the temporal and the eternal;

---

[362] Arthur Krentz, "Kierkegaard's Dialectical image of human Existence in the *CUP* to the *PF*." In Philosophy Today, Summer, 1997. p. 279.

and freedom and necessity. In the midst of this tension, these elements must relate to each other in a conscious and balanced way. The individual can not fall too much into the finite element, or the infinite element is stifled; neither can she float too much into the infinite element, for then the finite element suffers. A genuine human self is a concrete balance of these two opposite factors. A person that leans too much toward either the infinite or the finite is "disrelated"; her balance is off and the relation of these two factors cannot relate itself to itself properly. Despair ensues and she is not a self, as he writes:

> Man is spirit. But what is spirit? Spirit is the self. But what is the self? The self is a relation which relates itself to its own self, or it is that in the relation [which accounts for it] that the relation relates itself to its own self; the self is not the relation but [consists in the fact] that the relation relates itself to its own self. Man is a synthesis of the infinite and the finite, of the temporal and the eternal, of freedom and necessity, in short it is a synthesis. A synthesis is a relation between two factors. So regarded man is not yet a self. 363

In this passage, Kierkegaard argues that the ontological reality of the self consists in the internal reflexive relating of these conflicting elements. The self is the reflexive relating of the relation of these disparate elements to itself. The dialectic is the form of the relationship of these contradictory elements of existence as they are brought into dialogue with each other. This relation of the disparate parts then, relates to itself in a dynamic and dialectical way. This reflexive relating constitutes an individual. Kierkegaard writes, that it is a "dialectical fact that the self is a synthesis [of two factors], one of which is constantly the opposite of the other."364 Thus the individual is constituted by the dialectic relationality of the binary nature of elemental realities: finitude and infinity, etc. One's genuine inner life is essentially the relating of the relation of

---

363 Kierkegaard, *SUD*, p. 146.
364 Kierkegaard, *SUD*, p. 163.

the finite and the infinite to itself-- the inner element and the transcendent element.

But Kierkegaard is not done, for this self is such that this synthesis is "constituted by another."[365] Becoming of oneself is willing to become oneself in relation to one's disparate parts, as this relation relates to itself dynamically, **and** in relation to God and God's power. Thus, "the self is the conscious synthesis of infinitude and finitude which relates itself to itself, whose task is to become itself, a task which can be performed only by means of a relationship to God. But to become oneself is to become concrete. But to become concrete means neither to become finite nor infinite, for that which is to become concrete is a synthesis." [366]

This theme is continued in *CUP*, where Climacus says that existence is a mixture: "a synthesis of the finite and the infinite, and the existing individual is both infinite and finite."[367] In *CUP*, he emphasizes the impossibility of the task of human existence. He writes of the ideal task: "the simultaneous maintenance of an absolute relationship to the absolute, and a relative relationship to the relative."[368] The key is the relation that must "relate itself to itself"[369] dialectically. Climacus distinguish two different types of a dialectical method: quantitative, which is objective, and qualitative, which is subjective. Arthur Krentz explains that the subjective dialectic differs from the objective dialectic in that it "emphasizes not the nature of what is known (as does the quantitative dialectic) but, rather, how the 'knower' is related to that which he seeks to know. The shift is from the content of an idea to how one lives the ideas in one's life."[370] In *CUP*, Climacus develops subjectivity as the ideal form of existence. And this form of subjectivity is dialectical: processive and relational.

---

[365] Kierkegaard, *SUD*, p. 146.

[366] Kierkegaard, *SUD*, p. 162.

[367] Kierkegaard, *CUP*, p. 350.

[368] Kierkegaard, *CUP*, p. 386.

[369] Kierkegaard, *SUD*, p. 146.

[370] Krentz, p. 280.

Further, the relationship of objectivity and subjectivity is also dialectical. Kierkegaard believes that self-consciousness and subjectivity occurs through a dialectic, through the internal dialectic of spirit and matter. Kierkegaard's dialectic of faith is that of becoming subjective, of becoming oneself before God. Kierkegaard's dialectic of faith views the spirit in the process of becoming subjective/ becoming itself through objectifying itself and then returning to subjectivity. The movement from one pole to the other provides the depth of dimension and complexity that is appropriate to the human self. Louis Dupre' relates the religious sphere and subjectivity. I am intrigued with Dupre's view of the "trichotomic"[371] dialectic and movement from subjectivity to objectivity, as he elucidates,

> Our relationship with God is necessarily dialectical. The spirit cannot grasp its own essence (subjectivity) without continually objectifying itself; but since the resulting objectivity is not proper to the essence of spirit, spirit must always leave it again to turn back to itself. Objectivity, then, is a necessary pole for the ascent of the spirit. Spirit uses objectivity as the rungs of a ladder to which one clings and from which one loosens one's grasp to pull oneself up.[372]

Kierkegaard's process for becoming subjective, which is the task of becoming authentically oneself, is a dialectic movement between the two poles of subjectivity and objectivity. Dupre's view of this dialectical movement of back and forth is intriguing, but I am wary of his ladder metaphor, since it suggests that one climbs up the ladder, leaving the lower rungs behind and reaching a goal at the top. Kierkegaard's dialectic is a back and forth movement like climbing, but it is more like dancing the walk of life because one must never leave behind one's right foot, even when one is leaning on one's left foot. Further, one must continually be moving and progressing. There isn't a top rung that signifies the

---

[371] Dupre', p. 123.
[372] Dupre', p.124.

completion of the task of becoming subjective. Becoming subjective is a continuous process, a dialectical dance. This dialectic of subjectivity is parallel to the dialectical movement of the existential elements.

Let's apply this relational dialectic to the spheres of existence. I suggest that this dialectic be used to describe the relationship of the spheres to each other both externally, or quantitatively, and subjectively, qualitatively. Kierkegaard's view of the spheres of existence is dialectical in two ways. First, the individual moves progressively from the aesthetic to the ethical and then to the religious in a dialectical manner. And secondly, within the religious sphere itself, the aesthetic and the ethical are moving between each other in dialectical relationship.

As I explained earlier, I prefer the term, "spheres" to Taylor's term "stages." Let me expand on this here. While Kierkegaard's view of the spheres of existence is progressive, Taylor's emphasis on "developmental stages" is misleading. It suggests that they are phases that one passes through and then leaves behind. Further, it omits the dialectical relationship between the spheres. Spheres is a better term because it takes the processive and relational natures of the dialectic into account. Freedom of selfhood is so important to Kierkegaard that he refuses to establish a closed linear developmental system. One does not "progress" linearly from the aesthetic sphere, through the ethical sphere, and into the religious sphere, as if it were a fixed time line. Rather, the spheres reflect a spiraling complex movement to greater and greater complexity, each new sphere including the last one, transforming it, and bringing it into the dialectic. The spheres are concentric and overlap with each other to form the dimensions of human existence. They are progressively inclusive of each other and are related to each other.

It might seem that the ethical is in counter-distinction to the aesthetic sphere, given the contradictory characteristics of immediacy and mediation, and the particular and the universal. As Steven L. Ross says, "It is often said that *Either/Or* confronts the reader with two wholly self-contained and mutually exclusive world views."[373]   However, as Judge William's argument for the "Aesthetic Validity of Marriage" and his discussion of "The Balance Between the Aesthetic and the Ethical in the Development of the Personality" indicate, the ethical does not replace the aesthetic, nor does it annihilate the difference. Rather, the ethical takes the aesthetic into itself, thereby including the aesthetic within the ethical. The ethical can even be said to beat the aesthetic at its own game. Marriage, the Judge argues, is more aesthetically pleasing than the immediate happiness of Don Juan or the teasing of the seducer. The Judge says,

> The same aesthetic character which inheres in the first love must, therefore, also inhere in marriage, since the first love is contained in marriage . . .. Marriage has all this too; it is sensual and yet spiritual, but it is more; [374]

Thus, the ethical sphere includes both the ethical sphere itself and aspects of the aesthetic sphere as well. But the aesthetic sphere even as taken up into the ethical sphere is not destroyed by its inclusion in the ethical or the religious.

Also in this vein, I disagree with Dupre's claim discussed earlier, that the aesthetic sphere carries within itself the seed of its own destruction. This claim implies that the aesthetic is destroyed, and that the aesthetic sphere is a stage that must be transcended, and in fact, is transcended almost inherently in its own fulfillment of itself. It is not destroyed, but rather preserved in the ethical sphere. This point is a significant aspect of Kierkegaard's theology of redemption -- nothing of the human person is absolutely lost, but rather is transcended and transfigured, and included in the progressive movement toward becoming a Christian. Dupre's way of understanding the aesthetic sphere here, and thus also all the spheres together, misses the depth of the dialectic that Dupre' so insightfully brings out in his discussion of the dialectic of faith.

Like the inclusion of the aesthetic into the ethical, the religious sphere

---

[373] Kierkegaard, *Either/Or*, Abridged Edition, (San Francisco: Harper & Row, 1986). p. viii.
[374] Kierkegaard, *Either/Or*, Abridged, p. 152.

includes the religious sphere itself, the ethical sphere, and the aesthetic sphere. The movement from the ethical to the religious does not annihilate the ethical, but takes the ethical into itself, preserving it intact and adding more. For instance, the knight of faith makes a double movement -- first he makes the movements of ethics, the movements of infinity, and then he makes the movements of faith. The form of the religious sphere is the dialectical relating of all the spheres of existence. Thus the religious sphere includes all the spheres. A religious self brings all the spheres together in the dialectic movement of her existence like a spiral of transgressions and regressions -- fragmentary ambiguity mixed with fragmentary harmony.

In the highest human existence the self is related to itself dialectically. For instance, in the first part of *SUD*, a self is present only when the elements of existence are related dialectically. In the second part, faith, the opposite of despair, is present only as one realizes that one is both guilty as a sinner and forgiven and loved at the same time, each state dialectically relating to each other. In becoming subjective, one must also relate to oneself dialectically as described above. Finally, then, the religious sphere is also a dialectic in which the spheres relate to each other in the walk of existence. The religious self includes the awareness of her faults and finiteness. The subjectivity of the religious sphere is the dialectical interrelationship of the spheres of existence.

The process of becoming subjective and becoming a Christian is becoming what I call *multivalent integration*. The self is the coming together of factors that are in conflict and in opposition to each other. This internal conflict is what causes anxiety/dread of existence. Trying to placate this dread without uncovering the root creates the sickness unto death in its many forms of despair. Despair is not in the number of the parts a self has, nor in its malevolency. Rather despair is the insistence on singularity and homogeneity of substance. The unity of the self that Kierkegaard desires is not the homogenous one thing of Connell's contention. Rather, it is more precisely articulated as a related connection among the contrary aspects of the becoming human self: a multivalent integration.

In conclusion, I have discussed several ways of understanding Kierkegaard's spheres of existence and offered critiques of three major interpretations. My first critique centered on Taylor's excellent and comprehensive study of Kierkegaard's pseudonymous authorship. I object to his preference for the term stages and his emphasis on the developmental structure of the "stages" of existence. I maintain that the term spheres is a more apt choice because it calls attention to both the dialectical form of the spheres internally and externally, as well as the non-linear progression and movement from one sphere to the next. My primary critique of Connell is his exclusive use of the lens of unity through which he views the spheres. He is blinded to the religious sphere's harmonizing of multivalency and to the triune movement of the dialectic. I also touched on Dupre's insightful discussion of the dialectic of faith. I suggest that his primary limitation is that he misses the intricate inclusive relationship of the spheres of each other. The spheres progress inclusively, taking the previous one into the present one. I further suggested that Kierkegaard's dialectical structure, so clearly elucidated in *Sickness Unto Death* and in the *Postscript*, provides the key insight to interpreting the relationship of the spheres of existence to each other. The polar elements of existence are oppositional, and yet in the faith of the religious sphere they are brought together and held in balance. This dialectical tension is also the glue for understanding how the spheres are related to each other. Each sphere contains the previous sphere and its contents, going beyond it while not annulling it. This dialectical structure of back and forth motion of the spheres is the form of the religious sphere and the structure of Christian existence. This inter-relationality governs the dialectical movement between and within the spheres of existence internal to the individual as she moves toward becoming oneself before God. Religiousness B, the ultimate sphere, brings together all the spheres in an integrated whole. Integrated in that these conflicting characteristics

234

are connected all in one whole self. This multivalent integration of the self is only possible by "relating itself to its own self and by willing to be itself, the self is grounded transparently in the Power which constituted it." [375] In other words, how does one know oneself? Kierkegaard answers, By living as a Christian: in all the tension and ambiguity of life itself and still loving oneself and others, and knowing that one is loved by God.

---

[375] Kierkegaard, *SUD*, p.262.

"NO SUPERFLUOUS ADORNMENT:" TROELTSCH AND WEBER ON RELIGION AND THE ETHIC OF RESPONSIBILITY

Bradley E. Starr

One year before his death in 1923, Ernst Troeltsch produced an essay in response to a publisher's request for a description of his philosophical "system," a request calculated to allow the author an opportunity to set the record straight with respect to misunderstandings and errors on the part of his interpreters. This opportunity, however, presented difficulties for Troeltsch. "I have no system," he wrote in his opening paragraph, "and in that I am different from most other German philosophers." He continued:

> Of course I keep one [i.e., a system] in the back of my mind, as a basic presupposition, but only to correct it constantly as a result of specific research. I cannot display the system in such an unfinished condition. I can only explain the sequence of my books—which in the case of a systematically oriented person is in itself a kind of system.[376]

Accordingly, Troeltsch entitled his essay "My Books," indicating where he wanted to direct his readers' attention. Nevertheless, students of Troeltsch have long sought to bring to light that elusive system in the back of Troeltsch's mind. In the end, however, most have generally concurred with Troeltsch himself as to its unfinished and imprecise condition. So rather than examining Troeltsch's "system," this brief essay will take its start from Troeltsch's self-description as "a systematically oriented person." Working from the premise that the key to Troeltsch's "systematic orientation" is located in his understanding of the ethical dilemmas that he believed faced contemporary religious individuals and

---

[376] Ernst Troeltsch, "My Books," in Religion in History (Minneapolis: Augsburg Fortress, 1991), 365. I wish to express my gratitude to the editors for this opportunity to participate in honoring Jack Verheyden on the occasion of his retirement. It would be difficult for me to overestimate how much I owe him for his intellectual influence, wise counsel, and professional example.

institutions, my purpose will be to draw attention to the ethical framework that provided the central orienting feature of his metaphysical perspective.

I propose to bring this theme into sharper focus by juxtaposing Troeltsch's views with those of his friend and colleague Max Weber on the question of the relationship between religion and what Weber called "the ethic of responsibility" (Verantwortungsethik). Troeltsch's article, "Die Revolution der Wissenschaft," specifies the aspect of the intellectual relationship between Weber and Troeltsch that I want to highlight here. Written in 1921, the year following Weber's death, the piece was Troeltsch's contribution to the controversy that followed the presentation and publication in 1919 of Weber's disturbing lecture, "Science as a Vocation."[377] In his article, Troeltsch distinguished between three issues: (1) the nature of science; (2) philosophical attempts to "grasp the whole;" and (3) "the practical stance toward life in both the private and public spheres." It is in the middle area—attempts to grasp the whole—that Troeltsch located his departure from Weber, alleging that Weber's metaphysical skepticism is unwarranted. Still, Troeltsch cautioned, attempts to grasp the whole should not proceed undisciplined by the Weberian conception of science and practical life, both of which Troeltsch strongly affirmed. The practical stance of the serious person, Troeltsch wrote,

> Must rest upon a faith or a worldview, but it cannot with contempt and renunciation simply push aside the practical conditions of life. Instead, one's practical stance must enter into these conditions and situate itself in that which inevitably belongs to the economical, social, and political forms of the life of an age. Christians of all times must always experience this fact anew.[378]

What will concern me in this brief essay is Troeltsch's attempt to construct a theological perspective that allows for the agreement he claims with Weber in the area of ethics. My analysis will begin with a summation of the key features of

---

[377] Max Weber, "Science as a Vocation," in Max Weber, From Max Weber: Essays in Sociology, ed. and tran., H.H. Gerth and C. Wright Mills (Oxford: Oxford University Press, 1946), 129-156.

[378] Ernst Troeltsch, "Die Revolution in der Wissenschaft," in Gesammelte Schriften, 4 vols., Aufsätze Zur Geistesgeschichte und Religionssoziologie, ed. Hans Baron (Aalen: Scientia Verlag, 1981) 4: 672-73. This and all following translations from cited German texts are mine.

Weber's distinction between the ethic of conviction and the ethic of responsibility. This section will culminate in a summary sketch of his understanding of the close connection between religion and the ethic of conviction—what Weber labeled "die Gesinnungsreligiosität." In the second section I will discuss Troeltsch's perspective on the basic problems of religion and ethics, showing how Troeltsch's analysis of the religious apriori allowed him to produce a conception of religion that lends itself to the ethic of responsibility. Finally, I will suggest that Troeltsch's way of understanding religion and Christianity in both personal and institutional terms was oriented so as to render the ethic of responsibility a specifically Christian obligation.

PART 1: Weber on The Two Ethics and Religion

Not long before his death in 1920, Max Weber, summarizing his ethical perspective in a controversial lecture entitled "Politics as a Vocation," gave powerful expression to his concern over the fate of moral selfhood—Persönlichkeit—under the conditions of modernity.[379] In Weber's ethical framework, heavily influenced by neo-Kantian philosophy, one's basic task as an individual is to shape oneself into an autonomous moral personality through loyal commitment to values within the context of critical awareness of the social and historical situated-ness of one's life and conduct. Through committed moral engagement, one gives meaning, consistency, and ethical worth to one's life.

Over the course of his earlier sociological investigations, however, Weber had painstakingly revealed the soul-fragmenting conflicts that have attended ethical decision-making wherever the notion of the moral unification of the self and of the culture has taken hold within a given social and historical context. In his analyses, he had shown how the very notions of personal consistency and

---

[379] Max Weber, "Politics as a Vocation," in Gerth and Mills, 77-128. I have given a much fuller interpretation of Weber's ethical perspective in "The Structure of Max Weber's Ethic of Responsibility," Journal of Religious Ethics 27.3 (Fall, 1999): 407-434.

rationality in the service of moral ends are fractured into contradictory demands for morally principled action and instrumental effectiveness. These conflicts duplicate themselves on the institutional level where considerations of principle and feasibility—in Weber's terms, substantive and formal rationality—confront each other interminably and inevitably. Above all, Weber focused on the conflicts between value claims themselves and the competing obligations that parcel-out the souls of those attempting to live rationally consistent lives in devotion to values that cannot be united without contradiction or compromise. To be an ethically rational person, in Weberian terms, means to live consistently in accordance with principles of action and value. The problem, however, is that what is rational is relative to the individual values and forms of action that enter into the various individual and institutional spheres of life. Consistency in one area leads inevitably to violations of the obligations of another. What shape, Weber asked, could moral selfhood take in such a world?

Concluding his lecture, Weber presented his listeners with a choice between what he characterized as two mutually exclusive moral worldviews. On the one hand one can live from an "ethic of conviction" (Gesinnungsethik), which presents one with a world conceived as an orderly cosmos of values, imposing upon human beings the duty to structure their personal and institutional lives so as to coincide with "the order of things." The adherent to the ethic of conviction holds the view that beyond the competing rationalities of action, regardless of how anarchic they may appear, there is a higher rationality that coordinates moral demands and ultimate consequences, and provides a hierarchy according to which the spheres of value are to be ordered. Historically, versions of this supra-rationality have appeared in religious or philosophical movements, but they have also emerged in contemporary forms of secular Wissenschaft.

Weber labeled the other type of ethic the "ethic of responsibility" (Verantwortungsethik). For the adherent to this ethic there is no higher rationality beyond the conflicting rationalities that confront the ethically serious person. One becomes a moral personality not by surrender to a higher rationality, but by assuming responsibility for the axiological and teleological tensions that attend moral decision-making. One accepts that in the actual world, value claims conflict with each other. Cultural and personal unity are possible only on the basis of responsible human compromises between these ethical commitments. One holds oneself responsible for the value hierarchy that one constructs and for the resulting costs to subordinated claims and interests. In the face of such decisions, there is no relief to be gained from religion or science, although science can provide clarity as to the costs of one's decisions.

The difficulties of the ethic of responsibility for a universal monotheistic salvation religion such as Christianity seemed obvious to Weber, who had often shown that such religions inevitably produce an ethic of conviction, demanding that adherents lead a religiously consistent life within a universe imbued with orderly divine purpose. According to Weber, the adherent to a religious ethic of conviction, living in an intellectually closed universe, enjoys a certain "closure of the mind" with respect to the contradictions of the world.[380] Given this description, one might be tempted to assume that a universal religious outlook would be attractive to people precisely because of the sense of unity it offers within a potentially anarchic arena of values. Religion, in other words, relieves the tensions of value pluralism. Weber's point, however, was that universal religions create, or at least reveal, the problem even as they offer relief from it. Historically, Weber argued, religious developments have provided the impetus for people to turn away from both the pursuit of their own immediate material interests as well as from unreflective tradition, and toward the pursuit of spiritual values that demand the discipline of a morally consistent life. For Weber, however, when in general you demand moral consistency in yourself, others, and the world, your moral universe and the moral value of your soul are threatened because values inevitably conflict with each other in fundamentally irreconcilable

---

[380] Max Weber, Economy and Society, 2 vols., eds., Guenther Roth and Clauss Wittich (Berkeley: University of California, 1978) 1: 548.

ways. Thus when people demand religious consistency of themselves, they would seem to be threatened by the opposite of what religions promise: the loss of their souls on the rocks of competing obligations. Nevertheless, according to Weber, heretofore the religious demand for consistency in the face of the ethical inconsistency of the world has generally led people not to the rejection of religion, but to what Weber calls "religious rejections of the world."[381] For Weber, one of the most intriguing ironies in human history is that such rejections have had major world-forming significance, frequently providing the cultural basis for the intellectual rationalization of the world as well as epoch-making and persistently disciplined attitudes toward work, love, family, art, and power.

Though deeply respectful of those devoted to an uncompromising religious ethic of conviction, Weber took a dim view of the appropriateness of this practical stance for the institutional life of the present. Even so, he had long acknowledged what he referred to as the deeply rooted "metaphysical needs of the human mind," the "inner compulsion to understand the world as a meaningful cosmos and to take a position toward it."[382] Here, the issue becomes most acute. At the heart of religion is the demand for unity and meaning. Yet, Weber argued, no religion that demands absolutely consistent religious devotion can expand or endure in the world. It must compromise, and usually does so through the construction of a cosmological perspective that sets competing values into some kind of a tolerable order, typically hierarchicalizing them within a scheme of salvation. Sites of stubborn inconsistency provide openings for salvation, judgment, forgiveness, mercy, asceticism. All such schemes, however, inevitably represent systems of compromise in the midst of irreconcilable contradiction. Ultimately and inevitably, all value claims—including those central to religion—must accept the constraints of other competing demands. Otherwise, cultural life as a whole cannot endure. Acknowledgement of this situation leaves universal

---

[381] Max Weber, "Religious Rejections of the World and Their Directions," in Gerth and Mills, 323-359.

[382] Economy and Society, 1: 499.

monotheistic religions and their devotees in a peculiarly tense situation. "I believe," he wrote, "that unsettled conflict, and therefore the necessity for constant compromises, dominates the sphere of values. No one knows how compromises should be made, unless a 'revealed' religion will forcibly decide."[383] Indeed, Weber warned,

> Today the routines of everyday life challenge religion. Many old gods ascend from their graves; they are disenchanted and hence take the form of impersonal forces. They strive to gain power over our lives and again resume their struggle with one another.... Our civilization destines us to realize more clearly these struggles again, after our eyes have been blinded for a thousand years— blinded by the allegedly or presumably exclusive orientation towards the grandiose moral fervor of Christian ethics.[384]

Part 2- Troeltsch on Religion as a Valid and Autonomous Sphere of Value

Our question now is: How was Troeltsch able to agree with Weber on the practical and scientific aspects of his outlook and yet not proceed to the same skeptical perspective regarding "attempts to grasp the whole?" To answer this question, I will begin with Troeltsch's philosophy of religion, reveal the ethical dimension of his perspective, and, in the concluding section of the essay, consider the theological implications that Troeltsch draws from these considerations.

From the early days of his mature intellectual activity, indeed most thoroughly in his 1902 essay "Grundprobleme der Ethik," ("Basic Problems of Ethics") published long before Weber summarized his own perspective in "Politics as a Vocation," Troeltsch had analyzed and espoused what Weber later named the ethic of responsibility.[385] In his view, however, the "divided ethical consciousness" of contemporaries such as Weber is paralleled in the modern

---

[383] Max Weber, Letter of 2 April 1913 to Robert Wilbrandt, Weber papers. Quoted in Wolfgang Mommsen, Max Weber and German Politics, tran. Michael J. Steinberg (Chicago: University of Chicago, 1984), 44.

[384] "Science as a Vocation," 149.

[385] Ernst Troeltsch, "Grundprobleme der Ethik," in Vol. 2, Gesammelte Schriften, 4 vols., Zur Religiösen Lage, Religionsphilosophie und Ethik (Aalen: Scientia Verlag, 1981) 2: 552-672.

religious consciousness. This split is one of Troeltsch's primary concerns in his important notion of the religious apriori.

Concern over the nature and validity of values in general, and over the status of religion as a sphere of value in particular, provided an agenda for serious debate within the "Baden" school of neo-Kantians that formed the backdrop for Troeltsch's notion of the religious apriori. On one side of the question stood Troeltsch's older colleague at Heidelberg, Wilhelm Windelband, who argued that while the validity of religion is indisputably grounded in the apriori structure of the valuing consciousness, nevertheless, religion presupposed no distinctly autonomous sphere of value. The true, the beautiful, and the good are the only three "universal values" that constitute the epistemologically apriori basis of human consciousness. Hence, when we speak of the religious, or of the "holy" ("das Heilige"), we are not speaking of phenomena related to a fourth value, but rather of "the character of universal validity of these [three] values," of the relationship of "all these values together... to a supersensuous reality," and of the "metaphysical anchorage" presupposed in human value judgments.[386] Windelband's concern was that religion, if grounded in a fourth apriori sphere of value, would need to presuppose a further element as the ground of its unity with other values. In that case, religion would lose its character as the unifying dimension of the life of the human spirit.

One of our most certain convictions, Windelband argued, is the absolute validity of the three basic values. Our ability to make even distorted and imperfect value judgments depends upon these absolutely valid values. Accordingly, Windelband postulated the reality of a transcending "normative consciousness" of the absolute validity of values. "Conscience," he theorized, "presupposes the metaphysical reality of the normative consciousness (Normalbewusstsein), which of course is not to be identified with what we call empirical reality. It is, as soon as we consider the validity of absolute values, the most certain of our experiences,

---

[386] Wilhelm Windelband, An Introduction to Philosophy, tran. Joseph McCabe (London: Unwin, 1923), 324-26.

and precisely in this sense it is the normative consciousness of the holy." Indeed, he continued, "The holy is therefore the normative consciousness of the true, the good, and the beautiful, experienced as a transcendent reality."[387] Our experience of this transcendent absoluteness initially shatters and humbles us, revealing our imperfection, impotence, and dependence. The transformation of these norms into personal motives within our own souls is experienced as nothing less than the unmerited gift of a new and better self that strives to subordinate and unite all of life under the normative consciousness of that which ought to be. To this end, one may seek to activate the religious dimension that permeates all aspects of cultural life; or, for the sake of unimpeded fellowship with the divine, one may withdraw entirely from the distractions and corruption of cultural life. For Windelband, this dual impulse toward world-affirmation and world-rejection is ineradicably rooted in the apriori validity of the holy.

On the other side of the neo-Kantian debate about religion stood Windelband's student, Heinrich Rickert. Not content with general distinctions between the three value spheres, Rickert sought to derive from the data of consciousness the formal apriori "open system of values" presupposed in human thought and practice, and he concluded that in fact religion constituted not only a valid, but an autonomous component of consciousness.[388] Ingeniously manipulating intricately described logical polarities—infinite or eternal, present or future orientation, personal or impersonal, immanent or transcendent, active or contemplative, particular or universal—Rickert divided the apriori system of values into two basic classifications, and argued that religion forms the apex of both. On one side he scaled those values by which one defines and relates to objects in impersonal terms (science and art), culminating in the monistic sort of religion that centers on the impersonal contemplation of the whole and inclusion

---

[387] Wilhelm Windelband, "Das Heilig," in Präludien, 2 vols. (Tübingen: Mohr, 1907) 2: 304-305.
[388] See Heinrich Rickert, "Vom System der Werte," Logos 4 (1913): 295-327.

of the many in the One. On the other side are those values by which one defines and relates to objects as persons (institutional ethics and personal morality), culminating in theism, personal surrender to the will of God, and the permeation of the particular by the divine presence. Both kinds of religion participate in the validity and autonomy that religion enjoys, together representing a frequently realized tension within the religious consciousness itself. Moreover, both contain within themselves the tension between world-rejection and world-affirmation.

As a participant in this debate, Troeltsch credited Windelband with recognizing "the originating point [of religion]," affirming Windelband's connection of religion with the relation of values to the supramundane. Nevertheless, although Windelband had shown the validity of religion, he still had not advanced beyond Kant; indeed, what more had Windelband really done than to distribute religious "clinging" beyond the moral sphere to the other two apriori spheres? [389] For Troeltsch, any claim that religion is valid is not complete unless it includes the claim that religion is autonomous. In this respect, Troeltsch found the work of Rickert more to his liking. For Troeltsch religion involves an absolute obligation to surrender all else for the sake of specifically religious ends. In the life of Jesus, for example, this loyalty translated into a relative indifference to all other spheres of life and an exclusive concentration on total love of God and absolute love of other human beings in preparation for the coming reign of God. Hence, Rickert was correct to emphasize both religion's autonomy as well as its validity. On the other hand, with Windelband, Troeltsch saw in the religious apriori more than a merely formal epistemological grounding for religion. Troeltsch claimed that the religious apriori has metaphysical significance, representing a unifying "noumenal" presence within the human personality. For Troeltsch, the obligatory character of values, the human impulse toward unity of life, and the capacity for freedom in the formation of moral personality "appear to

---

[389] Ernst Troeltsch, "Religionsphilosophie," in Wilhelm Windelband, ed. Die Philosophie im Beginn des zwanzigsten Jahrhunderts: Festschrift für Kuno Fischer (Heidelberg: Carl Winters, 1907), 476.

point to an active presence of the absolute spirit in the realm of the finite, to an activity of the universe, as Schleiermacher says, in individual souls."[390]

With that affirmation, however, Troeltsch must now face Windelband's challenge. If religion is to be religious, it must express the transcendent unity and source of all values. If religion is to be an autonomous value, however, the price for this autonomy is that religion now becomes one sphere among others, its obligations only one of many equally valid obligations. For Troeltsch, this dilemma constitutes a "fundamental distinction" in the ethical life of religious persons and communities, involving "the highest, final, and most difficult problem of ethics."[391] Religious obligation is rooted in an "ethic sub specie aeternitatis:" "Take no thought for the morrow," and "Seek ye first the Kingdom of God, and all things needful shall be given to you." But, Troeltsch wrote, "Not only do Jesus' demands exceed human ability, they also exceed the human situation. Taken consistently, they rule out the possibility of the continued existence of the world."[392] In actual human ethical endeavor, we are confronted with an "ethic sub specie temporis." The inner worldly values, each with what Troeltsch referred to as its own "logic," subject the religious purpose to their own conditions. To the moral person, the spheres of politics, economy, family, art, or science, while rooted in the natural pursuit of interests and benefits, generate autonomous moral claims by which they are transmuted and elevated into fields of ethical obligation.

---

[390] Ernst Troeltsch, "On the Religious Apriori," in Religion and History, 41.

[391] Ernst Troeltsch, "The Formal Autonomous Ethic of Conviction and the Objective Teleological Ethic of Value," tran. Donald Miller, in William F. Groff and Donald Miller, eds., The Shaping of Modern Christian Thought (New York: The World Publishing Co., 1968), 235. This is a translation of a section of Troeltsch, "Grundprobleme der Ethik," 616-625.

[392] Ernst Troeltsch, The Christian Faith, ed. Gertrud von Le Fort, tran. Garrett E. Paul (Minneapolis: Augsburg Fortress, 1991), 164. English translation of Ernst Troeltsch, Glaubenslehre nach Vorlesungen aus den Jahren 1911-1912, ed. Gertrud von le Fort (Munich and Leipzig: Duncker and Humblot, 1925).

For Troeltsch, all such values are "born absolute." Each value at its inception as a consciously separate and obligatory sphere of life claims absoluteness over and against other value spheres. Each in turn (religion, science, politics, economics, etc.) sets itself up as an unquestioned norm that relativizes the claims of the others. This absoluteness is "a universal characteristic of the naive way of thinking." Speaking of the development of religion, Troeltsch claimed that religious "naive absoluteness" manifests an inner necessity of consciousness in its "unpolluted" form, in its "innocence."[393] The force of this inner necessity overturns ingrained conventions and customs, shuns reflection on consequences in the fervor of obedient purity of heart, feels no need for apologetics, proofs, or comparisons, and is uninterested in mutual restraint over and against other spheres of life. It emerges from a valid center of human consciousness as "an ineradicable recognition of a higher life of necessary and universal validity."[394] Certainly, then, naive religion is not delusory, not something to be eradicated. And yet purely naive absoluteness must be short lived.

> Thwarted expectations, disillusioning comparisons between what religion says about how things should be understood as over against ways of understanding that originate in other quarters, the clash and contradiction of ideas, and especially the opposition between different kinds of religions; all of this leads to comparisons and adjustments that result in a transformation of the initial naive position.[395]

Once shaken, believers are compelled to buttress their shattered sense of naive absoluteness with what Troeltsch referred to as "artificial absoluteness," a process in which rationalized systems of belief and practice are produced, assuring the faithful with an image of the cosmos that salvages religious

---

[393] Ernst Troeltsch, "Religion and the Science of Religion," in Robert Morgan and Michael Pye, eds., Ernst Troeltsch: Writings on Theology and Religion (Atlanta: John Knox Press, 1977), 91.

[394] Ernst Troeltsch, The Absoluteness of Christianity and the History of Religions, tran. David Reid (Richmond, VA: John Knox Press, 1971), 139.

[395] Ibid., 133.

absoluteness on the basis of revelatory, miraculous, or intellectual criteria. The tensions that shattered naive absoluteness are strategically transformed into doctrinal and institutional determinations of the proper hierarchies of values and the disordered failures of unredeemed humanity. Hidden within this doctrinal construction is the process by which naive religion necessarily hammers out its compromises between the poles of world-affirmation and world-rejection.

According to Troeltsch, the problem for many contemporary Christians is that these forms of artificial absoluteness are profoundly unconvincing within the actual practices of contemporary life. It has become difficult simply to assume the givenness of any one synthesis of values. Analysis of the "modern spirit" reveals our awareness of a world "full of inner contradictions and tensions."[396] In earlier historical periods, these contradictions and struggles found at least a relative synthesis in the great churches, but in the present, "the claims of the churches in this direction are not realizable."[397] "The praxis of life" shows us there is no "common spirit" that envelopes the multiple spheres of value in which we live. Religion pushes beyond the boundaries of the world, seeking to subordinate the penultimate and innerworldly "logics" of science, art, economics, political life, and the family. But these spheres in turn resist intellectual and practical assimilation into one another as well as into religion. Institutions and groups embodying these various values and interests come into inevitable conflict. Any attempt to find a key value that can provide an overarching rationality for the unity of values is, rather than a discovery of the order of values, "in itself an attempt to forge and create this unity."[398] Moreover, no such attempts can ever finally resolve the crisis.

> The hardest feature of man's fate, after all, is that the purity of the
> ideal is never fully practicable, that the highest conceptions of the

---

[396] Ernst Troeltsch, "The Essence of the Modern Spirit," in Religion and History, 240.

[397] Ernst Troeltsch, Christian Thought: Its History and Application, ed. Baron F. von Hügel (London: University of London Press, 1923), 119.

[398] "The Essence of the Modern Spirit," 240.

mind are vitiated more and more in the process of their material realization. But this feature also gives rise to the courage to decide and to assume responsibility, the daring to solve the problem of the particular case in the best way possible.[399]

Troeltsch was clear as to how this responsibility is to be exercised. The task, he argued, is to find ways to allow the various components in the conflict of values to set limits upon one another in the various situations of life, taking into account the relative validity of each while refusing to elevate any one into an absolute. Our ethic will thus always be characterized by incompleteness, rooted in "the acknowledgement that the ethical is not unified from the outset, but is many-sided; that human beings grow out of a plurality of ethical purposes whose unity is first the problem, and not the starting point."[400] Hence, one must avail oneself of the troublesome awareness of human possibilities and limitations, since, as Troeltsch wrote,

> Many ethical decisions are only possible on the basis of the firm grasp of the facts, and this firm grasp of the facts is an infinitely troublesome thing.... Here nothing is to be said merely out of the fullness of the heart and good intentions (guter Gesinnungen), nor merely on the basis of isolated, local, and personal observations.[401]

In response to this crisis, Troeltsch called for the formation of a third approach to religious life, rooted in a "scientifically reflective" outlook that preserved the naive sense of the validity of religion, but recognized the "practical objective... to organize and clarify what itself grows in naive and tangled form and to harmonize and to balance out one-sided tendencies with other factors in life."[402] Troeltsch's intention in this call for adjustment has been frequently misunderstood as a call for religious affirmation of and accommodation to the world as it is, but in fact Troeltsch ridiculed any religious ethic that had lost its

---

[399] Ernst Troeltsch, "Political Ethics and Christianity," Religion and History, 204-205.
[400] "Grundprobleme der Ethik," 657.
[401] Ernst Troeltsch, "Ethik und Kapitalismus." Christliche Welt 30 135 (August 17 1916): 323.
[402] "Religion and the Science of Religion," 93.

world-rejecting critical edge, reducing itself to merely "blessing the flow of business."[403] "Mediation," he insisted, "is not reconciliation."[404] For Troeltsch, while religion as such is valid, religious people and institutions are nevertheless accountable for the stance they take within the economy of cultural values, for the restraints they call for and accept from other cultural spheres, for their exercise of autonomy—in short, for the world their ideas and actions help to create.

Hence, in spite of the sense of obligation to a divine power that continually and radically calls human ethical endeavor into question, Troeltsch admonished religious people to devote themselves also to innerworldly values, somehow taking them up into their lives and acknowledging the presence of God in the moral commitment that they call forth. This mediation will most frequently emerge by way of the basic forms of religious community that religious people create. Religion cannot generate out of itself political, aesthetic, nor scientific norms anymore than these can originate religious norms. Hence, "in order to grasp and fix rational or accidental forms of regulation of the struggle for survival, religion must rely on forces within that struggle that are favorable to and compatible with religion. It will always be a question of compromises with, and adjustment to, the actualities of life."[405] The recognition that innerworldly values "spring from [God] and his life" solves no problems, but instead sharpens the dilemma between the ethic sub specie aeternitatis and the ethic sub specie temporis. Ultimately, religious ethical engagement can never move beyond mediation between the two kinds of ethic in accordance with what is possible in each situation.

---

[403] "Grundprobleme der Ethik,"668.

[404] The Christian Faith, 164-65.

[405] Ernst Troeltsch, "Religion, Economics, and Society," in Sociology and Religion, Norman Birnbaum and Gertrude Lenzer, eds. (Englewood Cliffs, NJ: Prentice Hall, 1969), 203.

Part 3: The "Dialectic of Faith" and the "Romantic Swindle"

As we have seen, for Troeltsch naive and artificial forms of religious absoluteness "solve" the tensions of religious life by building on the conviction that the world is "rationally" closed. Troeltsch's proposed "scientifically reflective" religious stance sees these contradictions as tensions the resolution of which is an open human task, theoretically and practically "realized" in never-ending adjustments, compromises, and risks for which we must assume responsibility. It is likely that Weber would find such a practical stance congenial. Certainly they shared a common ethical emphasis that can be generally subsumed under Weber's term "the ethic of responsibility." At two junctures, however, Troeltsch reported the personal response of Weber to his views. One involves Troeltsch's concept of the "dialectic of faith," a component of Troeltsch's theory of the religious apriori. The other concerned Troeltsch's notion of "development," a notion that Weber rejected outright. A look at these two issues will help us clarify the ethical orientation of Troeltsch's way of "grasping the whole."

In a 1910 essay, Troeltsch argued that religion, as an independent and necessary feature of human consciousness, contains its own "logic" not unlike the other spheres of value. Religion, he wrote, bears "within itself an independent law of its own movement."[406] Troeltsch argued that four basic formal categories of religion necessarily structure the development and expression of the religious consciousness, namely, God, the world, the soul, and redemption. These categories do not rise from outside impulses, he argued; they are not contingent. Writing toward the end of his life, Troeltsch reported that he had raised this point with Weber. "I used... to speak", he wrote, "of an independent 'dialectic' of religion, or art, and so forth, a theme I often discussed with Max Weber. He was uneasy with the concept, but did not want to simply reject it. In any case, every page of his sociology shows that that he actually worked with it. His notion of

---

[406] Ernst Troeltsch, "Faith," in Religion in History, 128.

'chances of expectation' was based on it, and because of this his sociology richly and vitally moves beyond positivism."[407]

Let us consider the implications of Troeltsch's report for the issue of religious world-rejection. Troeltsch was convinced that every religion, once it becomes a universal Gesinnungsreligion, necessarily structures its experience of the world in terms of the need for redemption, and thus in terms of the contradictions Weber had vividly canvassed under the rubric of the "religious rejections of the world." In other words, for Troeltsch the contradiction between the ethic sub specie aeternitatis and the ethic sub specie temporis is not a contingent development but a necessity of the religious consciousness. The various religious forms of the contemptus mundi that result are not superfluous aberrations, but necessary features in the apriori logic of religion. Thus, with his concept of the dialectic of the religious apriori, Troeltsch locates what for Weber was essentially an "ideal type" in the structural heart of religion itself. A fully realized religious consciousness necessarily both affirms and rejects the world.

For Troeltsch, then, the apriori structure of consciousness itself drives us to the conflict of values, but provides no final conceptual means to resolve this conflict. This perplexing situation, however, can be framed from another perspective: our awareness of the conflicting apriori structure of consciousness drives us to a deeper level of moral responsibility where historically informed decisions must be made and careful compromises worked out and risked. Indeed, for Troeltsch, this is the ultimate arena of the exercise of human freedom, the opening for both the development and the expression of moral selfhood in its fullest and highest sense. Note, however, that this arena is open most fully to the responsible religious person not because religion provides access to or reveals final or ready-made practical or theoretical solutions to the problems of value conflict, but rather because it is from the religious perspective that one has the

---

[407] Ernst Troeltsch, Historismus und seine Probleme, vol.3, Gesammelte Schriften, 4 vols. (Aalen: Scientia Verlag, 1981) 3: 657-58, n.348.

potential to experience, recognize, and grapple with life's contradictions most acutely, most seriously, and most humanely.[408]

This train of thought brings us to the final point of this brief study. Troeltsch attempted to express a theological vision of the whole that was compatible with the personalist ethical perspective outlined above. That Weber harbored grave doubts regarding the viability of Troeltsch's attempt Troeltsch himself tells us in a footnote in his Historismus und seine Probleme. Discussing the nature of historical development, Troeltsch made reference to "Max Weber's joining of voluntarism with the strictest historical-scientific orientation." Troeltsch then went on to report that Weber, "abruptly rejected the idea of development that I connected to this; in discussions on that theme he occasionally called it a 'romantic swindle.'"[409]

As noted earlier, Troeltsch was a notoriously fuzzy system-builder, but his orientation can be illuminated by relating his theological concerns to his ethical stance. Recall that at the heart of Troeltsch's theological perspective is his neo-Kantian understanding of moral personhood, the actualization of which demands the postulate of freedom. The cultivation and expression of responsible moral selfhood is the ultimate human calling and the heart of the Christian religion. Hence, moral freedom finds its highest expression in responsible mediation between the ethic sub specie aeternitatis and the ethic sub specie temporis. For Troeltsch, then, "ethics doesn't just flow from God, but leads back to God. The divine spirit is present in every moral demand. In every submission... we take a step toward God."[410] Further, for Troeltsch, the category of moral "Persönlichkeit" expresses not only that which is most profoundly human, but that which is most profoundly appropriate in our language about the nature of God.

---

[408] The Christian Faith, 154, 191; "Grundprobleme der Ethik," 656; Ernst Troeltsch, Christian Thought, 179.
[409] Historismus und seine Probleme, 189-90.
[410] The Christian Faith, 163.

This category also, however, plunges us even more deeply into the fissure between the two ethics.

In his 1910 article "Theodizee," Troeltsch discussed the construction of theodicies, understood in the broad Weberian sense as religious worldviews erected in response to unexpected consequences and frustrated religious expectations. "The issue of theodicy," Troeltsch wrote, in words which by now sound familiar, "is no mere piece of baggage or a strain upon religion, but the fountain without which religion is not religion. Some kind of struggle, some kind of tension is essential to the religious consciousness. Precisely in the claim to provide a solution to the struggle is a faith a religion."[411] For Troeltsch, however, such a solution can be neither "firm" nor "scientific." Though necessary, it is nonetheless always a "work of fantasy," a work of the religious imagination that unavoidably expresses itself in symbol and myth. Still, Troeltsch argued, the theoretical construction of a theodicy, if connected critically to scientific and ethical realities, can prove "quite helpful to purely practical-religious faith," providing a solid stance for religious ethical engagement. Thus the work of the religious imagination, while not specifically scientific, ought to be, as noted above, scientifically reflective.

Troeltsch's own work of "fantasy" appeared most fully in a somewhat startling form in his section on the doctrine of God in his Glaubenslehre. Keep in mind that in the Troeltschian program, the task of the Glaubenslehre is to systematize and express one's religious consciousness as it has been shaped by the religious tradition in tandem with one's historical and cultural horizon. Further, metaphysical statements are permissible, indeed required, by derivation from the historically ascertained tradition of the Christian community. Naturally, however, such statements reflect one's consciousness of God rather than God as God is. The latter is beyond the limits of human knowledge.

---

[411] Ernst Troeltsch, "Theodizee," in Die Religion in Geschichte und Gegenwart, 5 vols., F. M. Scheile and L.Zscharnack, eds. (Tübingen: J. C. B. Mohr [Paul Siebeck], 1909-1914) 5: 1187.

In the Troeltschian consciousness of God, then, we meet up again with the fissure between the sub specie temporis and the sub specie aeternitatis. Troeltsch proposes that we must think of God as the one who has presented us with the tasks incumbent upon the responsible person. It is God who has provided the "Spielraum" for this expansive exercise of human freedom. Hence, the tensions and contradictions that arise in moral life are not problems with religion, but rather tasks for the religious person. Not through access to some sort of divine blueprint, but through responsible constructive engagement within both the variegated historical continuum of Christian praxis and the complex stream of cultural life, the responsible Christian is drawn to active involvement in the ongoing work of affirmation, rejection, and compromise required for synthesis of character and community.

Thus, the plurality and antagonism of values, including the split between otherworldly and innerworldly values, are not symptoms of human sinfulness. Human sinfulness, for Troeltsch, is self-centered rejection of the imperative to commit oneself to God and others. Selfless moral concern with value tensions and contradictions assumes that one is set free from such egoism, and made free for responsible moral commitment. Redemption, then, in its personal dimension, is the experience of the moral seriousness and freedom needed for responsible ethical commitment. Nevertheless, the question arises: is value struggle and risk itself a feature of human life that will eventually be overcome? Is there to be a moment when the eternal ground and unity of all in God is fully realized, the eternal and the temporal harmonized? For Troeltsch, such a redemptive moment would take us beyond the conditions of time and history as we know them, since for us moral selfhood requires risk, struggle and tension. Nevertheless, redemption in the sense of the unitive cessation of value conflict and the advent of a fully affirmable world is the vanishing point of the dialectic of the religious apriori, and the fundamental orienting drive of the Christian consciousness—the ethic sub specie aeternitatis, expressed in the expectation of the coming Kingdom of God—but in the present it is a hope expressible only in symbol and myth.[412] Indeed, Troeltsch wrote,

> [The] history of Christianity is itself... in the long run... a tremendous, continuous compromise between the Utopian demands of the Kingdom of God and the permanent conditions of our actual human life. It was indeed a sound instinct which led its founders to look for a speedy dissolution of the present world-order.[413]

However, we have not yet exhausted Troeltsch's concept of redemption. For Troeltsch, the logic of the fissure between the ethic sub specie aeternitatis and the ethic sub specie temporis drives us to a final dimension in which the cleft is presented as one under which God suffers—indeed, a split traceable to the divine "personality" itself.[414] God's freedom is expressed in his creation of and partnership with free human beings. For the sake of the full expansion of the moral selfhood of his creatures, God has freely put himself at risk under the conditions of the religious ethic sub specie temporis. For Troeltsch, the divinely grounded unity of values provides the formal goal and impulse of all human attempts at value synthesis. The drama of history, however, driven by the human activity of synthesizing recalcitrant values and coordinating unruly consequences, is a divine and human partnership in which God voluntarily submits himself "to the spiritual and moral errors involved in the process of elevating the spiritual world to him."[415] Here lies the ultimate meaning of God's central ethical attributes of holiness and love. For under the rubric of God's holiness, the divine contemptus mundi is experienced within the religious consciousness as the relentless wrath of God toward all that contradicts the unity of and unity with the divine being. And yet God has at the same moment gathered the world into

---

[412] The Christian Faith, 179-180.
[413] Christian Thought, 177.
[414] "Grundprobleme der Ethik," 555.
[415] The Christian Faith, 178.

himself, lovingly rendering himself vulnerable to his creatures, affirming their world, sharing in their tasks and struggles. For Troeltsch, Christian mystics such as Eckhart, Angelus Silesius, and Böhme have most fully explored this dimension of the Christian God-consciousness. In our struggle to bridge the gap between God and God, to return to God, they teach, God struggles to return to himself. God's self–knowledge, under the freely self-imposed conditions of creation, is mediated in the relation of his being God-for-us. In the forms of unity we imagine, create, or fail to create, the divine personality is itself expanded or diminished. Hence the ultimate redemption—the harmonization of the eternal and the temporal, of the two ethics—is the return of God to himself, God's own self-redemption. Troeltsch offered the following summation of his perspective:

> God, in calling the creature to himself, actually grows and multiplies himself as the result of the creature's own activity. This thesis is absolutely unavoidable. Something is added to the life of God, something new. God is actually growing.... God raises up helpers for himself from among the finite spirits, which is how the spiritualization and ethicization of the world will be achieved. He reckons us as part of the household of his creation. We hold significance for him, for to omit the individual creature is to deny universality. What enables us to be helpers in this process is the freedom of the creature, which is no superfluous adornment that may or may not be put to use. Instead, if we refuse to use this freedom, we interrupt God's development.[416]

These are relatively unsystematized strands in Troeltsch's work toward a theology of responsibility. For Weber, they added up to a "romantische Schwindel," but they may also be, as I am suggesting here, symptoms of an acutely tuned ethical orientation toward the difficulties involved in establishing a conceptually viable "Verantwortungsreligiosität," with its conviction that the world is not rationally closed, but an open arena for responsible moral endeavor. Attempting to do justice to his unflinchingly honest sense for the intractable ethical pluralities and complexities of contemporary life on the one hand, and to

---

[416] Ibid., 192. My italics.

his equally unflinching religious convictions on the other, Troeltsch located the ethic of responsibility in a profound historical partnership between God with humanity. For those who enter into it, Troeltsch insisted, faith in this partnership "explains nothing," but "inspires and illuminates everything."[417]

---

[417] Ibid., 211.

On Friedrich Schleiermacher

THE ROLE OF THE IMAGINATION IN THE INTERPRETATION OF RELIGIOUS EXPERIENCE ACCORDING TO THE WORKS OF FRIEDRICH SCHLEIERMACHER AND LUDWIG FEUERBACH

Gayle D. Beebe

The purpose of this paper is to demonstrate the role of the imagination in the interpretation of religious experience. Of primary interest is the way in which Friedrich Schleiermacher and Ludwig Feuerbach identify this role and make their own unique contribution to its definition and discussion. In addressing this issue, three basic elements will be considered.

First, a brief definition of imagination and its role in the interpretation of religious experience will be considered. Of particular significance is the way in which Immanuel Kant's original synthesis offered a unique understanding of the role of the imagination in the interpretation of religious experience. Although there is a rich and varied history regarding the concept of imagination, this section will focus primarily on Immanuel Kant due to his enormous influence not only on these two writers, but also on all religious thinking in the 19th-century.[418]

Second, a significant comparison of the way in which Schleiermacher and Feuerbach use imagination will be considered. Of particular importance is the way in which Feuerbach uses the imagination to demonstrate why religious experiences are not real, but illusory while Schleiermacher uses the imagination to demonstrate the reality and reliability of religious experience.

Finally, the way in which the imagination functions to construct religious meaning and understanding will be considered. Of primary significance is the way in which experiences interpreted religiously form plausibility structures that

---

[418] There is a significant body of literature on the concept of imagination and especially its role in human understanding and theological thinking. For a selected overview of these resources consult the attached bibliography for relevant sources.

provide meaning and direction to one's life. Included in the purpose of this paper is the desire to demonstrate legitimate uses of the imagination in the interpretation of religious experience and the role these interpretations play in providing understanding of the nature and destiny of human life.

I. Towards a Working Definition of Imagination

Webster defines imagination as, "...the formation of a mental image or concept of that which is not real or present, a mental image or idea."[419]   Although Webster's definition is the one generally understood when speaking of the imagination, his definition reflects only one part of the contested discussion. In many respects, Webster's definition characterizes the contemporary disregard for the positive use of the imagination. It is true that the imagination can produce images and concepts that are not real, but only illusory. When put to such use the imagination operates to corrupt one's perception of reality and prevents one from knowing or understanding what is real.

This is not the only function of the imagination, however. The imagination also creates possibilities that are not present, but have the capacity to be realized. Imagination need not lead one astray. Instead, imagination can operate to open up domains of understanding and thought that lead one towards a greater comprehension of life as it is and can be.

As early as Aristotle a critical place was established for the imagination. In one telling passage, Aristotle distinguished the imagination from either perceiving (aesthesis) or discursive thinking (noesis).[420]   Here, Aristotle attempts to establish the way in which the imagination forms the bridge between our experiences of life and the way in which our mind reflects on and categorizes these experiences. Later, during the Renaissance, Pico della Mirandola argued that the imagination is the vehicle through which we connect the sensations we

---

[419] *Webster's Dictionary.* New York: Houghton Mifflin Co., 1969.
[420] *The Complete Works of Aristotle, vol. I, De Anima, 426 b.* Edited by Jonathan Barnes. Princeton: Princeton University Press, 1984.

have in life with the way in which we form ideas to make sense of these experiences. These two ideas fundamentally shaped the understanding of the imagination well into the 18th century.

In the 18th century, the imagination once again emerged as a dynamic concept. One of the most significant figures in this century is Samuel Coleridge. Coleridge makes a critical distinction between imagination and fancy. Imagination forms the vehicle for receiving divine truth. Fancy, on the other hand, only leads us astray.[421] Imagination, moreover, is critical for energizing the human mind with the ideals that can shape human destiny. In summation, Coleridge argues that what one believes fundamentally shapes how one behaves.[422]

In contemporary discussions of the imagination, John Bowker suggests that the imagination functions differently depending on one's religious orientation. Since each religion codifies information and experiences differently according to their ultimate outcomes, the imagination works to build the connections between the rituals, institutions and sacred understandings and our personal experiences that give meaning to these religious understandings.[423]

Jacob Bronowski extends this discussion when he writes, "...The act of imagination is the opening of the system so that it shows new connections. Every act of imagination is the discovery of likenesses between two things that were thought unlike..."[424] John Coulson further amplifies this point when he demonstrates the specifically religious use of the imagination. Coulson writes, "The theologian...if he is to make a real assent to the objects of faith...must use

---

[421] Baker, James Volant. *The Sacred River: Coleridge's Theory of Imagination.* Baton Rouge: Louisiana State University, 1957, pp. 115-116.

[422] Brett, R. L. *Fancy and Imagination.* London: Methuen, 1978, p. 31.

[423] Bowker, John W. *The Religious Imagination and the Sense of God.* New York: Clarendon Press, 1978.

[424] Bronowski, Jacob. *The Origins of Knowledge and Imagination.* New Haven: Yale University Press, 1978.

his imagination ... to [uncover what] lies hid in language."[425] Mary Warnock wraps up this discussion with her classic definition of imagination. In her important work, Warnock defines imagination as, "...our means of interpreting the world, and it is also our means of forming images in the mind."[426]

This final definition does more to return the discussion to its Kantian roots than virtually any other description. This return is significant since the synthesizing work of Immanuel Kant forms the integrating center not only for contemporary discussions of imagination, but also for its role in shaping the understanding of imagination in both Schleiermacher and Feuerbach.

Of critical importance to this discussion is the synthesizing work of Immanuel Kant. Kant defined imagination as that which extracts from lived experience the framework within which these experiences can occur.[427] It is the power within the human that generates possible explanations for how and why we experience life the way we do. It creates understanding. It clarifies meaning. It permits the noumenal and phenomenal selves to connect with one another. Without imagination, we would never be able to know,[428] understand or even conceptualize our experience of the world.[429] Imagination, then, operates to synthesize the specific experiences of our life into a unified, meaningful whole.[430]

In Kant's own work he was careful to distinguish between what he termed the productive and the reproductive imagination. The productive imagination produces an original representation of the object prior to experience. The reproductive imagination is the way in which a prior conception is retrieved to help make sense of a current experience. In this way, Kant offered a key distinction between sense-based imagination in which one identifies discrete

---

[425] Coulson, John. *Religion and Imagination.* New York: Clarendon Press, 1981, p. 168.

[426] Warnock, Mary. *Imagination.* Berkeley: University of California Press, 1976, pp. 194-195.

[427] Kant, Immanuel. *The Critique of Pure Reason.* Translated by Norman Kemp Smith. New York: St. Martin's Press, 1965, p. 28.

[428] Kant, *op.cit.,* p. 112.

[429] Kant, *op.cit.,* p. 127.

[430] Kant, *op.cit.,* pp. 142-43.

objects and the productive imagination that creates the conditions for
understanding one's experience.

Although his fascination with imagination accompanied him throughout his academic life, his concluding judgments on imagination came in the final edition of the *Critique of Practical Reason.* Here, Kant began the final edition by noting that imagination assumes an even greater role in producing a synthesis between judgment and reason. Moreover, in attending to this synthesis, Kant notes that the imagination works to unify discrete sense experiences into meaningful wholes by connecting an individual's new experience with the original apperceptions that gave rise to conceptual understanding.[431]

The significance of Kant's work cannot be underestimated. The loss of contact with his original thinking has created enormous problems in contemporary discussions of epistemology. The stumbling block in present discussions of imagination has been the overwhelming emphasis on empirical verification without adequate attention to the conceptual, unifying thought systems within which these empirical observations can find meaning and make sense. The grounds for epistemology generally and religious epistemology specifically have depended on the capacity of the human to verify one's knowledge empirically. By this is meant that what is accepted as plausible is only that which can be verified by human sense organs in coordination with the human mind.

This definition, however, limits the discussion unfairly and loses contact with Kant's very significant work on the role of imagination and his key influence on Schleiermacher and Feuerbach. Let me illustrate the importance of Kant's work and its relevance for our discussion by way of a practical illustration.

There are many effects impacting us that we do not notice normally unless we look for them specifically. For example, as I write this paper my sense of reality tells me that I am sitting in a stationary chair at a stationary desk typing on

---

[431] Kant, Immanuel. *Critique of Practical Reason.* Translated by Lewis White Beck. Indianapolis: Bobbs-Merrill, 1976.

my computer. When I pause to reflect I lean back and look out my window where a bird appears to be perched in a stationary position on the limb of a tree. All of this is real to me. When my wife enters my study and I ask her if she sees what I see she concurs with my description. Thus, at one level, there is agreement on my perception of reality.

Yet, this is not the only reality occurring. To apprehend other aspects of reality one must utilize both one's imagination and other instruments of human knowledge including technology to grasp levels of reality that are not immediately apparent to us. For example, as I sit at my desk I am also spinning at approximately 1,000 miles an hour. That is, as part of the earth, my larger sphere of reality is in a state of constant motion that I do not realize, but nonetheless experience. This is to suggest that there is more than the level of three-dimensional perceptual reality that a human experiences. But in order to understand and grasp this deeper level of reality, a perceptual reorganization leading to an expanded interpretation must occur that takes into account new discoveries and information.

Consider the following data. Scientists report that the earth revolves around the sun in 365.26 days.[432] The earth rotates on its own axis every 23 hours and 56.07 minutes.[433] The significance of these facts is that they document movements that we do not normally perceive or experience, yet have a very real effect on us. We experience day and night, spring and fall, but we do not perceive or experience moving at a constant speed of 1,000 miles an hour.[434] The lack of perception that we are simultaneously at rest and in motion is meant to suggest that the imagination, as the integrating faculty of the human, allows us to take perceptions we knowingly experience, conceptions that make new knowledge

---

[432] *World Book Encyclopedia, volume E-F.* New York: World Book Pub., 1975.

[433] Op. cit.

[434] To reach this conclusion I performed the following calculations: the earth has an average radius of 3,959 miles. The circumference of a circle is 2 x pi x radius. Therefore, 2 x (3.14) x (3,959) = 24,862.52 divided by 24 hours/day=1,035.94. Therefore, we are traveling at approximately 1,000 miles per hour.

available to us and is able to provide the tools to build an interpretation that integrates these perceptions and conceptions into a new and meaningful whole.

The significance of this development is the way in which it helps to build a framework of meaning that produces understanding. As we turn to Schleiermacher and Feuerbach it will be necessary to remember this development as we consider the manner each deployed in using the imagination to build very different interpretations of religious experience.

II. Schleiermacher/Feuerbach

Central to the thesis of this paper is the premise that Feuerbach's treatment of the imagination as presented in *The Essence of Christianity* is inadequate. His attempt to diminish the validity of experiences interpreted religiously misunderstands the primary and legitimate role the imagination plays in the interpretation of religious experience.[435] By contrast, Schleiermacher provides a reliable alternative to Feuerbach when he identifies both the significant role of the imagination in our interpretation of religious experience and the significance of the development of a religious understanding of life.[436] The imagination, as a central integrating activity of the human, helps one construct a religious interpretation of life. This construction in turn permits one to synthesize and understand a vast array of experiences that otherwise remain disjointed and confused. In order to substantiate this contrast it is necessary to show the respective use each man makes of the concept of imagination.

Schleiermacher develops his understanding of imagination by borrowing heavily on Kant's distinction between the productive and reproductive uses of the imagination. For Schleiermacher, the imagination and its activity provide the

---

[435] Feuerbach, Ludwig. *The Essence of Christianity.* Translated by George Eliot. New York: Harper and Row, 1957.

[436] Schleiermacher, Friedrich. *On Religion: Speeches to Its Cultured Despisers.* Translated by Richard Crouter. New York: Cambridge University Press, 1988.

necessary resources to understand and explain both one's experiences of life and
one's experiences, or intuitions, of God (Schleiermacher actually uses the
expression 'the intuition of the infinite' in his early works and then ceases to use
it in The Christian Faith*). The activity of the imagination is critical in the*
establishment of a conceptual framework in which experience interpreted
religiously can make sense. Such experience interpreted religiously becomes the
criterion by which the construction of religious knowledge can occur. In defining
his understanding and use of imagination, Schleiermacher writes,

> ...You will know that imagination is the highest and
> most original element in us, and that everything
> besides it is merely reflection upon it.[437]

Schleiermacher, like Kant, wants to demonstrate the way in which the imagination forms the bridge between the noumenal and phenomenal selves. For Schleiermacher, imagination demonstrates that knowing and desiring are not two distinct activities in the human, but one.[438] The desire to know and the event or activity of knowing is inextricably linked. The activity of knowing arises when one experiences an intuition of the infinite and seeks to understand the significance of this intuition. Imagination not only cultivates this desire to know, but also creates the plausibility structures that make knowledge possible.[439] It is these plausibility structures that help organize, interpret, and provide religious meaning for these experiences.

Imagination, for Schleiermacher, is the necessary tool for understanding
the true nature of religious knowledge. Following Kant's lead, Schleiermacher
rejects religious epistemology based on metaphysics. Schleiermacher, moreover,
does not stop with metaphysics, but proceeds to reject the moral foundation for
religious epistemology as well. Imagination is neither an isolated activity nor a

---

[437] Schleiermacher, *op.cit.*, p. 132.

[438] Schleiermacher, *op.cit.*, p. 25.

[439] For a definition of my use of plausibility structures see Peter Berger, *The Sacred Canopy*, 1966.

distinct category. It is a faculty whose basic operations permit one to apprehend, interpret, and understand the world and our experiences, including our religious experiences, in it.

Critical for Schleiermacher is the nature of one's encounter with the infinite. An encounter with the infinite is not something we produce on our own, although we may prepare for it. There are many boundary situations that awaken one to the reality of other dimensions and powers, including the experience of beauty and the reality of one's mortality. [440]

According to Schleiermacher, every experience of the infinite drives an individual to attempt to understand and articulate this experience.[441] This leads to interpretation. Imagination, then, giving rise to interpretation, makes understanding and articulation possible. Imagination acts to build detail, to add color, to conjure up possibilities that help one understand and interpret their experience. It is this 'inner creative drive' of the imagination that moves one towards greater apprehension of reality.[442]

Since the infinite is such an important concept how does one come to understand this reality? Schleiermacher states that this depends on the orientation of one's imagination. If we see the infinite as God it is because we need to personify the spirit that acts freely upon us. If not, then one envisions the infinite not as a personal being, but as the impersonal spirit of the universe.[443] Regardless of one's understanding of the infinite, however, Schleiermacher never views the concept of the infinite as a misguided use of reason or an ill conceived illusion or a misunderstood part of human nature gathered together and projected outside oneself.

---

[440] Schleiermacher, *op.cit.*, p. 14.
[441] Schleiermacher, *op.cit.*, p. 109.
[442] Schleiermacher, *op.cit.*, p. 122.
[443] Schleiermacher, *op.cit.*, p. 138.

Imagination both shapes and is shaped by our interpretations of the world. Imagination permits one to create perceptions of reality while adding depth and complexity to these perceptions. These are not sheer flights of fancy, novel attempts to deceive one's mind. Rather, they are efforts undertaken in order to understand the ultimate foundations of reality, its impact on us and our apprehension of how to structure our existence in accordance with these impacts.

Feuerbach, by contrast, is suspicious of the imagination. Imagination, though natural to the senses and an innate part of us, can be misleading. It causes us to believe in miracles, to reach beyond the boundaries of our finite existence to satisfy the spurious yearnings of the human heart.[444] These tendencies that operate without any possibility of empirical verification or causality distract the human mind from what is real.

Feuerbach is particularly intent on rejecting the role of intuition and feeling in religious epistemology. Feuerbach argues that the one who lives and moves only in their feelings is not refined or cultured, but naïve and crude.[445] Such individuals experience the operation of their imagination as involuntary activity. They have control neither of its operations nor of its capacity in comprehending an accurate view of reality, including the religious dimensions of reality.

What stimulates the activity of the imagination is not an intuition of the infinite, but an egocentric desire to be free from the laws of nature and morality.[446] In this activity, Feuerbach cites the particularly pernicious effect of the imagination. It does not bring one to greater apprehension and understanding of reality, but to greater distortion through the creation of a Christ-figure upon who is heaped "...all the joys of the imagination and all the sufferings of the heart..."[447]

---

[444] Feuerbach, *op.cit.*,

[445] Feuerbach, *op.cit.*, p. 133.

[446] Feuerbach, *op.cit.*, p. 143.

[447] Feuerbach, *op.cit.*, p. 148.

The question Feuerbach sidesteps, however, is whether a Christ-figure is simply a crude illusion or the fulfillment of a legitimate human need to understand how one encounters the infinite and can subsequently help one acquire knowledge of this encounter. Schleiermacher sees Christ as fulfilling our need for an individual who realizes perfectly an experience of the infinite in time. Thus, the Christ-figure forms the bridge between the dimensions of our human reality and the infinite reality of God.

Yet, Feuerbach disagrees. Because the heavens are closed to him, Feuerbach sees all such efforts as diversions of the human from what is real. For Feuerbach, Christ represents the "...ascent to heaven of the imagination."[448] It reflects all that is wrong with those distracted by their imagination from what is real. For Feuerbach, reason, not imagination, is omnipotent. It alone apprehends reality accurately.[449] Feeling, intuition and imagination are all real, but non-rational activities of the human. Consequently, all these activities must bow to reason. The activity of reason is the ultimate and accurate criterion for knowledge since reason is the ultimate and only reliable faculty of human nature.[450]

Since all reality for Feuerbach is strictly rational,[451] what cannot be apprehended rationally must be passed over in silence. For Feuerbach, the definition of what is rational is what can be proved by empirical verification. Yet, Feuerbach's position awakens a massive question: why is human reason considered supreme? If one accepts Feuerbach's thesis that the reality of the world is only that which can be grasped rationally, then the world and our experiences of the world must be compressed into the limits of human reason alone.

---

[448] Feuerbach, *op.cit.*, p. 149.
[449] Feuerbach, *op.cit.*, p. 195.
[450] Feuerbach, *op.cit.*, p. 150.
[451] Feuerbach, *op.cit.*, p. 195.

272

Clearly, Feuerbach believes no individual is capable of total apprehension or comprehension of reality. In part, this accounts for his advocacy of the individual actualized through participation in corporate society. Nevertheless, he implicitly assumes that the totality of human history is essentially uniform and therefore capable of being grasped by human reason.

Feuerbach furthers his position when he accepts Anselm's premise in the proof of God's existence, but then re-applies it.[452] The problem Feuerbach identifies is that if one accepts 'existence' as a predicate of 'God' then God must exist spatial-temporally. Yet, this cannot be proved.[453] Since God does not exist spatial-temporally, then God's existence is only a sensational impression within the spiritual realm, not an actual existence in space-time.

Such a nuance of meaning is produced by the imagination. Feuerbach writes,

> ...Only the imagination solves the contradiction in an existence, which is at once sensational and not sensational; only the imagination is the preservative from atheism. In the imagination existence has sensational effects...where the existence of God is a living truth, an object on which the imagination exercises itself, there also appearances of God are believed in.[454]

In contrast to such use, Feuerbach notes the positive effect when the imagination is no longer used in the service of religion. He continues,

> ...Where, on the contrary, the fire of the religious imagination is extinct, where the sensational effects or appearances necessarily connected with an essentially sensational existence cease, there the existence becomes a dead, self-contradictory existence that falls irrevocably into the negation of atheism.[455]

---

[452] Feuerbach, *op.cit.*, p. 198.
[453] Feuerbach, *op.cit.*, p. 200.
[454] Feuerbach, *op.cit.*, p. 203.
[455] *Loc.cit.*

Clearly, Feuerbach prefers the latter. Yet, Schleiermacher makes necessary allowances for such decisions when he notes that one must desire an intuition of the infinite for it to occur. Earlier, Pascal, in the tradition of Plato and Augustine, had written, "...there is enough light for those who want to see and enough darkness for those of a contrary disposition."[456] This observation captures the essence of Schleiermacher's concern that the orientation of the knower influences the knowledge that becomes known.

One must consider finally why Feuerbach is willing to accept the extinction of religious imagination as legitimate grounds for denying the possibility of an infinite reality that can be known and experienced. He is not willing to accept the exercise of religious imagination as legitimate grounds for God's proof. After all, it is the imagination that continually corrupts human reason and so deludes the individual who is vulnerable to its delusions.[457]

Yet, with this rejection no adequate alternative is suggested for the human's persistent need to complete its knowledge and experience of the world in order to derive guidance for their whole life. Feuerbach's chiding of religion never fully explains the way in which the human remains incurably religious despite the exercise of reason. The question Feuerbach must answer is why does the human feel incomplete in itself and search for a completing ingredient in its life. The search is never satisfied by simply calling for a review of the collective will and good of humanity. There must be something more and this something more awakens the question of God and of the possibilities of an infinite reality.

Such a question needs a reference point beyond the totality of the species, the solution proposed here by Feuerbach.[458] It needs an encounter or intuition of

---

[456] Pascal, Blaise. *Pensees.* Edited by Thomas Krailsheimer. New York: Penguin, 1966, F #149.

[457] Feuerbach, *op.cit.,* p. 206.

[458] Feuerbach, *op.cit.,* p. 208.

the infinite that goes beyond human experience and can mobilize human energies to grow continually as they reflect and refine their understanding of life and one's experiences in life. Life experiences give rise to reflection and reflection deepens and changes our understanding and interpretation of life. Ultimately, Schleiermacher believes such reflection and understanding can only come through the right use of the imagination in the interpretation of religious experience. Unfortunately, Feuerbach did not share such optimism.

In order to understand the full range of Schleiermacher and Feuerbach's treatment of imagination it is necessary to place this discussion within the broader framework of the way in which imagination is used to construct religious understanding through the formation of plausibility structures. Of particular interest is the ways in which these plausibility structures form the networks of meaning that provide interpretation and understanding of our experiences of life.[459] It is to this framework and its value to our discussion that we now turn.

III. The Use of the Imagination in the Construction of Religious Understanding

Imagination plays a key role in shaping and influencing the knowledge we obtain of our life. Imagination creates a structure of consciousness that permits the subject and object to interact through interpretation. The possibility of each to interact and influence the other makes the world in which we live subject to perpetual interpretation. These acts of interpretation form the bridge of understanding that provide a greater comprehension of our world and our life.

Although both Feuerbach and Schleiermacher make imagination a central piece of their work, Schleiermacher specifically strives to make imagination the central, unifying thread of his philosophy. Schleiermacher is concerned with the tremendous capacity different aspects of life have either to divert or to direct us to what is real. This diversion occurs when the imagination falls into corruption and disuse.

---

[459] Berger, Peter. *The Sacred Canopy.* New York: Doubleday, 1966. I am indebted to Berger's work and especially his definition and use of the concept of a plausibility structure.

On the other hand, the imagination operates properly when the will is oriented towards that which is good. The orientation of the will reveals the fundamental allegiance of our entire being. It is the will that influences the human by directing the imagination to that which it values. Because the human tends to do what is expedient, right action is based not on the strength of our will to choose properly in a given moment, but on the orientation of our will and the quality of our moral attachments.

Because the human is inherently egocentric it is necessary to exercise the imagination properly. The problem, however, is that the imagination is often corrupted by the ego-centrism that distorts one's apprehension of reality. This corrupted imagination turns into fantasy that results in a misleading general picture. It distorts our known world and our role in the known world. On the other hand, when imagination is used properly it creates not only structures of understanding for specific experiences, but also allows one to develop a proper perspective of all of life. This reorientation counteracts egocentrism and allows the individual to embrace the world as a center of value and to embrace a religious interpretation of our experiences in this world.

Imagination directs our attention to new possibilities and then forces us to construct a reasonable interpretation of their reality. Imagination presupposes that neither human perception nor perceptions of our experiences of God are adequate or complete. We stand with the capacity to be changed and with the possibility to influence this change. It is not a prepackaged reality we simply accept or receive, but a range of possible meanings and capacities that contribute to one's experience of life, the influence these experiences exert on life, and the meaning derived from the interpretation of these experiences.

Finally, one's perspective makes a significant difference in whether or not one comes to experience God. Overall, what a human includes and excludes in developing their perception of life fundamentally shapes what they know and experience. Austin Farrar, the great British philosophical theologian of the 20th

Century, highlights this reality when he identifies four essential categories of life and thought in the preface to *Interpretation and Belief.* In the preface to this landmark work, Farrar notes that even though all four categories have philosophical legitimacy, two of the four are often overlooked or ignored.

The first category is what he refers to as the special sciences. Here, one introduces artificial boundaries in order to study a particular aspect of life. For example, physics and chemistry function by introducing artificial boundaries and studying this part of the world on the basis of its physical dynamics or its chemical changes. It is strictly objective and attempts to be factual without entertaining any questions of human or ethical value.

Likewise, the second category seeks to remain scientific. Here, the human is the particular subject of study, but again only in categories that assess reality based on what is empirically verifiable. Psychological studies or sociological analysis are two examples where the human is considered objectively without regard for human or ethical values.

Categories three and four shift the issue of importance from fact-based reality to value-based reality. In these final two categories the object of supreme importance is that which pertains to human value. Category three addresses specific ethical questions that address human needs and concerns. It forces one to consider whether or not the facts we derive in categories one and two should be complemented or condemned. It asks us to make a judgment on life as we encounter and live it.

Finally, category four raises questions of religious importance. It deals specifically with the human before God. Farrar writes,

> ...Unless we sometimes see God as truth, and evasion of him as credulity, at other times the proved facts of the special sciences as truth, and the outrunning of them as credulity—unless this is so, we are not confronted with the specifically religious problem of truth.[460]

---

[460] Farrar, Austin. *Interpretation and Belief.* Edited by Charles Conti. London: S.P.C.K., 1947, reissued in 1976.

Farrar's work highlights the unique problem in one's interpretation of religious experience: often the specific nature of religious truth and a religious interpretation of reality is completely excluded from human consideration. Yet, without including category four, religious truth and a religious interpretation of reality is not even available as a legitimate explanation for human experience.

Often, the first two categories are the only two that are accepted as legitimate grounds for inquiry. Yet, both categories explicitly reject the human as a center of value worthy of consideration and respect. Categories one and two attempt to operate on the basis of objective fact, not subjective value. What is suggested, therefore, is that the human need for interpretations that make sense must include a consideration of all four categories if one's quest for truth and meaning is to find satisfaction and understanding.

IV. Conclusion

This paper has attempted to define the role of the imagination in the interpretation of religious experience. This role is a central, unifying one and not simply a flight of fancy from all that is real and meaningful. This paper has sought to show that the imagination plays a central role in constructing an interpretation of religious experience and providing one with an adequate framework for religious understanding. Central to this position is the premise that all humans are incurable religious. This dimension of life can be ignored, but it is not non-existent.

The dispute between the thought of Feuerbach and Schleiermacher demonstrates that one human faculty can generate two very different interpretations. This does not imply that one must accept both perspectives as equally valid, but does demand that one think through the criteria they use in establishing reliable interpretations of religious experience.

Clearly, both Feuerbach and Schleiermacher believe the imagination catapults one beyond the limits of human reason in seeking and producing understanding. For Feuerbach, such activity only produces false consolation. For Schleiermacher, by contrast, such activity opens one to religious experiences and activates the human's need to know, interpret, and understand these experiences. Ultimately, each individual articulates a perception of reality, an attitude towards God, a belief in a Christ-figure and an understanding of the role of reason that defends their understanding of the role of imagination in the interpretation of religious experience.

Finally, the concept of imagination creates a capacity to interpret certain experiences religiously and to build a plausibility structure that undergirds and strengthens these interpretations. All aspects of human life and thought must be taken seriously. If we imagine and have an imagination then our explanation must give an account that includes why the imagination is a part of us. We must illustrate the way in which this part of humanity helps ground the human in what is real. Ultimately, it is the role of the imagination in the interpretation of religious experience that stretches one to the limits of human understanding. By producing understanding in an area of life that eludes easy definition, the role of imagination in the interpretation of religious experience can enhance our knowledge and understanding of life, of life's experiences and of our participation in the full range of the realities of our world.

THE THEOLOGICAL SIGNIFICANCE
OF THE CHRISTIAN CHURCH IN SCHLEIERMACHER
Young Bok Kim

Friedrich Ernst Daniel Schleiermacher(1768-1834), unlike Kant and Hegel, as a Christian systematic theologian, successfully reinterpreted the whole Christian theology by using prominent logical coherence and innate creativity. In particular, Schleiermacher considers the idea of the Christian church as a foundation of all theological themes in the sense that they originate from it and develop in it. Schleiermacher defines theology once more as "ecclesiological" theology. Nevertheless, in calling Schleiermacher "the father of modern Protestant theology," scholars have focused on the aspects of his dogmatics other than his idea of the Christian church. Schleiermacher's ecclesiology, unfortunately, has seldom been examined in the major studies of Schleiermacher's theology.

After defining what the distinctive identity of the Christian church is briefly, this article introduces the theological importance of the Christian church in relation to the major theological themes of Christian faith, such as Christian religious experience, Christian theology, and Christian ethics. In doing so, one recognizes that Schleiermacher also can be called "the father of modern Protestant ecclesiology."

The Distinctive Identity of the Christian Church

In his major work *Der Christliche Glaube*, Schleiermacher, with the perspective of apologetics, interprets the Christian church as a particular religious community to explain its distinctive identity. Schleiermacher defines this as follows:

> Christianity is a monotheistic faith, belonging to the teleological type of religion, and is essentially distinguished from other such faith by the fact

that in it everything is related to the redemption accomplished by Jesus of Nazareth.[461]

What does the definition of Christianity as "a monotheistic faith" mean? Although all religious communities are related to each other by the common consciousness of piety (Frömmigkeit) in human nature, each one, Schleiermacher thinks, has different levels and different kinds in the sense that they develop according to their own particular perspectives on religion.[462] According to Schleiermacher, unlike Fetishism and Polytheism, the last stage of religious development is found in the religious communities of Monotheism. They have the religious self-consciousness of dependence on "One Supreme Being behind the plurality of higher Beings," in which the whole world is apprehended as a unity.[463] In this vein, Schleiermacher considers the monotheistic religious forms as the highest level of religious development, unlike all other kinds of religious forms destined to pass to the monotheistic forms and subordinated to them. Furthermore, Schleiermacher asserts that since the Christian community is the highest expression of the highest form of communal religious consciousness, it is

---

[461]. Friedrich Schleiermacher, *Der Christliche Glaube nach den Grundsätzen der evangelischen Kirche im Zusammenhang dargestellt*, (1821, 1830), (Berlin: 1835/36); *The Christian Faith*, English translation of the second German edition, H. R. Mackintosh and J. S. Stewart (Edinburgh: T. & T. Clark, 1986), 52. Henceforth this work will be cited as *CF*.

[462]. *CF*, 31.

[463]. *CF*, 35. In more detail, Schleiermacher describes three stages of religious development. Let us think of two stages before Monotheism. First, the lowest stage of religious development appears from the religious forms of "Idol-worship" or "Fetishism." In this level, the religious self-consciousness remains in "the confused animal grade," which cannot have the total consciousness to realize the distinction between the higher and the lower consciousness. The feeling of utter dependence is accordingly mirrored in "an individual object sensuously apprehended." The next stage of religious development, according to Schleiermacher, consists in the religious forms of "Polytheism," in which the local references of the different deities completely fade away and "the gods, spiritually defined, form an organized and coherent plurality." Here, unlike the case above, the religious self-consciousness can have an ability to distinguish subject from object, but the feeling of utter dependence is still reflected from "a plurality of beings," not a unity of Being. *CF*, 34. George Cross, *The Theology of Schleiermacher* (Chicago, The University of Chicago Press, 1911), 128.

the highest form of religious consciousness among monotheistic forms such as the Jewish and the Mohammedan.[464]

Next, why does Schleiermacher interpret the Christian community as "the teleological type of religion"? According to Schleiermacher, since the Christian community is a form of teleological piety, it stresses the value of ethical self-consciousness dominated by religious self-consciousness based on insights from the Kingdom of God toward which all Christian activities are always focused. That is to say, Christianity is a teleological religion regarding the moral forms of religious emotion as the fundamental type of piety, in which God's consciousness centers always on the fulfillment of a Kingdom of God.[465]

Lastly, Schleiermacher, as indicated above, considers Christianity as a particular religious community in the redemptive activity of Jesus of Nazareth. In other words, Christianity is the religious community of redemption accomplished in Jesus of Nazareth who is its Redeemer and therefore its Founder, for Jesus has shared His God-consciousness through the Christian church in a concrete human history.

Schleiermacher explains the meaning of the birth of Jesus Christ as the historical Redeemer through Ernst, one of the characters in the *The Christmas Eve*. According to Ernst, the "joy" of the Christmas festival comes from the appearance of the Redeemer because it gives us redemption.[466] Ernst considers the birth of the Redeemer as "the uniquely universal festival of joy" in the sense that "there is no other principle of joy than redemption."[467] In this vein, since the birth of "the divine Child" comes to be the inner ground of the Christian church, Ernst recognizes Jesus Christ as the historical Redeemer as well as the Founder of

---

[464]. *CF*, 34, 37, 38.

[465]. *CF*, 42, 43.

[466]. Friedrich Schleiermacher, *Christmas Eve: Dialogue On The Incarnation*, trans. Terrence N. Tice (San Francisco: The Edwin Mellen Press, 1990), 77-78. Hereafter referred to as *CE*.

[467]. *CE*, 78, 79, 80.

the Christian new life. This is a brief outline on why Christian community is essentially distinguished from other religious communities.[468]

The Christian Church and Christian Religious Experience

Since 19th century, the idea of religious experience has been a very serious topic of discussion by religious thinkers and Protestant theologians. Unfortunately, most of them have rarely ever thought about Christian religious experience in relation to the Christian community. In this way, since they have often ignored or easily criticized the theological importance of the Christian community in dealing with the issue of religious experience, it is true that the topic of Christian religious experience tends to fall into the wrong kind of individualism.

Where does the Christian religious experience come from and develop? I hold that according to Schleiermacher, it originates and develops from the Christian church. Namely, without thinking of the Christian church, we cannot speak of Christian religious experience. Of course, Schleiermacher, like William James,[469] seems to focus on individual religious experience in defining the

---

[468]. Schleiermacher explicates the natural heresies, such as the Docetic and the Nasarean, the Manichean and the Pelagian. According to Schleiermacher, Docetism denies the reality of the body of Christ, namely, the reality of Christ's physical incarnation in the sense that Christ's suffering and death were only apparent and not real. Since docetism rejects the redemptive activity of Jesus of Nazareth in ontological and historical dimensions, which constitutes the essence of the Christianity, it tends to be supernatural and therefore comes to be heretical. Secondly, unlike docetism, Schleiermacher insists, since the Nasarean or Ebionitic entirely regards Jesus as an ordinary man, it repudiates Christ's pre-emmence over all other men, namely, an exclusive and peculiar dignity of Jesus as the Son of God. Thirdly, since Manichaesim denies man's capacity for redemption on the basis of a natural dualism which claims that light is good, equated with God and darkness is evil, equated with matter, it annuls the essence of Christianity as the religion of redemption by Jesus of Nazareth. Fourthly, unlike Manichaesim, Pelagianism denies man's need of redemption in the claim that there were sinless human beings before the coming of Christ. That is to say, the Pelagian rejects man's need of redemption through Jesus Christ as Redeemer and therefore is called heresy by Schleiermacher because it refuses the original sin of a human being. *CF*, 97-101.

[469]. In his famous book *The Varieties of Religious Experience* (New York: Penguin Books, 1928), William James (1842-1910), as an American psychologist and philosopher, emphasizes individual religious experiences rather than the precepts of organized and institutionalized religions in understanding the nature of religion. James especially focuses on the plurality and the variety of individual religious experiences in world's religious life. In this sense, James defines

essence of religion in his famous book *Über die Religion*.[470] In its Second Speech, Schleiermacher, beyond Immanuel Kant,[471] recognizes the value of individual religious experience of the infinite and its plurality in the claim that the essence of religion is "neither thinking nor acting, but intuition and feeling," namely, immediate experiences for the infinite on the basis of the historical, theological, and cultural differences of the individuals.[472]

However, we cannot evaluate the reality of individual religious experience of the infinite without considering the religious community because in its Fourth Speech, Schleiermacher contends that since human beings are social and religious in their nature, necessarily individual religious phenomena come from the social context and develop by communal religious communication. Here Schleiermacher defines the nature of religion as "social."[473] In other words, Schleiermacher views the nature of religion as embracing interactive communication, namely, communal nature in the sense that human beings as social animals intrinsically hope to communicate or share their own religious

---

religion as "the feelings, acts, and experiences of individual men in their solitude, considering philosophical, theological, and ecclesiastical formulas or organizations as secondary processes. 31, 431.

[470]. The book *Über die Religion: Reden an die Gebildeten unter ihren Verächtern* was first published anonymously in 1799, and reissued in 1806, in 1821and in 1831 by Friedrich Schleiermacher. Fortunately, the text had been translated from the third German edition by John Oman in 1893 and Terrence Tice in 1969. Also, in 1988, it was first translated from the first German edition by Richard Crouter.

[471]. Immanuel Kant, *Religion Within the Limits of Reason Alone*, trans. Theodore M. Greene and Hoyt H. Hudson with a new essay "The Ethical Significance of Kant's Religion" by John R. Silber (New York: Harper Torchbooks, 1960). Kant, in the famous book, has simply reduced religion to morality in the definition that "Religion is (subjectively regarded) the recognition of all duties as divine commands." Kant claims that a religion as morality should not be in dogmas and rites but in the heart's disposition to fulfill all human duties as divine commands. In this vein, Kant insists that religion and morality must go hand in hand in the sense that to be religious is to be moral, and conversely, to be moral is to be religious. 142. Henceforth this work will be cited as *RWLRA*.

[472]. The sentences quoted here are from the translation by Richard Crouter of the first German edition. Friedrich Schleiermacher, *On Religion: Speeches to its Cultured Despisers*, translation, introduction, notes. Richard Crouter (Cambridge: Cambridge University Press, 1988), 102. Hereafter referred as *OR*.

[473]. *OR*, 163.

experiences with others.[474]   The religious feeling (Gefühl), Schleiermacher stresses, inevitably produces spiritual fellowship, that is, churches. Schleiermacher explains this in propositions 6 as follows: "The religious self-consciousness, like every essential element in human nature, leads necessarily in its development to fellowship or communion...a Church."[475] In this vein, unlike all other associations, such as the family, the school, and the state, Schleiermacher considers "piety" (Frömmigkeit) as the essential basis of all kinds of churches, which is "neither a Knowing nor a Doing, but a modification of Feeling, or of immediate self-consciousness."[476]

Furthermore, according to Schleiermacher, the term piety as "immediate self-consciousness" is specified as "the feeling of utter dependence" ("ein schlechthinniges Abhängigkeitsgefühl"), which means the religious self-consciousness of being absolutely dependent in relation to God.[477] Schleiermacher equates the feeling of utter dependence with the relationship to God in the belief that since "the *Whence* of our receptive and active existence" is to be named by the term 'God,' God is the place of the total self-consciousness.[478] Here, the direct inward expression of the feeling of utter dependence denotes the consciousness of God, namely, the highest immediate self-consciousness.[479]

If so, how can we experience the feeling of utter dependence as the God-consciousness?   According to Schleiermacher, only through the redemptive

---

[474]. *OR*, 163-165. Schleiermacher advocates this as follows: "...his first endeavor, when a religious view has become clear to him or a pious feeling penetrates his soul, is also to direct others to the object and, if possible, to communicate the vibrations of his mind to them."163-164.

[475]. *CF*, 26.

[476]. *CF*, 5. "Die Frömmigkeit, welche die Basis aller kirchlichen Gemeinschaften ausmacht, ist rein für sich betrachtet weder ein Wissen noch ein Tun, sondern eine Bestimmtheit des Gefühls oder des unmittelbaren Selbstbewußtseins." Friedrich Schleiermacher, *Der Christliche Glaube nach den Grundsätzen der evangelischen Kirche im Zusammenhang dargestellt, zweite umgearbeitete Ausgabe, vol.* 1 and 2. (Water De Gruyter & Co.: Berlin,1960), vol. 1, 14. Henceforth this work will be cited as *DCG*.

[477]. *DCG*, v. 1, 28. *CF*, 12-13.

[478]. *CF*, 12-17.

[479]. Schleiermacher describes self-consciousness in three levels: "the confused animal grade" as the lowest; "the sensible self-consciousness" as the middle; and "the feeling of utter dependence" as the highest. *CF*, 19, 20.

activity of Jesus Christ in the Christian religious community, all believers come to experience the Christian religious self-consciousness that is the highest consciousness of communal religious experience. As the Redeemer Jesus Christ possesses "an absolutely powerful God-consciousness" ("ein schlechthin kräftiges Gottesbewußtsein") in the self-consciousness, which constituted the personal existence of God in Him.[480] The power of God-consciousness in Him, according to Schleiermacher, exists in an absolutely perfect form, that is, in a perfect archetypal form (Urbildlichkeit), through which Christ comes to be distinguished from human beings in the claim that He has "His essential sinlessness and His absolute perfection."[481]

While Kant understands the term Urbild as "the idea of a person morally well-pleasing to God" in terms of moral and ahistorical dimensions, here Schleiermacher considers it in spiritual and historical ways.[482] In other words, from a practical point of view working within the limits of reason, Kant apprehends Urbild as the universally moral reasoning to fulfill the moral law given by God, in which Jesus Christ is considered only as a moral teacher. Yet Schleiermacher interprets it as the religiously productive forces working in history, through which as an historical individual Jesus Christ comes to be the Founder of the Christian religious community. Jack Verheyden explains the relationship between Jesus of Nazareth and the Christian church as follows:

> ...the Christian community is related both outwardly and inwardly to Jesus of Nazareth-outwardly as the determinate historical beginning from which the community continually derives, inwardly because it is the power of Jesus' unqualified dependence which is present as the new life. In this sense Jesus is the exemplar

---

[480]. *DCG*, v. 2, 45. *CF*, 385-387..
[481]. *CF*, 413. *DCG*, v.2, 45.
[482]. *RWLRA*, 56.

of Christian life and fulfills his vocation by communicating vitality and direction to the Christian church.[483]

This means that Jesus Christ, who is the Redeemer as well as the Founder of the Christian church, has fulfilled His archetypal God-consciousness through, with, and in the Christian church. Since, as a kind of religious energy, Christ's God-consciousness is also a kind of self-communicating consciousness, Christ leads believers into the power of His God-consciousness. By participating in Christ's self-communicating redemptive activity, all believers come to experience his sinless perfection and blessedness which is called redemption, namely, a new personality.[484] In this vein, Schleiermacher advocates,

> For since Christian piety never arises independently and of itself in an individual, but only *out of the communion* and *in the communion,* there is no such thing as adherence to Christ except in combination with adherence to the communion.[485]

Therefore, without the Christian church, we can never think of the Christian religious experience because to have a vital fellowship with Christ is to participate in the Christian church which is His organic body as well as His perfect image in the power of the Holy Spirit.[486] Here we can define Christian spirituality as a communal spirituality not as an individual spirituality in the claim that Christian religious experience comes from the Christian community and develops in it.

The Christian Church and Christian Theology

The Christian religious self-consciousness as piety, Schleiermacher advocates, is interpreted and expressed by theological works because although

---

[483]. Friedrich Schleiermacher, *The Life of Jesus,* ed. Jack C. Verheyden (Philadelphia: Fortress Press, 1975), xlvi.

[484]. *CF*, 425, 431.

[485]. *CF*, 106. (Emphases mine)

[486]. *CF*, 578. Schleiermacher says this in propositions 125: "The Christian Church, animated by the Holy Spirit, is in its purity and integrity the perfect image of the Redeemer, and each regenerate individual is an indispensable constituent of this fellowship." 578.

piety as "a state of Feeling" does not come from the Knowing and the Doing, it first emerges in the aspects of the Knowing, namely, thinking.[487]

If so, what kind of relationship is there between the Christian church and Christian theology as an aspect of the Knowing? Like the case of the relationship between the Christian church and the Christian religious experience, according to Schleiermacher, without speaking of the Christian church, we cannot think of Christian theology because Christian theology should proceed from and develop in relation to the Christian church. Schleiermacher defines theology as follows:

> Theology is a positive science, whose parts join into a cohesive whole only through their common relation to a particular mode of faith, i.e., a particular way of being conscious of God. Thus, the various parts of Christian theology belong together only by virtue of their relation to "Christianity."[488]

That is to say, in Schleiermacher, the term theology as a positive science means only Christian theology because in a reciprocal relationship between the whole and the particular, theology should focus on a particular religious consciousness of God which is present in the Christian community and pertains to the Christian church. In such a perspective, Schleiermacher defines Christian theology in more detail as follows:

> Christian theology, accordingly, is that assemblage of scientific knowledge and practical instruction without the possession and application of which a united leadership of the Christian Church, i.e., a government of the Church in the fullest sense, is not possible.[489]

According to Schleiermacher, Christian theology, which must center on the Christian church leadership in all kinds of theological themes, has a twofold

---

[487]. CF, 11. Schleiermacher says, "...so piety in its diverse expressions remains essentially a state of Feeling. This state is subsequently caught up into the region of thinking, but only in so far as each religious man is at the same time inclined towards thinking and exercise therein...." CF, 11.

[488]. Friedrich Schleiermacher, Brief Outline on the Study of Theology, trans. Terrence N. Tice (Richmond: John Knox Press, 1966), 19. Hereafter referred as BOST.

[489]. BOST, 20.

value. One of them is "an ecclesiastical value" which is interested in the Christian religious self-consciousness of the infinite through Jesus Christ within the Christian community.[490] More specifically, as we have already shown, the ecclesiastical interest serves to interpret a particular piety on which the Christian church is based. The other is "a scientific value" which depends on the theological interpretations of the former on the Christian self-consciousness because the role of the latter is to articulate the results of the former with a logical coherence. Schleiermacher describes the relationship between two:

> Now since every doctrine of the faith has, as such, an ecclesiastical value, and since these doctrines become dogmatic when they acquire a scientific value, dogmatic propositions are the more perfect the more their scientific character gives them an outstanding ecclesiastical value, and also the more their scientific content bears traces of having proceeded from the ecclesiastical interest.[491]

To be sure, if any theology does not stem from this ecclesiastical interest, in Schleiermacher, at least, it cannot be called theology or Christian theology as a positive science because Christian theology should come from the Christian community and develop in relation to it continually.

According to Schleiermacher, the task of Christian theology, then, is to try to figure out the distinctive nature of the Christian church from other churches based on different kinds of faith and the nature of its particular religious experiences in relation to all religious phenomena within human nature.[492] To fulfill the theological task, Schleiermacher explains the whole theological study in relation to the Christian church in three dimensions. The first is called "philosophical theology" which involves two sides, *apologetical* and *polemical* in investigating the distinctive nature of the Christian church with perspectives drawn from the philosophy of religion.[493] While apologetics tries to communicate

---

[490]. *CF*, 83, 84.
[491]. *CF*, 85.
[492]. *BOST*, 24.
[493]. *BOST*, 29-31.

persuasively the confidence of the particular piety of the Christian church with others outside the Christian church, polemics aims to criticize exclusively diseased deviations which are present in the Christian church through the process of a reconfirmation of its distinctive nature.[494]

However, philosophical theology is interdependent on "historical theology" because the former utilizes the material of the latter in its theological process and vice versa. According to Schleiermacher, like philosophical theology, as a theological discipline, historical theology also is closely related to the Christian church in the sense that it explores the original knowledge of the Christian church, its whole past, and its present.[495]

As a historical theology, exegetical theology analyzes the New Testament, the canon of the Christian church so that we can listen to God's words as Jesus Christ preached them to the earliest Christians.[496] Church history, as the second subdivision of historical theology, examines the particular meaning of Christian history through Jesus Christ who is the Redeemer and therefore the Founder of the Christian community.[497] As the third subdivision of historical theology, dogmatic theology, like the above two, has an essential relationship with the Christian church because as a theological discipline, it does not deal with social community or purely metaphysical things in character, but focus on the particular religious experiences of the infinite in the Christian religious community. In this vein, Schleiermacher demonstrates,

> Since Dogmatics is a theological discipline, and thus pertains solely to the   Christian Church, we can only explain what it is when we have become clear as to the conception of the Christian Church.[498]

---

494. *BOST*, 31, 32.
495. *BOST*, 45.
496. *BOST*,50, 51.
497. *BOST*, 64.
498. *CF*, 3.

Alongside philosophical theology and historical theology, Schleiermacher puts "practical theology." Practical theology is the culmination of theological study in the Christian church because it, as theological reflection, centers on "the immediate applicability of its results" in the particular piety of the Christian church.[499]

Therefore, without becoming concerned with the idea of the Christian church, we cannot consider Christian theology because, as we have already seen, Christian theology as a positive science should proceed from and develop in relation with the Christian church. In this vein, Schleiermacher apprehends Christian theology as "ecclesiological" theology.

The Christian Church and Christian Ethics

According to Schleiermacher, the Christian religious experience as piety, as we have already indicated, brings forth the Christian ethical activity because even though piety as "a state of Feeling" does not stem from the Knowing and the Doing, it produces the ethical activity of the Doing through the theological step of the Knowing.[500]

If this is true, what kind of relationship is there between the Christian church and Christian ethics as an aspect of the Doing? According to Schleiermacher, like the case of the relationship between the Christian church and Christian theology, Christian ethics has an essential relationship with the Christian church because Christian ethics also should stem from and develop in relation to the Christian church. This is because Christian ethics is only a theological system of Christian activity in Christian life, based on Christian piety within the Christian church. Schleiermacher asserts, "Since Christian ethics can contain nothing other than the description of the same form of behavior that

---

[499]. *BOST*, 91.
[500]. *CF*, 11.

develops naturally from the Christian principle, *it is always only in and for the Christian church.*"[501] (Emphasis mine)

In Schleiermacher, Christian ethics, unlike philosophical ethics or ethics in general, has its own particular characteristic by focusing only on the Christian principle of life in the Christian church.[502] However, here Sung M. Park affirms that Christian ethics also can be philosophical in relation to the Christian church. He explains,

> ...if philosophical ethics admits that the formation of the Christian religious community is based on the approval of rational ethics, then it must also acknowledge Christian ethics, which always wants to develop completely in the religious community. Christian ethics also acknowledges that the Christian life is in a religious community based on rationally ethical judgment.[503]

That is to say, even though Christian ethics and philosophical ethics have their own different principles, they are not exclusive, but are related to and support each other. If Christian ethics is based on the Christian principle of life in the Christian church, what then is the Christian principle? According to Schleiermacher, it is redemption through Jesus Christ in the Christian community. Schleiermacher considers redemption as "activity to please God" (Gottesgefälligen) based on the revelation of God in Christ's person.[504] Schleiermacher expresses,

---

[501]. *Friedrich Schleiermacher, Christliche Sittenlehre: Einleitung, nach grössenteils unveröffentlichen Hörernachschriften*, ed. and introduction by Hermann Peiter, afterword by Martin Honecker (Stuttgart: Kohlhammer, 1983). Henceforth references to Peiter's edition on the introduction of the Christian ethics will be cited as *CSE*. John Shelly translated this edition into English. Friedrich Schleiermacher, *Introduction to Christian Ethics* (Nashville: Abingdon Press, 1989). Henceforth references to this English translation will be cited as *ICE*. 38, 87, 96.

[502]. Friedrich Schleiermacher, *Die Christliche Sitte: nach den Grundsätzen der evangelischen Kirche im Zusammenhange darstellt*, Aus Schleiermacher's handschriftlichen Nachlasse und nachgeschriebenen herausgegeben von L. Jonas. 2nd ed (Berlin: G. Reimer, 1884), V. 2, 29. Hereafter referred to as *CS*.

[503]. Sung M. Park, *Christ and Christian Conduct* (Ph.D. diss. The Claremont Graduate School, 1995), 75, 76. Henceforth this work will be cited as *CCC*.

[504]. *CSE*, 40.

The idea of 'pleasing to God' has itself emerged in another way through the fact of the divine revelation in the person of Christ, and adhering to this revelation of God in Christ was also a manifestation of the idea of 'pleasing to God.' In that case it is clear that there must be a Christian ethics. What exactly is this that has continually emerged in the Christian church as the Christian consciousness? If we begin with Christ himself, he lays the most certain claim to the fact that he has knowledge of God that can be communicated only through him, and that he sets forth a knowledge of God's will that did not exist before him.[505]

In addition, Schleiermacher argues that without Jesus Christ, we cannot think of the Christian consciousness because only Christ has the archetypal God-consciousness in His personality. Christ's God-consciousness, as I have already demonstrated, is a kind of self-communicating consciousness, effective in the Christian church because Christ's God-consciousness is not a metaphysical reality, but it is the religiously productive force working in history. Here the archetypal person of Christ, to Schleiermacher, comes to be the source of His redemptive activity by which the Christian church was established and is developed. That is to say that since Christ's archetypal God-consciousness, as a kind of religious energy is *"already* present, and *continues* to be present" in His whole life, it influences the Christian church only through "all real vital fellowship with Him."[506] Thus, by participating in Christ's redemptive activity, all believers come to share in His sinless perfection and blessedness which is "His reconciling activity."[507] This means that all Christians hold redemption, namely, a new personality through the self-communicative influences of Christ in the Christian church. Schleiermacher explains Christ's self-communicative activity according to the Calvinistic tradition, but from a different angle. While most of the orthodox Protestant theologians influenced by the Calvinistic tradition center only on the death of Christ on the cross in understanding Christ's redemptive

---

[505]. *ICE*, 52.
[506]. *CF*, 371.
[507]. *CF*, 371, 431.

activity, Schleiermacher focuses on Christ's whole ministry through His redemptive self-communicating activity in explaining the work of Christ.[508]

Schleiermacher identifies Christ's archetypal dignity with His redemptive activity through His entire life.[509] In His God-consciousness, Christ's redemptive activity as "pleasing to God" is the central principle of Christian ethics that all Christians should follow. Schleiermacher defines this fundamental principle as "the pure Christian principle of life."[510] Since Christian ethics is just a descriptive form of Christ's self-communicative life, in which Christ's life itself comes to be the most important criteria in determining the ethical life of Christians, Christ is a model and a type of Christian activity which all Christians should imitate in the Christian church. Schleiermacher defines Christian ethics as follows:

> *Christian ethics* does indeed have connections to the person of Christ, but it also has another connection to the Christian church viewed as community. It will be truly valid only *in and for the Christian church*, and it will not solve the problem of behavior in a way that is universally binding. Rather, it will only show how it is treated in the Christian church in accordance with its spirit. It is, therefore, *the ethics of a particular community*."[511] (Emphases mine)

---

[508]. Let us consider Schleiermacher's idea of Christ's threefold redemptive activity briefly. First, Christ's prophetic activity includes "teaching, prophesying, and working miracles." These three are not separated, but are unified. The source of Christ's prophetic activity is "the absolutely original revelation of God in Him." In this sense, Schleiermacher considers Christ as "the climax and the end of all prophecy." Secondly, Christ's priestly activity consists in "His perfect fulfillment of the law (i.e. His active obedience), His atoning death (i.e. His passive obedience), and His intercession with the Father for believers." While in His prophetic activity Christ regards us as His antithesis in which we still do not have a complete union with Him, in His priestly activity, Christ leads us to a perfect union with Him through the living fellowship between Him and us. This union, to Schleiermacher, is defined as "absolute and eternal" by God. In this vein, Schleiermacher calls Christ "the end of priesthood." Thirdly, according to Schleiermacher, Christ's kingly activity refers to His vital fellowship with believers. This does not mean a special relationship with individuals, but with members of His religious community. In this community of believers, Christ has the creative power to develop its communion continuously, through which Christ controls this world in history. In this sense, Schleiermacher defines Christ as "the climax and end of all spiritual kingship." *CF*, 441-472.

[509]. *CF*, 377.

[510]. *ICE*, 50.

[511]. *ICE*, 53.

This means that Christian ethics also is a theological doctrine of Christian activity based on "the Christian moral feeling" derived from Christ in the Christian church.[512] Therefore, Christian ethics as "the ethics of a particular community," in Schleiermacher, should begin with the Christian church and develop in relation with it because Christian ethics is "a reality only for the Christian church."[513]

Concluding Remarks

We have seen that there is an essential relationship between the Christian church and the major theological themes of Christian faith, such as Christian religious experience, Christian theology, and Christian ethics in Schleiermacher's theological thought. Here, I hold that Schleiermacher can be called the father of the modern Protestant ecclesiology as well as "the father of the modern Protestant theology." In other words, without the Christian church, according to Schleiermacher, we can never think of Christian religious experience, Christian theology, and Christian ethics because they should stem from and develop in relation to the Christian church. Therefore, if we explore any religious experience, any theology, and any doctrine of activity without scrutinizing the Christian church, such a theological approach, in Schleiermacher, will never be "Christian."

---

[512]. *ICE*, 42.
[513]. *ICE*, 87.

SCHLEIERMACHER ON SACRED AND PROFANE HERMENEUTIC

David E. Klemm

It is a privilege for me to contribute an essay to a Festschrift honoring Jack Verheyden, who has done so much excellent work on Friedrich Schleiermacher. In this paper I focus on the fact that Schleiermacher, the founder of modern hermeneutic, is often credited with the theoretical breakthrough that in principle elides the distinction between sacred and profane hermeneutic. I intend to show that if we apply one of Schleiermacher's principles of interpretation to his own texts concerning hermeneutic, we can understand that Schleiermacher's hermeneutic restores in a higher dimension of reflection what it takes away at a lower dimension. The principle I have in mind is the ancient one of reading the parts of a text in light of the whole and the whole in light of the parts. If we apply this principle to Schleiermacher's own writings, we find that the principled distinction between sacred and profane hermeneutic in one part of his system is restored in another part. Let me explain.

In the past, sacred and profane hermeneutic were distinguished with reference to certain kinds of texts. Interpretation of the Bible constituted sacred hermeneutic; whereas interpretation of literary, philosophical, or legal texts constituted profane hermeneutic. Within each of these domains of scholarship, hermeneutic served as a subordinate discipline, which formulated local rules of thumb pertaining to a particular text tradition. The emergence of full critical consciousness made it impossible to draw the distinction on such an object-oriented basis, because there is nothing inherent in the text as a received object that would justify such a special status. Paul Ricoeur, among many others, wrote that Schleiermacher was the one who transformed such regional or special hermeneutic into a general theory of the universal activity of understanding.[514] Schleiermacher, according to Ricoeur, disengaged hermeneutical theory from any particular object domain, whether sacred or profane. According to Ricoeur,

> A general hermeneutic therefore requires that the interpreter rise above the particular applications and discern the operations which are common to the two great branches of hermeneutic. In order to do that, however, it is necessary to rise above, not only the particularity of texts, but also the particularity of the rules and recipes into which the art of understanding is dispersed.[515]

Ricoeur calls this subordination of the special rules of regional hermeneutic to the general problematic of understanding, "an inversion fully comparable to that which Kantian philosophy had effected elsewhere, primarily in relation to the natural sciences."[516] The inversion had many fateful consequences according to Ricoeur. Among the consequences were, first, Schleiermacher's hermeneutic followed the Kantian rule of subordinating ontology to epistemology, because according to the general spirit of critique "the capacity for knowing must be measured before we confront the nature of being."[517] Second, and for our purposes most important, Schleiermacher's hermeneutic loses the capacity to make any principled distinction between sacred and profane interpretation. Indeed, Schleiermacher himself says repeatedly that the principles for interpreting all discourse are the same.

---

[514] Ricoeur probably takes Schleiermacher at his word when Schleiermacher wrote, "Hermeneutics as the art of understanding does not yet exist in a general manner, there are instead only several forms of specific hermeneutics." Friedrich Schleiermacher, *Hermeneutics and Criticism*, translated and edited by Andrew Bowie (Cambridge: Cambridge University Press, 1998), p. 5. As a matter of fact, however, Schleiermacher did not produce the first universal theory of hermeneutic. See Jean Grondin, *Introduction to Philosophical Hermeneutics*, translated by Joel Weisheimer (New Haven and London: Yale University Press, 1994), chapters II and III.

[515] Paul Ricoeur, "The Task of Hermeneutic," in Paul Ricoeur, *Hermeneutic & the Human Sciences: Essays on Language, Action, and Interpretation*, edited and translated by John B. Thompson (Cambridge, England: Cambridge University Press, 1981), pp. 43-62, p. 45.

[516] *Ibid.*

[517] *Ibid.*, p. 46.

Arguably, conceiving the difference between sacred and profane hermeneutic becomes a problem following Schleiermacher. Is it possible to distinguish sacred from profane texts? Is it possible to distinguish sacred from profane acts of interpretation? Schleiermacher's general theory of interpretation seems to deprive us of criteria for making these distinctions. At stake in the problem is the very meaning of our being in the world. For if humans are primarily meaning-conferring and meaning-receiving creatures, then our inability to distinguish sacred from profane meanings registers our inability to understand events in our own lives as either sacred or profane. Our lives would hold only an emptiness that is beyond the sacred and profane, that has emptied itself of genuine humanity.

Hermeneutic in Relation to Rhetoric and Dialectic

The claim of this paper is that Schleiermacher restores in his dialectic precisely the conceptual capacity to distinguish between sacred and profane that he appears to confiscate in his hermeneutic. Schleiermacher himself insisted that hermeneutic be read in the context of his philosophical system as a whole and not as a freestanding and self-contained theory, so we cannot go too far afield in interpreting Schleiermacher's hermeneutic by following his own advice and relating it to dialectic.[518] In the early portion of the 1819 compendium on hermeneutic, Schleiermacher acknowledges the difficulty of assigning general hermeneutic its proper place among the sciences, but he ultimately relates hermeneutic both to dialectic and rhetoric as three fundamental philosophical sciences.[519] Most simply put, he calls hermeneutic is the art of understanding, rhetoric is the art of speaking, and dialectic is the art of thinking.

Hermeneutic and rhetoric are therefore simply the reverse sides of one another. In any conversation with another person, I am either uttering words

---

[518] Precisely the same thing can be said of Schleiermacher's theology; it must be read in the context of the whole.

[519] Schleiermacher, *Hermeneutics and Criticism*, pp. 5-6.

myself or listening to words uttered by the other. Living dialogue is the natural home of both arts, which are deeply rooted in everyday life. Although both speaking and understanding are purposive and rule-governed activities, we ordinarily do not have recourse to their principles and rules; we simply engage in the free but structured interplay of language as a back and forth movement between two interlocutors. Only when certain more particular interests arise—for example, aesthetic, historical, political, or religious interests—do we have recourse to the arts of hermeneutic and rhetoric. Hermeneutic and rhetoric primarily have to do with language in actual use. However, insofar as language is the necessary and universal medium of thinking—Schleiermacher calls language the exterior of thinking, and thinking the interior of language—they both in the nature of the case have reference to dialectic. The intrinsic reference to thinking reveals itself in the more precise definitions of the two arts in their twofold nature as both theory and method.

Hermeneutic is thinking about the principle and rules for true understanding of the meaning of judgments articulated in particular linguistic signs. As theory, hermeneutic is thinking about the relation between the universal structure of thinking and the particular meaning of the individualized thinking embodied in a text or other set of linguistic signs by an author and presented to an audience or reader to be understood. As method, hermeneutic is the set of rules governing the correct interpretation of texts or other such signs.

Rhetoric is thinking about the principle and rules for truthful and effective presentation of judgments in new discourse. As theory, it is thinking about the relation between the universal structure of thinking and the particular purposes, audience, and occasion of discourse addressed by a speaker or writer. As method, rhetoric is the set of rules used to produce truthful and persuasive arguments within specific contexts of discourse and for particular audiences.

Dialectic is thinking about the principle and rules of relating the forms of thinking with the material of being in true judgments. As theory, dialectic is thinking about the universal structure of thinking that intends to become a knowing. As method, dialectic sets forth the set of rules governing such thinking—rules used to construct true judgments in inquiry. Both the form and content of dialectical theory and method are utterly universal for all thinking beings.

According to Schleiermacher, dialectic, hermeneutic, and rhetoric are interrelated yet distinct arts (*Kunstlehre*). Hermeneutic and rhetoric are interrelated as the arts of understanding and producing discourse respectively. Both are subordinate to dialectic, however, as pure thinking about thinking that intends truth. Hermeneutic without dialectic is interpretive free association without ground in the author's intention. Rhetoric without dialectic is argumentative persuasion for personal ends without regard to truth. Interest in dialectic arises whenever there is interest in truth in understanding or speaking. Dialectic is thus the measure of both hermeneutic and rhetoric. Dialectic, however, is also reciprocally dependent on both hermeneutic and rhetoric, for dialectical thinking in the nature of the case has recourse to rhetoric when it is actually produced as discourse and to hermeneutic when it is understood as discourse. There is no actual instance of dialectic that is not itself produced through the principle and rules of rhetoric and understood through the principle and rules of hermeneutic. Moreover, the phenomenal starting point for Schleiermacher's lectures on dialectic is precisely the same as that of his reflections on hermeneutic and rhetoric, namely, the occasion of misunderstanding in dialogue. In contrast to hermeneutic and rhetoric, however, dialectic is its own measure. Dialectic alone gives human thinking access to the truth about truth, and interest in dialectic arises whenever interest in the difference between knowledge and opinion arises within dialogue. Let's turn now to Schleiermacher's notes and lecture material about hermeneutic to see what kind of structure Schleiermacher assigns to interpretation. Only then will it be possible to draw a distinction between sacred and profane hermeneutic.

The Structure of Interpretation in Schleiermacher

It is important to understand that everything Schleiermacher says about interpretation is intended to illuminate the natural everyday processes by which we do in fact come to know other persons. The problem of understanding texts from the ancient past is always derivative of the primary hermeneutical problem, which is how to understand others. Hermeneutical principles are therefore always rooted in the social character of life. Schleiermacher's intellectual procedure is always to begin with everyday discourse and then to discern the principles governing the social practice of conversation.

Schleiermacher does precisely the same thing in his dialectic, when he begins with the fact of two people conversing about a common topic. He does not begin with abstract principles derived from the structure of self-conscious mentality, then applying them to concrete situations. He always begins with concrete experiences of discourse and expands to the universal principles. In his hermeneutic, Schleiermacher time and again refers both to the mystery of a child's acquisition of language and to the experience of life-transforming significant conversations ("*bedeutungsvolle Gespräche*"). He tests his principles by our inability to deny their structuring presence in these events of language without ourselves deploying them.

But there is a twist in Schleiermacher's procedure. Schleiermacher runs against the received tradition in hermeneutic by distinguishing between a lax and a rigorous practice. The lax practice assumes that "understanding results as a matter of course and expresses the aim negatively: misunderstanding should be avoided." The rigorous practice assumes, by contrast, that "misunderstanding results as a matter of course and that understanding must be desired and sought at every point."[520] Previously, the lax practice reigned in hermeneutic; hence rules were constructed to illuminate the difficult passages by means of the easy ones on the assumption that understanding happens of a course for the most part and its light can drive out misunderstanding. With Schleiermacher, the rigorous practice

---

[520] Schleiermacher, Hermeneutics and Criticism, pp. 21-2.

is adopted in principle; he assumes that misunderstanding, rather than understanding, naturally takes place. Hermeneutic cannot rest on the apparent success of naïve practice but must be the vigilant philosophical critic of naïve practice.

Schleiermacher does the same thing with dialectic. In beginning with significant conversations about a common topic, he does not assume general agreement but rather the reverse. Dispute, not consensus, is the normal condition of everyday practice. Dialectic is not the art of producing agreement out of disagreement when such occasionally arises; it is the philosophical investigation into the possibility of disagreement. Given that we disagree about some topic, how do we know that we are talking about the same thing? What basic principles and concepts make dispute possible? This twist introduces an awareness of negativity into Schleiermacher's thought, which displays a keen sensitivity to the foibles and finitude of human thinking. Hermeneutic does not promise to produce understanding, but to make us aware of our misunderstanding; dialectic does not promise absolute knowing about knowing, but a knowing about our lack of knowing. This twist continues to make Schleiermacher interesting at the end of the 20th century.

Turning to hermeneutic, the most fundamental principles Schleiermacher extracts from the experience of misunderstanding other persons are those of sameness and otherness. In every instance of misunderstanding, there is nonetheless something common between speaker and hearer that binds them together and makes at least a partial understanding possible: minimally the interlocutors share a common humanity and a common language. In every instance of misunderstanding, something strange also intrudes: the otherness of the other is ultimately inexplicable and inexhaustible. To produce and understand meanings is a reciprocal, interactive task that is infinite in scope for finite humans who always find themselves in the middle of an ongoing conversation without the means to elevate themselves above their limited positions within it. Interpretation for Schleiermacher is a never-ending process, always inadequately approximating the ultimately unattainable truth of things.

What emerges with consistency over Schleiermacher's lectures and notes on hermeneutic is a structural analysis of meaning: an attempt to account for all the basic elements in the understanding and producing of meaning in relation to one another without purporting to explain them. He distinguishes two kinds of interpretive activity that we actually use to reduce misunderstanding—the grammatical and the technical/psychological. Furthermore, he specifies two methods of interpretation—the comparative and the divinatory. It is very important to understand that both the comparative and divinatory methods apply to both the grammatical and technical/psychological kinds of interpretation. Methodical interpretation oscillates between them. Let's briefly consider the two methods.

Comparison is the objective-analytic method of distinguishing the material element from the formal element for the sake of correctly subsuming particulars under universal concepts. *Divination,* by contrast, is the subjective-intuitive method of directly apprehending individuals as living combinations of formal and material elements, universal concepts and particular percepts. Now let's consider the two kinds of interpretation.

The task of *grammatical interpretation* is "to understand the sense of an utterance from out of the language."[521] It focuses predominately on what is common between speaker and hearer and hence objective in nature: the shared structure of language. The two rules of grammatical interpretation are variations on the principle of understanding the parts in light of the whole and the whole in light of the parts. First, "Everything in a given utterance which requires a more precise determination may only be determined from the language area which is common to the author and his original audience."[522] In other words, first refer

---

[521] Schleiermacher, *Hermeneutics and Criticism*, p. 232.
[522] Schleiermacher, *Hermeneutics and Criticism*, p. 30.

the apparent particular meaning of the words of the passage to the meanings universally present in the entire historical "linguistic sphere" of the author. Second, "The sense of every word in a given location must be determined according to its being-together with those that surround it."[523] In other words, following the initial determination of meaning, the interpreter should comprehend how the author further individualizes the meaning of his/her words within the text itself and its intertextual references. Use of metaphor and irony often depend on understanding highly individualized instantiations of meaning. The comparative method of grammatical interpretation deals primarily with formal considerations: various means of combining both words into sentences through connectives and particles and sentences into larger units through genre. The divinatory method of grammatical interpretation deals with material considerations in focusing on the distinctive meaning of what is combined.

In *technical/psychological interpretation* "the unity of the work, the theme, is here regarded as the principle which moves the writer, and the main characteristics of the composition as his individual nature which reveals itself in that movement."[524] Whereas grammatical interpretation focuses on what is common between the author and reader, speaker and hearer, technical/psychological interpretation pays particular attention to what is strange and unique in the work. Again, the interpreter has only language to work with, but this moment brings out the individual treatment of the theme by concentrating on the author's distinctive style and means of composition. Even when dealing with a primary idea that is well known in the tradition, the author will individualize that idea by means of his or her own addition of secondary ideas that enable the theme to be embodied as a distinctive reception and interpretation of that idea. For quite some time, scholars took Schleiermacher to use the terms

---

[523] Schleiermacher, *Hermeneutics and Criticism*, p. 44.
[524] Schleiermacher, *Hermeneutics and Criticism*, p. 90.

"technical and "psychological" synonymously in his lectures and notes on hermeneutic. Recently, however, it has become quite clear that there is a systematic difference. The technical moment understands the text through the comparative method by focusing on its discrete meaning as a work of art. In contrast, the psychological moment understands the text through the divinatory method as a creative event in the author's ongoing life.[525]

A fourfold structure of hermeneutical possibilities therefore emerges from Schleiermacher's analysis, and it is possible to construct a model of it as follows.

MODEL #1:

STRUCTURE OF INTERPRETATION:

Comparative-Grammatical[526]

Divinatory-Grammatical[527] +   *(Comparative)-Technical*[528]

(Divinatory)-Psychological[529]

The structure is derived from the basic experience of sameness and otherness. Just as sameness (the objective, grammatical, or comparative element) has in itself both sameness and otherness, so otherness (the subjective, technical/psychological, or divinatory element) has sameness and otherness in itself. The four corners of the structural cross simply articulate these four possibilities.

Schleiermacher says that the aim of interpretive activity is to circulate among these functional possibilities to produce at least a partial agreement among

---

[525] Timothy Clancy, S.J. has done important work in demonstrating this distinction in his recent paper on the "Significance of the Negative Formulation of the Hermeneutical Task" presented to the AAR Schleiermacher Group in 1998. The terms qualitative (referring to the comparative) and quantitative (referring to the divinatory) are crucial here.

[526] The comparative-grammatical element represents the objective meaning accessible to any competent speaker of the language.

[527] The divinatory-grammatical element is the subjective meaningfulness of the language for its original audience.

[528] The (comparative)-technical element focuses on the text as work of art, considering the correspondence between discourse and thought on the grammatical side.

[529] The (divinatory)-psychological element has to do with the text as an event in the author's life; emphasis is on how much weight or meaningfulness to ascribe to each passage.

their results. When the meaning understood by means of a comparative-grammatical inquiry begins to correspond to the meaning understood by means of a divinatory-psychological inquiry, and so on, then the interpreter is going in the right direction. When the results obtained in all four elements of the structure come into tentative agreement with one another, then the hearer or reader is formulating an internally coherent meaning. What is more, Schleiermacher believes that the meaning so understood is not only internally coherent, but comes into some partial correspondence with the meaning actually produced by the speaker or author. That is the best we can do in hermeneutic.

So what is the "true" meaning for Schleiermacher? Is it the psychological event? Is it the grammatical sense? It is vitally important to understand clearly that Schleiermacher assigns equal weight to each of the elements. Meaning is a composite structure with all four elements present. Some texts, for example personal letters, require more psychological and divinatory skills than grammatical or comparative skills. Other texts, such as scientific treatises, require more comparative and grammatical skills than psychological and divinatory ones. The genre of the text itself will determine in part what proportion of skills to bring to bear on the text. Schleiermacher recognizes that some people have more interpretive power in one domain than in another. Some can intuit individual vision with a gift, but they cannot understand the objective complexities of language. Others have a knack for translating sentences, but they cannot intuit the spiritual presence and the individual urgency behind the words. Schleiermacher advises everyone to identify where his or her own hermeneutical strengths lie and to develop their weaknesses without letting their strengths go dormant. But he insists that no one element in the structure stands in a preferential position over any other element in the nature.

So far, we have seen how Schleiermacher's project to construct a universal hermeneutical theory and practice has resulted in a complex four-fold structure of interpretation. We must know relate that structure to its ground in dialectic.

The Dialectical Ground of Hermeneutic

In Schleiermacher's notes and lectures on hermeneutic, it is clear that the four elements of the structure of interpretation each presuppose the other. None of the operations analyzed in each of the four locations on the grid can be described without recourse to the other elements. We can and must distinguish them intellectually for purposes of theoretical construction, but we cannot separate them practically speaking. This recognition gives rise to a hermeneutical problem: If we cannot distinguish these elements, how are they different? In particular, how are the grammatical and technical/psychological forms of interpretation different one from the other? Andrew Bowie argues that for Schleiermacher, when we are interpreting a text we are always presented with an ineffable yet thought-provoking individual, a combination of universal and particular elements whose ground cannot be fully mediated.[530] The individual work of art itself has both a givenness and an inexhaustibility about it that ultimately defy complete explanation.

And so it is in the hermeneutic: the structure of interpretation is simply posited as the structure it is. But in dialectic, Schleiermacher does not leave it at that. He tries to cast a light of intelligibility further than he does in hermeneutic. In his lectures and notes on dialectic, Schleiermacher presents a disciplined thinking about thinking, that refers the specific modes of thinking in the hermeneutic both grammatical and technical/ psychological, both comparative and divinatory, to the nature of thinking itself.[531]

---

[530] Andrew Bowie, "Introduction," to Schleiermacher, *Hermeneutics and Criticism, pp. vii-xxxi.*

[531] Schleiermacher lectured on the topic of dialectic at the University of Berlin in the years 1811, 1814, 1818, 1822, 1828, and 1831. He always intended to prepare these lectures for publication, and he produced an introduction to his intended book in 1834, but he died before seeing the project through to completion. Editions of the lecture notes, supplemented by student notes are as follows. *Dialektik* (1811), edited by Andreas Arndt (Hamburg: Felix Meiner Verlag, 1986); *Dialektik* (1814), edited by Andreas Arndt (Hamburg: Felix Meiner Verlag, 1988); *Dialektik* (1814*): Aus Schleiermachers handschriftlichem Nachlasse,* edited by L. Jonas (Berlin: Reimer, 1839) (in *Sämmtliche Werke,* Part III, Volume 4, pt. 2; *Dialektik* (1822), edited by R. Odebrecht (Leipzig: Hinrichs, 1942; reprint Darmstadt: Wissenschaftliche Buchgesellschaft, 1976); *Dialektik* (1831), edited by Halpern (Berlin: 1903), *Dialektik* (1814), edited by Andreas Arndt (Hamburg:

Recall that hermeneutic is thinking about understanding particular meanings embodied in particular linguistic expressions. Understanding is one form of thinking among others; it is a species of the genus "thinking." Thinking, for Schleiermacher in the dialectic, is a rule-governed, structured, and purposive activity. To think well, we must know the rules, structures, and purposes of thinking; we must think about thinking. The aim of the dialectic is precisely that: to think about the structure, limits, and first principle of all thinking. To understand understanding, we must engage in dialectic, because we must understand the general form of thinking, of which understanding is one instance among others, just as we must understand the genus "canine" in order to understand the species of American Eskimo that I have in my house. Hermeneutic necessarily has recourse to dialectic in order to think itself.

Thinking, according to Schleiermacher's dialectic, is always a combining of sameness and otherness into a unified thought. For example, in articulating a judgment, such as "Chloë is a dog," I combine an common abstract concept ("dog") with a concrete image derived from perception, here denoted by the distinct name "Chloë," which is a singular term that picks out one dog among others. Sameness and otherness are brought together in the thought. Moreover, each side of the combination of sameness and otherness is itself a combination of sameness and otherness. The concept "dog" is intelligible by reference to its sameness with the concept "mammal" and its otherness from other non-doglike mammals. Similarly, I can use the proper name "Chloë" only she is like other properly nameable creatures, but in doing so I distinguish her from other named creatures in my world. Even tautologies, such as "A dog is a dog," combine sameness and otherness when repeating the same concept in the different logical positions of subject and predicate. Therefore, when we are thinking the sameness

---

Felix Meiner Verlag, 1988). I use the Odebrecht edition for citations here as "Schleiermacher's Dialectic, Odebrecht."

of something, we are also thinking the otherness of that thing, and vice versa. Consequently, nothing can be thought that is absolutely self-same or wholly other. Sameness and otherness are mutually co-implying logical terms in the sense that although they are distinct, they are nonetheless co-dependent; think one and you think the other.

Now, according to Schleiermacher, the condition of the possibility of thinking both sameness and otherness in the human being is the twofold structure he calls the intellectual function in relation to the organic function. Through organic function, I receive chaotic sense impressions through bodily senses and affective capacities of emotion, and I form an image as a means of achieving an initial state of organization.[532] Through the intellectual function, I apply general concepts according to rules of synthesis to the images formed in response to the manifold of received sensations and emotions.[533] Once again, according to Schleiermacher, I can distinguish these two functions as different in kind: one is predominately active and intellectual; one is predominately passive and bodily. But the two functions always occur together. There is no pure thinking in utter absence of sensory data formed into images, for I must think in language and language provides me with auditory or visual stimulation. There is no pure sensation in utter absence of thought, for to be aware of the chaos of sensory stimulation I must apply the concept "chaos of sensory stimulation." The intellectual and organic functions always occur together. The human being is itself an already-combined combination of sameness ("the intellectual function") and otherness ("the organic function") whose essence is the ongoing activity of combining sameness and otherness. I am a unity of opposites who being is to unify opposites. Everything that has been said so far about thinking applies to understanding as the combining of sameness (through grammatical interpretation)

---

[532] Schleiermacher's *Dialectic*, Odebrecht, p. 139.
[533] Schleiermacher's *Dialectic*, Odebrecht, p. 141.

and otherness (through technical/psychological interpretation) in hermeneutics. Dialectic and hermeneutic are another instance of sameness and otherness.

According to Schleiermacher, when we think about thinking, we are thinking about something that intrinsically divides into sameness and otherness. Thinking is both the activity in which we are now engaged (what I am doing) and that about which I am thinking (the being that is thought in thinking). Thinking about thinking therefore divides into thinking and being. The primordial structure of thinking is that thinking thinks about something, namely, being. More precisely, thinking is the activity of mediating between the external or objective opposites of "ideal being" (the intelligible form obtained through the intellectual function) and "real being" (the sensible content obtained through the organic function). The thinking activity itself is likewise and internal and subjective mediating between "thinking in the narrow sense" (the temporal activity dominated by the intellectual function) and "perceiving" (the activity dominated by the organic function that adds spatial content). Consequently, we can now construct a model of the structure of thinking.

MODEL #2:   STRUCTURE OF THINKING

Thinking   *Ideal Being*

\+

Perceiving   *Real Being*

Let us go one step further and ask the question, What is the essence of the being about which we think? Essence is the principle through which a thing can be determined in its sameness and otherness. Any thing is, first, the same as all other things (the thing is a being like other beings). Second, it is the same as itself (the appearing thing is the same as its concept). Third, it is other than all other things (the thing is specifically different from other things). Fourth, it is other from itself (the appearing thing is in a certain regard different from its concept). Now, we all know from school that the essence of a thing is signified in its definition. Schleiermacher asks, not entirely rhetorically, how is thinking the essence of a thing possible?

According to Schleiermacher's dialectic, it is only possible to relate the elements of sameness and otherness within concepts and judgments if the related elements are in principle originally the same. In other words, to think the essence of something it is necessary to posit a primordial common ground, an absolute sameness of sameness and otherness that makes possible the acts of combining and distinguishing sameness and otherness in concepts and judgments. Moreover, according to Schleiermacher, the common ground must be formulated as an absolutely first principle of thinking, otherwise thinking would not occur. What status does this first principle have?

According to Schleiermacher, the first principle of thinking has a transcendental-logical status as the formal condition of the possibility of actual instances of thinking about being. But in addition, the first principle of thinking must also be a transcendental-ontological principle, in order to prevent the collapse of the otherness of being from thinking into non-dialectical sameness with the concepts by which thinking thinks real beings. In other words, the absolutely first epistemological principle of thinking must be the absolutely first principle of being as well. It is an original knowing (*"ein Urwissen"*) that *is* in and of itself.[534] The ultimate first principle must be the absolute identity of the sameness and otherness of thinking and of being in their identity and difference. It is the essence of essence, the divine essence, the being of God. It must be so, because within the structure of dialectic, this first principle of thinking and being is also that than which none greater can be conceived.[535]

---

[534] Schleiermacher's *Dialectic*, Odebrecht, p. 115, p. 171.

[535] Schleiermacher himself reserves the term "God" for the ultimate origin point of thinking, and "world" for the ultimate "about which" of being. Nonetheless, systematically considered the absolutely first principle as *"Urgrund"* is the God-term of the dialectic. Here, in the dialectic, I think we see the deep Augustinian and Anselmian roots of Schleiermacher's thought, because the dialectic is an elaborate working out of the ontological argument.

Schleiermacher does indeed arrive at the idea of an ultimate and unknowable ground of thinking and being. But he also refers us to a conditioned and finite ground of thinking and being in the human self: immediate self-consciousness, or "feeling." This finite ground appears not only mediately through the intellectual function, but a ground that appears immediately in feeling through the organic function.[536] Immediate self-consciousness, or feeling, denotes an original unity of thinking and being in the self. It is the awareness that I am the one thinking when I think, that I am the one feeling when I feel, that I am the one willing and acting when I will and act. And this finite, embodied, immediate self-consciousness has ingredient in it the awareness of its utter dependence on the infinite and ultimate transcendent-transcendental ground. Let me try to add some further detail to the model of thinking, including both the infinite and finite ground of thinking and the unities of thinking-perceiving and ideal-real being, namely intuiting and the totality of being respectively.

MODEL #3:

STRUCTURE OF THINKING

Thinking	*Ideal Being*	
Intuiting	+	*Totality of Being*
Perceiving	*Real Being*	

|

Finite Ground

["I" of Immediate Self-Consciousness (Feeling)]

|

Infinite Ground

["God"]

---

[536] Schleiermacher's *Dialectic*, Odebrecht, pp. 286ff.

At this point, let us recall the question of this essay, so that we can come to some conclusion. Does Schleiermacher provide in the dialectic the means to restore the distinction in principle between sacred and profane hermeneutic that he elides in the hermeneutical reflections themselves? The answer to the question is yes, as I briefly explain in the final section.

The Sacred and the Profane in Schleiermacher's Hermeneutic

Schleiermacher provides us with two structural analyses—one of interpretation in the hermeneutic and one of thinking in the dialectic. The structure of interpretation he leaves groundless, but the structure of thinking is grounded finitely in the self's immediate self-consciousness and infinitely in an original knowing that is. Because interpreting is a species of thinking, we may infer that the finite and infinite grounds of thinking are also the grounds of interpreting. If so, then we have a warrant for constructing a theological model of interpretation on basis of Schleiermacher's own systematic constructions. The intention in my constructing a model that Schleiermacher does not himself produce is purely to understand Schleiermacher properly; that is, to apply the maxim "understand the author better than he/she understands him/herself."

To conclude this paper, I shall present is my proposal as to how Schleiermacher distinguishes between sacred and profane hermeneutic in principle. Hermeneutic that engages only in the elements that included in the structure of interpretation, along with the finite grounds of subject and meaning, but which ignore or neglect reference to the infinite ground of interpretation ("God") is *profane hermeneutic*. Hermeneutic that engages in the structural elements of interpretation, but additionally makes explicit reference to the infinite ground of interpretation ("God") is *sacred hermeneutic*. Profane hermeneutic can be literary hermeneutic or philosophical hermeneutic, depending on whether the texts interpreted are literary or philosophical and whether they are interpreted using literary or philosophical methods. Sacred hermeneutic by contrast is theological hermeneutic. Theological hermeneutic has no natural textual domain of its own, not even the religious. It simply adds reference to the infinite depth of meaning in the structure of literary, philosophical, or for that matter, scientific hermeneutic. Theological hermeneutic of philosophical texts has two possibilities: it either interprets the explicit references to the infinite ground of thought and experience, or it makes explicit the implicit ultimate presupposition of the infinite ground that have not been made explicit by the author.

JESUS' GOD-CONSCIOUSNESS IN FRIEDRICH SCHLEIERMACHER
John S. Park

To Schleiermacher, the idea of Christ is the positive center of his entire theological and philosophical system. David Friedrich Strauss, regarding Schleiermacher's Christology as a fervent attempt to make the churchly Christ acceptable to the modern world, says that the doctrine of faith (*Glaubenslehre*) of Schleiermacher has actually only one single dogma, the person of Christ.[537] According to Schleiermacher, Christianity is a monotheistic faith, belonging to the teleological type of religion in which everything is related to the redemption accomplished by Jesus.[538] Christianity, therefore, has a predominating interest in the meaning of Christ (we can call this "a doctrine of faith" in Christ) and its applied moral task ("an ethical teaching") constituting the fundamental type of religious affections. The meaning of Christ and its ethical importance was the consistent and central concern in Schleiermacher's theological journey.[539]

From the beginning of his early pious life in the Moravian Herrnhut community, Schleiermacher was challenged by this life long meaning to him. Even before he left the community, Schleiermacher's personal meaning of Christ was already transcending the community's idea of Christ, especially on the necessity of Christ's vicarious sacrifice and his divine sonship.[540] At that time, to Schleiermacher, the meaning of Christ is only the illusion of the imaginary fantasy with its supernatural meaning. Nevertheless, the problem of how to

---

[537] David Friedrich Strauss, *The Christ of Faith and the Jesus of History: A Critique of Schleiermacher's Life of Jesus*, trans. and ed. Leander E. Keck (Philadelphia: Fortress, 1977), 4.

[538] Friedrich Schleiermacher, *The Christian Faith*, translated by H.R.MaCkintosh and J.S.Stewart (Edinburgh: T. & T. Clark, 1986), 52.

[539] In other place I highlighted this important Schleiermacher's theological systematics. Sung M. Park, *Christ and Christian Conduct: A Study of Christology and Theological Ethics of Friedrich Schleiermacher*, Ph. D. Diss., Claremont Graduate University, 1995 (Ann Arbor: UMI, 1995).1

[540] Martin Redeker, *Schleiermacher: Life and Thought*, translated by John Wallhauser (Philadelphia: Fortress, 1973), 13.

interpret the meaning of Christ kept confronting Schleiermacher from that time on. His interpretation of the meaning of Christ always affects particular attention in his followers and opponents.[541]

Schleiermacher understands and expresses his personal Christ in many ways as he expands and develops his theological systematics. In his early Christology, Christ is elaborated respectively as the Mediator among many mediators and as the Christ Child in *On Religion* and *Christmas Eve*. His later Christology in *The Christian Faith* and *The Life of Jesus* centers on Christ as the Redeemer and as the *Urbild* (or *Vorbild* in his *Christian Ethics*). In these later works, Schleiermacher tried to be au fait with development of Jesus' divine God-consciousness.

I

Before Schleiermacher used the word, *Urbild*, archetype, or "the ideal of moral perfection," Kant in *his Religion Within the Limits of Reason Alone* famously uses the word to refer to the idea of "an example of a man well-pleasing to God."[542] After he discusses the very nature of humanity, Kant proceeds to define a Christology based on his notion of "Christ as archetype." Through faith in this archetype, a "practical faith in this Son of God," we are acceptable to God. This human faith has moral worth in Kant. In other words, a human being who has faith is morally good. According to Kant, this faith is present in Jesus, a historical figure and a morally perfect teacher, who is also the content of the archetype. The universal idea of duty as an archetype, according to Kant, is, from a practical point of view, already present within us, especially in the form of reason. According to Kant, a human being has to elevate ourselves to moral perfection, to become in accord with an "archetype of the moral disposition in all its purity--and for this the idea itself, ...can give us power."[543] This elevation to the

---

[541] Ibid., 131.

[542] Immanuel Kant, *Religion Within the Limits of Reason Alone*, trans. Theodore M. Greene and Hoyt H. Hudson with a new essay "The Ethical Significance of Kant's *Religion*" by John R. Silber (New York: Harper Torchbooks, 1960), 56.

[543] Ibid.

archetype is a human being's universal duty. A human being is indeed created for moral perfection. Consequently, according to Kant, a human being is responsible for one's own salvation or the reception of the grace.

In the very beginning of the book, Kant makes a significant statement on Biblical theology:

> Were Biblical theology to determine, wherever possible, to have nothing to do with reason in things religious, we can easily foresee on which side would be the loss; for a religion which rashly declares war on reason will not be able to hold out in the long run against it.[544]

From this statement, we can easily conclude that for Kant, Jesus Christ is the one who acts morally within the limits of reason. Strictly speaking, there is no place for Jesus Christ with his divinely given God-consciousness in Kantian moral religion. The role of Jesus Christ, in Kant, is very alienated from a traditional understanding in Scripture, a text full of stories that human beings cannot understand with their reason.

Schleiermacher, along with many of his contemporaries, however, interprets the meaning of archetype differently from Kant. Kant, in his interpretation of Christ, lost the meaning of the consciousness of the self, which Schleiermacher rediscovered.[545] In his *The Christian Faith*, Schleiermacher clearly distinguishes himself from Kantian interpretation by saying that Jesus Christ is archetypal only in his personal God-consciousness. This archetypal ideal of Jesus Christ, according to Schleiermacher, has become "completely historical"[546] and this perfect historicity of perfect ideality in Jesus is demanded.

---

[544] Ibid., 9.

[545] Thandeka, "Schleiermacher's Dialektik: The Discovery of the Self that Kant Lost," *Harvard Theological Review* 85 (October 1992): 433-52.

[546] Friedrich Schleiermacher, *Christian Faith*, 377. Cf. Maureen Junker, *Das Urbild des Gottesbewusstseins* (Berlin: Walter de Gruyter, 1990), 176-180.

318

In all Christian common life, all Christian activities are always and only from "an ever-active susceptibility" to this Christ's perfect God-consciousness.

The power of God-consciousness in Christ is also in perfect archetypal form determining his historical activity. If this absolute power were lacking in Christ, it would also be impossible to have such an archetype in communion of his self-consciousness. In Christ, God-consciousness possesses absolute control over his being, even though he cannot escape from sinful common life; this is an "absolutely miraculous fact" and "perfectly natural" (the Redeemer does possess the same human nature, but freed from sinfulness).

If the person of Christ is archetypal, then God was present in him as a person. However, we cannot say that God is in humanity, which may imply division within God. Instead, we say that the presence of Christ is in the world. We are not conscious of God, a revelation of God, unless we first see it in Christ, in whom God-consciousness is personally present as his own person and innermost self. Thus, we may say that all revelation of God is mediated through Christ and the Christ, as an original act of humanity, is also regarded as the completely perfected creation of the human nature. Schleiermacher confirms that the physical nature of the first Adam, an uncompleted human nature, is now completed in the spiritual nature of Christ. In the archetypal Christ, both physical and spiritual human natures are perfectly completed creation.

In this archetypal person and work of Christ, all Christian activities are always and only from "an ever-active susceptibility" to Christ's perfect God-consciousness in Christian common life. In our imperfect (or immoral) God-consciousness, we aspire our hopes and wishes to subordinate our personal self-consciousness to this perfect ideality; Jesus' absolutely perfect God-consciousness, as the mirror of our imperfection. The possibility of a continuous progress in the potency of God-consciousness is open to us. Commenting on Schleiermacher's lecture: "The Life of Christ Before His Public Appearance" in *The Life of Jesus*, Verheyden says, "Although Schleiermacher insisted upon the historical actuality of the archetype of humanity in Jesus Christ, he was not unmindful of the difficulties which this raises for systematical thought."[547] Emphasizing the importance of Christ's archetypal God-consciousness in the Christian community, Verheyden concludes:

> Schleiermacher's historical judgments about the public activity of Jesus and his systematic construction of Jesus' archetypal God-consciousness enabling his public work to have such efficacy for the Christian become tightly intertwined.[548]

II

We now look more closely at the historical meaning of the humanity of Jesus in *The Life of Jesus*.[549] In the beginning of his lecture of the life of Jesus, Schleiermacher first presupposes faith in Christ and tries to maximize Christ's practical validity with his powerful God-consciousness in its communal sense. He distinguishes Christ from all other human beings, since he has a specific and peculiar dignity, as we previously studied. Christ is given to us as an example (*Vorbild*) for practical individual life, for the practical application of the knowledge of Christ in Christian community. In order to take Christ as our example, Schleiermacher thinks that we have to fathom "his way of acting." As early as 1794, Schleiermacher used the word *Urbild* in his preaching. From that time on his preaching, particularly with respect to Christ, focuses on the perfect image of Christ that we must "imitate."

---

[547] Friedrich Schleiermacher, *The Life of Jesus* ed. Jack C. Verheyden and trans. S. Maclean Gilmour (Philadelphia: Fortress, 1975), l.

[548] Ibid., li.

[549] Schleiermacher was the first theologian to give a public lecture on the subject of the life of Jesus in 1819. He lectured on the topic five times during his career: in 1819/20, 1821, 1823, 1829/30, and lastly in 1832. Three main issues, according to Verheyden, are what we must primarily scrutinize in Schleiermacher's *The Life of Jesus*: first, "the hermeneutical question of the principles of historical knowledge" of Jesus; second, his new study on the nature of the person of Jesus Christ, even if it overlaps his position in *The Christian Faith*; and third, the content of Jesus' preaching and his life events. Jack C. Verheyden, "Christology and Historical Knowing: A Study based on the Thought of Friedrich Schleiermacher and the New Quest of the Historical Jesus" (Ph.D. Diss., Harvard University, 1968), 260-61.

320

Schleiermacher also has a different view from traditional Christology in his interpretation of the two natures of Christ. Schleiermacher calls Christ's divine and human nature "the interest of faith in associating the divine in him" or "an object of faith, a central point of the world" and "the practical necessity of conceiving of Christ in purely human terms" respectively.[550] We are here at one of the most difficult points in our theological study. How can these two natures be interpreted without leaning to either Docetism or Ebionism? It is true that the doctrine of the person of Christ should be in between these two heresies. But how or how can the divine be properly understood in human terms in a human context? In order to reach a human view of the life of Christ, Schleiermacher clearly states from the beginning of his lecture on the life of Christ that this dilemma is not without contradiction.[551]

Schleiermacher develops his on the idea of Christ by using many illustrations from traditional Christian doctrines. First, the Orthodox Church has fallen into an almost Docetic understanding of Christ simply by overemphasizing Christ's divine nature. Next, as one nature "cancels" the other one, if they exist in unity, so the human nature manifests itself as a definite and limited consciousness, but divine nature is not bound in its definite limit and excludes all that is limited.[552] For example, if we say that the divine nature is *apathes* (incapable of suffering), then it would be meaningless, because we, then, would have to determine that Christ is without suffering. In spite of that, Christ's suffering is one of the main divine agendas given by God. Finally, one nature is more dominant than the other or they merge together. Schleiermacher calls the two natures of Christ "divine understanding and divine will" and "human understanding and human will": "unlimited and limited." However, how can a divine will be a human will, or vice versa, when Christ must possess logically only one will? Schleiermacher takes objection to the margining of the divine and human natures, because "there is no

---

[550] Friedrich Schleiermacher, *The Life of Jesus*, 81-82.
[551] Ibid., 30.
[552] Ibid., 82 and n. 15.

relationship in God between essence and properties such as exist in finite things but both are the same."[553]

The union between divine and human loses its value. If we view a two-fold nature of Christ, then Christ within him has a divine understanding and will with his human understanding and will. According to Schleiermacher, two controversies exist here: either the unity of the person rests on the unity of the will, "only one will" or two natures can be maintained if they always "wills only one things." Here Schleiermacher questions how a human will can be the same thing as a divine will and yet remain in a human will and vice versa. Therefore, Schleiermacher does not favor a traditional orthodox creed on the two natures of Christ, which confesses that God took upon himself the human nature without ceasing to be God; because God can do something that we confess we cannot fathom.

Schleiermacher considers that if we regard Jesus as the "absolute model" and "absolute teacher," then he must be capable of being expressed in human terms. Schleiermacher has difficulties with the divine side of Jesus, saying "it is not to be denied that the more strictly one undertakes to demonstrate that Christ must be perfectly comprehensible to us… the more easily one reaches the point of denying that specific dignity in its eternity."[554] Schleiermacher confirms that all these aids are not enough to explain the possibility of putting both divine and human tasks into one at the same time. Schleiermacher's bottom line is that this dichotomy is an either/or proposition and can never be a both/and one. He believes that combining these two natures is an impossible task, as we have simply believed and traditionally always agreed to the same conclusion, whenever we try to solve this dichotomy in unity.

---

[553] Ibid., 83.
[554] Ibid., 84.

However, Schleiermacher interpretatively uses the concept of the Holy Spirit here. This impossibility of understanding is completely possible when the Holy Spirit dwells in a human being as a positive God-consciousness. Because we receive the Holy Spirit at the point of conversion, it is not something pre-existent in us. Then we cannot accept this positive consciousness as something that pre-existed. If this is true, then this positive consciousness is not pre-existent in Christ. Therefore, Schleiermacher argues that what appears in Christ as human is something definite and limited, which needs development of God-consciousness in a certain historical time, even though we must view Christ's development in terms of "complete innocence to an ever more perfect consciousness."[555] (Here innocence is state of an underdeveloped consciousness, which opposes sin, virtue, and merit.) This is the reason why Schleiermacher is always hesitant to use the term incarnation, because he depicts Jesus who could become God with the help of the Holy Spirit in its positive God-consciousness, rather than God becoming a human being.

What then are Christ's self-consciousness in Schleiermacher and its relationship with his God-consciousness? Is the God-consciousness different from Christ's total self-consciousness? Or how does Christ's self-consciousness reflect God-consciousness to the human being? Schleiermacher thinks that the God-consciousness in Christ was not fully developed in his earlier life. Schleiermacher believes, unlike traditional orthodox Christology, that the consciousness of Christ was not in the form of full God-consciousness. In the beginning, Christ's relationship with God was not completely developed, even if the relationship between Christ and God was a special one. Schleiermacher focuses on the Gospel story, which represents Christ as a child who increased in wisdom [and became strong] and in favor with God and people. [Luke 1:80; 2:40, 52] If we accept, as Schleiermacher acknowledges, that the God-consciousness in Christ began to develop at a certain time in his earlier life, or that his peculiar

---

[555] Ibid., 99.

relationship with God was only introduced to us by his disciples or by their interpretation of faith, then we must admit that Christ also confirmed that God-consciousness had been developed within himself. However, this is the same case in human consciousness. Human self-consciousness is also developed gradually in each individual, as the doctrine of sanctification teaches us, even if the consciousness may not make a developed appearance. Schleiermacher says: "The concept of God can be very different, but the consciousness of a relationship to the object of these different concepts is essentially the same."[556] Therefore, the problem is a matter of degree in the relationship. Even if both human beings and Christ have the same God-consciousness and the same relationship with God in their consciousness, Christ's God-consciousness is a perfect and complete one.

Schleiermacher further explicates the relationship in his own way. "The actually perfect maximum" in the relationship between God-consciousness and self-consciousness is the condition of the God-consciousness as the element in every human being's self-consciousness. Whenever the God-consciousness is linked with human self-consciousness and becomes a maximum impulse, the latter reaches a certain complete or maximal relationship. On the other hand, when a person requires an external impulse in order to develop this consciousness within itself, or when the person struggles against the development of this consciousness, this is a minimum impulse.[557] With reference to these two poles, rather than proving this further, Schleiermacher simply urges us to presuppose that Christ must have stood on the maximum side. We must presuppose in Christ, according to Schleiermacher, a maximum of sensitivity in his God-consciousness. The God-consciousness in Christ is a constituent of all human consciousness, but to a very different degree.[558]

---

[556] Ibid., 93.

[557] Ibid.

[558] Ibid., 95.

III

We now turn our attention to Christ's God-consciousness in its relationship with human self-consciousness and in its importance with regard to the second person in the Trinitarian relationship. The question now is whether we can think of Christ's consciousness as both human self-consciousness and the consciousness of the second person in the Godhead. In the creedal form, we have said that Christ's self-consciousness is the divine God-consciousness as the second person in the Godhead. Therefore, Christ's consciousness is in the form of a divine pre-existence before all Christ's temporal experience. However, Schleiermacher says that we cannot solve this dilemma of Christ's having human and divine consciousness without giving up one side. A definite divine consciousness of Christ cannot be conceived except as "an operative one."[559] This operative function of human consciousness and divine consciousness is assumed in Christ's consciousness. From the creedal formula this is not acceptable, because in Christianity Christ's character has a tendency to be interpreted as divinely unchanging or inoperative. Schleiermacher himself gives up the creedal interpretation of Christ's divine consciousness, regarding the unity of the two characters or natures as an impossible one.

But Schleiermacher does not fully give up interpreting Christ's consciousness in the divine sense. Following and slightly modifying the Sabellian Trinitarian interpretation,[560] Schleiermacher assumes that the activity of the Holy Spirit is also working and dwelling both in Christ and in human beings. This divine Spirit, not conceived as a pre-existent divine consciousness, "is not conceived in the form of a real, discrete consciousness, but only as something that lies at the basis of the total consciousness"[561] to carry out the divine will. The willingness of the divine will in human self-consciousness, given by the activity

---

[559] Ibid., 96.

[560] Cf. Schleiermacher, "On the Discrepancy Between the Sabellian and Athanasian Method of Representing the Doctrine of a Trinity in the Godhead," trans. Moses Stuart, *Biblical Repository and Quarterly Observer* 6 (1835):1-116.

[561] Friedrich Schleiermacher, *The Life of Jesus*, 97.

of the divine Spirit, is "the perfect pure principle" in human moral action. Furthermore, when we accept the activity of the divine Spirit in human self-consciousness, the pure principle must rule the actual human being and doing. However, we know that a human being is, especially in all decisions, imperfect or immoral, even if one wants to be perfect or moral. We then face another problem. Is the activity of the divine Spirit less powerful or influential than natural human self-consciousness, so that the imperfect nature still remains, even if a human being wills to do the divine will? Schleiermacher thinks that the question has not yet been answered in Christian doctrine. Nonetheless, Schleiermacher does not give up attempting to solve the problem.

Schleiermacher goes back again to his proposition that Christ's self-consciousness is something that develops from within. Like the activity of the divine spirit, this developing character in Christ is also both in human beings and in the entire community, as the principle of the temporal consciousness. In the individual and in the community, God-consciousness or the activity of the divine Spirit is in conflict with the originally existent self or sensuous consciousness, which is the sinful element. This is, in fact, not the case with Christ's self-consciousness, because Christ has no sensuous consciousness. Christ is, according to Schleiermacher, in "complete innocence to an ever more perfect consciousness," opposed to sin as "the state of an underdeveloped consciousness."[562] Schleiermacher does not tell us here, however, when Christ is in a condition devoid of consciousness or whether Christ has no consciousness at all, either God-consciousness or self-consciousness. In Christ, this moral demand under moral consciousness is without a state of sin. These two principles of Christ--the consciousness of his innocence and sinlessness--are specific

---

[562] Ibid., 99.

differences between Christ himself and other people.[563] The fact that the existence of the divine Spirit was in Christ from the very beginning is another presupposed difference. From this condition of innocence and sinlessness, Christ's self-consciousness began to develop with a divine "power imparted to him from the beginning adequate to make the God-consciousness (or the activity of the divine Spirit) continuously, purely, and absolutely effective" in the individual and in the Christian church.[564]

---

[563] "As soon as we assume that these two things were in Christ from the beginning, we have assumed in him the specific difference, without having put an end to the essence of man as the concept represents it." Ibid., 100.

[564] Ibid., 102.A

HOW CAN WE FIND A LANGUAGE WHICH MAKES THE DOCTRINE OF JUSTIFICATION CLEARER TO THE PEOPLE OF OUR TIME?

(Wie lässt sich eine Sprache finden, die geeignet ist, die Rechtfertigungslehre auch den Menschen unserer Zeit verständlicher zu machen?)

Hermann Peiter

Am 31. 10. 1999 haben die Katholische Kirche und der Lutherische Weltbund in Augsburg (Deutschland) eine Gemeinsame Offizielle Feststellung zur Rechtfertigungslehre unterzeichnet. Unabhängig davon, wie einig beide in der Rechtfertigungslehre tatsächlich geworden sind, dürfte ein Einvernehmen da-rin bestehen, daß Katholiken und Lutheraner sich gemeinsam darum bemühen sollten, „eine Sprache zu finden, die imstande ist, die Rechtfertigungslehre auch den Menschen unserer Zeit verständlicher zu machen."[1] In einem 1. Schritt soll hier das vermeintliche Goethe-Wort „Gott gibt die Nüsse, aber er bricht sie nicht auf" erörtert werden. In einem 2. Schritt soll dargelegt werden, dass die Frage „Wie bekomme ich einen gnädigen Nächsten?" ein schlechter Ersatz ist für Luthers Frage „Wie bekomme ich einen gnädigen Gott?" In einem 3. Schritt soll daran erinnert werden, dass für F. Schleiermacher Lehrdifferenzen insofern kein Übel sind, als sie keine kirchentrennende Wirkung haben müssen.

I

„Gott gibt die Nüsse, aber er bricht sie nicht auf". Diesem simpel wirkenden Wort wird nachgesagt, von J. W. von Goethe zu stammen. Es ist von S. Macht vertont und einem launigen Anspiel zum Erntedankfest zu Grunde gelegt worden[2].

Wäre dies Wort lediglich ein Erntespruch, wäre es banal. Jeder Bauer oder Gärtner, der Gott für eine gute Ernte dankt, muss sich nicht darüber belehren lassen, dass es nicht Gottes, sondern seine, des Menschen, Sache ist, die Ernte einzubringen und zu verwerten. Kein ernst zu nehmender Mensch hat es nötig, darüber aufgeklärt zu werden, dass Gott kein Nussknacker ist.

1. If God gave nuts without breaking them open (a word attributed to J. W. von Goethe), God's omnipotence would result in nothing but hard nuts and unsolved problems for man.

Nur auf eine andere als die natürliche Ebene übertragen ist das Nuss-Wort diskutabel. In ihm wird unterstellt, der Mensch habe mit Gott zu kooperieren; ohne einen solchen Synergismus seien alle Nüsse wertlos.

In dem Nuss-Wort wird so getan, als sei 1. Gottes Handeln unvollständig und auf Ergänzung angewiesen, als liesse 2. nur der Mensch sich rechtfertigen, der Gott nicht allein wirken lässt, sondern sich das Handeln angelegen sein lässt, das zu bewerkstelligen Gott nicht tatkräftig genug ist, und als wäre 3. eine Nuss zu nichts gut, wenn nicht tatkräftige Menschen in Aktion träten, die, da sie, was die Lieferung genießbarer Lebensmittel betrifft, Gott nichts zutrauen, Nussknacker zur Hand nehmen bzw. selbst zu Nussknackern werden. „Selbst ist der Mann!" wird die Losung derer, die eine von außen kommende göttliche Hilfe ablehnen.

2. The doctrine of justification is the decisive criterion for all Christian doctrines.

In der Gemeinsamen Erklärung zur Rechtfertigungslehre heißt es unter Nr. 26: „Nach lutherischem Verständnis rechtfertigt Gott den Sünder allein im Glauben (*sola fide*)." [3] Aufschlußreich ist die Antwort der Katholischen Kirche vom 25. 6. 1998: Während für die Lutheraner die Rechtfertigungslehre „eine ganz einzigartige Bedeutung erlangt hat, muß, was die katholische Kirche be-trifft, gemäß der Schrift und seit den Zeiten der Väter die Botschaft von der Rechtfertigung organisch in das Grundkriterium der ‚regula fidei' einbezogen werden" (S. 27, Nr. 2). Der Unterschied tritt auch hervor, wenn man liest, dass die Lehre von der Rechtfertigung für die Katholiken ein unverzichtbares Kriterium ist, das die gesamte Lehre und Praxis der Kirche unablässig auf Christus hin orientieren will, und dass die Lutheraner die einzigartige Bedeutung dieses Kriteriums betonen (S. 5, Nr. 3, 18). In „Justification by Faith" wird klargestellt, dass die reformatorische Lehre von der Rechtfertigung allein durch den Glauben als Kriterium dient, an dem alle kirchlichen Bräuche, Strukturen und Traditionen gemessen werden [4]. In einer Stellungnahme (ohne Datum) theologischer Hochschullehrer zu der für den 31. 10. 1999 geplanten Unterzeichnung der Gemeinsamen Offiziellen Feststellung zur Rechtfertigungslehre wird beanstandet, diese Feststellung interpretiere die Formel „allein durch den Glauben" gegen ihre reformatorische Bedeutung in römisch-katholischem Sinn (Nr. 3). Gewiß ist in dem Anhang (Annex) zu der Gemeinsamen Offiziellen Feststellung des Lutherischen Weltbundes und der Katholischen Kirche [5] davon die Rede, Rechtfertigung geschehe allein durch Glauben; doch ist man damit gar zu schnell bei der Heiligung, statt mit F. Schleiermacher darin der Lehrweise der evangelischen Kirche treu zu bleiben, dass man die Heiligung von der Rechtfertigung absondert. [6]

Der Mensch lebt davon, dass er gerechtfertigt ist. Wenn es in dem Nusswort um mehr geht als um Nahrungsmittel, wenn es in ihm wirklich um Lebensmittel geht, wird so getan, als ob der Gottes Handeln komplettierende Nussknacker etwas Wesentliches zu seinem Leben beiträgt und gewinnt. Wenn die Alleinwirksamkeit Gottes in Abrede gestellt und suggeriert wird, dass der Mensch die Probleme seines Lebens selbst löst und harte Nüsse selbst aufbricht, entspricht das nicht der lutherischen Rechtfertigungslehre, nach der bei der Menschwerdung des Menschen Gott alles und der Mensch nichts leistet.

Eine harte Nuss zu knacken ist eine Leistung. Nach der Rechtfertigungslehre lebt der Mensch nicht von dem, was er selbst aus eigener Kraft leistet - entgegen der landläufigen Auffassung, dass beide, sowohl der Nussknacker als auch der Nusskern, der eine nicht hohle Nuss auszeichnet, die Rettung sind.

Die lutherische Deutung, dass der Mensch allein durch den Glauben gerecht wird, ist eine Absage an alle Versuche des Menschen, sich in der Schöpfung bzw. im Rechtfertigungsgeschehen zum Mitarbeiter Gottes aufzuspielen. Gewiss ist der Mensch Gottes Mitarbeiter, z. B. dann, wenn er sein Bestes dafür tut, die göttliche Schöpfung zu bewahren. In Sachen Selbstverwirklichung freilich ist der Mensch völlig unproduktiv - wie der Lehm, aus dem Adam im Schöpfungsakt gebildet wurde. Gott war mit sich und dem Lehm völlig allein, als er Adam schaffen wollte. Der Lehm war kein Mitschöpfer, sondern ein bloßes Material, um nicht zu sagen: ein Nichts. Auch in der Rechtfertigung ist das, woraus dann alles wird (der gerechtfertigte Mensch hat und ist alles, was er vor Gott braucht), ein Nichts. Als Sünder ist der Mensch ein Nichts.

Mit dem christlichen Glauben kann man sich ähnlich überfordert fühlen wie mit dem Knacken einer zu harten Nuss. Mitunter hat ein Mensch den Eindruck, als beschränke Gott sich darauf, ihm unlösbare Probleme zu bescheren, ihn mit seinen Sorgen allein zu lassen und von ihm einen Glauben zu fordern, von dem er, der Glaubende, nichts hat. Der Glaube gleicht dann jenem Nusskern, der, solange man sich an ihm nicht die Zähne ausbeißen will, einem verschlossen und entzogen bleibt. Wenn einem Menschen das Glauben Mühe macht und er sich anstrengt, das für wahr zu halten, was er eigentlich gar nicht für wahr halten kann, wird sein Glaube zu einem Werk, also genau zu dem, was er nach M. Luther gerade nicht ist.

3. Rather than difficult problems, the best things that God offers is the spirit which does not leave people alone with their problems or when they are distant from God.

Hat man harte Nüsse vor sich, wenn man Buchstaben vor sich hat, mit denen man nichts anzufangen weiß? Hüten die Buchstaben und deren Sammlung, al-so die Heilige Schrift, den Geist, wie eine Nussschale den Nusskern schützt?

Der Geist wäre der Inbegriff der Beliebigkeit, wenn man seinetwegen darauf verzichten wollte, den Buchstaben in Ehren zu halten. Nichts versteht, wer nicht lesen kann. Was es zu lesen gibt und zu lesen gilt, sind Buchstaben. Geist und Buchstaben gehören ebenso zusammen wie die christliche Verkündigung und die Heilige Schrift, die nicht nur auf den Altar, sondern auch auf die Kanzel gehört. Ein Prediger geht von der Heiligen Schrift aus, wenn der Geist über ihn kommt. Ohne den Buchstaben käme er ins Schwärmen. Ein Schwärmer tut den Buchstaben Gewalt an, wenn er sie nach seinem Geschmack umdeutet, bis sie ihm gefallen.

Es ist ein unglückliches Unterfangen, den Buchstaben mit der Schale einer Haselnuss zu vergleichen. Eine Haselnussschale wird zerstört, wenn der Nusskern freigelegt wird. Der Buchstabe der Heiligen Schrift bleibt hingegen unangetastet, wenn der Geist ins Spiel kommt. Die Bibel wird nicht jedesmal umgeschrieben, wenn sie neu gedeutet wird. Im Unterschied zu einem Code gleicht ein biblischer Text nicht einer zu knackenden Nuss. Ein geknackter Code läßt sich verstehen – etwa so, wie der Kern einer geknackten Nuss sich verspeisen läßt.

Wer einen biblischen Text knacken zu müssen meint, geht von der falschen Voraussetzung aus, die Bibel enthalte keine Offenbarung, sondern sei eine Geheimschrift. Die Bibel besteht aber nicht aus absichtlich verschlüsselten, kodierten Texten. Sie ist nichts für religiöse insider, sondern für Menschen, die aus sich herausgehen und sich herauslocken, ja provozieren lassen. Gott gibt nichts, ohne zugleich zu öffnen und zu erschließen.

Es ist ein Rätsel, was unter einer Schale verborgen sein kann. Das Rätsel ist gelöst, wenn die Schale entfernt ist. Gottes Wirken ist kein Rätsel, sondern ein Geheimnis. Im Unterschied zu einer Nuss oder einem Code lässt ein Geheimnis sich nicht knacken. Ein Geheimnis will gewahrt sein.

Wissenschaftliche Probleme können eine harte Nuss sein. Die Theologie ist eine Wissenschaft. Welche harten Nüsse hat die Theologie zu knacken? Gottgegebene? Ihr von Gott gegebene? Oder hausgemachte? Die Theologie hat Probleme mit sich selbst. Manch ein Theologe hat Probleme mit seinen

Zunftgenossen, gegenwärtigen wie toten. Er hat Mühe, auf das Niveau der theologischen Klassiker zu kommen.

Für die Probleme, die Gott uns gibt, ist nicht direkt die theologische Wissenschaft, sondern ist der Geist zuständig. Probleme, die etwas mit Gott zu tun haben, sind nicht nur vernünftig, sondern geistvoll anzugehen.

Wer einen Nussknacker benutzt, wendet, wenn er eine Nussschale aufbricht, Gewalt an. Doch gewaltsame Problemlösungen (von den polizeilichen und militärischen Aktionen einmal abgesehen, die auf einem anderen Gebiet nötig sein mögen) sind keine Lösungen. Wirkliche Probleme, die einem zu schaffen machen, erfordern Geist und Geduld. Gott gibt die Kraft, mit schweren Problemen zurande zu kommen. Diese Kraft ist der göttliche Geist.

Was hat man ohne den göttlichen Geist vom Leben? Antwort: Nüsse, an deren Kern man nicht herankommt. Trost, der einem verschlossen bleibt. Kraft, die nicht zur eigenen Kraft wird. Einen Glauben, der eine einzige Last ist. Kerne einer Nuss, die bei einem falschen Öffnen zerstört, d. h. ungenießbar werden.

4. The Holy spirit is a gift which would not be so if one had troubles with it.

Der vom Geist gewirkte Glaube ist ein göttliches Geschenk, aber kein menschliches Werk. Darum läßt er sich schlecht mit einer harten Nuss vergleichen. Eine harte Nuss aufzubrechen macht Arbeit. Ein fertiges Geschenk macht keine Arbeit.

Ein Geschenk ist keine Forderung. Umgekehrt ist eine Forderung kein Geschenk. Wer in die Pflicht genommen wird, dem wird nichts geschenkt. Wenn eine Nuss, auf die man Appetit hat, an einen das Ansinnen stellt: „Öffne mich! Gib dir so viel Mühe und Arbeit, wie ich dir Mühe und Arbeit mache!", kann der die Nuss knackende Mensch sie mit den Worten öffnen: „Jetzt mach ich dich erst zu einem Geschenk. Wer mich beschenkt, bin ich selbst!" Auf einen Menschen, der zum Glauben kommt und der durch den Glauben ganz gewiss nicht faul und bequem wird, kommen keineswegs die Arbeit und die Anstrengungen zu, die eine ungeöffnete harte Nuss, d. h. ein halbes Geschenk macht.

Ein Geschenk ist eine Umschreibung für das Evangelium, eine Forderung eine Umschreibung für das Gesetz. Evangelium und Gesetz sind nicht mehr wie bei M. Luther unterschieden, sondern miteinander vermengt, wenn R. Bultmann die Einheit von Kraft und Forderung zur Geltung bringt. [7]

Wer von einem Beschenkten Dank fordert, wird weniger Dank ernten als der, der keinen Dank erwartet. Auf ein Geschenk, das richtig ankommt, folgt nicht nichts, sondern der Dank. Wenn der Dank ausbleibt, ist das Geschenk nicht richtig angekommen. Schuld daran können das Geschenk oder (und) der Schenkende, kann aber auch der Beschenkte sein. Das ethische Handeln der Menschen ist ein Ausdruck ihres Dankes (und keine Antwort auf eine Forderung).

Was Gott gibt, gleicht, wenn denn schon Vergleiche mit Nüssen angestellt werden sollen, keiner geschlossenen, sondern einer offenen Nuss. Wenn behauptet wird: „Gott gibt die Nüsse, aber er bricht sie nicht auf", läßt sich zurückfragen: „Wozu soll Gott geöffnete Nüsse aufbrechen?"

5. The doctrine that states that God justifies the sinner means that those who have learned nothing will pass God's exam.

Ein Mensch, dem eine harte Nuss gegeben wird, befindet sich in einer Prüfungssituation. Auch in Gottes Schule gibt es Prüfungen.

In einer landläufigen Schule wird einem Schüler zunächst das erforderliche Wissen beigebracht bzw. eingetrichtert. Erst danach wird er in die Prüfung geschickt, in der er zu beweisen hat, wieweit er das zu Lernende verinnerlicht und sich angeeignet hat. Wer erst in der Prüfung zu lernen anfangen wollte, käme mit seinem Lernen zu spät.

Bei Gott gibt es indessen kein Zu-spät. Gottes Prüfung gleicht einer solchen Prüfung, vor der man rein gar nichts gelernt hat und in die man völlig unvorbereitet geht, die aber von dem Prüfer so gestaltet wird, dass man in ihr noch etwas lernt. Dass Gott den Sünder rechtfertigt, bedeutet, dass er einen

Menschen die Prüfung bestehen lässt, der keinerlei Voraussetzungen dafür mitbringt, erfolgreich durch die Prüfung zu kommen.

Freilich muß der Prüfling dann schnell im Lernen, d. h. geistesgegenwärtig sein. Ohne die Gegenwart des Geistes wäre er alles andere als lernfähig. Geistesgegenwart bedeutet nach S. Kierkegaard: flinke Willigkeit. [8] Abraham, der Vater des Glaubens, war nicht verlangsamt, als der rettende Engel ihm das Gegenteil von dem gebot, was Gott verlangt hatte (Gen 22, 11 – 13). Abraham schaltete im Handumdrehen, ohne lange darüber nachzudenken, wie sich all die Widersprüche, aus denen unmöglich klug zu werden war, auf einen gemeinsamen Nenner bringen ließen.

In einer göttlichen Prüfung ist Geistesgegenwart keine menschliche Tugend. Die Geistesgegenwart wird von eben dem Gott gewirkt, der den Seinen seinen Geist gibt. Mitten in einer Prüfung ist Gott nicht nur ein Prüfer, sondern vor allem ein Helfer, bei dem es noch immer viel zu lernen gibt.

Wie kann Gott eine Hilfe sein? Nach H. Gunkel, schließt der Anthropomorphismus, dass Gott den Abraham versucht habe, die göttliche Allwissenheit aus, was dem Erzähler selber nicht zum Bewusstsein gekommen sei [9]. Schlimmer als das, was dem Erzähler nicht zum Bewusstsein gekommen ist, ist freilich das, was H. Gunkel nicht zum Bewusstsein gekommen ist. H. Gunkels liberale Theologie ist ebenso einfältig wie die klassische Physik, in deren Augen die Art der Beobachtung (das mit „versuchen" übersetzte hebräische Wort heißt nach H. Gunkel eigentlich: „zusehen, wie jemand oder etwas beschaffen sei") unwesentlich sei für den Ablauf des beobachteten Vorgangs.[10] Dagegen spielt in der Quantentheorie die Störung, die mit jeder Beobachtung des atomaren Geschehens verbunden ist, eine entscheidende Rolle. Wenn ein Mikrokosmos einer Beobachtung unterzogen wird, reagiert er darauf empfindlicher, als etwa die Welt der Planeten darauf reagieren würde.

Die Prüfung, der Abraham unterzogen wurde, bedeutete sehr wohl eine Störung in seinem Leben. Diese Störung hat ihn verändert, ihn über sich selbst hinauswachsen lassen und ihm einen Erkenntnisgewinn gebracht. Gott ist kein unbeteiligter Zuschauer, sondern wirkt, indem er zusieht.

Dass durch Zusehen das verändert werden kann, was einer Beobachtung unterzogen wird, lehrt nicht erst die moderne Physik, sondern bereits die alltägliche Erfahrung. Der eine Mensch errötet, wenn er merkt, dass er beobachtet wird; ein anderer Mensch spreizt sich wie ein Pfau, wenn ihm aufgeht, dass er nicht allein ist, sondern Zuschauer hat.

Abraham war dessen gewiss, dass sein Prüfer nicht der Teufel, sondern Gott war. Der Teufel ist ein Prüfer, für den von vornherein feststeht, dass sein Prüf-ling durchfällt. Jeder halbwegs überlegene Prüfer ist in der Lage, so zu prüfen, dass sein Prüfling die Prüfung nicht besteht. Jeder Prüfling wird mit Angst in die Prüfung gehen, wenn er weiß, dass sein Prüfer ein Teufel ist. Seine Gewissheit, von Gott geprüft zu werden, ließ den Abraham über sich selbst hinauswachsen. Abraham leistete in der Prüfungssituation mehr, als er in normalen Situationen geleistet hätte. Obwohl er allen Grund hatte, Angst zu haben, gehörte er nicht zu den Prüflingen, denen in einer Prüfung die Angst alles ver-dirbt. Auf die Frage: „Hat dein Prüfer nicht einen Pferdefuß?" hätte Abraham geantwortet: „Meine Angst ist bewältigt!"

In einer landläufigen Schule hat ein Prüfling selbst und allein die Lösung einer ihm gestellten Aufgabe zu finden. Der Prüfer sagt nichts vor. Nur das zählt, was der Prüfling verinnerlicht bzw. „drauf" hat.

In einer göttlichen Prüfung bekommt der Prüfling Anteil am göttlichen Geist. Gott sagt dem Prüfling etwas vor. Dass Isaak nicht geopfert werden muss, hat Abraham sich zwar gewünscht, sich aber nicht selbst gesagt. Das hat er sich vorsagen lassen. Das lösende, das erlösende Wort kam nicht von dem Prüfling, sondern, wenn auch mittelbar, von dem Prüfer.

II

Wolfgang Steck und Hermann Timm entdecken bei den theologischen Laien ein weitgehendes Desinteresse an der Rechtfertigungslehre: „Nichttheologische 'Laien' wissen sehr wohl, was protestantische und katholische Christen sind, was sie voneinander unterscheidet und wie sie gleichwohl zusammenleben. Von der Rechtfertigungslehre ist dabei nicht die Rede. ... Im konfessionellen Unterscheidungsbewußtsein spielt der Rechtfertigungsartikel jedenfalls keine Schlüsselrolle." [11] Lässt die Rechtfertigungslehre sich in kleinen Münzen weitergeben? Hat sie etwas mit der Lebenswirklichkeit zu tun, in der die theologischen Laien sich zu bewähren haben?

6. Luther's question "How do I get a gracious God?" does not coincide with the question "How do I get a gracious boss?" Asking for justification liberates.

Lassen wir uns einmal darauf ein, Luthers vermeintlich überholte Frage „Wie bekomme ich einen gnädigen Gott?" durch die anscheinend aktuellere Frage zu ersetzen: „Wie bekomme ich einen gnädigen Nächsten?"! In der Tat fragt ein Arbeitnehmer, der um seinen Arbeitsplatz bangt und seine Kündigung fürchtet, weniger nach Gott als: „Wie bekomme ich einen gnädigen Arbeitgeber, einen gnädigen Vorgesetzten?" Diese Frage, die nichts Befreiendes an sich hat, ist die Frage einer sich entwürdigenden Untertanenseele. Dieser Untertan legt großen Wert darauf, sich die Gnade und Gunst dessen zu erwerben, von dem er sich abhängig weiß bzw. von dem er sich abhängig macht.

Empfiehlt es sich, den Vorgesetzten, von dem man außer einer vernichtenden Kritik nichts zu hören bekommt, zu wechseln und sich einen anderen Vorgesetzten auszusuchen? In einer Arbeitsgesellschaft mit vielen offenen Stellen und im Polytheismus kein Problem. Ein Anhänger des Polytheismus muss sich nicht verschlechtern, wenn er den einen Gott gegen einen anderen Gott austauscht. Irgendwie göttlich erscheinen im alle Götter. Wenn Gott jedoch Einer ist, gäbe man sein Ein und Alles auf, falls man sich allen Ernstes nach einem Gottesersatz umtut.

Ein Vorgesetzter gibt Arbeit und Lohn. Aber er fordert auch eine Gegenleistung. Kein Lohn ohne Arbeit. Die Arbeitsplätze, deren Inhaber nichts oder kaum etwas zu leisten brauchen, werden mehr und mehr abgebaut und bekommen Seltenheitswert.

7. Luther's question "How do I get a gracious God?" does not coincide with the question "How do I get a gracious landlord?" The apartments in the house of our heavenly father are condominiums.

Auch ein Vermieter ist ein Herr - besonders dann, wenn die Wohnungsnot groß ist. Selbst wenn Menschen ein Dach über dem Kopf haben: in geistlicher Hinsicht können sie obdachlos und unbehaust sein (vgl. Joh 14, 2).

Wer auf Wohnungssuche ist oder fürchtet, „seine" Wohnung seitens des Vermieters gekündigt zu bekommen, fragt: „Wie bekomme ich einen gnädigen Vermieter?" Ein Vermieter gibt Wohnraum. Aber er fordert auch eine Gegenleistung. Keine Mietwohnung ohne Miete.

Im Hause des himmlischen Vaters sind die Jünger keine Mieter. Christus will sie zu Eigentümern der Wohnungen machen, die er für sie bereitet und hergerichtet hat. Nicht die Jünger waren die Bauherren. Die Wohnungen sind Christus zu verdanken. Die Seinen wohnen bei ihm gratis und mietfrei. Dass er die Seinen zu sich nimmt (Joh 14, 3), bedeutet, dass er sie aufnimmt, annimmt, akzeptiert, bejaht und rechtfertigt.

Wer aus Gott einen Vermieter macht, nimmt Gott in die Pflicht. Wer Miete zahlt, kann erwarten, dass die gemietete Wohnung in einem ordentlichen Zustand ist und bleibt.

Wenn Gott aufhört, einem Mietzahlungen fordernden Vermieter zu gleichen, tritt das Evangelium auf den Plan. Im Evangelium werden keine Forderungen (auch keine Gegenforderungen) und keine Ansprüche gestellt. Ein Vermieter freut sich über den pünktlichen Eingang von Mietzahlungen. Er freut sich aber auch, wenn ein Mieter ihm ohne jeden Hintergedanken etwas schenkt (z. B. einen Blumenstrauß zum Geburtstag), wozu ihn der Mietvertrag überhaupt nicht verpflichtet. Dann besteht die Chance, dass der Vermieter in dem Mieter nicht nur den Mieter, sondern den Menschen entdeckt. Dann kann aus einem Mietverhältnis eine Freundschaft werden.

Ähnlich werden im Geschehen der Rechtfertigung Gott und Mensch zu Freunden. Als Freunde wohnen sie in demselben Hause. Das von Christus hergerichtete Haus ist sowohl das Haus der Seinen, d. h. der Söhne (und natürlich auch der Töchter) Gottes, als auch das Haus der himmlischen Vaters.

8. In the right sense God is no „Arbeitsgeber" (= employer) but an „Arbeit-Abnehmer" (= employee). It is his work that makes Christ the Lord.

Gott nimmt den Seinen die vergebliche Liebesmüh der menschlichen Selbstrechtfertigung ab. Es ist eine vergebliche Liebesmüh, wenn der Mensch im Geschehen der Rechtfertigung sich besser zu machen sucht, als er ist. Wenn ein Mensch sich selbst vor Gott rechtfertigt, wird er dank seiner Selbst-rechtfertigung nicht besser, sondern schlechter.

Einen Sünder zu rechtfertigen, und das will heißen: aus etwas Bösem etwas Gutes zu machen, bedeutet harte Arbeit. Wenn Gott den Menschen rechtfertigt, ist Gott in dem Sinn ein „Arbeitnehmer", dass er ein Arbeiter ist. Wen Gott für gerecht erklärt, wird nicht zu dem, der er ist, sondern zu dem, der er vorher noch nicht war. Zu sagen, was (Sache) ist, macht nicht unbedingt Arbeit. Doch Gott arbeitet, wenn er spricht und zugleich durch dieses sein rechtfertigendes Wort jemanden und jemandes Lage verändert.

Hört, wer ein Herr wird, damit auf, ein Knecht und Arbeiter zu sein?

Was Christus zum Herrn macht, ist dessen Arbeit. In M. Luthers Kleinem Katechismus heißt es: „Ich gläube, daß Jesus Christus ... sei mein HERR, der mich verlornen und verdammten Menschen erlöset hat, erworben, gewonnen ...

nicht mit Gold oder Silber, sondern mit seinem heiligen, teuren Blut und mit seinem unschüldigen Leiden und Sterben ... " [12]

Wollte Christus wie ein Herr unser Herr werden, müßte er uns freikaufen, müsste er uns, wie Luther sich ausdrückt, mit Gold oder Silber gewinnen. Die Herren haben Gold und Silber, eine harte Währung, und sind gute Herren, wenn sie ihr Kapital in den Dienst einer guten Sache stellen.

Ein Arbeiter hat kein Geld zu geben und - (das zeigt er bei harten Tarifauseinandersetzungen) kein Geld zu verschenken. Ein Arbeiter gibt seinen Schweiß. Wenn man schon drastisch reden will, hat man nicht nur von dem Blut Jesu Christi zu reden, sondern auch von seinem Schweiß. In einem späteren Zusatz heißt es im Lukasevangelium: "Und sein Schweiß wurde wie Blutstropfen, die auf die Erde fielen." (Lk 22, 44) An diesem Schweiß erkennt ein Christ seinen Herrn.

9. To justify God is not work but child's play.

Gewiss hat auch der Mensch an seinem "Heil" zu arbeiten. Der Mensch hat Gott zu rechtfertigen. Das ist freilich keine Arbeit. Während es eine harte Arbeit ist, aus etwas Bösem etwas Gutes zu machen, ist es ein Kinderspiel, etwas Gutes gut zu nennen. Gott ist gerecht. Ihn gerecht zu preisen ist keine Kunst und fällt einem leicht. Nicht nur Künstler loben und preisen Gott. Wenn ein Mensch seinen Gott rechtfertigt, bleibt Gott der, der er ist. Wenn dagegen Gott einen Menschen rechtfertigt, wird wie gesagt aus „alt": „neu". Aus „alt" „neu" zu machen bedeutet Arbeit.

Gott zu rechtfertigen bedeutet nicht, zu rechtfertigen, was sich nicht rechtfertigen lässt. Gott ist nicht die Welt. Die Welt steckt voller Ungerechtigkeiten. Ein gegenwirkendes ist eines der drei wesentlichen Elemente des christlichen Handelns. Weil das Christentum „ein irreligiöses Princip als überall verbreitet voraussetzt, weil dies einen wesentlichen Theil der Anschauung ausmacht, auf welche Alles übrige bezogen wird, ist es durch und durch polemisch." [13] Gott wird nicht sanktioniert, wenn der Mensch ihn rechtfertigt. Gold hat es nicht nötig, vergoldet zu werden.

10. Luthers question "How do I get a gracious God?" does not coincide with the question "How do I get a gracious customer?" Now and then a customer has his moods. God has grace.

Wer Waren produzieren oder Dienstleistungen erbringen will, ist auf Nächste angewiesen, darauf, dass dieselben ihm nicht davonlaufen. Diese Nächsten pflegen als „Kunden" bezeichnet zu werden. Wichtiger als die Frage „Wie bekomme ich einen gnädigen Gott?" kommt einem kundenfreundlichen Anbieter, dem sein Geschäft alles bedeutet, die Frage vor: „Wie bekomme ich ei-nen gnädigen Kunden?"

Wer, statt ihm zu dienen, Gott bedient, macht aus Gott einen Kunden, z. B. beim Musizieren. So werden auch mit dem ausgestrahlten Programm zufriede-ne Rundfunkhörer zu Kunden der Rundfunkanstalt ihrer Wahl. Ein Kunde will bei guter Laune gehalten sein. Schließlich ist er der König.

Ein Kunde ist nur dann ein König, wenn ein Anbieter ihn dazu macht. Er ist ein König von Anbieters Gnaden. Anbieter sind Königsmacher, aber auch Königsmörder. In Zeiten der Not und des Mangels, in denen es mehr Kunden als Waren gibt und die Höhe der Einnahmen unabhängig ist von der Anzahl der Kunden, legt manch ein Kaufmann die Höflichkeit ab, die er vorher seiner Kundschaft entgegengebracht hat. Wenn es dem Anbieter nicht mehr beliebt, ist der Kunde kein König mehr.

Gott ist nicht wirklich ein König, wenn er nicht mehr ist als ein allseitig umworbener und heiß begehrter Kunde.

Bisweilen (z. B. beim Einkaufen oder bei der Auswahl des abendlichen Fernsehprogramms) achtet ein Kunde nicht auf Qualität, sondern hält sich an seinen eigenen mitunter schlechten Geschmack.

Im Unterschied zu einem bloßen Kunden hat Gott keine Launen. Gott hat Gnade. Das Wichtigste an der Gnade ist, dass auf sie Verlass ist. Gottes Gnade ist keine

Willkür. Liebe ist sein Wesen. Gott hat nicht nur Liebe. Er ist Lie-be (1. Joh 4, 16).

Wer sich auf die göttliche Gnade nicht verlassen will und ihrer nicht gewiss ist, sucht in seiner Ungewissheit Gott gnädig zu stimmen und ihm etwas Gutes zu tun - wie auch ein Anbieter sich bemüht, einen Kunden, von dem er nicht weiß, ob er bereits ein treuer Stammkunde ist, bei guter Laune zu halten.

Wenn der Kunde, den man pflegt und bei Stimmung hält, „Gott" heißt, bezeichnet man diese Pflege als „Kultus". Kultus ist der gottesdienstliche Betrieb, der in den Kirchen abzulaufen droht. In den mittelalterlichen Klosterkirchen vollzog sich der Kultus auf einem beachtlichen Niveau. Manch ein Klosterbruder und religiöser Virtuose konnte sich weitgehend auf die Ausübung des Kultus spezialisieren.

Der Kultus ist ein Fach, in dem ein Mönch namens Martin Luther ein Meister war. Die befreiende Erkenntnis eben dieses Martin Luther war, dass er, der Meister seines Fachs, vor Gott und in Gottes Augen ein unbeholfener Berufsanfänger und Stümper geblieben war. Luther fühlte sich regelrecht befreit, als er erkannte, dass man, um vor Gott zu bestehen, kein Meisterstück vorlegen und keine Meisterprüfung ablegen muss. Vor Gott kann man es sich leisten, ein Stümper in der Kunst zu sein, Gott gnädig zu stimmen. In der Religion gibt es immer nur Anfänger. Darum haben sogar religionslose Menschen bei Gott eine Chance. In der Religion kommt es auf Bescheidenheit an. Dem allgemeinen Priestertum aller Gläubigen entspricht das Bewusstsein der Priester, Laien zu sein und, was die Frömmigkeit betrifft, nicht höher zu stehen als die Laien.

11. An „Anbeter" (= worshipper) is no „Anbieter" (= provider). God provides the new man.

Wer Gott anbetet, geht auf die Knie. Ein Anbeter ist kein Anbieter. Wenn Gott Gott, aber kein Kunde ist, gibt es gegenüber Gott keine Anbieter. Der Mensch hat Gott nichts zu bieten. Damit ist nicht gesagt, dass der Mensch arm ist. Im Gegenteil! Arm wird der Mensch dadurch, dass er etwas bietet, was gar nicht gefragt ist, wonach Gott gar nicht fragt. So wäre es reine Zeitverschwendung, wenn beispielsweise ein Zigarettenhändler seine Zigaretten unter konsequenten Nichtrauchern an den Mann bzw. die Frau bringen wollte. Ebenso wenig wie ein Nichtraucher Freude an Zigarretten hat, findet Gott Gefallen an den Offerten der Leute, die "anbeten" mit "anbieten" verwechseln.

Was ist im Verhältnis zwischen Gott und Mensch im Angebot? Nicht das, was der Mensch, sondern das, was Gott zu bieten hat.

Welcher Mensch ist reich? Der Mensch, der sich selbst hat. Der Mensch ist verloren, wenn er sich selbst verloren hat. Gott bietet ihm die Chance, ein glücklicher Finder zu werden und sich selbst zu finden.

Wer Gottes Angebot, d. h. sich selbst annimmt und akzeptiert, ist nicht mehr verloren, sondern kann voller Freude bekennen: „Ich bin nicht mehr verloren. Ich habe mich. Ich habe mich aus Gottes Hand empfangen. Wer Gott hat, wen Gott hat, hat sich. Ich bin das, was ich habe. Ich habe nicht nichts. Ich habe mich. Ich bin kein Nichts. Ich war im Angebot, in einem großzügigen Angebot. Auf dieses Angebot habe ich mich eingelassen. Ich habe mich gewonnen."

Gott hat den Menschen im Angebot, der nach Gott fragt und zu ihm betet. Dieses Angebot ist ein Sonderangebot - ein Billigangebot, weil es den Menschen nichts kostet, kein Billigangebot, weil es Gott teuer zu stehen kommt.

III

In seiner Vorlesung über Christliche Sittenlehre (1826 /27) sagt F. Schleiermacher über das Verhältnis von evangelischer und römischer Kirche: Der „Angel, worum sich die ganze Streitigkeit drehte, war die Lehre von der Rechtfertigung durch den Glauben, worin eingeschlossen war die vom Werth oder Unwerth aller äußern Werke. Dies ist offenbar ein gestaltendes Princip für die ganze Ansicht der Sittenlehre." [14] Keine Rede von mehreren Angeln oder, wie sich auch sagen ließe, von mehreren Kriterien (s. o. unter Punkt 2).

12. The abolition of genuine religious differences is a sign of religious indifference.

Der in der evangelischen (sei es der lutherischen, der reformierten oder der unierten) Kirche waltende Geist wäre der einer bloßen Sekte, wenn die evangelische mit der katholischen Kirche sich in nichts mehr eins wüsste. Bereits die Taufe ist ein Beispiel dafür, wie auch in einer Kirche des Wortes ein Sakrament in Ehren gehalten wird. Andererseits wäre es ein Ausdruck religiöser Gleichgültigkeit, wenn echte konfessionelle Gegensätze kleingeredet oder verschleiert werden. Der eigentümliche Charakter der evangelischen Kirchenlehre ist unzertrennlich „von dem durch den Ausgang der Reformation erst fixierten Gegensatz zwischen der evangelischen und römischen Kirche" [15].

Keine Einheit der Kirche ohne konfessionelle Gegensätze. Selbst innerhalb der evangelischen Kirche heißt es mit Spannungen zu leben. Eine „gänzliche Übereinstimmung ... ist in der evangelischen Kirche deshalb nicht notwendig, weil auch zu derselben Zeit bei uns Verschiedenes nebeneinander gilt." (KD § 196) Lehrverschiedenheiten und Gemeinschaft schließen einander nicht aus. „Die evangelische Kirche ist groß und das Haus des Vaters, in welchem gar viele Wohnungen sind, und so muß es bleiben" [16]. Es lässt sich in einem Hau-se und zugleich in einer seiner Wohnungen leben. Erst dank seiner Wohnungen wird ein Haus wohnlich. Im Haus des Vaters ist keine Wohnung wie die andere. Wozu auch? Eins wird ein Haus nicht durch die Gleichheit seiner Wohnungen.

13. A difference in Christian doctrine has not resulted in schism in the occidentalchurch and does not stand in the way of Christian unity.

Aus einer spezifisch evangelischen Wahrheit, der Rechtfertigungslehre, lässt sich keine allgemeingültige, sowohl in der evangelischen als auch in der katholischen Kirche gültige Wahrheit machen, ohne dass diese Wahrheit Schaden nähme. Nicht eine Lehrverschiedenheit hat im Zeitalter der Reformation zur Auflösung der Kirchengemeinschaft zwischen evangelischen und katholischen Christen geführt. Deswegen ist es eine trügerische Hoffnung, dank der Beseitigung einer Lehrverschiedenheit, von der lediglich behauptet wird, aber nicht erwiesen ist, dass sie zur Spaltung der abendländischen Kirche geführt hat, die kirchliche Gemeinschaft von katholischen und evangelischen Christen wieder herstellen zu können.

In seinem Kollege über christliche Sittenlehre (Wintersemester 1826 / 27) sagt Schleiermacher: Die Trennung von der katholischen Kirche „entstand nur durch die Ausschließung von katholischer Seite und lag gar nicht in den Prinzipien derer, die als Reformatoren auftraten. ... Die christliche Kirche ist nie ohne Verschiedenheit in der Lehre gewesen, und es ist klar, daß sie ohne diese auch gar nicht sein kann. Will man also den Satz allgemein aufstellen, so hebt man die Kirche überhaupt auf, sondern jeder für sich ist isoliert. Auf jeden Fall muß hier ein Bedingnis eintreten, und da fragt sich: Gibt es innerhalb der christlichen Kirche Lehrverschiedenheiten, welche Grund zur Trennung geben? Wir gestehen, daß wir keine solche konstruieren können, denn gesetzt auch, einer sagte, er glaube gar nicht an Christum, so existiert freilich für ihn keine Kirche, und er wäre außerhalb derselben." (CL, Bd 1, S. 157, 16 – 29)

14. Christian doctrine is free from polemic. Polemic has its place in Philosophical theology. Polemic turns inward.

Im Gefolge der evangelischen Rechtfertigungslehre ist es zu Lehrverurteilungen gekommen. Die Verfasser der Gemeinsamen Erklärung halten dieselben für überholt; in den Grundwahrheiten der Rechtfertigungslehre bestehe zwischen der evangelischen und der katholischen Kirche ein Konsens (Nr. 5, 40).

Lehrverurteilungen zur Sprache zu bringen ist Aufgabe der Polemik. Die Darstellung der Lehre, wie sie jetzt ist, ist die theologische Disziplin, welche „Dogmatik" heißt [17]. Die Dogmatik ist selbst keine Polemik. Die Polemik ge-hört zur Philosophischen, die Dogmatik zur Historischen Theologie. Die Historische und die Philosophische Theologie sind auseinanderzuhalten. Je mehr

Lehrverurteilungen sich in der Dogmatik finden, desto weniger ist die Dogma-tik bei ihrer Sache.

Nach KD § 41 geht die Polemik nicht nach außen, sondern richtet sich nach innen. Polemik gegen die eigene Kirche bzw. gegen die eigene Konfession ist fruchtbarer als Polemik gegen andere. Die Polemik der Reformatoren des 16. Jahrhunderts gegen die Missbräuche, die sie in der damaligen katholischen Kirche entdeckt hatten, nahm „ihre Richtung nach innen, weil die Reformatoren noch in derselben Kirche mit den Katholiken stunden." (Enzyklopädie, S. 47) Die Polemik richtet sich nach innen, solange die Schwestern und Brüder auf der Gegenseite nicht als Nichtchristen, sondern als Mitchristen in derselben Kirche angesehen werden. Die katholische Kirche ist alles andere als nur ein Inbegriff von Verirrungen und Deformationen. Sie ist sehr wohl eine eigentümliche Gestaltung des Christentums (C Sl 11 f, 16 ff), der mit Lehrkom-promissen auf halbem Wege entgegenzukommen kein Fortschritt wäre.

15. In presenting itself to the public the Protestant church is not inter-ested in polemics but in corrections, i. e. apologetics.

Außenstehende, die für die Kirche bzw. für die eigene Konfession gewonnen werden sollen, lassen sich nicht durch Polemik, sondern dank der Apologetik überzeugen und innerlich überwinden. Die Apologetik will vom Nichtverstehen bzw. vom Noch-nicht-verstanden-haben zum Verstehen führen. Dem entsprechend ist auch das Missionswesen von niemandem als Polemik angesehen worden (Enzyklopädie, S. 45). Die Apologetik hat ihren Grund „in dem historischen Umstand, daß das Christenthum von Anfang an ist angegriffen worden." (Enzyklopädie, S. 43) Die Apologetik stellt richtig. Das eigene Bekenntnis (auch das evangelische) bedarf, sobald es von außen angegriffen wird, der Verteidigung, der Apologie - ein Umstand, dem sich, um nur ein Beispiel zu nennen, die Apologie der Augburgischen Konfession verdankt. Seit der Spaltung der abendländischen Kirche spielen evangelischerseits Lehrverurteilungen und

Polemik im Gegenüber zur römisch-katholischen Kirche nicht die wichtige Rolle, die die Apologetik spielt. Ihre eher defensive als offensive Haltung hätte die evangelische Kirche nur aufzugeben, falls die katholische Kirche mit ihrer Ansicht in die evangelische Kirche eindringen wollte (CL, Bd 1, S. 148 f, 19 ff).

16. Christian unity begins in Christian life.

Die christliche Einheit kommt nicht von einem Lehrkompromiss, sondern von dem gemeinsamen christlichen Leben, das es beispielsweise in einer sog. „gemischten" Ehe, bei einer Abendmahlsfeier oder bei der Wahrnehmung politischer wie sozialer Verantwortung zu bewähren gilt. „Die evangelischen Kirchen heißen schon heute ihre katholischen Mitchristen am Tisch des Herrn willkommen im Sinne der Rechtfertigung allein aus Glauben." [18] Der christlichen Einheit würde ein Bärendienst erwiesen, wenn man die Lehre über das Leben setzt und das gemeinsame Leben als etwas Zweitrangiges ansieht und - erschwert.

17. Christian life gains its clarity by forming doctrines and by self-assertion leading to clarity.

Obwohl die Lehre nur ein Teil des gesellschaftlichen Zustandes einer Kirche ist (KD § 195), geht es nicht an, nicht nur die Lehrkompromisse, sondern auch die Lehre abzuwerten, zu der die jeweilige Kirche steht. Schleiermacher versteht unter Bildung der Lehre: sich zur Klarheit bringendes frommes Selbstbewusstsein (KD § 166. 180). Die Lehre hat etwas Klärendes. Die Lehre ist eine reinigende Macht. [19] Aus ihr bezieht das Leben seine Reinheit. "Quando enim doctrina pura manet, spes est vitae facile corrigendae. Radii solis puri manent, etiamsi in stercus" (Dreck) "cadant et splendeant" [20].

Notes

1 Antwort der Katholischen Kirche auf die Gemeinsame Erklärung zwischen der Katholischen Kirche und dem Lutherischen Weltbund über die Rechtfertigungslehre vom 25. 6. 1998. In: Texte aus der velkd 87 / Juni 1999, Nr.

8, S. 29. Für die Übersetzung des Inhaltsverzeichnisses meines Beitrags habe ich Dr. Hartmut Krüger (Gymnasium Lütjenburg) zu danken.

2 E. Lade: Kreative Schulgottesdienste, Neue Ausgabe, WEKA Fachverlage, Nr. 6 / 4. 7

3 Texte aus der velkd, Nr. 87, Juni 1999, S. 7

4 Deutsche Übersetzung. In: Rechtfertigung im ökumenischen Dialog, hrsg. von Harding Meyer und Günther Gaßmann (= Ökumenische Perspektiven Nr. 12), Frankfurt / M. 1987, Nr. 160

5 epd-Dokumentation 24 / 99, S. 50 unter C

6 Der christliche Glaube [1] , § 129 Anm. b; ed. H. Peiter; KGA I / 7, 2, S. 109, 20 – 25

7 Theologie des Neuen Testaments [2], Tübingen 1954, S. 333

8 Die Tagebücher X [4] A 338, hrsg. von H. Gerdes, Bd 5, Düsseldorf / Köln 1974, S. 30

9 Genesis [7] , Göttingen 1966, S. 236

10 Vgl. W. Heisenberg: Wandlungen in den Grundlagen der Naturwissenschaft,[9] Stuttgart, 1959, S. 36

11 Deutsches Allgemeines Sonntagsblatt, Nr. 8 vom 20. 2. 1998, S. 26

12 BSLK [5], S. 511, 23 - 33

13 F. Schleiermacher: Reden [1], Berlin 1799, S. 294

14 Meine Ausgabe der Christlichen Sittenlehre, Stuttgart / Berlin / Köln / Mainz 1983 (im Folgenden = C Sl), S. 34, 16 – 19

15 Kurze Darstellung des theologischen Studiums [2] (im Folgenden = KD), § 212

16 Keine Ormig-Ausgabe „Das christliche Leben", Berlin (Humboldt-Universität) 1968 (im Folgenden = CL), Bd 1, S. 161, 5 - 7

17 F. Schleiermacher: Theologische Enzyklopädie (1831 / 32), ed. W. Sachs, Berlin / New York 1987, S. 99

18 Punkt VI des gemeinsamen Papiers von (zunächst) 141 deutschen Theologieprofessoren. In: Deutsches Allgemeines Sonntagsblatt, Nr. 6 vom 6. 2. 1998, S. 30

19 Vgl. meine Ideologiekritik, Göttingen 1977, S. 75

20 M. Luther: WA 13, 688, 13 – 15

Appreciative Response from Jack Verheyden

SCHLEIERMACHER'S HERMENEUTICS OF THE HISTORICAL JESUS

Jack Verheyden

Friederich Schleiermacher's position as a major figure in the rise of modern theology has long been recognized, although at times quite differently evaluated. He has also become known as a philosopher, mainly through his lectures published posthumously as part of his collected works. These philosophical reflections range over a number of topics, one of which is a theory of language and interpretation, the hermeneutics, which is carried out with special attention to the New Testament. However, the ideas of these lectures are applicable generally and not only to theological subject matter. In the last half of the twentieth century attention to Schleiermacher's hermeneutics has been by far the most prominent subject singled out for discussion from his lectures. Indeed, he has attained the status of a "classic" figure in the history of the development of this topic.

Along with his systematic work in theology and philosophy, Schleiermacher also was an historian of considerable accomplishment in both classical and theological literature. He spent nearly three decades in the translation of the dialogues of Plato into the German language, a translation still widely used today, while he also engaged in New Testament studies concerned with the Gospel of Luke, I Timothy, and other books. In addition, his collected works include lecture material over the life of Jesus, a topic which Schleiermacher is held to have initiated as a public academic presentation.

This lecture material over the history of Jesus is not easy to read because it contains brief statements from Schleiermacher's lecture manuscript combined with lecture notes from several listeners organized around the date the lecture manuscript was expounded upon. A series of several student notebooks have then been conflated into a single account. Perhaps for this reason comparatively little attention has been paid to Schleiermacher's lectures on the life of Jesus, but the neglect has prevented some worthy reflection from being considered. Apart from the account of Jesus' history as seen in 1832, the introductory material displays the application of Schleiermacher's hermeneutical theory to the knowledge of an individual of the past in a manner not found elsewhere in his corpus. Furthermore, the lectures show Schleiermacher wrestling with the relation of faith to historical knowing, issues that have stretched across the generations from his time even into the present. The fact that the Jesus of history unites in such an exceedingly sharp fashion the relation of faith to historical knowledge has called forth endless reflection and variety of positions taken. In Schleiermacher's lectures on the life of Jesus we have an early attempt by one who unites dogmatic, historical, and philosophical capabilities in his exploration of this subject. Naturally, there have been many changes in the critical handling of the gospel material since 1832, but the principles that Schleiermacher explores in his introduction have great worth transcending the state of critical discussion of his era. I am going to present closely the structure and progression of his thought.

The Rejection of Legitimizing Unbelief

In his Brief Outline for the Study of Theology Schleiermacher elaborated in schematic fashion the organization of the areas of theology in relation to the historical character of the Christian church. One consequence of this historical character are issues pertaining to the Jesus of history. In the introduction to the Life of Jesus Schleiermacher takes up this theme by maintaining that unless Christian theology recognizes the importance of historical-critical investigation into the life of Jesus theology is legitimizing unbelief. "Since our faith is faith in an event, it is thus also dependent on that event; but just for that reason it must be in the interest of faith to bring this event to view in such a way that it is seen as the source of faith."[565]

---

[565] Leben Jesu, p. 20. This reference is in the student notebooks. When I cite Schleiermacher's own manuscript the page number will be followed with the designation (S). This volume is part of

This event is the source of faith in its having the kind of concreteness that any historical subject must have; therefore, Schleiermacher intends that the solution of this historical task must be pursued ". . . as in the solution of any similar one, as in regard to a man who is not in any way a subject of faith for us."[566] Yet the risk implied in this is plain to him. It also rests upon his conviction that the person of Jesus Christ is constitutive of the essence of Christianity, and that if his person was not held to as intrinsic to it, then Christianity as such must be given up.[567] And this is a possibility that is obviously risked in holding that faith is dependent on a concrete historical subject which can and must be dealt with in terms of the general rules of historical knowledge. In historical research the testing of all views is always necessary, and in the case of Jesus Christ no exception can be made. Positions which oppose him and the uniqueness of his person have to be considered.[568] If we attempted to say that we would not take into consideration that which is put forward as a result of critical observation into the life of Jesus, we would not be proceeding theologically. To say that historical judgments have no consequence for faith is really to give up the Christian theological standpoint.[569] This is pointedly expressed in the following words: "If we wish to maintain the 'scientific' standpoint we are not permitted to shrink from investigation. If we wish to be theologians, it is necessary that a 'scientific' orientation and Christian faith be compatible. But if we out of a dark concern attempted to be able to know the results of investigation in advance, we would deceive ourselves. This is something that we can only reject for it would already be a product of unbelief, so

Schleiermacher's <u>Sämtliche Werke</u>, I, 6 (Berlin: C. Reimer, 1864): The English translation is <u>The Life of Jesus</u>, ed. J. Verheyden (Philadelphia: Fortress Press, 1975). References will be to the German text.
566 Ibid.
567 Ibid., p. 22(S).
568 Ibid., p. 21.
569 Ibid., p. 23.

that rather than extinguishing unbelief we would legitimize it and, therefore, be in contradiction to ourselves."[570]   Unbelief would be legitimized or justified precisely because the standpoint would be denying that the locus of the origins of Christianity could stand open investigation. Faith would be in contradiction to itself because implicit within it is the confidence that this concrete historical subject is the one which is the transforming activity directed toward all times and places. While historical investigation can never establish the claims of faith regarding this historical subject, it can never be expected to uncover truth which would be inimical to the reality of faith precisely because the Church is convinced that its mode of faith is true. For that reason, a theological position falls into contradiction to itself if it tries to predetermine the results of critically controlled historical evidence. Rather, it can only expect what is gained from critical investigation to have a positive and beneficial result to the understanding of Jesus Christ. Thus: "There is nothing other remaining than that we must employ investigation and incorporate its results into our presentation (of Christianity)."[571]

On the other hand, Schleiermacher warns that theology must be cognizant of the fact that there are views which preclude the results in advance from the other side. This kind of position is one which denies that Jesus can be part of the essence of Christianity because universal truth is not dependent upon specific and unique occurrences.

This is the issue which evokes Schleiermacher's most sustained debates in the pages of the Life of Jesus. It is the prosecution of his case against the Hegelians, or any transcendentalist position which projects: ". . . that it is necessary to establish the demand that what is true and divine in Christianity be separate from the person of its founder."[572] When Schleiermacher says that one must not legitimize unbelief by attempting to know the results of investigation in advance, it is an orthodoxy apprehensive of the new situation of historical

---

[570] Ibid., p. 24.
[571] Ibid.
[572] Ibid., p. 30.

knowledge which is the ostensible partner in the discussion. But the positive theological point which results from this attention to historical concreteness is also a built-in counteroffensive against a strictly transcendental reading of the essence of Christianity. Without this interest in critically controlled historical evidence and the corresponding emphasis on the specific locus of the source of Christian faith, the Christian Church would have no leverage to exert against the weight of such transcendentalism. And these issues come to their brightest focus in the interpreting of the person of Jesus.

To Schleiermacher's mind, the matter finally comes to this. If the occurrences of history have been such that a representation of Jesus Christ is produced which is not compatible with Christian faith, a faith which in Schleiermacher's opinion rests upon the foundation of the person of Jesus Christ, then it has to be said:

> Special circumstances have prevailed so that out of this which was not authentic such a manifestation as the Christian Church has come about and it is necessary that we give notice that God's direction of the human race has been such that a great part of the human formation has been erected upon a well-meaning error. The task would then be to remove the errors in the smoothest possible way and turn back to the truth.[573]

If this were done, then, perhaps, the religious community which is now the Christian Church could be so established that it included the truth in itself. If so, the case would be one which was indifferent to the person of Jesus Christ and in place of the false view which had directed itself upon him, an accurate one could prevail.[574] It might be that Jesus could have a role here in that he was a bearer of a proposition concerning an insight into a mode of life which was relevant to his time, but that he is not required for another period of history.[575] Or, this

---

573 Ibid., pp. 23-24.
574 Ibid., p. 24.
575 Ibid., p. 27.

interpretation could say that certain hopes and desires of the Jewish people were fastened upon him, a person who was intrinsically unable to fulfill them, so that the whole matter arose out of the seed of the error to which we know the human soul is liable in its longings.[576] Still further, it could be said that the reports we have of Jesus are completely false.[577] Yes, there are many varieties and angles which may be explored in an interpretation of Christianity which attempts to separate the truth of Christianity from its founder. But it can only be done at the cost of violence to the religious consciousness which is the faith of the Christian Church and the special worth which Jesus Christ has for that self-consciousness. For that reason Schleiermacher holds that it is Christianity itself which is abolished when the uniqueness of the person of Jesus Christ and the special relationship in which he stands to the Christian Church and the human race generally is removed.[578]

Of course, there is a considerable variety of ways of representing Jesus Christ in the New Testament itself and part of the task of a life description of Jesus is to attempt to bring some unity to the diversity which is found there.[579] Some hold that New Testament Ebionism provides scriptural justification for the transcendentalism of the day. But Schleiermacher is convinced that even representation of Jesus which, from the standpoint of subsequent church doctrine, is to be considered Ebionite, that the difference from transcendentalism is clear. An Ebionite view of the person of Jesus still held him to be unique in relation to all other people. This position in its New Testament version was held by people who were Jews and thus people who already participated in a faith which adhered to the prophetic revelation of God in a manner that could only be held to be miraculous from the standpoint of transcendentalism.[580] The latter could not accept the Ebionite's interpretation of Jesus "as one decisively sent from God,

---

[576] Ibid., p. 19.
[577] Ibid., p. 84.
[578] Ibid., p. 22(S), p. 27.
[579] Ibid., p. 23.
[580] Ibid., p. 25.

who people had to follow in order to find salvation, and in respect to which everything earlier had been a preparation."[581] Such New Testament Ebionism did not separate what was true and divine in Christianity from its founder in the manner which is the mark of the modern transcendentalist.

It was the consistently intelligible treatment of the physical miracles which was the siren call of the transcendentalist in Schleiermacher's day. They said that people of the first century had virtually no comprehension of scientific matters, and that the Apostles and authors of the New Testament were no exception. This means that: " . . . the Christian Church, then, rests upon the statements of such people, whom we today must regard as men of very little power of judgment."[582] Schleiermacher was prepared to journey a good distance with this interpretation of physical miracles himself. Yet, at the same time, he thought: " . . . that this sphere is more or less the physical one concerning the manner in which a phenomenon is situated. Their lack of judgment in this does not do any great damage as long as they have correctly transmitted the teaching of Christ."[583] The latter is directed to the religious self-consciousness of human beings and not to the area of the scientific knowledge of nature.

A further consequence of the demand that the truth of Christianity be separated from the person of its founder in the transcendentalist mode is that the first century man Jesus of Nazareth becomes one who practiced a deception upon his fellows. This has to be said because critically controlled historical evidence bears out the fact that Jesus made claims about his own person in relation to God which the transcendentalist says is a denial of the nature of truth.[584] Even if this was done out of a good intention on Jesus' part, the fact would remain that he has represented his self-consciousness, his higher vocation, and his special relation to

---

[581] Ibid.

[582] Ibid., p. 26.

[583] Ibid.

[584] Ibid., p. 84; cf. p. 79(S).

God in a way which could only have been a lie.[585] Of course, since we have only reports of Jesus, it can always be said that these are so uncertain: " . . . that they are not able to be used to produce a definite picture of him because the original narrator has throughout imported his own view into the speech of Christ, and then it is not possible to pursue the subject historically." Schleiermacher thinks that it is the case that:

> In every narrative, even in those which only mean to be reports, the judgment of the narrator, nevertheless, joins in with them, for it is his apprehension; but if we accept that nothing of the speeches of Christ is communicated without also being falsified through the erroneous and exaggerated opinion which arose against his own will, then naturally nothing remains; but this itself is of the highest improbability.[586]

It is of the highest improbability from the standpoint of critically controlled historical evidence so that one can only return again to the view that if the truth of Christianity is separable from the person of its founder, then Jesus himself has perpetrated a deception.

This discussion with a transcendental rendition of Christianity highlights the kind of issues which theology must have an eye toward in being cognizant of the position which deals with critical questions, but really rests upon a foundation which precludes the results in advance. But the basic point still remains. While the awareness of Christian theologians that Jesus Christ can only be correctly approached from the standpoint of faith should make them sensitive to those presuppositions which would preclude the uniqueness of Jesus in advance, they cannot foreclose concrete historical investigation. This would throw them into contradiction with themselves. The picture of Jesus which was retained in those who stood nearest to him must be continuously probed and clarified for it is this which is the ultimate aspect of the normative presentation of Christianity. Without this kind of questioning Schleiermacher thought the Church would be in

---

[585] Ibid., p. 26, and p. 31.
[586] Ibid., p. 84f.

danger of placing its own fantasy in the place of Jesus Christ, and then his normativeness would most certainly be abolished.[587] These reports of Jesus and the initial form of the Christian religious self-consciousness presented in the New Testament are: " . . . at the same time the temporal basis of the Christian Church and the origination of Christian faith generally."[588]

For these reasons, it is necessary that critical inquiry into the life of Jesus be carried out and the introduction to Schleiermacher's lectures on this subject are devoted to the hermeneutical principles and formal considerations which are appropriate to this field of inquiry. The refusal to legitimize unbelief leads Schleiermacher to develop further the issues involved in the knowledge of the historical Jesus.

The Understanding of Intentional Unity

We noted above that Schleiermacher says that the task of knowing the historical Jesus must be pursued just as with the similar one concerning a man who is not the subject and mediator of Christian faith. Therefore, Schleiermacher asks the question, What is it that one seeks to accomplish in a description of a life? One must be clear about this for it is the goal to be accomplished in regard to the person of Jesus.[589] Since it is a life description, it falls under the province of the historical, and here there is a distinction fundamental to all historical productions. This distinction is the one between a real history and a chronicle. Since life is something that changes in time in its appearances, it can be approached in more than one way. If one proceeds on the assumption that time is divisible, then the entire life of a person would consist of a series of single

---

[587] Ibid., p. 16.

[588] Ibid., p. 25.

[589] I will use the name Jesus whereas Schleiermacher most often uses Christ. However his meaning in using this name is consonant with our use of the name Jesus for it is clear that he is speaking of an individual of history who must be approached in terms of the categories of historical knowledge. He is not speaking of the transcendent "heart" of God or only of the Christian principle.

360

moments which, correctly or incorrectly, can be separated from one another. If the account deals simply with how these moments are filled out in terms of their observable content in temporal appearance, one has a chronicle. This aspect is in some sense indispensable to a description of a life, but since the divisibility of time is limitless from a practical standpoint one is always involved in embracing the separated moments by a selection in order to bring the whole or unity of the subject matter to representation. This selection presupposes a standard by which one passes over the insignificant in order to present that which is important. This standard contains the seed of something more than the mere representation of observable particularities because it must be an idea in reference to which the changes occurring in time are measured. Since this is a historical procedure, Schleirmacher concludes, a naked chronicle of a person's life cannot be formulated in an understandable manner. Something more must be considered than the observable particularities. Further, the more historical a representation is, that is, the more adequately the unity of the subject is grasped, the more the observable particularities in their separation recede. This selection which is fundamental to the engendering of the historical must in some way reside in the one presenting the matter, that is, in the knower. "The depiction of the subject will only be observed from a certain point of view, and much will appear significant to him, therefore, which would be unimportant from another point of view."[590] Schleiermacher concludes his first point in the discussion, then, with the affirmation that if a presentation is to be a real history it must not be allowed to stop short with externally observable particularities for it is constituted by interpretation.

At this point Schleiermacher introduces a distinction which he feels is already implied in the remarks dealt with above; namely, that there is a twofold differentiation involved. There is the particular as something separable standing contrasted with the unity as something indivisible, and then, there is also the

---

[590] Leben Jesu, p. 2.

externally perceptible object as contrasted with an internal reality.[591] This internal reality is the resolution or intention which is explored in Schleiermacher's theory of hermeneutics. This internal reality is not directly perceptible, but can only be grasped in another way. It can only be grasped by reconstructing the intention of the person in one's own self-consciousness.[592] Now the greater the distinction is in the subject between its unity as that which is indivisible, and that which in it stands separate, and the greater the distinction is between the internal reality and that which is externally observable, then the distinction is greater between the kind and mode of historical representation which directs itself primarily to the externally separate and the mode of representation concerned with the intentional unity.[593] Schleiermacher illustrates the import this has for the matter of a description of a life in the following manner.

> Think of an individual which you especially observe from such a point of view that he fills out a definite place, but he fills out his place in such a way that you at the same time can think of many others who would have filled out the same place in the same way. When you do this, you think of the intention, the continuity of the individual life as something receding, and he becomes a subject for you only with respect to his externality.[594]

Schleiermacher holds that this is what is done when an individual is placed under a general category, a proceeding which must always be done with caution because of the possibility of erroneous application. Externally observed, the general affairs of the situation are reflected in the individual. Since the intentional unity is not a subject of observation, we think of a great quantity of individuals as being the same, ascribing to them only a very minimum of individuality. "But the more we describe the single one from the viewpoint of individuality, we must

---

[591] Schleiermacher uses this distinction in the Brief Outline in respect to the history of Christianity.

[592] This, of course, is the basic motif of the psychological interpretation.

[593] Leben Jesu, p. 2.

[594] Ibid., p. 3.

understand the task as finding the unity by means of which just this individual in all his varied appearances is distinguished from every other individual."[595]

Therefore, a description of a life is a history and it is that kind of history in which one must attempt to bring the intentional unity of the life to consciousness in such a way that one is able to maintain : "If the single episode and its circumstances would have been different than they actually were, nevertheless we would be able to relate to the same unity; that is, the contrast between the external and the intention is only real insofar as we are able to think of the same externals with various intentions, and the same intentional reality with various externals."[596] This can be illustrated by the fact that one can think of moments in the lives of two persons who, considered externally, are virtually indistinguishable; yet, the life determination, the moving power or intentionality of that moment, is something very different in one life than it is for the other person. This means that the external itself is always a product of two factors.

Every emerging life moment originates and traces back to another, that is, the life moment allows itself to be regarded as a reaction and in that case it presupposes an action. Something effects a person and the next moment of his life appears as a reaction to that cause. Again, one is able to regard that moment of life as an original action, but in its external appearance it appears as determined by the object against which it is reactive. As a result,

> If we merely apprehend that which is externally observable in the activity of a man, this relation [the original action] is lost, and the external can be completely presented without the describer knowing more than the least of the intention—"the individual has performed that and that and this"—but the authentic life determination which is the foundation the observer does not know. Evidently, he has not grasped the individual man himself at all, and he cannot say that he knows him if he only knows the external, just because he assembled these pieces together.[597]

---

[595] Ibid.
[596] Ibid., p. 4.
[597] Ibid.

A man's own characteristic being is always one coefficient of that which is external; but if an interpreter is completely incapable of distinguishing the external and the intentional unity in any way, then a man's active nature can never be grasped. This is the same point made in the hermeneutics that the external circumstances alone are not sufficient to explain the resolution.[598] Schleiermacher's second point, therefore, is that the task of a description of a life is to seek the unity from the particularities and to seek the intention from the external.[599]

Does this mean that the unity to be sought is identical with the intention of that which is externally observable? Not entirely, according to Schleiermacher. In one sense the intention does remain the same. This is the case when it is the same factor for various results; if so, it can be identified with the unity of that which is isolated. But the matter takes on a different form when one considers the question of how it comes about that a man in the development of his life remains the same. "That is to say, we say in one sense that a man always remains the same, but in another sense we say that he becomes different. If we only meant this as an external appearance, the matter would not belong here for then it would be the external that had become different, but we mean also that his intention becomes a different one."[600] Even internally a person changes in the ongoing course of life. Yet one does not hesitate to say that it is the same person who is changing in some way. Schleiermacher here is pointing to the importance time has for the intentional reality of a person's life and how the relations a person has with others in its life cannot be confined to externally observable matters. The "intersubjective" social relations into which one steps and the manner of one's

---

[598] Cf. Hermeneutic und Kritik, Sämtliche Werke, I, 7, p. 157.

[599] Leben Jesu, p. 5.

[600] Ibid.

response to these qualify one's intention.[601]   Because of this, the intentional reality itself is not simply a constant and a person can become different in this respect. Thus, the question of the unity of particular life moments of a person is not strictly identical with the question of the distinction of the intention and the external, however much they may at first have in common in the differentiation of history and chronicle. A description of a life must finally deal with the question of the unity of this intentional reality in the variableness which it too may undergo.

The variety that is possible for the intention of a person is not to be understood solely in terms of the change connected with different periods of life. It is also brought about by the fact that in a given life moment of a person a certain aspect of his or her activity will step forward and become prominent in a way consonant with the situation; thereby occasioning another aspect to retire even though it is still fundamentally present.[602] While this distinction of unity and intentionality must be borne in mind, Schleiermacher does not usually burden his statements with this differentiation and usually uses them as a compound. Consequently, he concludes the first section of the discussion of the issues involved in the description of a life by stating that: "The task is to find the intention in the course of a person's life as a unity so that one can determine results also under the assumption of other coefficients."[603] That is, one attempts to grasp the intentional unity of a person in such a way that one could say something about this person's external action even if that which had influenced him or her in the person's circumstances and how the person had modified them had been different than that which is simply given as externally observable.[604] Only when one can do this, Schleiermacher maintains, does the interpreter of a life ". . . have an authentic knowledge of his subject's intentional unity" for he is able to

---

[601] Schleiermacher illustrates this by the difference between the child and the matured adult. Ibid., p. 6.

[602] Ibid.

[603] Ibid., p. 1(S).

[604] Ibid., pp. 6-7.

construe the person's way of acting as it would appear in different circumstances. This is the index to the person in its individuality, that which is characteristic to the person's own identity. The construing of a person's way of acting Schleiermacher often designates with the phrase, "calculating" the person. It is also what is indicated by the phrase "knowledge of human nature." As such, it provides a kind of prophecy so that one knows in advance something of how a person will present her or himself under certain given conditions.[605]

This is fundamental to Schleiermacher's understanding of a description of a life. By grasping this dimension of a person's being, its active nature or deed, one is apprehending the subject in the person's freedom, that by which he or she is distinguished from others. Yet, immediately a qualification has to be made. At the same time that one recognizes that the task of a life description is to discern the intentional reality of a person as a unity so that one comes to an appreciation of the person in its freedom, a freedom that the interpreter appraises in being able to realize his or her subject's way of acting in different external situations, one is aware also of the limits of this procedure.

> But this task has maximum limits in terms of which it can be conceived: namely, it is a nil and empty undertaking if one attempted to think of one and the same man among a different people, or in a different age. This becomes something completely idle, since the individual man in a different people and a different age would no longer be the same man . . . one cannot think of an individual man without at the same time thinking of the general conditions of his existence.[606]

One cannot rip a person out of these general conditions of his life for the individual becomes who it is only in and through the common life in which he or she participates. Consistent with the principles of the hermeneutics, the person is in one sense a result of this common life. One may grasp the life unity of a

---

[605] Ibid., p. 8.
[606] Ibid.

person and come to estimate its free activity, but this can only be done in terms of the conditions that shape that life. It is vacuous to attempt to calculate Julius Caesar in terms of the Cold War, but the task of apprehending the life unity of Julius Caesar in such a way that the intentional reality of his externally observable actions can be constructed in terms of other circumstances of his time is ingredient to understanding the man in his free activity.[607]

This discussion, then, presents Schleiermacher's view on what a description of a life should accomplish. It seeks to understand the intentional unity of a person as a freely acting being. One is to consider Jesus in this perspective just as with any person who is not in any way "a subject of faith for us." Nevertheless, a problem emerges here for there is a definite scope within which intentional unity is concretely meaningful. This problem is Schleiermacher's next topic.

The Dominant Person and the Antinomies of Historical Knowledge

After formulating his principles for a description of a life, Schleiermacher pauses at this point of the discussion to reflect whether he has not painted himself into a corner. He set out to clarify what a description of a life is in order to provide a basis for the investigation and interpretation of Jesus of Nazareth. But now principles have come to be established which seem to militate against understanding Jesus in the way essential for Christian faith.[608] The possible contradictions to faith in Jesus Christ that have emerged spring up from two sides. On the one hand, is not the very attempt to calculate Jesus' way of acting a placing of ourselves above him so that his freedom is somehow less than ours, his normative worth and resulting dignity being placed at our disposal? Even as we consider this difficulty, Schleiermacher observes, it should be evident that Christian faith cannot entirely eschew calculating Jesus for: "We could not take

---

[607] The illustration of Julius Caesar and, of course, the Cold War is mine, but the principle is discussed by Schleiermacher. Ibid., p. 15.
[608] Ibid., p. 8.

him for an exemplar if we were not able to construe his way of acting."[609] Therefore, an antinomy seems to be established where a Christian needs to be able to calculate the intentional unity of Jesus Christ, and yet the very attempt to do so seems to detract from the Christian claim of how Jesus, who in his normative worth is distinguished from all other persons, is the master of the disciple.[610]

A possible contradiction to faith in Jesus Christ seems to emerge on the other side, also. This contradiction is manifest in relation to the maximum limits in terms of which an intentional unity can be construed. That is, if the limits of the task of a description of a life are set by not being able to tear a person out of the general conditions of its individual existence as defined by the person's nationality and age, what are we to make of Jesus Christ? We are in another age, and belong to another common life. If we are not able to construe Jesus' way of acting for our age and common life, then the knowledge of him would have no practical or existential worth for us in the manner religious conviction must have.[611] Put another way, does not the very conditions of a definite age and people produce a diminution of the special value of Jesus Christ? Here, then, is the antinomy from the other side. The task of a description of a life must respect its temporal, spatial boundaries; yet, if we were to limit the practical application of the knowledge of Jesus to the particularities of his own life visibly at hand, the practical application would be as good as nil. "it would be something entirely powerless and completely empty for us."[612] It might be an interesting report from the past, but it would have no contact with the living interests of our own lives.

Schleiermacher attempts to resolve these antinomies by a closer scrutiny of the conditions of historical life, a scrutiny which displays the motifs of his hermeneutics. He first turns to the question of the second antinomy by a further

---

[609] Ibid., p. 10.
[610] Ibid., p. 9.
[611] Ibid., p. 10.
[612] Ibid., p. 9.

analysis of the relationship of the individual person to the general conditions of the course of his or her life. And, consistently, he says that this must be understood in a twofold manner: "namely, on the one hand, the individual stands under the power of the common life to which he belongs; but then, on the other hand, the common life stands under the power of individuals."[613] If the first of these was not true, the very conditions of history would be taken away. Everything that fell under the category of natural and human influence would be abolished and the only category that would remain through which continuous powers could be interpreted would be the one of sheer accident. But if the second side was false, " . . . there could be no historical progression."[614] Without the emerging and transforming newness that arises from the individual, history would be frozen, it would lose its dynamic. These two sides represent in the most general way the very structure of history. And if certain people have particular importance it must be grasped in these terms. There are persons whose capacity exceeds their people and their time, and whose achievements pass over into the common life. In such a case, " . . . the individual advances the common life through the outcome of his work," a contribution " . . . which previously was not there but subsequently became a common good."[615] In this way, the whole of the common life stands under the power of the individual.

While a person may surpass her people and exercise a directing influence upon the common life in which she exists, there can be no one who while she may direct in one respect, does not in other respects stand under the power of the common life. "This is a duplexity which must be recognized in its universality."[616] Of course, one readily can think of a great crowd of individuals in whom it is virtually impossible to detect a directing influence upon the common life, but this standing under the power of the common life is no less true

---

[613] Ibid., p. 11.
[614] Ibid.
[615] Ibid.
[616] Ibid.

for even the dominant and directing person. Different individuals are differently related to the various forms of human activity, both in the sense of their specific orientation to a form of activity and in the sense of the quantitative power which they possess.[617] Consistent with this, then: " . . . the individual can only exercise a directing influence on those forms of activity in which it is dominant in himself, but in respect to other forms of activity he stands under the power of the common life."[618] Indeed, it follows that even in that activity in which he is directing he reflects the power of the common life as a very presupposition of his directing activity.

This finds illustration by turning back to these matters in regard to Jesus Christ. Schleiermacher notes that many well meaning theologians of his day have opposed his Christological position in The Christian Faith where he has insisted upon recognizing the influence of the Jewish nationality and first century age upon Jesus' self-consciousness. This was interpreted by some theologians as reducing the unique dignity of Jesus Christ.[619] But Schleiermacher insists that this is a misunderstanding. Jesus' relationship to the common life was of such a kind that he exercised a dominant influence, and a dominant influence is certainly greater the more its effects extend over a people and an age than is the case if it immediately disappeared. But to attempt to say that Jesus only stands in a dominant relation and does not stand under the power of the common life would really remove Jesus' possibility of being dominant and directing. Unless Jesus has borne in himself the age and the nationality in which he lived and under whose power he existed: "Each activity of Christ which we thereby would conceive in a denuded way would have been to those people surrounding him something absolutely strange; such a thing could only always be an object of

---

[617] Ibid., p. 12.
[618] Ibid.
[619] Ibid.

contemplation; it could not be more."[620] It could not be more because it could not have extended into their lives in any shaping and transforming way, a feature of the dominant man. It could not be more because there would have been no framework to appropriate that which was unique and powerful in Jesus. In the language of the hermeneutics, there would have been no point of contact. Therefore, the receptivity of Jesus in standing under his common life was requisite to his dominant activity. Without this intrinsic relation to the common consciousness of the general conditions in which he lived he could neither have been human nor could he have been the Redeemer. Rather than the conditions of these two being opposed, they must be apprehended in terms of one another. But it must not be done in such a way that the individuality of Jesus is sacrificed for this would abolish his humanity from the other side. A dominant man must retain his distinct activity. As much as his common language, his nationality, and his age must be emphasized as ingredient to the work that Jesus accomplished, it was not the language, the nationality, or the period of history which simply evolved the consciousness of God. Rather, they are the concrete specificities in which what was distinctive in Jesus came to expression.[621] As such, the power of the common life both contributes to the work of Jesus and is transformed by him in his dominant and directing activity.

The category of the dominant man, then, is the one through which Schleiermacher wants to approach Jesus Christ. Obviously, however, this alone does not answer the possible contradiction to which Schleiermacher is attending. This indicates the framework for understanding a significant historical life, but it does not specify how the maximum limits of an age and a people function in regard to the religious interest in construing Jesus' way of acting in another age and people. If this is to receive an answer, it cannot occur on the basis of formal principles alone. It can only be viable by a consideration of the specific content of Jesus' activity, as well as what is communicated by this activity. The former is

---

[620] Ibid., p. 13.
[621] Ibid., pp. 13-14.

treated in the section of the Life of Jesus dedicated to the message of Jesus and the events of his life. The latter is dealt with in The Christian Faith. But even this material may have its import for a discussion of the formal principles of historical knowing, that is for hermeneutics. So Schleiermacher thought.

Concerning the question of the dominant man and Jesus Christ whose life unity must have a practical import for a people and an age other than his own, Schleiermacher says that the maximum limits he has imposed " . . . are valid also for Christ, even though only in a certain sense."[622] The maximum limits were that it would be something completely empty if one asked the question how this or that outstanding man of another people and age would have acted under present circumstances. This emptiness applies to Jesus if one attempts to represent his life in a concrete fashion outside the connections of his time and people. A concrete picture only results when one conceives him under the relationships of his own time.[623] Yet, it is still true that the exemplary pertinence of Jesus Christ would cease if we could not transpose anything at all about him to our time and place. Therefore, Schleiermacher says: "Since the exemplary proceeds entirely from his disposition . . . we must say that we do not at all need the concrete visibility of his relationships under wholly different circumstances; but what matters is to convey his disposition in those relationships to us without superimposing our relationships upon him."[624]

In these lines, Schleiermacher expresses his conviction that Jesus Christ must be understood as a man of his own time, yet precisely in his being this we are able to grasp the life unity of his intention as something which has exemplary power for us. His disposition, his attitude, his character is communicable to us in an efficacious way that is not confined to the conditions of Jesus' own time. But why would the same not be true of, say, Julius Caesar, to recall our illustration?

---

[622] Ibid., p. 15f.
[623] Ibid., p. 16.
[624] Ibid.

What is it about Jesus' intention which enables it to carry exemplary consequences for us in a way that the intention of Julius Caesar or that of another dominant person cannot do?

Jesus Christ and the Resolution of the Antinomies of Historical Knowledge

The resolution of the historical antinomies that Schleiermacher finds between the requirements and scope of historical knowledge, on the one hand, and the practical necessity of calculating Jesus' way of acting in another era than Jesus' own, on the other hand, focuses the question of the relation of Schleiermacher's hermeneutical principles to the dogmatic convictions of Christianity. That is, Schleiermacher's attempt to resolve these antinomies is at the same time a statement of the relation of faith to historical knowledge. The understanding of intentional unity and the dynamics of the dominant man do not require the standpoint of faith, but the resolution of this antinomy does require the conviction of Christian faith.

We have seen that Schleiermacher holds that different individuals are differently related to the various forms of activity which mark the human scene, and, further, that a dominant man is so in the specific relation he has to one of these activities and the quantitative power that he possesses. Jesus' dominant and directing activity concerns the religious self-consciousness of human beings which is founded in the consciousness people have of being in relation to God. Every person, Schleiermacher maintains, takes up an active orientation to this dimension of life, as misdirected and minimal as it may be. Founders of religion are those who are dominant persons in this sphere of human life.[625] This sphere of the religious self-consciousness is anterior to the activities of the self in reference to the world.[626] Rather than being only a specific form of activity such as is found in politics, science, art, etc., the religious self-consciousness arises out of the very unity of the self, and this means that it is present in all the various activities of politics, science, art, etc. in which human life is engaged. Therefore,

---

[625] CF, #13, 1.
[626] Ibid., #4.

as an institution religion is another form of activity alongside other forms, but as founded in the unity of self-consciousness itself religiousness is present in and through all forms of human activity. As a man whose activity refers to the religious self-consciousness, Jesus' intention is not restricted to the general conditions of his people and age in a manner that is exactly equivalent to the dominant person endowed with a transforming power over another aspect of the common life. This is one ingredient in Schleiermacher's answer to the question as to why Jesus' intention carries consequences for us in a way that the intention of Julius Caesar cannot do.

But this does not comprehend Schleiermacher's treatment of the question. There is another ingredient. The concept of revelation found in the introduction to The Christian Faith reflects the principles of the dominant person. In speaking of the dynamics of history Schleiermacher says:

> Every outstanding endowment of an individual, through whose influence any spiritual institution within a particular circle takes shape anew, is such a starting point . . . No one will object to the supposition that in all founders of religion, even on the subordinate levels, there is such an endowment, . . . But if this is to be applied in the same sense to Christ, it must first of all be said that, in comparison with him, everything which could otherwise be regarded as revelation again loses this character. For everything else is limited to particular times and places, . . . Anyone who does not take Christ in this universal way as divine revelation cannot desire that Christianity should be an enduring phenomenon.[627]

Therefore, the intentional unity of a man of another people and another age can carry practical consequences for those in very different historical conditions if that intention is at the same time universal. As history's fundamental newness,[628] what appears in Jesus Christ is the transforming activity directed toward humanity itself in its historical course. Jesus Christ is the universally dominant and

---

[627] Ibid., #13,1.

[628] Revelation in Schleiermacher's view signifies the originality of the historical given which lies at the foundation of the religious communion for the adherents of that communion.

directing man through whose specific orientation and quantitative power a new form and energy is given to the common life in which he stood and then through it to the whole developing course of man.[629]

However, to speak of an individual of history as being a universally directing man transcends what is embraced by the content of a general description of a life and goes beyond the limits of historical investigation generally. The same hermeneutical principles of historical knowledge may apply, but to universalize what is known through this intentional unity is to enter another domain. It is one thing to discern the intentional unity of a historical figure in such a manner that one could construe his way of acting within the general conditions of his common life even under circumstances not empirically presented. It is another thing to say that this intention is efficacious in other times and places, including the interpreter's own age and people. The activity of Jesus upon the religious self-consciousness of his common life is universalized, and by means of this universalisation an ontological claim is made about the humanity of Jesus Christ.

The two ingredients in the difference which Schleiermacher finds between the intentional unity of Julius Caesar and that of Jesus Christ is reflected in the terminology used in the Life of Jesus, as well as The Christian Faith, to explicate the person of Jesus Christ. The terms which Schleiermacher draws upon are Vorbild and Urbild. Vorbild points to Jesus as the mode, the exemplar. His Vorbildlichkeit lies in the disposition which the Christian attempts to transpose into the latter's own time and circumstances. Jesus Christ's Urbildlichkeit, on the other hand, results from the conviction that what Jesus communicates is universally dominant and directing, that what appears in him embodies that which effects the whole of humanity. The Urbildlichkeit or archetypal ideality of Jesus Christ is an ontological term which denotes the transforming activity directed toward the human race. Therefore, Jesus Christ is the universally dominant man

---

[629] Leben Jesu, p. 13.

not, first of all, in the sense that all men shall come to view him as exemplary, so that Jesus Christ shall be universally dominant at some future time; rather, for one who attempts to transpose the disposition of Jesus the humanity of Jesus Christ displays what is universally dominant and directing now, and in all times and places.

In Schleiermacher's theology Vorbild and Urbild indicate different aspects of the person of Jesus Christ. The terms, the exemplar and the ideal, both refer in post-Ritschlian theology to the same Christological ingredient. They refer to that in Jesus Christ which the disciple is to repeat as an ethical movement in his or her life. In Schleiermacher, however, archetypal ideality is an ontological term which denotes the productive power which is constitutive for the course of the human world. As such, ideality can only result from the unique presence and activity of God in Jesus Christ.

This, then, is Schleiermacher's answer to the antinomy that emerges in face of the requirement that the historical task of a description of a life is to grasp the intentional unity of a person in such a way that one could envision him under other empirical conditions, yet only within the maximum limits of his own age and people; and the practical necessity of the Christian's being able to construe Jesus' way of acting in the present. It is empty to remove Jesus from the conditions of his common life; nevertheless, due to the specific activity which he has in that form of human orientation referring to man's religious self-consciousness, and the fact that faith recognizes this intentional unity as the transforming activity directed toward history itself, the antinomy is resolved. But it is resolved only from the standpoint of faith. It cannot pretend to be a neutral solution, even though it approaches the historical material with impartial procedures.[630]

---

630 Ibid., p. 19f.

The fact that it is not a neutral solution and that faith in Jesus Christ as the universally dominant man is ingredient to understanding him is illuminating for Schleiermacher's handling of the first possible contradiction. This antinomy was occasioned by the situation in which the interpreter is in a position to calculate Jesus' way of acting so that the master's freedom is put at the disposal of the disciple. Does this mean a placing of ourselves above Jesus Christ? Schleiermacher says that it does not for the basic reason that knowing another person's intentional unity is dependent on the activity of that person. That is, the other person's own act is the condition of knowing him or her and being influenced by that person's activity.[631] This is valid for the knowledge of that which is distinctive in any person, and is preeminently true for the one whose activity is of universal import. Thus in calculating him:

> . . . so that one would be able to maintain that he could know in advance how Christ would have acted in this and that case, that would only be the impact of Christ himself, and in a subordinate way we could apply that upon all similar cases. The relationship in which the disciples were placed to Christ was his work. It was the beginning of his directing influence. The first consequence of that must be that such a picture of him gradually came to position in them, and this places them in no way above him; and if we with complete knowledge of his life could completely calculate him, the attaining of this goal would not enable us to stand above him, for it was his work.[632]

These sentences bring to light Schleiermacher's fundamental conviction that participation in the influence of Jesus Christ is a necessary condition of understanding him.

The principles of the relation of Christology to historical knowledge which Schleiermacher projects in the introduction to the Life of Jesus are exceptionally significant. These principles evidence the uniting of Schleiermacher's philosophical, historical, and theological thinking in regard to the hermeneutical

---

[631] Ibid., p. 17.
[632] Ibid.

problem of the historical Jesus. The resolution of the historical antinomies stated above requires elucidation in many directions. Such explanations go beyond the tasks here. My purpose is to show that Schleiermacher's lectures on the <u>Life of Jesus</u> contain reflections that should not be simply ignored because they contain dated critical judgments from the past; rather, these lectures manifest some of the most penetrating discussion concerning the relation of Christian faith and historical knowledge, and, as such, invite much more engagement than they have ever received.